The Piano in America,
1890–1940

CRAIG H. ROELL

The
University
of North
Carolina
Press
Chapel Hill &
London

The Piano in America, 1890–1940

The paper in this book meets the guidelines for
permanence and durability of the Committee on
Production Guidelines for Book Longevity of the
Council on Library Resources.

93   92   91   5   4   3   2

Library of Congress Cataloging-in-Publication Data
Roell, Craig H.
    The piano in America, 1890–1940 / by Craig H.
Roell.
       p.   cm.
    Bibliography: p.
    Includes index.
    ISBN 0-8078-1802-X (alk. paper)
    ISBN 0-8078-4322-9 (pbk.: alk. paper)
    1. Piano—Marketing.   2. Consumers—United States.
3. Music and society.   I. Title.
ML661.R64   1989
381′.4568181621—dc19   88-14326
                          CIP
                          MN

Contents

Tables and Figures

Illustrations

Preface

"There is probably no country in the world where piano playing is so widespread as in the United States," Louis C. Elson wrote at the turn of the century in *History of American Music* (1904). "Almost every home, even among the humble, possesses its instrument and some amount of piano music. . . . The universal gift or habit of playing the piano, or playing at piano music, in America is undeniable."[1] Indeed, the piano throughout most of its history has commanded a respect as "the basic musical instrument," delighting the senses of both cultivated musicians and the untrained majority. It satisfies the demands of the most skillful, yet allows the beginner gratifying results. Thus the piano, as the French composer Halévy put it, "is of all instruments the one which has contributed the most toward popularizing a taste for music and facilitating its study."[2]

This popularity was expressed even in slang. One could "soft pedal" a suggestion, use a forum as a "sounding board" for ideas. "Ivory thumpers" could "tickle the ivories" when playing the instrument. The steam calliope was also known as the "horse piano." In the period before the First World War, to "play the piano" could mean to be fingerprinted, while during the Second World War, the phrase described the release of bombs from a plane one by one. In some restaurants "piano" signified spareribs, because the bones resembled piano keys. Similarly were dominoes and horses' teeth called "piano keys." The railroad industry referred to the control box that operated track switches as a "piano box." The difficulty and pain associated with traditional piano lessons most likely helped to coin "piano bench" to mean a convict's workbench. The piano's association with domesticity and women is echoed in the late-nineteenth-century phrase "playing the piano," or "playin' the pianner," which described the shifting of rows of mineral-water bottles by women workers from a ship's hold into baskets that were then hauled onto the wharf by cranes, and it was hardly a compliment for a woman to be called "piano legs." Neither was it praise when Victorian men were considered "rather too piano," implying that they were effeminate—too gentle, weak, and mild.

When player pianos became popular, card players described a hand that was easy to play or required no skill as a "pianola" (originally a trademark of the Aeolian Company of New York). The expression also meant cash register, no doubt because the coin-operated player piano enjoyed a lucrative market, but to give a "pianolaed performance" was to render without life or emotion as if automated. Even the coining of "Chicago piano" to mean the submachine guns used by gangsters in the 1920s, especially in Chicago, is derived from the expressionless rat-a-tat performance of many player pianos.[3]

Before the advent of radio and the high-fidelity phonograph, the piano not only spread music appreciation; it added to the prestige of the home. It symbolized the middle-class values of the Victorian age—the treasured canons of the work ethic, the morality of music, and domesticity. The piano and music industries became a big business in an age that, with the exception of an occasional barrel-operated music box or dulcimer, knew only live music and whose entire value system was based on work, sacrifice, and saving. The "strenuous life" was a survival technique elevated to a virtue. As industry and society mechanized and electrified, however, and workers in the twentieth century labored for fewer hours per week, work and sacrifice became less valued in a culture that increasingly honored leisure, recreation, and consumption.

"The quickened tempo and increased leisure time of today have brought with them a gradual change of tastes, and have expanded enormously the number of ways of satisfying the urge for recreation," Julius Weinberger wrote in the *Harvard Business Review* for 1937. He estimated that Americans were spending more than one-sixth of their incomes available after the purchase of living necessities on recreation, most of this on "what may be called *passive* recreation," in which the participants were spectators and listeners exerting little physical energy.[4] Passivity did not eclipse active participation in modern society, however; consumers could be active workers and shoppers, or passive recipients of persuasive advertising and mechanized production. But work became more important and meaningful as a means of buying products, rather than providing an opportunity for self-expression or imparting a sense of accomplishment, independence, and moral fulfillment. Mechanical production eased labor, encouraged consumption, promoted obsolescence, and created dependency.

"We Americans are mercurial and changeable, and forever craving something new," declared another writer in 1932 about the related phenomenon of mechanically reproduced music. The "canned music" generated by the player piano, phonograph, radio, and "talkies," "has become a craze exceeding any movement of the kind in the entire history of music."[5] Indeed, these devices brought music into the homes and lives of millions who had never enjoyed it because they lacked the ability or desire to work at learning to produce tunes by hand. On the other hand, these inventions also uniquely affected the industry whose financial and social foundation was rooted in *active* participation.

By the 1920s this "consumer culture" had emerged as the dominant ethic, despite a deceptive (though not necessarily feigned) devotion to Victorian values. This was the conflict of the Progressive Era. Bureaucratic government and big business (with its professional managers, mass production and distribution, and national advertising) threatened local government and small businessmen. Urban life was seen as a danger to rural values. Peer groups and outside interests became more influential than home and family life. Women's liberation challenged tradition and caused social upheaval. Mechanization jepardized the pride and satisfaction of production by hand. Purchase by credit and the limitless variety of products for sale eroded the old reverence for thrift. The new consumer bought more than products and services; he consumed a new ideology, a new image—but one that was peculiarly destructive. The expenditure, waste, dependency, and deliberate obsolescence created by consumerism were both exciting and discomforting. The values of the waning age seemed to offer solace and stability.

This study examines the transition from the nineteenth-century Victorian to the twentieth-century consumer culture through a focus on the American piano industry from 1890 to 1940. This transition involves the examination of a number of interrelated themes: the erosion of the home as the center of family life; the transformation of the population from producers to consumers following the rise of industrialization; the impact of mechanization upon self-expression and production in the home; the rise of mass media, manipulative advertising strategies, and the democratization of public taste; and the development of a consumer culture, with its emphasis on leisure, recreation, and fulfillment through consumption. The piano and its industry linked music, technology, business, politics, and society, and therefore are particularly suited to providing a better understanding of the transition to the modern world.

While at one level this study examines the piano and its industry, it is fundamentally concerned not so much with the piano as with ideas about the instrument, with tracing the piano's function and stability as a cultural totem, a symbol for an age. The piano is significant as a foundation of Victorian middle-class values, reigning as a center for family life and an indicator of social respectability. Within this value system the instrument is also a medium for cultural uplift and a conduit for music appreciation and moral rejuvenation. It is particularly associated with the role and place of women. Consequently, this study is about changes in a value system as it encountered the emerging consumer culture.

But just as a study of business cannot ignore the cultural background, a cultural and intellectual analysis of the piano cannot be isolated from the business and industrial concerns that propelled the instrument into prominence. Thus this book also presents a case study of an industry important in American culture. It examines general business trends, marketing and merchandising techniques, product acceptance and rejection, and the connections among politics, business, and culture, in relation to the development of consumer motivation and consumption habits. This inquiry pursues the changes in American values (evident especially in the 1920s) as industrialization and the consumer society gained momentum and studies the efforts of the most prominent element in the music trade to survive these changes.

The American piano industry was both a promoter and a representative of Victorian philosophy. But in its quest to establish what I will term a "musical democracy," in which music would become universally accessible (a goal that would both widen sales and extend the moral and cultural benefits of music), the trade adopted and helped develop the business strategies characteristic of the emerging consumer culture. Achieving success initially through the sale of the revolutionary player piano, the industry soon met with disaster from the same technology that it was promoting. As radio, movies, and other amusements and products increasingly competed for consumers' attention, as music making became more automatic and passive while becoming less necessary socially and less associated with the piano, the music industry found itself facing financial catastrophe. "When one can hear at any time the best professionals perform music, if only on the gramophone and the wireless," as one writer expressed this dilemma, "it is reasonable to expect that many people may be discouraged from indulging their own poor efforts."[6] Ironically, though more people were exposed to music during the 1920s than ever before, the piano and music industries suffered near extinction.

Eventually, however, trade leaders adjusted to and even exploited the cultural changes of modern society. During the country's greatest depression they redesigned their product and touted the very Victorian values that were seemingly being undermined. Once the piano was streamlined to accommodate modern tastes, it was marketed as symbolic of traditional home and family life, as an avenue of self-expression, as a channel for the moral and uplifting value of music. The strategy appealed to a society searching for order and meaning in a period of rapid social change, to a depression-ridden people questioning the homage paid to modernization that characterized the "New Era."

This study is among the first to approach the changes wrought by the emergence of the consumer society by studying an industry whose economic, social, and cultural foundations rested within the Victorian culture that was being replaced, an industry that also helped the new ethic to emerge. Indeed, the American piano industry pioneered many business practices characteristic of consumerism: promotion of brand name loyalty and buying on credit, consignment sales, persuasive advertising on a national level, mechanization of factories, distribution through dealers, and ready accessibility of products. Because of the special nature of its topic, this work is one of the few studies examining the politics and business of promoting art in addition to products by an industry as concerned with uplifting society as with profiting from it. Such an approach reveals the crucial work of the American piano trade in encouraging music appreciation, and provides a more balanced and realistic account of the growth of American musical awareness than those that exclusively emphasize radio, phonograph, or the Federal Music Project of the Works Progress Administration.

Business history has only recently begun to explore this kind of interaction between business and the larger culture. Advertising, the small firm, and relations between business and government are likewise receiving attention long overdue. The piano trade, though not a "big business" comparable to steel, coal, railroads, and oil, nevertheless was the largest and most influential element in the music industry. As such it was closely involved with the federal government, especially in the areas of international trade, the development of modern copyright acts (the 1909 bill was the first to deal with mechanical reproduction of music), the attempted formation of a national conservatory of music and a federal department of fine arts, and national legislation regulating brand name usage. Furthermore, the piano trade's experience under the "Blue Eagle" of the National Recovery Administration provides a new perspective on the encounter of American business with the depression and the New Deal.

The twentieth-century consumer culture, though having roots in the previous century, gained potency in the years preceding the

First World War and became manifest in the decade of the 1920s. These are the years in which a recognizable consumer consciousness unfolded, manipulative advertising strategies developed, and mass appeals were sought through emerging mass media. They are appropriately the decades dividing Victorian and modern America. This study chronicles the fate of a nineteenth-century institution in transition and traces the process by which the American piano industry adjusted to the cultural changes of the consumer age.

I am deeply grateful for the assistance and encouragement that helped bring these efforts to conclusion. The manuscript originally was my doctoral dissertation, completed at the University of Texas at Austin under the inspiring, able, and sympathetic direction of Lewis L. Gould. Other members of my committee, all of whom assiduously offered constructive criticism, were William M. Stott, Robert A. Divine, Clarence G. Lasby, and especially Standish Meacham, who provided particularly insightful comments that tightened my argument considerably. In addition, Forest G. Hill, Richard K. Simon, and Harold S. Smith helped shape earlier versions of some chapters. The Bess Heflin Fellowship, University of Texas at Austin, and a scholarship from the National Society of the Colonial Dames of America in Texas allowed me the luxury of writing without interruption. Grants from the Dora Bonham Fund, History Department, University of Texas at Austin, and the Graduate School, University of Texas at Austin provided needed traveling funds.

I especially benefited from the considerable insight of Henry Z. Steinway and John H. Steinway, who generously opened their private family and business papers, and provided invaluable illustrations. Their kindness made researching this project particularly enjoyable. I appreciate Janet Wurlitzer Stites's sharing her time and private papers with me and making sure my stay in Cincinnati was pleasurable. Anne Shepherd's knowledge of the Baldwin-Wulsin papers in the Cincinnati Historical Society was exceptionally helpful; her efforts to locate appropriate illustrations enriched this book. Deborah Wythe happily aided my use of the

Steinway Factory Archives. Walter Merchant provided access to the archives of the National Guild of Piano Teachers. I owe special thanks to the interlibrary-loan staff and especially Richard Holland and Joe Ellison of the Perry-Castañeda Library, University of Texas at Austin, for their help in securing microfilm and other crucial materials. I commend the staff of the New York Public Library, Music Division at Lincoln Center, and the many people in the Fine Arts Library, the lonely Collections Deposit Library, the Humanities Research Center, and the Barker Texas History Center, University of Texas at Austin.

I frequently benefited from individuals giving me useful materials or information. David Rubin, formerly of Steinway & Sons, recounted his personal recollections of Theodore E. Steinway and Lucien Wulsin II. R. S. Harrison shared his valuable time while negotiating the successful separation of the Baldwin Piano and Organ Co. from Baldwin United; I am grateful for his permission to reproduce the Baldwin and other brand names, which are registered trademarks of the Baldwin Piano and Organ Company. E. F. Brooks, Jr., of Aeolian American, and T. H. Krumwiede of Story & Clark made available histories of their respective companies. William W. Kimball kindly provided information about his father, C. N. Kimball. George M. Otto, of the National Piano Manufacturers Association, and William R. Gard, of the National Association of Music Merchants, extended the applicable resources of their organizations. Robert Lindsay, of the Graduate School of Business Administration, New York University, kindly shared his current work on professional music in the 1920s and the rise of the singing trombone. Annemarie V. Sandecki, archivist for N. W. Ayer & Son, suggested relevant materials on Steinway advertising. Henry R. Roell, a professional photographer of distinction for over fifty years, together with Ruth M. Roell, reproduced most of the illustrative material for this book. John McClellan, through his collection of restored reproducing pianos, increased my appreciation of automatic musical instruments. The Austin chapter of the Piano Technicians Guild provided an eager forum for part of this material. J. W. Rose, who patiently taught me the craft of piano tuning and probably induced this study in the first place, shared his forty years of experience in the music trade. Harvey N. Roehl of the Vestal Press generously allowed me to reprint illustrations from *Player Piano Treasury*, and I appreciate Robert L. Hill's extending permission to reproduce the Gulbransen Baby trademark, and also the assistance of Charles L. Greiter, Trademark Counsel–RCA, in securing permission from the General Electric Company to reproduce the "His Master's Voice" trademark. Other contributors include Jan B. Whitlock, Tom Haley, Mariann H. Clinton, Cynthia Adams Hoover, Jerome Hershman, and Donald W. Dillon.

Working with the University of North Carolina Press has been a delight. I am grateful to Iris Tillman Hill, the editor-in-chief, for her encouragement and faith in this project even in its first drafts and for locating readers able to comment so knowledgeably about my topic. Dale Reed is an adept and sensitive copyeditor, whose acute sense for clarity of style, together with her enthusiasm, substantially improved this book. Ron Maner, the assistant managing editor, and Marjorie Fowler, head of the composition department, steadily guided me through the mysteries of final manuscript preparation. My thanks to the entire Press staff.

I owe my deepest appreciation to my parents, Henry R. Roell and Ruth M. Roell, who by advice and example have continuously buttressed my faith and enriched my life with their friendship. It is with gratitude, respect, and love that I dedicate this effort to them. I am especially grateful to Becky Roell Hirschhauser for her devoted solicitude, to Kim Drescher Roell for her discerning critique of the manuscript and her fellowship, and to Deborah Schwartz for her help in proofreading and for her support. For their support I am also grateful to Doug and Jennifer Barnett, Colleen Kain, Cecil Harper, Larry Cundiff, and Lew Gould.

October 1987
Austin, Texas

ABBREVIATIONS

FMP   Federal Music Project of the
Works Progress Administration

MSNC   Music Supervisors National
Conference
(later Music Educators National
Conference, MENC)

MICC   Music Industries Chamber
of Commerce

MTNA   Music Teachers National
Association

NAMM   National Association of
Music Merchants
(formerly Piano Dealers
of America)

NPMA   National Piano Manufacturers
Association of America

NRA   National Recovery Administration

WPA   Works Progress Administration

The Place of Music in the Victorian Frame of Mind

Show me the home wherein music dwells, and I shall show you a happy, peaceful, and contented home.
—Henry W. Longfellow

We cannot imagine a model New England home without the family Bible on the table and the family piano in the corner.
—Vice President Calvin Coolidge

His only outward evidence of prosperity was the purchase of a piano.
—B. A. Williams, Saturday Evening Post

A young woman who has been seated on her lover's lap at the piano starts up upon being reminded of her lost innocence by the tune being played, her conscience thus called to higher things. Such is the scene in William Holman Hunt's famous painting, *The Awakened Conscience* (1852–54). Hunt captured various ideological themes prevalent in Victorian society, themes immediately recognizable to the conscientious middle class. The painting depicts a moral drama and depends on the viewer's assumptions about woman's sexual purity (she is dressed in white), her social grace, and the home as the cornerstone of society. Implicitly the painting suggests the moral and spiritual value of music. The parlor piano was an easily understood symbol for all of these Victorian tenets. To play it demanded toil, sacrifice, and perseverance —fundamental virtues in a preindustrialized economy. Faith in the dignity of labor and the moral worth of a productive vocation sustained all types of handicraft, even after the increased development of mechanized production.

The complex intertwining of these notions—whose goal was the maintenance of moral health—formed an ethos that permeated nineteenth-century life and manners. In part, the significance of these Victorian attitudes lies in their persistence into the present century. The American piano industry, its merchandise the product of skilled labor and requiring practiced use, continued to promote these values long after the environment in which they were formed had been supplanted by a new ethos: the consumer society. Understanding the struggles of piano makers in that emerging culture, however, requires a grasp of the peculiar interaction of the work ethic, domesticity, and the morality of music with the piano industry.

Although the term "Victorian" generally describes British society from about 1830 to 1880, it is equally adaptable to (and often used to depict) American society as well.[1] For the United States, the term usually denotes the late nineteenth century, though in many ways it also defines the periods historians call the Age of Jackson and the Progressive Era. In this respect, "Victorian" is less a term of periodization than a collection of interrelated attitudes characteristic of a way of life. Emancipating the term from its restrictive boundaries allows the tracing of its collective ideas through time, and provides a better understanding of the erosion of those beliefs when confronted by a new and stronger value system. Hence it is appropriate to speak of "twentieth-century Victorians," or a "producer ethic in the consumer culture."

"Victorian" is an elusive term that usually conjures up images of prudery, hypocrisy, middle-class stuffiness, domesticity, sentimentality, earnestness, industry, and pompous conservatism. The moral severity that lay at the center of the Victorian code was a complex response to the needs of an emerging industrial society. Emphasis on work, duty, and effort was a reaction to the new opportunities industrialism provided. The snobbery of the age resulted from the rise of new classes attempting to break into a presumed hierarchy. Victorian hypocrisy developed because ideal standards of conduct proved impossible to maintain consistently. The earnestness and prudery of this code were a reaction against the drunkenness, uncleanliness, debauchery, and wastefulness the Victorians saw in the "uncivilized" preindustrial world they were leaving behind. The "cult of domesticity,"[2] with its elevated concept of the home and woman, was an attempt to establish order in a rapidly changing world. This code of moral severity defined the character of individuals as well as the mores of society. Centered upon the middle class and evangelical religion, this morality diffused both downward and upward in the social structure. It influenced politics, government, philosophy, literature and the arts, architecture, education—virtually every aspect of American life. It distinguished Victorian society from the more easygoing ways of the eighteenth century and from the consumer culture emerging in the twentieth century.

Many historians have focused on the nineteenth-century cult of domesticity, with its elevating yet restrictive conception of woman's place and duty and its notion of the moral superiority of women. Other scholars have analyzed the moral dimensions and extent of the work ethic, noting the interaction of these two cults in Victorian society. Social historians have identified the importance of the piano in middle-class culture, particularly as a symbol of social respectability and as a means of female accomplishment. Still others have demonstrated the cultural importance of music in American life. Yet no one has pointed to the moral interrelation of the work ethic, the cult of domesticity, and music through the medium of the piano. This is crucial to an understanding of the piano—"the altar to St. Cecilia"—as a foundation of Victorian middle-class life.

The significance of the piano in Victorian culture rested on a substructure much more intricate than historians have realized. While it is true that the piano *was* a token of respectability, its importance transcended mere considerations of class or social mobility. The piano became associated with the virtues attributed to music as medicine for the soul. Music supposedly could rescue the distraught from the trials of life. Its moral restorative qualities could counteract the ill effects of money, anxiety, hatred, intrigue, and enterprise. Since this was also seen as the mission of women in Victorian society, music and women were closely associated even into the twentieth century. As the primary musical instrument, the piano not only became symbolic of the virtues attributed to music, but also of home and family life, respectability, and woman's particular place and duty. Indeed, most piano pupils were female, and both music making and music appreciation were distinctly feminized. The glorification of the piano was no mere fad; it was a moral institution. Oppressive and opulent, the piano sat steadfast, massive, and magnificent in the parlors and drawing rooms of middle-class homes, serving as a daily reminder of a sublime way of life.

Music and Work

The glorification of work as a supreme virtue and the consequent condemnation of idleness remain among the strongest legacies of the Victorian era. Central to this ideology were the notions that nothing in this world was worth having or doing unless it meant pain, difficulty, and effort; that one had a social duty to produce; and that hard work was also morally purifying because it built character, fortitude, self-control, and perseverance. This elevation of work above leisure permeated American life and manners in the nineteenth and early twentieth centuries, resulting in countless warnings against the evils of idleness. Praise for work came from Protestant middle-class property owners: farmers, merchants, ministers, professionals, craftsmen, and industrialists. And because the middle class controlled the schools, business enterprises, and publishing houses in America, it also set the tone for society.[3] The work ethic promised solid rewards, independence, self-advancement, self-respect, contentment, and many other virtues. Throughout the industrial age, respected authorities preached the virtue of work: from Currier and Ives to Horatio Alger, from Ralph Waldo Emerson to Theodore Roosevelt.

In an age glorifying work and worshiping the virtuosos of the work ethic—the Carnegies, Rockefellers, and other captains of industry—American audiences flocked to hear the great piano virtuosos of their day. Not surprisingly, the goal of music teachers was to produce such titans; performance and technique took precedence over all else. In the nineteenth century, the virtuoso achieved heroic stature, often eclipsing the composer. American audiences, perceiving that no native virtuosity yet flourished, eagerly applauded the stream of European artists who just as eagerly toured the New World. The first to arrive was the "Lion Pianist," Leopold de Meyer, who appeared in about sixty concerts during the 1845–46 season from Boston to New York to St. Louis. In 1850 P. T. Barnum brought the "Swedish Nightingale," soprano Jenny Lind (with her "angel from heaven" pitch), on a successful tour of America. The pianist Henri Herz achieved similar success from 1845 to 1851, as did Louis Moreau Gottschalk, who returned to his native America in 1853. From 1856 to 1858, American audiences thrilled to the most celebrated virtuoso, "Old Arpeggio" himself, Sigismond Thalberg. It was no coincidence that one industrious entrepreneurial piano maker chose the name "Thalberg" for some of his instruments. America's love affair with the virtuoso was becoming big business. "It is a pity," wrote one American reviewer, "but 'tis true that our people generally would just as soon hear one pianist as another, provided he or she has a name or reputation (honestly acquired, or fictitious, it matters but little)."[4]

Following the Civil War, professional performances increased, audiences became more sophisticated about music, and promotional techniques became more elaborate. But the virtuoso still reigned supreme. American piano manufacturers, very conscious of the possible financial benefit from endorsement by or association with a great artist, took upon themselves the task of securing and backing concert tours of various musical virtuosos. Beside such efforts, the tours of Herz, de Meyer, Gottschalk, even Thalberg seemed insignificant. Steinway & Sons brought the hypnotic Anton Rubinstein to the United States in 1872, a highly successful promotion that set the pattern for future ventures. Chickering & Sons' sponsorship in 1875 of Hans von Bülow and in 1879 of the brilliant Rafael Joseffy, while not as financially successful (Joseffy would soon switch to the Steinway piano), further whetted the American appetite for virtuosity. Weber Piano Co. delighted Americans still more by sponsoring the eleven-year-old prodigy Josef Hofmann in 1887, while William Knabe & Co. absorbed the expense of bringing Tchaikovsky to New York in 1891 to open Carnegie Hall as guest conductor.

But it was Steinway & Sons who consistently supplied Americans with laureled musical heroes. In 1891 Steinway invited the famed Ferruccio Busoni on his first American tour. Later that autumn the piano manufacturer brought over Ignacy Paderewski—hypnotic, aggressive, lordly, legendary—who was to be the reigning virtuoso for thirty years. The most financially successful of all, the pianist had netted half a million dollars by his third tour in 1896. In an age worshiping the virtuoso, Paderewski was the virtuoso extraordinaire. All over America crowds attended his concerts in record numbers and gathered at railroad crossings to glimpse his profile. And the ever-growing reputation of the House of Steinway was of course simultaneously secured.[5]

The artists who toured Victorian America would have achieved their well-deserved fame regardless of the cultural mentality of the American people, but the significance of the work ethic in that culture should not be overlooked. Questions of art aside, the vir-

tuoso—whether musical, industrial, or financial—achieved success through "luck and pluck" (in Alger's timely phrase), but especially through hard work. The phenomenon of the virtuoso was
a phenomenon of the Victorian frame of mind. The work ethic and
the accompanying premium placed on virtuosity formed the basis
for teaching music, especially piano, not only in newly established
American musical conservatories, but among private teachers as
well. Increasingly common throughout the mid to late nineteenth
century was the trend to turn amateurs into performers. The goal
of music teachers was to produce the virtuoso.

Since most piano pupils were female because music lessons
were considered essential to their education and social graces,
such a music teacher was as inevitable in the life of a well-
brought-up child as was castor oil. As one historian points out,
"the American 'piano girl' was a recognizable type" by 1840.[6] But
as one teacher admitted, "Taking lessons on the piano had no
equals in the realm of torture."[7] Though few prescribed the mania
with which Hans von Bülow practiced ("I crucify, like a good
Christ, the flesh of my fingers, in order to make them obedient,
submissive machines to the mind, as a pianist must"[8]), most professional pianists—who inevitably also taught—did follow Men-
delssohn's dictum: "Progress is made by work alone."[9] Piano instruction in nineteenth- and early twentieth-century America followed the so-called "Klavier Schule" of Siegmund Lebert and
Ludwig Stark, coauthors of the historic *Method* (1858). Descen-
dant of the Czerny-Clementi-Reineke school, the Klavier Schule
became standard in the United States as German pianists drilled
in the method came to this country seeking disciples.[10] By 1884
the *Method* was in its seventeenth American edition and had been
expanded to four volumes. Though it was imported from Europe,
it was exactly suited to the American work ethic and glorification
of the virtuoso.

The main objective of the Klavier Schule was strengthening
the fingers by rigidly playing studies, scales, and exercises "with
power and energy." This demanded practice of several hours a
day, regardless of whether the pupil aspired to a concert career or

merely enhanced social graces. As Ernest R. Kroeger asserted, "the piano was a steed to be conquered by the most forceful means."[11] The writings of Amy Fay, Mississippi-born author of the widely read *Music Study in Germany* (which was published through the influence of Henry Wadsworth Longfellow and went through about twenty editions), demonstrate the extent to which the Klavier Schule was assimilated in America. In one of her "master rules for successful piano practice," she wrote, "Five-finger exercises are the things which most pupils dislike and shirk, and only the severest discipline on the part of the teacher will *make* the pupil take the daily dose of them which he requires." Her prescription required half an hour of exercises and scales, followed by an equal devotion to the études of Czerny, Bertinior, or Cramer, finishing with Clementi.[12]

Certainly this was a rigorous regimen, but in the culture of the time, idleness was a vice; work of some sort was a virtue, even in leisure: "When you play, play hard," said Theodore Roosevelt, "and when you work, work hard." The Cable Piano Co., echoing the best sentiments of this notion, advertised in 1915: "You can play hard on a Conover piano. It's built to last a lifetime."[13] By the late nineteenth century, the severe Klavier Schule method of teaching piano to the morally and socially inclined young lady had itself become an institution. "When I was a boy it was part of the destiny of the American female child to spend countless hours incarcerated in the parlor, pounding the piano," Gerald Johnson recounted in 1938. "This torture was inflicted with as calm an indifference to the feelings of the victim as was the binding of the feet of the Chinese female child, and for the same purpose—to increase her social prestige when she grew up."[14]

Such methods were unnecessarily severe for the great majority interested in playing only as a means of attaining popularity and social grace. Nevertheless, private teachers as well as those at conservatories stressed piano as a professional and performing art. Even the first lesson emphasized execution. "Technique became the sine qua non of all effort," declared Arthur L. Manchester in his 1908 report for the U.S. Bureau of Education. "The aim of music teaching has been the making of players and singers or the development of composers." For those not measuring up, the "less fortunate majority, music is a sealed book."[15]

In his memoirs R. F. Delderfield recounts this hysteria, which "struck savagely at the mothers of growing children," a hysteria he calls "Mozartitis": "My mother's insistence that I could, if I concentrated, become a musical prodigy, was particularly fierce, amounting almost to a mania. . . . So it was I who had to bear the accumulated weight of her frustrated ambition." At age seven he began piano lessons from "a Miss Dixon, a sweet, uncomplaining little spinster, who was only one in an army of suburban music teachers supplementing their incomes (and in some cases actually supporting themselves) by instructing the children of the avenues to 'play nicely.'" While enduring the efforts of Miss Dixon (and her contemporaries) to bring their pupils up to virtuoso standard, Delderfield relates, "each of us fairly wore out pianos with an endless repetition of scales and exercises."[16] Though British, Delderfield might just as well be describing the American experience, which was equally frustrating. Generations of music teachers faithfully subscribed to the tenets of the Klavier Schule; pupils throughout the first four decades of the twentieth century were well acquainted with its rigid demands. In private music education the Victorian work ethic transcended its age.

Thus, the impact upon music of a philosophy exalting the dignity of labor affected if not burdened the lives of countless musical amateurs. Yet the relationship between the work ethic and music was hardly one-sided. Music, indeed all art, was a valuable support for the idea of the morality of work, capable of inspiring workers to dignity and morality through beauty. "Life without industry is Guilt," wrote John Ruskin, but "Industry without Art is Brutality."[17] The impact of this philosophy in the United States was the refurbishing of factory architecture with designs and interiors that combined practicality with beauty. Piano manufacturer D. H. Baldwin & Co., for example, surrounded its buildings with flowerbeds and hung flowerboxes from windows. Work spaces were enlarged and kept scrupulously clean. Spacious offices were decorated with examples of Greek and Roman architecture to train workmen to appreciate beautiful form. Reportedly, an "air of refinement permeates the entire establishment and gentlemanly behavior is a characteristic of the Baldwin employees."[18] The obvious intimacy Baldwin workers enjoyed with the art of music was enhanced by the Cincinnati firm's growing reputation in the concert world.

A more specifically musical application of this moral prescription of art and beauty for factory life in the United States was the so-called "music-in-industry" crusade following the Great War of 1914–18. This movement offers additional evidence that Victorian notions continued to influence modern culture. Progressive reformers sought to remedy the adverse effects that a mechanized industrial economy inflicted upon the character and constitution of workers, and consumers as well. The supposed replenishing quality of music was particularly suited to this task. Many progressive industrialists encouraged workers to form singing and instrumental ensembles, which would provide a means of self-expression and recreation to counteract the boredom and tediousness of the assembly line. Lunch hours became music feasts, and monotonous work routines were injected with new life with music. If the work itself had ceased to provide moral replenishment, the work environment nevertheless could be revitalized. If mechanization threatened to destroy character and fortitude, music provided the necessary respite.

While seemingly unrelated, the notions of music *as* work (the Klavier Schule) and music *in* work were both vestiges of the Victorian work ethic, whose goal had been not only production, but also moral replenishment. Though perhaps more indicative of the therapeutic and moral value of music itself, the adoption of music by industry was no coincidence. Rather, it was a conscientious application of Victorian ideas about music and work, which were merged with a decidedly modern concern for recreation.

Receiving the endorsement of Secretary of Labor James J. Davis and the American Federation of Labor, music in industry was regarded as a spur to production and as a remedy for industrial unrest. The program varied widely, from singing to use of bands, pianos, and phonographs. According to official reports, pianos

played during working hours noticeably freshened workers' interest and increased their output. The power of music to instill confidence, aspiration, and fidelity in workers resulted in a 6 percent
increase in average per worker output, an 8 percent increase in
efficiency, and a 34 percent decrease in absenteeism (with an 87.5
percent decrease in Monday morning absentees). Music's apparent power to soothe nerves, increase metabolism, reduce fatigue,
aid digestion, and spur production of monotonous tasks produced
greater company loyalty, happier workers—and more work.

For industrial giant Charles M. Schwab of Bethlehem Steel, music in industrial life was "irreplaceable as a great humanizing
agent." In an interview with *The Etude* magazine, Schwab outlined his steps after taking over a steel plant: first, improve the
conditions of buildings to induce work within fine surroundings;
second, establish a musical interest within the plant by organizing
band, chorus, piano, or other music. To Schwab, an unhappy mind
would not produce fine work, and music seemed to be the most
effective means of promoting happiness.[19]

Schwab was hardly alone in this philosophy. In a two-year survey of music in industry published in 1929, the National Bureau
for the Advancement of Music found over 500 major industries
involved in the program and estimated the total investment value
of the activity to exceed $5 million. Efficient music departments
(pianos, phonographs, bands) were maintained at Simmons Bed
Co., General Electric Co., Shredded Wheat Co., Ford Motor Co.,
Dodge Motor Co., Reo Motor Co., Chevrolet Motor Co., American
Steel and Wire Co., Armour Packing Co., Corona Typewriter Co.,
Western Electric Co., Pullman Palace Car Co., Texaco Oil Co.,
Standard Oil Co., Elgin Watch Co., Pennsylvania Railway Co., and
of course Bethlehem Steel Co., to name only a few.[20]

The enduring legacy of the Victorian work ethic was its condemnation of idleness.[21] That this philosophy lost neither its appeal nor its effectiveness until well into the twentieth century is
clearly evident in the methods of teaching piano and in the crusade to establish music in industry. The Victorian legacy, however,
is even more apparent in the cult of domesticity.

The Cult of Domesticity

To Victorians, home was both a shelter *from* the anxieties of industrial society and a shelter *for* the moral and spiritual values that the commercial spirit was threatening. "Home Sweet Home" was called an "oasis in the desert," a sanctuary where man could recover his humanity from the selfish, degrading, immoral business and industrial world. The home nourished love, morality, religion, and culture.[22] These convictions continued to appeal to twentieth-century leaders. "Home is never a place," said Eleanor Roosevelt; "it is an atmosphere." The Victorian home was built, Mrs. Roosevelt reminded her listeners, on the principles of family integrity and durability. It was a self-sufficient unit supplying most of its own material and intellectual needs.[23]

It was the woman's task to provide this beauty, this oasis of calm. The cult of domesticity was essentially a social ethic. The woman headed the family and the home and was responsible for social stability, morality, and the transmission of culture. This was a philosophy of utility, which did not advocate women of leisure, who were simply decoration and helpless. As domestic manufacture diminished, as the home lost its productive function to the factory system, the work ethic was merely transferred to this new situation. Motherhood became woman's vocation. Her maternal duties, her influence on men and children, served as a positive social role. The cult of domesticity, which saw women as happy making others happy, was a Victorian middle-class ideal.[24] But within domesticity women gained new recognition and authority. Catharine Beecher, writers in *Godey's Lady's Book* and other magazines, and ministers celebrated the components of the female character: piety, purity, and moral superiority. And apparently, husbands accepted this notion.[25] The moral power of woman rested in her moral influence over man and in motherhood. The cultivation of manners, education, and the accomplishments was accepted as a necessary part of this role. "Beautiful manners are the first test" of morality, cautioned the author of *Girls and*

Women (1890), a handbook for young women. And "no class monopolizes fine manners."[26] Another nineteenth-century handbook, *The Habits of Good Society*, stressed the merits of the female accomplishments: they console the woman in seclusion, arouse her in grief, compose her in joy, and preserve her from ennui by giving her something constructive to do.[27]

Historians have missed an essential point by stressing musical cultivation as no more than an ornamental accomplishment denoting a well-mannered woman. Certainly this notion is accurate, but it is only a part of a complex ethos. The interaction of the work ethic, the cult of domesticity, and the moral value of music formed a crucial Victorian canon. Part of the moral value of music lay in its socializing effect, and part of the moral power of woman lay in her ability to integrate man socially and restrain him from antisocial behavior. Music "carefully played" compels listening, aids conversation, and soothes the troubles of work, claimed "the matron" who wrote *The Habits of Good Society*. A husband or brother "may be made almost domestic by the cheerful notes."[28]

Girls and Women asserted that music added much to woman's happiness.[29] Such happiness upheld woman's morality. In addition, music allowed expression that was otherwise frowned upon. Woman's speech must remain guarded, wrote one Victorian, yet she could speak "freely in the ecstacy of the music she made [at the piano] ... without care or hindrance."[30] In this way music could be a liberating, almost sexual experience for women. Her heart aching, she "groped after great chords" and "gathered strength and comfort as she played," Lilian Bell wrote of her main character in *A Book of Girls* (1903). "Emboldened from within, she burst forth into such a fanfare, such a glorious hallelujah of revolt and emancipation, that the aisles trembled, even the foundations of the great church seemed to rock, and under the exhilaration of the moment, the man in the pews, who loved and understood her, felt that this was his supreme hour."[31]

The ubiquitous Klavier Schule, with its emphasis on discipline, was obviously successful with talented students. With others, however, its moral virtues did not prevent, and indeed seem to have caused, musical failure. One music teacher lamented that people "thunder at the piano, because they are . . . so entangled in the meshes of pietism, prudery, foppishness, and pedantry . . . all that kid-glove gentility and tea table enthusiasm" that they fail to achieve music's ideal elevation. Thus, the value of music is lost in practicing technical exercises or pieces "devoid of character." This sad fact is seen nowhere "so plainly as in the wide-spreading branch of pianoforte-playing."[32] Oscar Wilde sarcastically agreed: "The typewriting machine, when played with expression, is not more annoying than the piano when played by a sister or near relative. Indeed, many among those most devoted to domesticity prefer it."[33]

Good music and self-expression, however, were not really the point. They were valued if they appeared, but it was not necessary that the proper woman play well. *Girls and Women* noted that the ability to play simple things well on the piano was rare, and even "with all her piano lessons she will stumble over the simplest march if any one is listening to her. . . . Nevertheless, she would everywhere at once be recognized as a cultivated lady."[34] Accomplishment was secondary to the dignity, graceful manner, and moral replenishment inherent in learning music.

The middle class demanded modesty of its women, and the piano—even with its "freedom of ecstasy"—"still keeps its pre-eminence as the instrument best fitted for society." The harp, no longer fashionable in the late nineteenth century, caused curvature of the spine, warned the author of *The Habits of Good Society*. The piano "cures this posture problem." The guitar was not forbidden, but it was considered more appropriate for a man. The horn, violin, and especially the cello were definitely unsuited to modest young ladies and would cause "detriment of their feminine attractions."[35] But at the piano, Arthur Loesser infers, her feet kept "demurely together," posture perfect, "there she could sit, gentle and genteel, and be an outward symbol of her family's ability to pay for education and her decorativeness, of its striving for culture and the graces of life, of its pride in the fact that she did not have to work and that she did not 'run after' men."[36]

Twentieth-century Victorians maintained this idea that a girl must learn music. The cult of domesticity accepted motherhood as the primary fulfillment of woman's moral destiny; and raising children correctly, nurturing them in morality, provided a rear-guard against the harshness of industrial society. The musical training of the young girl was a significant part of this nurturing. In 1929 *The Etude*, a very popular magazine that provided a forum for music teachers and was devoted to cultivating a "contagious enthusiasm" for music among amateurs, could declare unabash-edly that the greatest opportunity of America's music clubs was to encourage mothers to give a musical education to their children. Failure to do so was "almost as serious an error as failure to teach [the child] to read or write." To be musically illiterate, *The Etude* warned, was to be "classed with those who leave their spoons erect in their cups and spell cheese with a 'z'—that is, those who have not made the most of their chances."[37]

The close association between the Victorian woman and music, especially the piano, predictably gave music an effeminate cast. "Piano" even crept into the language as meaning gentle, mild, or weak, usually a disparaging remark reserved for men—"James Benwick is rather too piano for me," Jane Austen wrote in *Persuasion* (1818). This feminization of music directly resulted from the place of music within the home, within woman's separate sphere. Acknowledging this, most men were either ignorant of or even prejudiced against musical study for themselves. This notion of separateness carried into the Victorian twentieth century, though many modern writers lamented both the sissy label attached to the boy musician and the way men looked upon music as effemi-nate and unmanly, a softening influence in a strenuous age. The separateness of the spheres could be breached by genius—the male musical virtuoso—but male musicians generally were seen as undependable, unable to support a family. "Only a trifling mu-sician" went the phrase, and "piano" remained an uncomplimen-tary observation. Victorian society did not encourage a man to excel in music, but rather to be a good provider for his family.[38]

The music-in-industry movement of the 1920s began to chal-lenge this dogma. Steel executive Charles M. Schwab, for exam-ple, openly confessed a love for music, declaring that a "favorite saying" among men—"music is for women"—was just not so.[39]

Nevertheless, surveys continued to find music the domain of woman. Harold Randolph regretfully reported to the Music Teachers National Conference in 1922 that 85 percent of music students were girls and that 75 percent of concert audiences were women.[40] Even as late as 1978, a Gallup survey revealed that 57 percent of all musical amateurs were women, and of all amateurs playing the piano, 79 percent were female.[41]

Following the Great War, women joined the crusade for "America First" by promoting the "Americanization" of music and thereby American society as well. The National Federation of Women's Clubs and National Federation of Music Clubs sought to rescue music "from the hands of the infidel foreigner." *Arts and Decoration* reported in 1923, "Never before in the history of the world have so many women actively participated in one project. It is as though the now emancipated feminine voice would proclaim its destiny only through melody."[42] However emancipated was the modern woman, she and the cultivation of music remained bound together. "The hope of music rests with women," declared New York Symphony conductor Walter Damrosch in 1922, and he urged them to "bribe, cajole, and tempt" their fathers, husbands, sons, and brothers into cultivating an appreciation of music.[43] Damrosch's musical democracy, however, had to wait until the advent of the radio and the dissemination of the consumer culture. The Victorian grip was yet too strong.

The Moral Value of Music

The idea that music has an inherent power of moral elevation is at least as old as the Orpheus myth. Celebrating this story, William Congreve penned his famous: "Music hath charms to soothe a savage breast, to soften rocks, or bend a knotted oak."[44] But the tradition is hardly unique to the Greeks. Music and musicians generally have been attributed special moral or spiritual distinction. "Besides theology, music is the only art capable of affording peace and joy of heart," wrote Martin Luther; ". . . the devil flees before the sound of music almost as much as before the word of God."[45] Sir Arthur Conan Doyle even allowed his famous detective to decipher a woman's character from the apparent effects of music: "There is a spirituality about the face, however ... which the typewriter does not generate. The lady is a musician."[46] Such examples of the power of music are ubiquitous in literature.

In Victorian America, music lost none of its ascribed virtues. "The chief value of music ... will be social and moral," declared Lowell Mason. Music should be taught "as a sure means of improving the affections and of ennobling, purifying, and elevating the whole man."[47] Mason and his contemporaries upheld the virtues of music in their fight to make music an integral part of the public school curriculum. Music, especially vocal music, "may be employed to great advantage, as a means of discipline, of health, and of intellectual and moral advancement," Louis Harding said at the 1837 meeting of the Western Literary Institute of College and Professional Teachers in Cincinnati. Timothy B. Mason and Lyman Beecher's son Charles supported Harding, asserting that music would be of physical, intellectual, and moral benefit in the schools.[48] The movement for music in the public schools gained momentum rapidly, with the subject becoming an integral part of the curriculum in cities from Cincinnati to Boston by the early 1840s. Still, attempts to gain a definite place for music in public education were of limited success until the early 1850s and were achieved at great expense.

Nevertheless, throughout the nineteenth century and into the twentieth, enthusiasts regularly preached the moral value of music. The American Association for the Advancement of Education affirmed in 1855 that music "is one of the best means of quickening the moral sensibilities and elevating the affections of the young."[49] *The Habits of Good Society* elaborated on this theme, echoing the best of Victorian sentiments: music refines character, indeed; but it also has the power to bring back "home-born thoughts" and even "in some degree the absent, the kind, the forbearing, the loving, the honoured."[50]

Such remarks were widespread and were not confined to the Gilded Age. Twentieth-century Victorians likewise honored the moral value of music. In 1909 *The Musician* advocated "The Formation of Character through a Proper Study of Music." Thomas Whitney Surette wrote in 1917 that music was "pure spirit," an escape from the "thraldom of everyday." "Music frees us."[51] The latter-day Victorians who sought to end war and make the world safe for democracy that same year considered music to be essential to the war effort. The government of the United States held that music was vital ammunition. Walter R. Spalding, chairman of the Harvard Music Department, declared that "a victorious army will be a music-loving army" and music is "as much a part of the equipment of our fighting men as weapons, uniforms, and rations."[52] Following such advice, the War Department organized the National Committee on Army and Navy Camp Music, and began training musicians and supplying music to our fighting men. The War Work Council of the YMCA purchased pianos and other musical instruments, phonograph records, and player piano rolls for the troops with proceeds collected by civilian organizations. One such group, the Music Trade Exhibitors' Association, sponsored the National Music Exposition at New York's Grand Central Palace during the first week in June 1918. Showing the evolution of the piano, the exposition was billed as the "largest display ever assembled," and was apparently very successful.[53]

These various efforts resulted in what conductor Walter Damrosch called "an epidemic of music at the front," with the piano even making its way into the trenches.[54] With radio broadcasting still in its infancy and not yet generally available, soldiers sang songs around the piano at YMCA huts behind the lines, and civilians did the same back home in the parlor. And through the strains of "Keep the Home Fires Burning," "Till We Meet Again," and "Over There," Americans held together.

Neither Progressivism nor the Victorian spirit was dead in the decade following the Great War. With the support of William Jennings Bryan, Thomas Edison, George Eastman, John Philip Sousa, Kansas senator and former governor Arthur Capper, commissioner of music for the Bureau of Education Philander P. Claxton, and other prominent Americans, *The Etude* magazine launched its "Golden Hour Plan" to use music in the schools in a program of "regular, systematic instruction in character building." Music would be useful to the state, *The Etude* declared, for its potential power to diminish the growing crime problem and remedy the ills of modern society. The key was to reach children with music before they were contaminated by modern society, for "Music and Music only, is the art which so elevates, edifies and enraptures the child mind, that it becomes responsive to suggestions of high ideals." "Good principles of morality, integrity, sobriety, truth, honesty, clean living and patriotism, planted daily in the child mind while that mind is elevated, enthused and spiritualized by means of inspiring music, means that . . . our crime problem will diminish enormously with oncoming years."[55] Similarly, Herbert Witherspoon, before the Music Teachers National Association in 1926, pronounced music to be "a vital factor in education." Music, he said, speaks to all, both the individual and the group, with a common language. It develops ideals as nothing else can. It can "conquer the bad and redeem the good." Music educates the sense of "proportion, good taste, high moral sense, love, companionship, brother and sisterly affection—unless it is debased to lower ends."[56] Progressive reformers particularly supported character education through music, at least music that was considered respectable: the classics, hymns and many folk tunes, and childhood melodies.

The historical traditions supporting the moral value of music assured its significance in the Victorian cult of domesticity, though historians have largely ignored this aspect. According to *The Habits of Good Society*, music is the "medicine of the soul; it soothes the wrinkles of a hard life of business, and lifts us from thoughts of money, intrigue, enterprises, anxieties, hatred, and what not, to a calmer, more heavenly frame of mind."[57] Was this not the essence of the cult of domesticity? Were not women to maintain a home environment that provided essentially the same respite from the ills of industrialization?

Furthermore, serious teachers of music considered their profession a calling in the clerical sense of the word. They felt obliged to teach the proper kind of art music to students—especially to what one teacher called the "excitable and sensuously inclined" woman—in order to promote the Ideal in the life of the people, to elevate them and keep them there.[58] Like religion, music could save souls. But this power was not confined to hymns. Childhood melodies, the kind that are reminiscent of home, were of equal value here. "Many a hardened sinner has come back repentant at the sound of a melody from the distant years of early life," wrote one music teacher. "No man who . . . hums the melodies of his boyhood, need be mistrusted."[59] Music weaned the mind from sensual and vicious indulgences, providing instead a kind and generous heart. Though music also was promoted as pleasure and cultural refinement, its role in the moral rehabilitation of adults and the moral education of children was of greatest importance in Victorian philosophy.[60]

With music cloaked in such virtues, it was inevitable that the youthful, idealistic, middle-class social workers who sought to bring education, culture, and hope to urban slums would incorporate music as part of their settlement house movement. It is significant that most of the settlement workers were women. Given the place of music in the cult of domesticity, the moral value of music itself, and the essential part music played in middle-class female education, the use of music in the settlements was a natural extension of the middle-class home. Hull House, Chicago, established the first Music Settlement School in 1893, teaching music not as an adornment, but as a liberating, educative, humanizing force. By 1922 settlement workers had established more than eighty such schools.[61] In at least one instance the virtue of music translated through the piano was a successful redeemer. One settlement family had a piano, the mother refusing to sell it even though the money would have paid overdue bills. The reason? Her two girls played that piano, and they, unlike many neighborhood girls who "have been in trouble by being out on the streets late at night," stayed out of such trouble by having good, clean, moral fun at the piano.[62]

The therapeutic application of music in Victorian culture of the early twentieth century already has been noted in the crusade to establish music in industry. Music educators and physicians also saw the benefit of music in treating mental and physical illness. In

New York, for example, pianists and other musicians were employed in the sixteen hospitals of the New York Tuberculosis Association with positive results. Mental hospitals had parallel success. Similarly, the powerful Music Industries Chamber of Commerce, whose major component was the piano manufacturers, promoted music as an antidote to city and factory noise. Working with the New York Federation of Music Clubs, the Chamber launched a campaign in 1922 to "bring music into every home." The "only statistics available" sadly suggested that only a third of New York homes had a piano or other musical instrument.[63]

By the 1930s music educators saw the moral power of music less as an intrinsic quality and more as a potential quality, depending entirely upon the situations and reactions of those people involved. Nevertheless, given the right situation, music could still cheer, soothe, give confidence, develop self-discipline and physical coordination, gratify creative and aesthetic urges, and even "open the gates of heaven."[64] Such thinking would have been a comfortable philosophy for any respectable Victorian.[65]

Music in the American Home: The Pianoforte

It is significant that when Catharine Beecher and Harriet Beecher Stowe devised their floor plan for "a Christian House" and published it in *The American Woman's Home* (1869), they were careful to provide space in the drawing room for the inevitable piano. Music, they wrote, is an "elevating and delightful recreation."[66] As another popular book concurred twenty-one years later, "No home is complete without music," because singing and playing, being both "delightful" and "morally and physically uplifting," sustain family life.[67] For middle-class Victorians, the family circle and its home were the cornerstone of society. Throughout the nineteenth century the home increasingly became materially and emotionally significant as a refuge and a source of stability. As Nancy Woloch confirms, the home was increasingly depicted as "an insulated, privatized, feminized shrine," attesting to the power of the cult of domesticity.[68]

But the middle-class home also was becoming a display case of social status, elaborately decorated with upholstered furniture, carpets, and draperies. In the drawing room, kitchen, and even bathroom, Victorians sought to fill space with solid, heavy pieces.[69] The emphasis was on comfort; but permanence was the philosophy. Thus, much of Victorian furniture was designed not to fit into a room, but to dominate it. And as the center of the home changed from the kitchen to the parlor (where the family assembled and guests were entertained),[70] the ornate, massive piano became the most conspicuous and fundamental parlor piece. As Arthur Loesser insightfully suggested, the piano's "inertia, if nothing else, made it the focus of the domestic musical life."[71] Even so, pianos were expensive, and quite naturally became symbols of a family's ability to afford both the instrument and lessons to play it. The piano retained this connotation of status—clever salesmen perpetuated the association—despite the arrival later in the century of less-expensive, mass-produced pianos known as "thump boxes."

In Gilded Age America, the expanding middle class supported the arts: eastern and midwestern urban areas increased newspaper coverage of operas, symphonies, and distinguished virtuosos; they built and supported fine concert halls, and established impressive schools of music in Oberlin, Chicago, Boston, Cincinnati, and Baltimore.[72] Music-hungry, class-conscious Americans filled their urban parlors with mass-produced, enormous upright pianos in oak cases, highly ornamented (sold on the installment plan) as testimony of their increasing wealth, improving taste, and moral superiority. Even as early as 1867, James Parton could write in *The Atlantic Monthly* that "almost every couple that sets up housekeeping on a respectable scale considers a piano only less indispensable than a kitchen range."[73] But the phenomenon was not limited to urban areas. The piano was truly ubiquitous and by the 1880s began reaching rural areas as well. As piano technician and scholar William Braid White revealed, "cynical salesmen used to say that farmers bought their pianos as they bought their hogs—by the pound."[74] However, traditional interpretations that see such middle-class piano purchase merely as symbolic of status or respectability obscures the complex interaction of the work ethic, the cult of domesticity, and the assumption of the moral value of music in Victorian America, and are as incomplete as the other common ideas about pianos in the nineteenth century: that the infamous skirting of the piano's "limbs" revealed Victorian prudery.[75]

In an age of idealism, the ideal woman replenished an ideal morality in an ideal home filled with ideal sentiment and musical nurture. The freestanding suburban house provided the ideal home for the expanding middle class of the late nineteenth century, offering both isolation and insulation from the vice-ridden urban, commercial world.[76] Within this temple of repose the parlor was the main social area (sociability was considered a virtue), the repository of sentiment, and the room most revealing a family's wealth, culture, and dignity. "This room should convey a sense of elegance, good taste, recognition of the polite arts, and of graceful, social amenities," wrote Mary Gay Humphreys in 1896.[77] The contents of such homes remained unaltered for generations, while social life rested upon the family and neighborhood, with woman presiding.[78] Permanence was the philosophy.

Evening was the family time, when all gathered together. Ideally, all looked forward to it as an established part of an ordered universe. James Truslow Adams asserted that such practice was uniform and universal throughout the United States.[79] From the family of the mother in the settlement house to that of the First Lady in the White House, such a gathering also inevitably included music played upon the piano. The Sunday night hymn singing in the Hayes administration, in which Lucy Webb Hayes played hymns on the Chickering while guests, "a crowd of people, sang with heart and soul,"[80] was no isolated incident. "It was accepted as an unavoidable feature of a small soirée," Ralph Dutton somewhat callously wrote, "however tedious it might be."[81]

Such gatherings were primarily social, not ornamental. Etiquette books of the period advised decorous behavior: the proper way a lady seats herself at, plays, and leaves the piano; the proper way a gentleman escorts the lady to the piano, turns her pages "if he be competent," and cares for her gloves, purse, and other articles; even the proper music—the short piece is best fitted for society, declared *The Habits of Good Society*. In *Our Manners and Social Customs* (1892), Daphne Dale advised ladies to master a few pieces to play from memory, as "to carry your music with you is to suggest that you expect to play."[82] Furthermore, most girls enjoyed playing the piano as an accompaniment to singing. Accompanied vocal music, until the age of ragtime, was apparently the forte of Victorian amateur musicians.[83] Accommodating this trend, music publishers increasingly turned out "brilliant but not difficult" music, songs with passages that lay comfortably beneath a lady's hand. "The Lost Chord," "Last Hope," and "The Maiden's Prayer" continued to be best-sellers even into the "Victorian" twentieth century.[84]

In 1909 *The Musician* considered a concerned fifteen-year-old reader's question, "Why should a young girl take up the study of music?" The editor, reinforcing traditional Victorian values, replied that the girl should "be prepared to do her part in the scheme of social pleasure [because] the social element is strong in the life of young women." Furthermore, music study "makes common ground" with her companions. And though he stressed the value of music in the social circle, music in the home received added emphasis: "In the home life the daughter who can contribute to lighten the hours free from the cares of business and the household is a boon to her father, to her mother, and to her brothers. 'Give us a tune, Sis,' is a common request." The girl musician was not just cultivating a pastime or social grace; she was playing her proper role. She provided a musical oasis in a workaday world. "Don't make them go out of the home for lack of this pleasure," warned *The Musician* sternly. "Music is wanted in the home." Finally, the editor advised that music study could be profitable; at age twenty the girl could become a self-supporting woman. Financial independence, however, was beside the point.

The essential reason a young girl should study music was "that she prepared herself to minister to the joy and pleasure of others, thus fulfilling the social ideal."[85]

Music also was an important part of Victorian courtship. The girl who could sit at the piano and sing sentimental songs to gentlemen callers was at least popular and at best had a greater chance of a good marriage. The piano—symbol of Victorian morality and respectability—naturally lent itself to romance, serenade, and betrothal. "In many a humble home throughout our land the piano has gathered about it the most sacred and tender association," remarked President Grover Cleveland. "[W]ith its music each daughter . . . touched . . . the heart of her future husband."[86] When Catharine Beecher and Alexander Fisher began singing and playing the piano together, it was recognized as the beginning of a serious courtship. Within a year the two were engaged.[87] Piano manufacturer George P. Bent fondly acknowledged, "I courted my wife over a [Henry F.] Miller piano," and even the "father of radio," Lee De Forest, fell in love with the woman playing the piano in the apartment next to his, as "propinquity led to aquaintance."[88]

Playing the piano also had its comparatively licentious reward. Many Victorian sentimental songs required the couple to cross hands, thus providing the opportunity for touching.[89] *The Habits of Good Society* reminded young ladies that piano music "vibrates on a chord of sympathy between the sexes when possibly there is no other."[90] Wright Morris fondly recalled his girlfriend's playing "Lotus Land" by Cyril Scott, "a piece to my taste." But "even more than the music my girl liked to play," Morris continued, "I loved to see her seated at the piano, her body swaying slightly, as she was carried away by the music. At these moments I liked to fancy myself at her side, turning the pages of music, waiting for that moment when she would turn, gaze into my eyes, and I would embrace her. An embrace was a good deal more than a kiss."[91]

Perhaps such intimacy explains both Elizabeth Stuart Phelps's vision of heaven in her best-selling *The Gates Ajar* (1868), in which young girls play the piano,[92] and also William Holman Hunt's symbolic painting, *The Awakened Conscience* (1852–54).

The piano thus played a dual role, as an aid to flirtation but also as a monument to the moral value of music and the morality inherent in the cult of domesticity. By the late 1890s, Victorian prudery had dissolved enough to allow couples to be alone in the parlor with the doors closed, but even then a popular song warned the vulnerable young lady to "Keep Your Foot on the Soft Pedal."[93] The piano might have aided flirtation; but the moral code it symbolized was as steadfast as the piano itself. The American "piano girl" became a Victorian ideal, an intriguing blend of the work ethic, the cult of domesticity, the moral value of music, and of course, middle-class social life.

The continuity of Victorian traditions extended beyond the Victorian age. This ethos, in which the piano figured so prominently and in which the American piano industry prospered, was apparently still highly regarded into the 1920s. "The possession of a piano presupposes that it is housed in the home of people of comfortable means," declared Byron H. Collins in *The Etude* in 1922. "Most of us," contended Mrs. Somerset Maugham in 1925, are "people who possess a piano because life wouldn't be worth living without it." Other writers lamented the silent, inarticulate home devoid of music, which could easily be made vibrant and warm, "a welcoming place where one is glad to be," with the addition of a piano. "A fine piano is one of the most 'worth-while' investments in our interesting modern life," echoed James Francis Cooke in 1929, who insisted that the instrument was still the "center of the home culture." As such, "it brings mental stimulus, imagination, inspiration, entertainment, solace, poetry, color, love of home, and a hundred and one priceless advantages without which our much mechanized and 'forced-draft' existence might lead to a mere whirligig of restless activity with no ultimate elevation of the soul."[94]

Pronouncements such as these were common in the Victorian culture of the early twentieth century. They were also dangerously deceptive. By the time of the Great War, a new ethos, the consumer culture, had already gained irreversible momentum in the United States and was rapidly undermining Victorian values. The meteoric rise in popularity of the automatic piano, with its emphasis on playing without effort, illustrates this change. Ironically, the American piano industry innocently helped bring about this revolutionary transformation. Adopting modern persuasive advertising techniques, the piano trade sought to bring into every home a piano that anyone and everyone could play, without tedious lessons and time-consuming practice. It was a dream of a musical democracy that offered effortless access to the virtues of music. Yet, such a vision was not only contradictory to the Victorian frame of mind; it was peculiarly destructive of the very foundation upon which the American piano industry was built.

CHAPTER TWO

The Origins of a Musical Democracy

It is only a question of time when practically every piano will carry a player mechanism.
—William Geppert,
  The Official Guide
  to Piano Quality

"O mamma, come into the drawing room; there is a man in there playing the piano with his hands!"
—John Philip Sousa

The Pianola Piano is the Short Cut to Musical Enjoyment.
—Aeolian Company
  advertisement

Mechanization is essentially a story of values, not inventions. The two decades preceding the Great War produced an acceleration in the transformation of values from the Victorian age to the consumer culture. It was a time of pursuing old dreams with new technology, turning to new challenges, but with a traditional reference. In 1911 President William Howard Taft, himself caught between the challenges of the Progressive Era and the more conservative Victorian mentality, symbolized this transformation of values when he opened the annual convention of the National Piano Dealers of America in the Chicago Coliseum. The dealers had placed an electric piano in the president's hotel suite and connected it by wire to the Coliseum. "Seating himself at the instrument," reported the *New York Times*, "Mr. Taft struck a chord, and simultaneously the doors of the exposition swung open and the lights flashed on."[1] In this enlightened age the piano trade proudly offered the means with which to make music accessible to all—the mechanical player piano.

This notion of a *musical democracy* was both reformist and commercial. A wide appreciation of music could counteract the evils of industrialization, yet provide the means to large and successful business enterprise. The American piano industry set out to establish a democracy of music lovers, in which music would be consequential if not indispensable in *everyone's* life, thus insuring a morally healthier society, and also wider sales. Victorian culture provided a firm groundwork for this maneuver. The importance of music in the nineteenth century had engendered public school singing programs, music schools and conservatories, the mass publication of easy-to-play sentimental songs, and the production of inexpensive upright pianos sold increasingly on credit terms. But this foundation was restrictive, being essentially a feminine, middle-class phenomenon that was further limited by difficult and discouraging piano lessons, the inequality of talent, and a lack of universally available professional concerts. Still, middle-class piano manufacturers sought to expand their trade and extend their social philosophy.

The convergence of four developing factors in the 1890s created a musical revolution in American society. Though products of the

Victorian age, their consequences were indecipherable to the Victorian frame of mind. They contributed in an unprecedented way toward the formation of a musical democracy by making music a consumable object available to all, without the need of painstaking cultivation. These revolutionary factors were the contagion of ragtime music, and the invention of the mechanical player piano, the phonograph, and the motion picture. While each of these inventions in time effected change (however minimized by the invention of the radio), it was the player piano—with its significant link to Victorian culture, its superior fidelity, and its mass-production by an influential industry already entrenched in American musical and industrial life—that was the most powerful force toward establishing a musical democracy in the Victorian twentieth century.

The Contagion of Ragtime

The American heyday of the piano, when young people were most likely to gather around it and sing, was from the late nineteenth century to the beginning of the First World War. From 1870 to 1890 piano production increased at a rate 1.6 times faster than population growth. This ratio increased to 5.6 times from 1890 to 1900, and to 6.2 times the following decade.[2] The industry's peak year in production was 1909, with 364,545 pianos valued at $58.5 million. Alfred Dolge, renowned inventor and manufacturer of piano-making machinery, listed 295 separate piano makers and 69 piano supply manufacturers by 1911.[3] This decided increase in production was merely a part of a much more significant phenomenon overtaking Victorian America: modernization and the rise of the consumer culture. As America modernized, as it became progressive and faster paced, popular music also speeded up both in production and in tempo. A new type of music infected American parlors and spread like a contagion; it was called ragtime.

Irving Berlin, who capitalized on the mood with his song "Everything in America Is Ragtime Crazy," noted the kinship between modern American music and modern American life. The "speed and snap" of American ragtime was influenced directly by the automobile, Berlin remarked in 1924. The motor car "introduced to motivation a new method of movement. All the old rhythm was gone," he stressed, "and in its place was heard the hum of an engine, the whirr of wheels, the explosion of an exhaust. The leisurely songs that men hummed to the clatter of horses' hoofs did not fit into this new rhythm—the new age demanded new music for new action. . . . The country speeded up."[4]

Developed from folk songs and plantation banjo tunes, ragtime's peculiar and distinctly American style sprang up in the 1890s under the talented hands of black musicians in saloons, brothels, and casinos (blacks were denied the right to play elsewhere). At first the "refined" sections of American culture condemned the music. In 1901, for example, the American Federation of Musicians forbade its members to play ragtime, and most American composers were outspokenly hostile to what Edward MacDowell called the "nigger whorehouse music."[5] There were exceptions, of course, in the American musical establishment. Charles Ives used the idiom in his own works, and described ragtime as "something like wearing a derby hat on the back of the head, a shuffling lilt of a happy soul just let out of a Baptist church in old Alabama."[6] But Victorian respectability forbade most from indulging in such perceived immoral frivolity. "In Christian homes, where purity of morals are stressed," warned Leo Oehmler in the *Musical Observer*, "ragtime should find no resting place."[7] Among blacks this attitude also persisted. "I started playing what I heard about me," Eubie Blake remembered. "My mother was very religious and hated ragtime like all the high-class Negroes. . . . When I played it at home my mother would yell, 'Take that ragtime out of my house. As long as I'm here, you don't play ragtime in this house!' I had to go somewhere else to practice. *She* knew where it came from."[8]

Such judgments did not persist, however. By about 1910 ragtime had lost not only its sinful implication, but its association with black musicians as well. Middle-class America adopted the invigorating music into its own social life, white composers offered their own renditions of the form, and New York's Tin Pan Alley publishers developed it into big business. Though the musical establishment (including most private teachers) continued to denounce the "unbridled," "devilish," and "undignified" quality of the infectious new music, ragtime was accepted by the general American public.[9]

Popular music is not so much a musicological category as it is a sociological phenomenon.[10] In a hardly subtle way, the contagious popularity of ragtime both contributed to and resulted from the revolutionary change occurring in late nineteenth- and early twentieth-century America. It involved the big businesses of piano manufacturing, Tin Pan Alley songwriting, sheet music publication, and not least, the emerging consumer mentality, with its emphasis on recreation rather than work. Without the aid of radio (the phonograph was yet in its infancy and fidelity was primitive), sound movies, or television, ragtime spread across the United States and to other countries from the 1890s to the 1920s largely through traditional means: dance bands, pianists, sheet music, and "song pluggers." This was much the way music had always been popularized, played by hand from musician to audience.

But this time the phenomenon was aided by mechanical reproduction and a developing ideology of consumerism. Chiefly written for piano, ragtime music was successfully transcribed to perforated rolls and played mechanically on the player piano. Its delightful strains were popularized as much by pumping feet or electric motors as by hand. Player pianos were in fact an essential element of the contagion.[11] Given the limited fidelity and recording time of the pre–World War I phonograph (few piano solo recordings were made on disc until the 1920s), perforated rolls allowed the unprecedented dissemination of piano music, especially among the nonplaying public. Thus, the music was "consumed" as well as "produced." In this way ragtime became a product much like any other in the emerging consumer society. These products became characterized by their uniformity: they were all easily accessible, all short-lived, and all sold in a market of intense promotion and competition. The society itself became distinguished by an emphasis on the consumer's passive use of machine-made products. Ragtime was not popular because it was played by hand, but because it was well promoted and easily consumed.

Although ragtime was apparently the rage as early as the 1893 Chicago World's Fair, the first published piece was white composer William Krell's "Mississippi Rag" in 1897. Texas-born black composer Scott Joplin composed his famous "Maple Leaf Rag" in 1897 and published it with John Stark two years later. Although it was a slow seller initially—John Stark said that it took a year to sell 400 copies—in the fall of 1900 the rag suddenly became a financial success for both publisher and composer. Eventually it would be the first sheet-music piece to top a million sales. Apparently, everyone knew it. Joplin became the acknowledged "King of Ragtime."[12]

The so-called classic ragtime that Joplin and his followers (notably James Scott and Joseph Lamb) so carefully cultivated was soon overshadowed by products of Tin Pan Alley writers, which were easier to play and were heavily promoted in an attempt to capitalize on the craze. Joplin himself was already fighting this competition as early as 1908, when he wrote within a set of ragtime exercises: "That all publications masquerading under the name of ragtime are not the genuine article will be better known when these exercises are studied. That real ragtime of the higher class is rather difficult to play is a painful truth which most pianists have discovered."[13]

It is no coincidence that Joplin wrote technical exercises and stressed painful study of his music. His goal was to make ragtime respectable. The King of Ragtime, much like the era's president, Theodore Roosevelt, was a Victorian out of his time, product of a producer ethic, but also very much contributor to a progressive, modern culture—the consumer society. Ragtimers, like President Roosevelt, became celebrities, products to be consumed.[14]

Neither is it coincidence that ragtime was predominantly a piano form. Piano music was the socially and morally accepted form of musical expression for the American middle class. Piano manufacture, sheet music publication and distribution, and piano purchase were Victorian middle-class institutions. If Irving Berlin's attribution of ragtime's success to modernization is correct, this success had to come from middle-class acceptance. Ragtime, the first music of modern America, changed American musical culture.

Ragtime offered a pleasant alternative to Czerny excercises and the demands of the Klavier Schule, a relief to thousands driven to "play nicely" and practice "painfully." Its fast, syncopated pace reflected the changes in daily life. It was meant to be enjoyed, not to build character. It is essential to see ragtime's progress from the early view that it was immoral and sinful to its subsequent unprecedented national popularity in terms of this change in values.

The immediate effect of ragtime's popularity was the mass production of rags and ragtime songs, primarily emanating from New York's Tin Pan Alley district (especially from the Jerome H. Remick company, which issued over 500 rags, about one sixth of the entire published output). Scholars generally agree that the modern American music industry came to power during the revolution of ragtime.[15] Ironically, the most successful, the most widely played, sung, and danced "rag" was no real rag at all save for the title: Irving Berlin's "Alexander's Ragtime Band" (1911). But to ears of 1900–1915, ragtime was ragtime, whether it was the "Maple Leaf Rag," "Moonlight Bay," "Hello, Ma Baby," "Dill Pickles Rag," or "Put on Your Old Grey Bonnet."[16] Scott Joplin appropriately described ragtime, if played correctly, as having "that weird and intoxicating effect."[17] The Progressive Era was the Ragtime Era. As one song put it:

> I got a ragtime dog and a ragtime cat,
> A ragtime piano in my ragtime flat;
> Wear ragtime clothes, from hat to shoes,
> I read a paper called the "Ragtime News."
> Got ragtime habits and I talk that way,
> I sleep in ragtime and I rag all day;
> Got ragtime troubles with my ragtime wife,
> I'm certainly living a ragtime life.[18]

The Revolutionary Player Piano

In 1903 Axel Christensen advertised in the *Chicago Daily News*: "Ragtime Taught in Ten Lessons." By 1918, Christensen Schools had spread from Chicago to twenty-five cities, from San Francisco to New York, inducing people to "learn to play ragtime and be popular."[19] Capitalizing on the ragtime craze that engulfed the United States, Christensen significantly aided the spread of the contagion. Yet, the Christensen method—even if only ten lessons—still required the individual to learn to play the piano, to *produce* music with effort. Thus, his audience remained limited.

Moreover, despite the importance of playing the piano in Victorian culture, few amateur pianists could play well. This prompted *Fortune* magazine to assess the piano as the "crowning-adornment" in the American home, "as essential and often as nonfunctional as the fringe on the parlor lamp shades."[20] *The Atlantic Monthly* similarly described the Victorian piano as standing "for the most part . . . silent, majestic like an inanimate footman, testifying with polished rosewood to the opulence and taste of its possessor."[21]

Commentators lamented the frequent inability among girls and women to play even simple things on the piano well, and cited such depressing ratios as "94 percent" and "nine-tenths" as the dropout rate among piano students.[22] One irate father wailed that despite a year of lessons, his daughter, "who is of at least average intelligence I hope, knew absolutely nothing about music, although she was able to play a few stumbling passages on the keyboard after an hour's diligent practice daily during this period."[23] The British novelist R. F. Delderfield concurred, indicating the trans-Atlantic dimension of this problem: "I never encountered one of my fellow pupils in later life who could play a recognizable national anthem on a piano, or even one who wanted to, and it frightens me to conjecture where all those hours and hours of practice went, or what they accomplished in terms of achievement. One would imagine that *something* would have stuck, a phrase or two of one of the 'pieces,' a tiny residual of the technicalities we imbibed, but it didn't."[24]

Fathers frequently referred to daughter's efforts to "play nicely" as her "$400 piece," indicating that the financial investment in piano and lessons was lacking a gainful return. "I don't play accurately," said the heroine in Oscar Wilde's *The Importance of Being Earnest*, "but I play with wonderful expression. As far as the piano is concerned, sentiment is my *forte*. I keep science for life." Perhaps it was just such spirited attempts at "expression" that drove George Bernard Shaw to declare, "Hell is full of musical amateurs: music is the brandy of the damned."[25]

This unfortunate condition in an age in which music was so morally and socially important was relieved considerably as ragtime ignited a new interest in music. But more important was the change brought about by the mechanical player piano, the instrument that introduced ragtime itself to hundreds of thousands if not millions of ears and helped to spread it across the land. To many music educators, businessmen, and consumers, the real intoxication with this innovative instrument was with its unprecedented ability to encourage and elevate music appreciation, to allow the unmusical the opportunity for and benefit of musical expression, to redeem the rusty talents of the musically "fallen"—to provide music for all.

"The so-called mechanical piano player is destined to do more toward popularizing good music the country over than the three great orchestras of Chicago, New York, and Boston combined," proclaimed Charles I. Rice, supervisor of music in the public schools of Worcester, Massachusetts, in 1907. Music educators foresaw a golden age of musical creation and appreciation. The player piano inspired a new music education movement in the public schools, even in districts that had shunned such efforts before. And in schools whose music education program had been limited to vocal music, the player piano for the first time allowed an appreciation of piano, even orchestral, literature.[26] Virtually all music could be transcribed for perforated roll.

In an article for *The Musician* in 1917, Yolanda Mero affirmed that in the preceding twenty to twenty-five years, the number of

pianists in the United States had increased "at bewildering proportions." "The growth of musical appreciation plus American
prosperity has made the piano our national musical instrument,"
Mero continued, "a common part of household furnishings out-
numbered only by rocking chairs and kitchen tables." Music
teachers, piano manufacturers, and music publishers were all rejoicing in this musical emancipation, this step toward the democratization of art.[27]

Similarly rejoicing, *The Outlook* magazine in 1917 was confident that mechanical music would resolve the contradiction
in American thinking that music was either light entertainment
or art reserved only for the few. This discrepancy between concert and popular music, between amateur and cultivated music,
emerged in post-Civil War America as a direct result of the virtuoso phenomenon and the increased professionalization of the
music industry. *The Outlook* commented that Europeans, unlike
Americans, regard good music as part of everyday life, a necessity rather than a luxury. "In America, we have been too busy
with other things to study music as the Germans do," professed
an Aeolian player piano advertisement in 1908; and of course,
Aeolian had the answer in easy monthly payments. *The Outlook*
agreed, indicating that the perfection of mechanical music had
led to an almost universal music education in America: there
seemed to be a talking machine or player piano in every home,
whether its owners played or not. "These inventive and progressive manufacturers are literally 'putting music into every home,'"
and furthermore, the "most progressive" manufacturers were
spending thousands of dollars on "interesting and instructive literature" to raise the level of the public's musical taste, to help
them distinguish "good music from mere 'ragtime.'"[28]

Such enthusiasm was evolutionary, however, even among the
piano manufacturers themselves. The development of the modern
pneumatic piano-playing device was concurrent with the rise
and spread of ragtime. M. Welte & Söhne of Freiburg-im-Breisgau,
Germany, patented the pneumatic action activated by a perforated
paper roll in 1887. But it was an American, E. S. Votey, who in 1897
perfected this system in the Pianola piano-player, a cabinet-en-

closed "push up" device whose "fingers" rested upon the keys of a traditional piano. Manufactured and promoted under the direction of Harry B. Tremaine and his father, William Barnes Tremaine, founder of the Aeolian Company of New York, the impact of Pianola (a registered, copyrighted trademark name) was swift: "pianola" became the generic term for all "cabinet" or "push up" piano-players.[29] Manufacturer George P. Bent, however, claimed to have sold the first piano-player in the United States, a Wilcox & White Co. machine, in Chicago, May 1897, to M. E. Cook of the Chicago Board of Trade. He claimed that his "enthusiasm" and "attentive service," had caused other members of the Board to follow suit. Nevertheless, "the idea of such an invention was cruelly criticized by the trade in general," Bent related in 1924. "It was the universal acclaim that such a thing as a 'machine' to produce piano playing was not only ridiculous, but the very *idea* was preposterous."[30]

Perhaps to an industry reared in traditional Victorian values, such automation at first did seem preposterous. But most remaining piano manufacturers and many music educators were soon infected by the same ideal of a musical democracy that moved Welte and Aeolian to rekindle musical study in those who had given up hope, to interest men in music (what could be "unmanly" about operating a machine?). This is made obvious by the sheer number of manufacturers that turned to production of automatic pianos, and by the number of pianos produced as well.

Harry B. Tremaine, who succeeded his father as president of Aeolian Company in 1898, fostered the popularity of the Votey Pianola piano-player by running an advertising campaign that, according to trade historian and manufacturer Alfred Dolge, "stunned the old timers in the piano trade." "Before the advent of the 'Pianola,'" wrote Dolge in *Pianos and Their Makers* (1911), "there was neither competition nor encouragement from the piano trade."[31] By 1902, however, Aeolian had prepared the general strategy in player-piano advertising: "The Pianola solves the problem of music in the home. . . . every member of the household may be a performer," read an impressive four-page, two-color advertisement in *The Cosmopolitan* magazine. "The Pianola is the universal means of playing the piano. Universal because there is no one in all the world, having use of hands and feet, who could not learn to use it with but little effort. To operate it is simplicity itself. . . . a little child can do all this and give correct expression to the composition played." Rooted firmly in the Victorian ethos, the Aeolian ad also stressed that, "the piano is available to all. In its rhythmic tones the busy man forgets his cares. The hostess finds relief from thoughts concerning entertainment for her guests; and happy young folks respond with feet or voice and in a dance or song find wholesome recreation under the family roof."[32]

Popular only briefly (1900–1905), the 65-note "push up" player successfully introduced mechanically produced music to the public. It was clumsy, fragile, and rather a nuisance when one wanted to play the piano by hand. And as Arthur Whiting remarked in the July 1919 *Yale Review*, "The early models of the player had the exuberant spirits of a machine gun," because it lacked phrasing or volume controls.[33] But a rash of player manufacturers developed nevertheless to capitalize on the wave of the future, with Pianola, Angelus ("It Will Play Any Piano"), Cecilian, Pianista ("Knows No Technical Difficulties"), Simplex ("Anybody Can Play Anything"), Maestro, and Paragon being among the best known.[34] According to a product investigation authorized by Lucien Wulsin I, president of D. H. Baldwin & Co., the Pianola was the most satisfactory "at present," the Simplex was "hard to pump and rather cumbersome," while the Cecilian was "more artistic" because it had two buttons which controlled bass and treble volume. "It [the button control] does away with the mechanical thumping of the bass in an artistic piece of music." Such "thumping" apparently was a weakness in the Pianola, as Wulsin's memo indicated its bass was "very often heavier" than the treble. In addition, the Wulsin investigation found the Cecilian "*very* easy to pump."[35] Nevertheless, by 1909 the "push up" piano-player market was dead, long overtaken by the self-contained player piano.

Alfred Dolge suggests in *Pianos and Their Makers* that R. W. Pain produced the first self-contained pneumatic player piano (a 39-note instrument) as early as 1880 for Needham & Sons, New York. By 1888 Pain apparently also had manufactured a 65-note electric player. But Melville Clark Piano Co. (Chicago) produced the first documented player piano in 1901, and within a year the Aeolian Company brought out its own version. Capitalizing on the success of its "push up" model, Aeolian advertised the new self-contained instrument as "The Pianola Piano—The First Complete Piano."[36] It, too, would be an enormous success.

In 1902 Melville Clark introduced the first 88-note player piano, and by 1904 offered a self-contained pneumatic player action for grand pianos. In time, almost every maker made players or fitted pianos with player actions acquired from action factories. Since manufacture of actions and piano rolls was not standardized, however, chaotic conditions greatly hindered the industry. This situation was alleviated at a 1910 convention in Buffalo, New York, when player and music roll manufacturers agreed to abandon 58-, 70-, and 82-note players and produce only 65- or 88-note machines. This important move insured interchangeability among the many different makes.[37] Also by 1910 the piano trade had developed impressive merchandising campaigns. Hardman, Peck & Company, for example, presented their Autotone in monthly concerts in New York City, the piano in duet with vocal and violin soloists. Roll companies transcribed orchestral pieces, dance music, hymns, and popular songs (with words). In 1915 Sears, Roebuck offered the Improved Beckwith Player Piano with twenty rolls and a silk scarf for $397 (or $8 a month). And in its best Victorian phraseology, the American Player Piano Co. advertised, "The American Player Piano in the Home is the Delight of the American Girl." Likewise did Standard Pneumatic Action Co. proclaim, "A Player Piano is the Heart of a Happy Home."[38]

The ultimate in mechanical music technology and sound recording fidelity was the "reproducing" piano (originally an Aeolian trademark name). Introduced in a piano-player cabinet about 1904 by the German firm of M. Welte & Söhne and marketed in the United States about 1907 as Welte-Mignon (or "little Welte," to distinguish it from the huge mechanical orchestrions for which the manufacturer was famous in Europe), this instrument was capable of reproducing the full virtuosity of the artist—the nuances, the phrasing, and all the shadings. Practically all the great artists of the day recorded for Welte, including Grieg, Debussy, Strauss, Respighi, Bartók, Leschetitzky, and Paderewski. American production of the Welte-Mignon mechanism began in 1911, but Welte's assets were seized under the Alien Property Act during the First World War. Subsequently, the company was reformed as the Welte-Mignon Corporation, a subsidiary of the Auto-Pneumatic Action Co., which was itself a division of Kohler & Campbell Industries; the Welte patents were then used under license. Welte-Mignon Licensee actions were fitted to 112 makes of American pianos, including Baldwin, Bush & Lane, Conover, Kimball, Kranich & Bach, Mehlin & Sons, Stief, Hardman, and Sohmer. In 1913, the Aeolian Company of New York introduced the Duo-Art, the first American version of the reproducing piano, and installed the mechanism in its Aeolian, Stroud, Wheelock, Steck, and Weber pianos, and in special piano cases that the firm purchased from Steinway & Sons. The American Piano Co. (also of New York) produced its own Ampico in 1913, though it was not formally presented to the public until 1916. The company offered the Ampico action in its Mason & Hamlin, Knabe, Chickering, J. & C. Fischer, Marshall & Wendell, and Haines Bros. pianos.[39]

Ampico's "spark chronograph technique" of recording was capable of transcribing onto the piano roll not only all the artist's movement of keys and pedals, but the exact measurements of hammer velocity at the moment of impact with the strings as well. Thus, the company proudly stated, the instrument offered "perfect recording plus perfect re-enactment."[40] *The Piano and Organ Purchaser's Guide for 1919* similarly proclaimed the Duo-Art's prowess: "The remarkable patented mechanism of the Duo-Art reproduces not only the notes, tempo, phrasing and attack, but also every tone gradation precisely as originally played and recorded by the artist, including all the dynamics of his rendition with the innumerable gradations from pianissimo to sforzando, all crescendos and diminuendos, whether of abrupt or extended length; also all pedal effects of the artist in the use of the sostenuto and soft pedals; also all other expression effects so true to the individuality of the respective artists who recorded the original Duo-Art rolls that their style and identity is unmistakably to be recognized in their performance by the Duo-Art Pianola." Welte-Mignon advertising, which coined the popular slogan "The Master's Fingers On Your Piano," accurately and simply stated: "When you hear Welte-Mignon (Licensee) the artist himself is playing."[41]

As part of the unprecedented promotional campaign that both the Aeolian and American Piano companies devised, the Duo-Art and Ampico appeared as unmanned soloists with many of the leading orchestras of the day, including the Philadelphia Orchestra under Stokowski, the New York Symphony under Damrosch, and the San Francisco Symphony under Hertz. Another favorite promotional technique was the "immediate comparison." Leo Ornstein, for example, was soloist with the Metropolitan Opera House Orchestra, Artur Bodanzky, conducting, in June 1918 at Carnegie Hall. "Mr. Ornstein at first sat quietly on the stage while, in the popular phrase, 'the [Ampico] piano played itself,' " reported the *New York Times*. The pianist finished the final two movements of the Rubinstein D minor concerto himself "with no audible difference." In an illustration of yet a third technique, pianist Harold Bauer was "heard" on the Ampico with the New York Symphony in November 1917 while he performed live in Chicago.[42]

Every concert artist of any prominence made rolls for Welte, Duo-Art, or Ampico, and attested to the faithfulness of their reproduction. "For fidelity in reproduction the reproducing piano has no equal," reported *The Piano and Organ Purchaser's Guide for 1919*. "A reproducing piano is the highest expression of the artistic and mechanical genius of the musical instrument industries."[43] Until the advent of the high-fidelity phonograph and magnetic tape recorder, there existed no more advanced technology for recording piano music than the reproducing piano. Those fortunate enough today to hear a restored instrument perform a recording cut by Gershwin, Rachmaninoff, Paderewski, Debussy, Scriabin, Grieg, Busoni, or others will be shocked by the ghostly realism.

In the present age, comfortable with frequent manned spaceflight, computer technology, seemingly endless sound and visual special effects in its motion picture industry, and sophisticated advertising puffery, the word "revolutionary" has lost its impact. If something is not credited with revolutionary qualities, our interest quickly wanes. The miracle of sound reproduction—the piano-player, phonograph, player and reproducing pianos—was indeed revolutionary in the truest sense to the Victorian twentieth century. Prior to these inventions, the musician was human—active and creative—and the music was live. The ideology of the entire musical experience was derived from the producer culture. The revolutionary nature of the player piano changed these concepts forever, for increasingly the musician was a machine. The musical experience was becoming passive.

Passive Music for a Consumer Society

The American piano industry, of course, was not the only industry caught up in the revolution occurring in American culture, the journey from a producer ethic to a consumer one. By the turn of the century "consumption communities"[44] began to form around other institutions as well. Increasingly, people sought to be identified, and were identified, not by who they were or what they made, but by what they purchased and consumed. A new community, a new fellowship developed as these people came to use similar objects similarly branded. The unique became unpopular, even undesirable. The common use of common objects became commonplace; the undistinguishable became ideal.[45]

By the age of ragtime, the commercial use of the sewing machine by clothing manufacturers and individuals at home had successfully revolutionized American dress, homogenizing it, democratizing it. Like music recorded on player piano rolls, the best was now as inexpensive, as readily available as the common; every man, woman, and child could look like the best of their betters. Factory-made clothing—suits, coats, shirts, trousers, hats, caps, dresses, undergarments, shoes—became the standard

American dress. No longer were clothes "made"; they were "consumed."

The new consumer found limitless numbers and kinds of products in the new department store chains, which linked city to city, coast to coast. Sears, Roebuck; Montgomery Ward; Lord and Taylor; F. W. Woolworth; and A & P were just a few such junctions which created a democracy of consumption by making available to virtually everyone factory-produced, mass-marketed, nationally advertised, brand-named products, from food to clothing, from hardware to furniture. Similarity was the goal, uniformity was the price, democracy was the result. The middle class more than ever dominated American life.

Victorian values were based on the premise that each moment of life was unique, never to be relived. Mechanization, however, replaced the unique with uniformity and made the reproduction and duplication of experience a commonplace. People came to expect to buy the same clothing, food, and many other products again and again. Among the more artistic outgrowths of this phenomenon were the development of photography and, later, recorded music on phonograph cylinders, discs, and piano rolls.

The evolution of photography, according to one historian, was "the first giant step toward democratizing the repeatable experience."[46] Photography enabled anyone—artist as well as nonartist—to capture a moment of experience. George Eastman made anyone a photographer with the Kodak "Brownie" box camera, just as Aeolian made anyone a pianist with the Pianola. And in the same way piano manufacturers would promote their revolutionary player piano, Eastman advertised his camera: "You press the button—we do the rest."[47] Ease of accessibility, ease of operation, instant gratification—these were the hallmarks of the new value system undermining the Victorian sensibility.

The miracle of the repeatable experience also occurred in sound production with the Edison phonograph, or "talking machine." Patenting it in 1877, the inventor dismissed any serious ideas of recording musical experiences; letter dictation seemed to him the only real marketable use for his invention.[48] Nevertheless, a musical application of the phonograph occurred within a decade: in 1888 the twelve-year-old Josef Hofmann made the first recording by a recognized artist. By the 1890s the coin-operated cylinder phonograph provided the most sales, as the invention was still priced beyond the means of most families.[49]

As early as 1895, magazine advertisements promoted phonographs as fashionable, entertaining, and, like Eastman's camera and Aeolian's piano-player, easy to use: "so simple that even a child can make it pour forth the most enchanting selections of the world's greatest Musicians, Singers, Actors, and Speakers," read one Columbia ad.[50] The two leading companies, Edison and Columbia primarily promoted their products for the amusement of a "not too discriminating public." By 1901, however, not only was the technology of disc recording surpassing that of cylinder recording, but the Victor Talking Machine Company, maker of the Red Seal Record, was the first company in the United States to record "high class" music. The great tenor Caruso was the mainstay of President Eldridge Reeves Johnson's campaign to make Victor preeminent among phonographs as Steinway was among pianos.[51]

To overcome aesthetic objections to his phonograph, Johnson designed instruments that would be accepted, like the piano, as fine pieces of furniture. In a piano culture, he advertised his Victrola as "a musical instrument, like a piano" in "piano-finished" mahogany, and consumers made Victor (with its trademark "His Master's Voice") the most successful phonograph company in America.[52]

Though ragtime was primarily a piano, player piano, or band phenomenon, the phonograph also helped increase its popularity. "Rag Time King of the World" Mike Bernard recorded "Everybody Two Step" for Columbia in December 1912, the first documented piano ragtime recording for a phonograph.[53] Ragtime played on band instruments, however, had been recorded much earlier.[54] At any rate, Americans were very aware of the musical potentiality of the phonograph. One enterprising devotee suggested that the device could be used to give music lessons. And in all seriousness a letter to the editor of the *New York Times* proposed in 1910 that the phonograph should be the national musical instrument. "Do you play the piano?" "No, but I do play the phonograph," went the old vaudeville joke.[55] Perhaps even the twentieth-century Victorian piano industry, an industry consciously bringing about the cultural revolution in America, but unaware of the new value system that was eating away Victorian sensibilities, found humor in such wittiness.

Before the Great War, the fidelity of the phonograph remained limited, especially in recording the piano. In addition, disc time for the phonograph was only about four minutes, which greatly limited its recording potential. "To do it [record for the phonograph] is stupid and a strain," remarked an exasperated Busoni in 1919. "They want the *Faust* Waltz (which lasts a good ten minutes) *but it was to take only four minutes.* That meant quickly cutting, patching and improvising, so that there should still be some sense left in it. . . ; how can there be any question of inspiration, freedom, swing or poetry?"[56]

Many pianists, such as Fannie Bloomfield-Zeisler, refused to record for the phonograph altogether, preferring instead to preserve their art via the far superior technology of the reproducing piano. For most Americans of the Victorian twentieth century, the phonograph remained a novelty of the new age, though an immensely popular one, and considerably cheaper than the piano. By 1914 more than 500,000 phonographs were being produced each year, with a value of $27 million. But in 1914, a record 323,000 pianos were also produced, valued at $56 million.[57] Piano manufacturers, who were selling unprecedented numbers of pianos, were hardly worried by the possible threat of competition. Some even began to compete with phonograph manufacturers as basic patents expired: Aeolian marketed the Vocalion phonograph in 1914 and became a major contender with the big three, Victor, Edison, and Columbia.[58] Besides, the piano trade—morally, socially, and financially buttressed by the Victorian ethos—was developing its own novel sound-reproducing device: the player piano. "The player piano is an accepted musical instrument," wrote William Geppert in *The Official Guide to Piano Quality* (1916), "and it is only a question of time when practically every piano will carry a player mechanism."[59]

Automation, however, also increased the price of "practically every piano." For those not able to afford the luxury of mechanical piano music, or for those wanting to enjoy it outside their homes, the piano manufacturers, in their quest for a musical democracy, pioneered and developed the coin-operated music business. The Rudolph Wurlitzer Co. ("Manufacturers, Importers, Wholesale and Retail Dealers in Everything Musical") introduced coin music to the United States in the 1890s, and was among the first to market an 88-key electric player piano with coin slot for commercial use.[60]

During the heyday of the coin-operated player piano (1904–20), some sixty-five makers, according to one estimate, managed to put "well over one hundred thousand machines" in active service.[61] Wurlitzer and the J. P. Seeburg Piano Co. remained the two largest manufacturers, and the former offered the widest variety of electric, roll-activated, automatic music machines. Wurlitzer's 1910 catalog of eighty-two pages listed fifty different "nickel grabbers," from $1,500 to $10,000. "Wurlitzer Has Just the Right Instrument For *Your* Business," the company advertised, and it placed them in bowling alleys, excursion boats, cafes, clubs, cigar stores, department stores, grocery stores, hotels, railroad depots, restaurants, ocean liners, skating rinks, ice cream parlors, and brothels. "Good Music makes the Drinks Taste better," read a window placard. "Drop a Nickel. There's A Wurlitzer Instrument Here."[62]

In furthering a musical democracy in America, the coin-piano industry grew into big business, not only for the manufacturers, but for their customers as well. Selling the concept of "Music as a Revenue," Wurlitzer stressed that "nothing is more profitable than music in public places. The American people are very fond of music, and when the opportunity presents itself do not hesitate to loosen their purse-strings to hear their favorite march, or the latest popular song, or some sweet strain from . . . well-known Operas."[63] *The Coin Slot* magazine—"Devoted to Increasing Profits from Electric Pianos"—stressed that businessmen must keep their machines equipped with up-to-date music rolls in order to maintain public interest. Consequently, coin pianos not only increased business profits, but they paid for themselves in a very short time.[64] According to one estimate, in only six months the machine could return a 50 to 300 percent profit on the initial investment! Given such financial success, live bands and orchestras often found themselves replaced by coin pianos.[65] To these unfortunate few, the consequences of the new age were painfully obvious.

The coin piano significantly aided the development of a musical democracy in America, inducing or awakening a musical interest in countless numbers of people. George Gershwin, for example, first became interested in piano music when he heard a coin piano at a neighborhood store.[66] Most public reactions, however, were much more passive. The American piano industry thus encouraged the maturation of a new value system alien to the producer culture in which the industry itself was rooted. "Music ... to be cultivated among the masses should be in all public places where it will burst upon the ear uninvited," stressed Wurlitzer. But the piano manufacturer, Victorian-minded as ever, also stressed "The Charming Influence of Music": "Nothing is more soothing than the refined and elevating influence of music. . . . Let us once more impress upon the Proprietors of . . . public places, that you must have MUSIC to attract the better element [of the community]."[67]

Another significant factor in the evolution toward a musical democracy, toward passive music for a consumer society, was the invention and development in the 1890s of the motion picture, a contribution again of Thomas Edison and especially his assistant W. K. L. Dickson.[68] The novelty of moving pictures, however, was limited; it would be the American piano industry that gave life through sound to the silent celluloid.

"There is no question at all that music is essential to the pictures," said William Brandt, president of the Theater Exhibitors' Chamber of Commerce in 1921. He credited music with influencing 40 percent of the audience attendance for good films, and 95 percent for bad ones.[69] Supplying this crucial element became big business. Although in time large metropolitan theaters would use the giant pipe organ (such as "The Mighty Wurlitzer") or even employ an orchestra, most motion picture establishments used a piano to add life to love scenes, anxiety to chase scenes, or zest to transitions. From 1905 to 1925, nearly every manufacturer of coin-operated player pianos also made "photoplayers," instruments designed especially for movie houses. Such devices as Seeburg's "Pipe-Organ Orchestra," American Photo Player Co.'s "Fotoplayer," or Wurlitzer's "Motion Picture Theatre Orchestra" could supply piano, pipe organ, and percussion effects, as well as auto horn and exhaust, bird whistles, cowbell, wind, waves, telegraph key, crackling flames, horse's hoofs—all operated by pushing footpedals and buttons, and pulling handles. "Seeburg value quickly seen as music changes on the screen," read the J. P. Seeburg Piano Co. (Chicago) motto. Lyon & Healy, another Chicago piano manufacturer, provided a school for aspiring photoplayers (although employment was not guaranteed). For smaller theaters, which could afford only a regular piano or player piano, there were instruction books, such as L. C. Turner's *How and What to Play for Moving Pictures* (1914).[70]

"Movies are an emotional experience and you have to be spontaneous," recalled silent-film pianist Charles Hofmann. "I prefer to compose everything on the spur of the moment." Rather than memorize themes, Hofmann memorized the frames of film and responded as they appeared. (Not all movie pianists had to be so spontaneous. Motion picture studios commissioned scores for feature films and distributed the sheet music with the movie reels.) Employed Friday and Saturday afternoons, Hofmann found the theater "also wanted me to play on a Sunday, but my parents were strict Methodists, and you just didn't attend movies on a Sunday. But I did. I knew my mother's friends wouldn't be in the theater."[71]

A musician was not always necessary, however. The Link Piano Co. (Binghamton, New York) advertised its "Self-Playing Piano for Moving Picture Theatres" as: "CONTROLLED FROM THE PICTURE BOOTH / REQUIRES NO MUSICIAN." "The ordinary automatic piano is almost worse than useless for the picture theatre," continued a Link advertisement, "on account of lack of music control." Why? "INSTANTANEOUS CHANGES from one selection of music to another with change in tempo at the instant the scenes are shifted on the screen are the most important factors for the successful display of a film. In this the ordinary piano player is deficient and the effects desired are oftentimes spoiled." Thus, "THE RIGHT MU-SIC AT THE RIGHT TIME is the most vital for the success of the picture house." And with its piano cabinet holding four separate music rolls, each with eight to fifteen selections, Link made it so easy: "If the scene is a sad one and you want sob music, all you have to do is touch a button for the roll containing sob music. When the scene changes to a heavy dramatic picture, push the button controlling the dramatic music and the change is made instantly."[72]

Movie theaters commonly experienced a "music problem," but the installation of such automatic photoplayers apparently solved the problem quite well. "We simply turn on the current in the morning and shut it off at night and the instrument does the rest," reported the manager of the Grand Theatre, Atlanta, in 1916. "We have used an operator a few weeks, but we find that we get as much satisfaction from the automatic operation."[73]

The end of the ragtime era coincided with the end of the First World War. Various composers chronicled the changes taking place in American society in their song titles: James Scott's "Suffragette Waltz" (1914), J. S. Zamecnik's "Movie Rag" (1913), Harry H. Raymond's "Movie Trot" (1916), Otto Welcome's "Pianola Concert Rag" (1921), though the popularity of Irving Berlin's "I Love A Piano" (1915) showed the basic musical instrument still reigned. The player piano industry had become big business. In 1918 authorities estimated that 800,000 player pianos were in operation east of the Mississippi River alone, with 75,000 piano rolls sold each month just in Philadelphia.[74] And in 1919 the National Piano Manufacturers Association proudly declared that the piano industry had to operate at full capacity just to keep up with demand.[75] The "silent piano" was being rendered almost obsolete; the benefits of music would soon be enjoyed by all.

For the first time in history unprecedented numbers of people were exposed to music. Although the family still gathered around the mother or daughter playing the piano in the parlor, more and more people experienced passive music automatically produced: the phonograph and player piano in the home, the coin-operated player in restaurants, bars, hotels and other public establishments, and the photoplayer in the movie theater. Increasingly music, like clothing, was "consumed," not "made"; the experience was becoming instantaneous and easy, requiring no investment of time.

But for the moment at least, the American piano industry was locked within its Victorian culture. Twentieth-century Victorians were genuinely worried about the changes surrounding them. Reformers sought to redress the ill effects of factory production. Authorities challenged the moral consequences of the mechanization of household chores—the washing machine, water tap, sewing machine—as causing the deterioration of woman's health. Others advocated music as a cure for America's trend toward materialism.[76] And yet music itself was a significant part of that trend, an integral part of the uneasy transition from Victorianism to consumerism. This is especially evident in the debate between live and canned music, a debate comprising nothing less than a fight within the developing consumer culture for the Victorian frame of mind.

Canned versus Live Music: The Debate Begins

In December 1908, members of the Music Teachers National Association who gathered in Washington, D.C., for their thirtieth annual convention, listened anxiously to the remarks of guest speaker Dr. Charles W. Needham, president of George Washington University. "You can photograph the face, but not the soul," the president declared; "you can copy sound, but not the interpretation." Needham was only one speaker decrying the disturbing if not harmful effects of the new technology revolutionizing the music industry, one of many voices before the music teachers, whose thirtieth convention was almost entirely given over to warnings against insidious, mechanical music. Earlier that year the National Association of Piano Dealers had held its annual convention in New York City. Speakers before the June meeting of the dealers, rather than fearing that the player piano would supplant the pianoforte, had claimed that the automatic instrument would encourage people to take lessons by spreading music more widely, disseminating the gift—democratizing it. Earl B. Bartlett of W. W. Kimball Co. had told his audience that the player piano "stimulates knowledge," and that "just as many children [are] learning the piano as ever." Paul Brown Klugh of the Cable Co., noting that the sales of players were rising (even during the 1907 depression when sales of regular pianos were down), had been even more optimistic, declaring that the mechanical invention would take music "to new excellence."[77]

Such battle lines inevitably resulted when the Victorian-producer ethic clashed with the culture and technology of consumption, and when the advertisments of a Victorian-rooted industry espoused the advantages of "easy-to-play" technology. John Philip Sousa's celebrated diatribe, "The Menace of Mechanical Music," which first appeared in *Appleton's Magazine* in September 1906 and was reprinted the following month in *Current Literature*, marks one of the earliest protests against what became commonly called "canned music."[78] Sousa foresaw "a marked deterioration in American music and musical taste, an interruption in the musical development of the country, and a host of other injuries to music in its artistic manifestations, by virtue—or rather by vice— of the multiplication of the various music-reproducing machines." Talking and playing machines threatened to "reduce the expression of music to a mathmatical system of megaphones, wheels, cogs, disks, cylinders, and all manner of revolving things, which are as like real art as the marble statue of Eve is like her beautiful, breathing daughters." Sousa predicted amateur musicians would disappear entirely ("under such conditions the tide of amateurism cannot but recede"), and forecast the doom of many music teachers as well, for whom would they teach? An influential Victorian, the bandmaster emphasized that music teaches all that is beautiful in the world. Mechanized music diminishes the ideal by producing the same after same, with no variation, no soul, no joy, no passion.[79] In a response, the *Musical Courier* admitted Sousa's point, but also acknowledged that the absence of parlor tenors "with their violet voices," and of children practicing scales on the piano, would be a nice change.[80]

Despite the forebodings aired at the thirtieth conference of the Music Teachers National Association and by John Philip Sousa, many music teachers (and no doubt many disgruntled audiences as well) agreed with the *Musical Courier* and saw the development of the player piano—a hybrid artifact of both producer and consumer ethics—as a godsend. The obvious positive qualities of the invention seemed to outweigh by far its less obvious long-term, negative effects. Before the advent of the player piano, music appreciation could be developed only by attending concerts (which were few), or by spending much time learning two- or four-hand arrangements for piano of orchestra pieces (which demanded more skill than most players possessed). Though the invention of the phonograph promised to increase the American appreciation of music, its recording time and fidelity were limited and both major manufacturers, Edison and Columbia, demonstrated only a superficial interest in the musical potentialities of the invention.[81] The invention of the player piano removed all these obstacles. For the first time a wide musical education was possible, and made possible through a preeminent Victorian institution: the piano.

Readers of a variety of periodical literature experienced a frequent barrage of support for mechanical music. In 1908 Leo Rich Lewis asserted in *The Atlantic Monthly* that despite the question of whether automatics played with feeling or not, whether such playing was art or not, player pianos allowed the musically inexperienced to come into contact with art. And in a progressive age of efficiency, Lewis could declare that players were "the most efficient" means of musical education yet.[82] In 1907, *Current Literature* impressed its readers with an article, "The Democracy of Music Achieved by Invention," which argued that such machines, especially the player piano, were bringing music to more people, no longer keeping it the expensive pastime of the rich. Such instruments could not fail to educate and uplift the public taste, to popularize musical art, to make way for a democracy of music.[83]

Robert H. Schauffler made the point more forcefully in "The Mission of Mechanical Music," which appeared in the December 1914 issue of *Century Magazine*. "The influence of these machines is progressive," Schauffler declared, and mechanical music will bring evolution, not devolution, of musical taste. Eventually, this process will lead to the cultivation of the best music. The player piano enables those to play who could not play before. And while most merely "take lessons in the subtle art of manipulating the machine," the author continued, the most musical will pursue lessons in order to play the real thing. Thus, the passive will become active. Teachers need hardly fear this kind of technology, because the supreme value of mechanical music lies in its educational value, its ability to awaken latent interest and to inspire. Now, the best music will be as inexpensive as the worst, and machines will not unemploy musicians any more readily than public libraries killed booksellers. Schauffler suggested another virtue of the player piano, that it did much to cheapen the glamor and theatrics of mere technical display, "redeeming us from the thraldom of the Liszt school." The razzle-dazzle and display of the virtuoso must now take a back seat to "sound musicianship."[84]

As player piano sales continued to climb in the years before the Great War, a number of books appeared to teach people the "Art of the Player Piano," perhaps the most well known being William Braid White's *The Player Pianist* (1910) and Gustav Kobbe's *The Pianolist—A Guide for Pianola Players* (1907; 4th ed., 1912).[85] Many music teachers seemed to be recovering enough from the threat of technological unemployment to find the player an aid which stimulated the desire to play among the musically uneducated, who then sought lessons. According to Gertrude Borchard, the player piano, "if it has done nothing else, has made music more fully known—made it a more every-day possession of everybody." The child began lessons voluntarily, not simply under parental compulsion. Furthermore, the teacher could use the player to supplement her teaching, or even better, use the reproducing piano (the "triumphant alliance of art and science"), which played the exact interpretation of great artists. "Every nuance of Hofmann's shading, every detail of Paderewski's pedaling is there for the pupil's analytical study." Finally, Borchard reminded her readers that the player piano freed the teacher from the drudgery of keeping up on all compositions she teaches.[86]

The mechanization of art did not begin with machines, however; and criticism of the mechanization of music did not await the invention of the phonograph and player piano. Some were already deploring the consequences: the masses were imitating their betters, people were learning songs devoid of character and never learning the true value of music, and the means was being mistaken for the end. Idealistic piano teachers and socially aspiring families who insisted their daughters cultivate their musical talents were at least aware of the discrepancy between the ideal and reality. Social critics were more keenly aware. One nineteenth-century music teacher lamented that the "lower levels" of society, "even down to the small shopkeeper and tradesman," were copying the "cultivated" class in order to acquire a position in society: "And all that has thus everywhere been learned and practised flows in over-abundance into the domestic circles, attempts to make a display at evening parties. . . . It is a moving in a circle without beginning or end; every one learns music because music is heard everywhere, and music is heard everywhere because everyone has learned it—and too often nothing else." Thus, "art is made mechanical," the teacher concluded, by "fast and furious amateurs."[87]

A few generations later, R. F. Delderfield related a similar story, though from the piano pupil's point of view. "If you chanced to pass along the avenue on a summer evening in, say, 1921," Delderfield reminisced, "you could in effect have anticipated the radio and television eras. Identical snatches of melody issued from every open window. They were all at it, one eye on the music . . . the other on the mantelshelf clock."[88]

The invention of the phonograph and player piano, however, brought the conflict between mechanization and art under greater scrutiny, and infused it with a new, more sinister threat. What would happen to the moral value of music if the musical experience were trivialized, if it were no longer something to be painstakingly cultivated? When music became merely one more universally accessible, democratic, consumable experience, would it not lose its distinctiveness, its uniqueness as an experience? And if music became available to everyone everywhere, would the experience be impoverished by the very act of democratizing it?[89] Many critics thought so.

In 1919 Arthur Whiting offered a cynical review of the mechanical player in the *Yale Review*. The "horseless pianoforte" is becoming a very common sight, making "handplayers" aristocrats, the author declared. And although "plain people" could now encounter formerly inaccessible music, their experience was most superficial. Whiting wryly noted (and salesmen guaranteed) that the player granted immediate articulation free from irksome practice: "indeed, the intelligent running of an automobile in and out of town is a natural preparation for the auto of the drawing-room, which further insures against all lapses and contingencies by being fool-proof. Provided that our young musical chauffeur has the use of his feet and has passed the right and left test he is ready for a spin directly the machine is assembled. . . . [Soon] son has found himself, his natural gifts are now realized. His mother was right." The mechanical "insensate artist" puts all handplaying to shame with its security, Whiting continued, "it never hesitates, it surmounts the highest difficulties without changing a clutch. Always masterful and headlong, it can, if required, utter notes faster than the human ear can follow. Bouquets of adjectives, thrown by the excited audience towards the unperspiring, unexhausted performer, fall unnoticed at its feet. Since that memorable first appearance, poor sister has hardly touched the keys." After several months of mechanical music, the author warned, father finds that the "brazen readiness of the mechanical genius" no longer attracts him, and he longs "to hear once again the bashful, hesitating sounds which once charmed him, that human touch which said something to him although imperfectly," sounds that no "expression button" can give.[90]

"Who has not suffered from the over-cautious (or insensitive) amateur who knows not the proper way to operate accent and tempo levers, either dragging listlessly or racing like an automobile?" asked *The Atlantic Monthly* in 1913. "Such is hard to bear," and the unenlightened should "improve their musical taste in solitude."[91] Indeed, the struggle between the mechanical player and "the art of pianoforte playing" was often compared to that between the automobile and the horse.

The Music Teachers National Association continued to debate "the pros and cons of the mechanical player," and when the *The Literary Digest* reported Professor G. H. Bryan's remarks before the Physical Society of London in April 1913 that mechanical pianos could never duplicate human touch, it touched off a debate with the piano manufacturers. "Printed correspondence has been accumulating rapidly," announced the editor, "and *The Digest* has on file more manuscript material than it can print, from all points of view."[92]

A Square Deal for Composers: The 1909 Copyright Act

The controversy between art and machine, between the producer ethic and the emerging consumer system of values, became even more complicated as artists, legislators, and manufacturers debated copyright laws. "Our copyright laws urgently need revision," declared President Theodore Roosevelt in his December 1905 message to the Congress. "A complete revision of them is essential . . . to meet modern conditions."[93] Those conditions were unprecedented. By law, composers of music were paid a royalty upon the purchase of their sheet music. The law, however, had been written before the introduction of the player piano and phonograph.

Manufacturers of perforated rolls and discs freely recorded the latest hits, often at the request of music publishers and composers, who were quite aware that the new media would greatly aid both the popularity and sales of sheet music. But these manufacturers were not required by law to pay royalties to composers upon the sale of a recording. Manufacturers, music publishers, and even many composers viewed the mechanical reproduction of copyrighted music as an aid to sales, a form of advertising.[94] By

1905, however, the Roosevelt administration advocated a "square deal" for composers. Following the President's directive, legislators in both houses of Congress simultaneously introduced a copyright bill the following year, a bill intended to give composers exclusive right to their copyrighted music, including payment of royalties upon the sale of roll or disc recordings. What neither the President nor Congress knew was that the passage of such a bill would have brought about a monopoly between Harry B. Tremaine's Aeolian, Weber Piano & Pianola Co., then the largest company in the piano trade and maker of the famous Pianola, and the Music Publishers' Association, which controlled music publishing in the United States. Such a monopoly would have had disastrous effects on the American piano industry.[95]

Hearings of the joint Senate and House Committee on Patents in June and December 1906 and in March 1908 exposed Aeolian's intention to gain monopoly. As early as 1889 a suit had been brought in Massachusetts against a maker of perforated music rolls for violation of copyright, but the circuit court had ruled that a roll was not a copy within existing law. In 1891 a new international copyright act had passed Congress, but despite the absence of any specific language regarding mechanical reproduction, Aeolian's attorneys had advised that "there was serious doubt about whether a perforated roll was a copy within the meaning of the law." The company, they continued, should test the case in the Supreme Court.[96] In 1894 Congress had again attempted to address the problem of infringement of copyright by mechanical instrument makers, but the measure, the Troller bill, had failed to pass. Anticipating the eventual passage of such a bill, and wishing to protect its $10 million investment in the production of perforated rolls (by late 1904 Pianola music catalogs listed 12,978 recorded compositions[97]), Aeolian had approached the Music Publishers' Association with an offer to test the copyright law in exchange for some kind of protection. (If the Court ruled for the composer, Aeolian would be hit with countless suits from composers demanding royalties for past recordings.) The publishers had agreed to give Aeolian complete immunity for all past infringements, and Aeolian had agreed to pay the complete cost of carrying the case to the Supreme Court, an expense no one composer or publisher could afford.

But these secretly negotiated contracts also would have formed the basis for a music trust should the Supreme Court rule for the composer or should Congress pass a new bill preventing what proponents were calling the "indiscriminate 'canning'" of copyrighted music. Upon the passage of a new law or ruling, the publishers, by contract, would give Aeolian exclusive rights for thirty-five years to reproduce their sheet music on perforated rolls. Aeolian in turn would give the publishers as much as 60 to 80 percent of the profit from the sales of rolls. By 1899, Aeolian had negotiated eighty-seven contracts with leading American publishers of sheet music, most of whom were members of the Music Publishers' Association. In effect, the largest piano combination and the most powerful music-publishing organization would monopolize the music recording industry. Aeolian then completed the monopoly by negotiating contracts with its retail dealers of music rolls. In these agreements Aeolian reserved the right to raise the prices of rolls to include any royalty the company would have to pay the composer under a new law. Another clause forbade the roll dealer to lower the price or sell any other roll except Aeolian's.[98] Thus the dealer had to maintain price as well as exclusive dealership or Aeolian would cancel the franchise. In this way Aeolian negotiated a monopoly by tying up both the music publishers and the music roll manufacturers. And by monopolizing a one dollar music roll, the company also monopolized a $250 piano player, and this would effect control of the entire mechanical player industry. The scheme seemed almost complete. None of these secret contracts would go into effect, however, until the Supreme Court or Congress changed the copyright law.

With this intricate network in place, "the Aeolian Company poured out money like water," according to one witness,[99] to convince the courts to rule for the composer by requiring the manufacturers of rolls and discs to pay royalty. Indeed, Aeolian spent a reported $40,000 in a three-year preparation and public relations campaign. Composers inspired to activity (but wholly ignorant of the secret contracts) lobbied Congress through the Authors' and

Composers' Copyright League of America. Impressed with their cause, President Roosevelt urged Congress to pass a new copyright bill in December 1905. Meanwhile, Aeolian secured the widely respected talent of Charles Evans Hughes to present the case for the music publishers before the Supreme Court.

Both houses of Congress introduced a copyright bill giving the composer exclusive right in May 1906. The next month hearings of the joint Senate and House committee on patents discovered that such a bill would grant Aeolian a monopoly. The eighty-seven secret contracts were entered into the record when the hearings reconvened in December. Although the proposed copyright bill was intended to benefit the composer (J. L. Tindale of the Music Publishers' Association, for example, proclaimed that the practice of recording without compensation to the composer was "a moral wrong"[100]), representatives of the piano industry demonstrated that no composer had initiated the movement or been present at the introduction of the bill. They further showed that the music publishers framed and introduced the details of the mechanical reproduction clause. These piano manufacturers asserted that monopoly between the Aeolian Company and the music publishers was the clear intention. After the 1906 hearings, both House and Senate committees on patents decided to consider the matter separately.

In February 1907 the Supreme Court ruled in *The White-Smith Company* v. *The Apollo Company* that the existing copyright law was insufficient to cover mechanical devices, declaring, "These perforated rolls are parts of a machine . . . we cannot think that they are copies within the meaning of the copyright act."[101] Despite the financial efforts of the Aeolian Company and the arguments of Charles Evans Hughes, the Court ruled that the composer had no rights in the mechanical reproduction of his music. Aeolian proceeded to spend an additional $35,000 to convince the composers and Congress that a new copyright bill—one which would include a mechanical reproduction clause—was necessary.

The piano manufacturers opposing the monopoly found support in Frank D. Currier, Chairman of the House Committee on

Patents, who introduced a copyright bill which eliminated the mechanical reproduction clause. A. B. Kittredge, Chairman of the Senate Patents Committee, however, took up the cause for the composers and introduced a bill giving the composer exclusive right and payment of royalties for the sale of music rolls and discs. The 59th Congress ended with no settlement. In December 1907 Currier reintroduced his bill to the 60th House, and this time Reed Smoot, who had succeeded Kittredge as chairman of the Senate committee, submitted a bill substantially like Currier's. The Kittredge bill, which included the mechanical reproduction clause (and thus would create the Aeolian monopoly) was introduced again in the Senate. A. J. Barchfeld submitted an identical bill in the House. A heated debate ensued, pitting composers against producers of mechanical music, monopoly against free enterprise.

"This whole mechanical copyright agitation is a most ingenious attempt to monopolize the musical creations of mankind when reproduced mechanically," declared the president of the American Musical Copyright League before the hearings of the joint House and Senate committee on patents in March 1908.[102] The National Piano Manufacturers Association, the Player Manufacturers' League, Steinway & Sons, W. W. Kimball, Winter & Company, Wurlitzer, Mehlin & Son, Q.R.S Music Roll Co., Lester Piano Co., Estey Piano Co., Melville Clark, and other piano companies asserted their collective strength to prevent the passage of the Kittredge-Barchfeld bill, favoring instead the Currier-Smoot version. Under the fiery leadership of Victor Herbert and John Philip Sousa, the Authors' and Composers' Copyright League of America, of course, continued to press for the Kittredge-Barchfeld bill. *Musical Age* picked up the story and discussed its international effects in the February 29 and March 7, 1908, issues, revealing that Aeolian apparently had tried unsuccessfully to bring about a similar monopoly in England in 1906.

The resulting Copyright Act of 1909 was a compromise, and like *White-Smith* v. *Apollo*, an apparent victory for the piano manufacturers. The Currier-Smoot version of the bill formed the basis for the 1909 Act. Smoot noted that the object of the new copyright law was to protect the composer's composition, but not to grant the composer exclusive right or a particular company a monopoly. A composer now could prohibit the mechanical reproduction of his music, but if he chose to reproduce his music mechanically, or allowed anyone else to do so, then *any* maker of rolls or discs could reproduce his music upon payment to the composer of two cents on each roll or disc sold. Disappointed composers bewailed the meager royalty, but admitted, "two cents was better than nothing."[103]

Historians tend to overlook the 1909 Act of Copyright, and they have failed to discern the fundamental role the American piano industry played in its passage. The law was a landmark. It created a new property right, established a universal royalty which allowed any manufacturer equal right to reproduce a composer's music, and successfully undercut Aeolian's attempt to establish a music trust with the Music Publishers' Association, a trust which, according to a spokesman for W. W. Kimball, would have wiped out "the major portion of the mechanical instruments industry of this country."[104] Wurlitzer made the threat even more graphic, predicting the demise of 624 businesses if the Kittredge bill passed.[105] Testimony shows that the 1909 copyright law primarily involved the mechanical player piano, especially the coin-operated model.[106] The law is yet another measure of the revolutionary nature of this instrument, of the unprecedented change it brought about in American culture and life. "The art of music is the most democratic art in the world," Senator John W. Daniel said before the Congress in 1909. "It has given more for the benefit of the whole people than any other blessing we receive.... If you could put some good music free in everybody's home, you would do a great blessing to all mankind."[107] The American piano industry agreed completely. It also had demonstrated collectively that this condition would not be monopolized.

By the outbreak of the war that was to make the world safe for democracy, the battle lines were already entrenched in the war for a musical democracy. Like the war in Europe, the musical war was flawed by idealism and naivete. The participants in both were Victorians out of their time, pursuing an ethos no longer applicable in an age of modernization and new values. One was ignorant of the destructiveness of modern warfare, the other ignorant of the vicariousness and inconstancy of the consumer culture. And though both wars were waged successfully, the apparent victors in both were the ultimate casualties. The Great War brought down the optimism and morality of the Victorian and Progressive eras, while the piano manufacturers were defeated by the very musical democracy they had helped to create. The defeat, however, would not become evident until the mid-1920s. Until then, ragtime continued to spread, and interested parties continued to press for a revision of the copyright laws and to debate the merits of canned music. Until then, Americans increasingly entertained themselves at the coin piano and thrilled to the sounds of the photoplayer at the silent movies. Until then, piano manufacturers, convinced of their purpose and encouraged by their success, drove on to sell record numbers of pianos—most being players—to record numbers of people. A musical democracy was at hand, and along with it, a new culture, a new system of values both foreign and pernicious to the Victorian frame of mind. Ironically, American piano manufacturers had helped to bring about both.

CHAPTER THREE

Halcyon Years of the American Piano Industry

The piano is the greatest single factor in the development of musical art and the dissemination of musical knowledge.
—Francis L. York, MTNA

The introduction of the player piano mechanism has opened up a market for the piano which cannot be measured at the present time, as it seems to be almost unlimited.
—Alfred Dolge

We have never felt more optimistic about the future, and we think that 1923 is going to show tremendous gains in the standing of music stores all over the U.S. and the standing of piano salesmen.
—The Music Trades

Fifty-two "reputable" piano dealers, reportedly "disgusted with the prevailing ethics (or lack thereof) of the retail piano business," accepted the invitation of the National Piano Manufacturers Association of America (NPMA) to air their grievances at the manufacturers' fifth annual meeting in 1901. In the hope of eliminating cut prices, unethical advertising, and department store competition, the fifty-two dealers formed the National Association of Piano Dealers of America later that year. Their 1901 platform called for "the blacklisting of incompetent salesmen, banning the press from all meetings and protecting American women from the dangerous power of the department store ad writer." Caretakers of Victorian sensibilities, the piano manufacturers and dealers of America now had developed through their national organizations a powerful medium through which they could coordinate and spread their social philosophy. In 1902 both infant organizations (the manufacturers had organized only five years earlier) met simultaneously in Baltimore. The manufacturers exhibited a few pianos, thereby laying the basis for the annual trade show, which became one of the best barometers for measuring the industry's health. The dealers addressed problems of their business, such as piano rental programs, dishonest retailers, unethical promotional standards, and discount houses. As a forum for airing and solving the particular dilemmas of the piano industry, the dealers' convention remained considerably more important than the piano trade show, which gained ascendency only in the early 1970s.[1]

As the period from 1900 to 1923 brought unprecedented (and seemingly unlimited) prosperity to the industry, however, the annual conventions primarily became social clubs. Special trains brought piano men and their wives to the convention city, and members became accustomed to elegant theater parties and fancy dinners in posh hotels (the Hotel Astor in New York was a favorite). The men teed up in the annual tournament of the Piano Trade Golf Association as a preliminary to the serious work of the convention. Their wives enjoyed other diversions, such as an automobile excursion along the Hudson River.[2] The executive officers of a piano firm often held memberships in a variety of business-social clubs.

In February 1916 the executive committees of the National Piano Manufacturers Association, the National Association of Piano Dealers, and the National Piano Travelers Association held a joint convention in New York. One of their goals was to establish a national organization representative of the entire music industry to coordinate its various branches and provide a united political voice on issues important to the trade. The organization would include the piano manufacturers, dealers, travelers, and tuners, sheet music dealers, music publishers, music trade press, talking machine jobbers, music roll manufacturers, and band instrument makers. That summer members of the piano trade established the Music Industries Chamber of Commerce. This institution would become increasingly vital in addressing such issues as copyright, the tariff, and music as an essential war industry.[3]

The summer convention was an especially eventful one. Although piano production had fallen from 364,545 in 1909 to 322,652 in 1914, the secretary of the NPMA happily reported that piano sales in 1916 were climbing again despite increased prices caused by a scarcity of steel. The spirits of the group remained undampened, as over a thousand voices "lustily" cheered President Wilson's efforts in the crisis in Mexico. But the high mark of the 1916 convention was a trip to West Point. About 1,200 members, with their wives and daughters, sailed up the Hudson River on the *Albany*, and a specially commissioned dirigible dropped souvenir white carnations to the women on board. Upon their arrival the women travelled to the Point by auto. The men, however, followed a band in a "preparedness march" to the Point, again showing their support for Wilson.[4] The president, who had recently declared a policy of preparedness in the wake of the *Lusitania* crisis, was busy promoting preparation for armed defense should the United States be pulled into the European war. Selling preparedness had become for Wilson a political and national necessity.[5]

The piano industry, armed with the moral value of music, was confident that the government would consider music—and hence the music industry—as essential to the war effort in the event that war became a reality. Manufacturers were encouraged by unprecedented sales of instruments and the universal popularity of the player piano. These businessmen dared to attempt world leadership in piano export (a position then held by Germany). Unabashedly resting on what Alfred Dolge called its "accomplishment of such startling results," the American piano industry proceeded "in the hands of strong men" to seek its "destiny."[6] These were halcyon years, a time when white carnations dropped from the sky and laureled the makers of a musical democracy.

Anatomy of the Piano Industry

Several trends emerged in the last two decades of the nineteenth century that propelled American industry into big business, trends that were primarily a response to developing urban markets. Technological innovations spurred the mass production of standardized parts, and an increasing railroad network aided the mass distribution of finished products to a growing national market. To control this process more efficiently, the structure of American business shifted away from proprietorships and partnerships to corporations. Because a corporation could obtain large sums of capital by issuing stock and could limit the liability of stockholders to the amount of money they had invested in the company, this type of organization had become increasingly common by the late Victorian period. Furthermore, in an effort to gain greater market control or to expand production, businesses consolidated; industry combined, integrated, and diversified. One result was huge companies and oligopolistic industries. Very often, however, the attempts to establish trusts failed. Recent research has demonstrated that, while combination was universally attractive, certain types of businesses were predisposed to form successful trusts, but for others failure was almost certain. The research distinguishes "center" firms from "peripheral" ones, and underscores both the complexity and the fundamental characteristics of the movement toward trusts.[7]

Accompanying this move toward monopoly capitalism were the trend toward a wider dispersal of ownership among many small stockholders, the increasing separation of ownership and management, and the rise of a class of professional managers and salaried experts who governed the operation of a company by order of an executive committee. This development has been appropriately called, "the managerial revolution in American business."[8]

In order to see the American piano trade as a part of the larger industrial culture, it is necessary to understand both the way a piano company manufactured and distributed its product, and the extent to which large, vertically integrated holding companies and corporations came to control the trade.[9] The story of the industry's confrontation with the consumer society, however much influenced by changing cultural, social, and moral values and technological advancements, cannot properly be considered as isolated from the trade's industrial idiosyncrasies. This chapter examines the anatomy of the piano industry during its most productive years.

In *The Book of Complete Information about Pianos* (1897), Frank L. Wing of Wing & Son Piano Co. wrote that American companies produced the best and also probably the worst pianos in the world.[10] Ironically, both resulted from a very effective system of manufacture and distribution. This system was not monopolized by large firms, however. The last three decades of the nineteenth century also saw the rise of the piano supply industry, which in turn provided actions, keys, iron plates, strings, hardware, and even soundboards and cases to companies not having sufficient capital to manufacture the complete piano "in shop." The requirements for such capital were met as they were in the early automobile industry—by shifting the burden to the manufacturers, distributors, and dealers of standardized, machine-produced parts.[11] Thus, entry into both the automobile and the piano industries was rather easy in the early days and required only a minimal amount of capital or managerial expertise. Moreover, given the piano's apparently unlimited market and secure place in social, cultural, and moral tradition, there was plenty of room for competition. The American piano industry was built into a big business upon the sales of moderately priced uprights for the home.

Both major contemporary authorities paid tribute to the "kindred branches" of the industry in their respective histories of the piano trade. In his *History of the American Pianoforte* (1890), Daniel Spillane described "the benefits that accrued to the whole trade from the establishment of separate [supply] industries" as "incontrovertible, for specialists necessarily can produce better results than manufacturers that aim at doing everything at the same time." "A few large firms are, however, excepted," he continued, "for obvious reasons."[12] Alfred Dolge, writing twenty-one years later, concurred: "Perhaps no other class of manufacturing depends more largely upon auxiliary industries, each of itself of considerable magnitude, than the piano industry. It is furthermore true that the piano industry could not have made its marvelous progress, had not the auxiliary industries kept pace with the inventive piano maker, oftentimes anticipating his wants and providing superior material which permitted the improvement of the piano."[13]

In his 1911 survey of the industry, Dolge listed sixty-nine separate piano supply manufacturers in the United States, of which all but twenty-one had been established by 1890. These "kindred branches" allowed the small manufacturer to compete very successfully with the larger firms by avoiding the prohibitive cost of producing parts in-house. This made many piano companies less factories than assembly plants. According to Dolge, "as a matter of commercial and industrial evolution, the specialists, such as case makers, key and action makers, have become indispensable to the industry. They have made possible the production of a reliable, satisfactory instrument, at a price within the reach of the masses."[14]

Authorities traditionally have categorized the products of the various companies into three grades. The high-grade instrument makers were few, with names like Steger & Sons, Bush & Lane, Baldwin, Mason & Hamlin, Conover-Cable, and of course Steinway & Sons. These pianos were among the best of the piano maker's art, instruments intended for artistic and professional use, but also for the drawing rooms of the wealthy or the aspiring middle class. According to *The Official Guide to Piano Quality* an upright of this class sold for about $600 in 1916 (grands of course were "much higher").[15] Much more common were pianos of good quality intended for proficient amateur musicians, or as Byron H. Collins wrote in *The Etude*, a piano "as good a value as possible in a lower priced instrument" for those who couldn't afford the best.[16] In 1916, an upright of this grade sold for about $400. Many firms, such as Kohler & Campbell or Story & Clark, made medium-grade pianos exclusively. Others produced them as a second line below their expensive high-grade product. Baldwin manufactured the Hamilton and Ellington pianos to meet this particular market. Frank Wing, noting the consistent moderate quality that characterized this grade, admitted that these "commercial" pianos were good, but there was "nothing particularly artistic or special to recommend them."[17]

At the bottom were the notorious low-grade pianos, uprights costing less than $200. According to Collins, manufacturers (or more often, assemblers) of this grade "make and sell pianos of little or no merit, . . . give no thought to serving the public. . . . [They] get as much as possible for their products, and give as little as possible in return," according to Collins. Wing concurred, warning that there was no attention to quality, tone, construction, or durability except as needed to sell the piano. Price was the ultimate object.[18]

Within this category fell the infamous "stencil" piano, a product not traceable to its manufacturer because no name was placed on it, and therefore no responsibility either. "The stencil piano represents the fraudulent side of this piano business," declared William Geppert in *The Official Guide to Piano Quality* (1916), "and the good is made to suffer with the bad. The name of the manufacturer upon the piano, no matter whether it is hid or not, just so the origin of the piano can be traced and the maker held responsible for its guarantee, places that piano out of the stencil class, no matter what name it may bear."[19]

Generally, dealers stenciled their own names (or that of their city, state, or a famous composer) to these nameless pianos to sell as a discount line. In many cases the quality of these pianos was adequate, and some dealers obtained a trademark for a name they proudly used on a piano made especially for them. Many times, however, the stencil piano was inferior and unsatisfactory. To insure customer satisfaction (and therefore protect the industry), consumer guides advised the prospective buyer to avoid the 1,100 or more stencil names in favor of a legitimate trademark: "always it is best and safest to buy the legitimate pianos offered by any house . . . for then there is that protection of name as to workmanship that insures the best the manufacturer can give, no matter the grade," advised *The Official Guide to Piano Quality*: "It can be assumed that the manufacturer who is not responsible for a stencil piano because it does not bear his name, does not pay that attention to the making of it that he does to the piano that bears his own name. This applies to all stencils, no matter whether they be pianos or anything else. . . . The manufacturer whose name is not upon the instrument that goes out has no responsibility at stake, the responsibility is handed over to the one for whom the stencil is being made."[20]

The manufacture of stencils for dealers and mail-order houses was an accepted part of the piano industry by the late-nineteenth century.[21] William Tonk, one of the few manufacturers to write memoirs, estimated that 70 percent of the industry manufactured nameless pianos or affixed names other than their own to instruments in an effort to offer cheaper merchandise.[22] But the practice tended toward compromised quality and even fraudulence. Often there appeared a name carefully chosen to make a customer think the stencil to be a legitimate, well-respected trademark: "Stenger & Sons" for Steger & Sons, "Baldin" for Baldwin, "Webar" for Weber, "Bush & Gaerts" for Bush & Gerts, or "Steinweg," "Steinwebb," or "Steinvey" for Steinway & Sons.[23] Since the 1870s manufacturers of good pianos made strenuous efforts to end what Dolge called "the nefarious traffic in stencil pianos." "It has opened the door to fraud and deception by unscrupulous dealers and caused the mushroom growth of a large number of concerns, more or less irresponsible," he continued, "who use the cheapest kind of materials, employ the lowest-priced labor, and compile so-called pianos, marketing their stuff under all sorts of names, preferably such as would have resemblance to the names of makers of good pianos. The piano-buying public has no means of judging the intrinsic value of a good piano, as compared to a cheap stencil piano, and frequently low-grade instruments are foisted upon the public as superior goods at high-grade prices."[24]

The campaign against the stencil piano became more intense and directed as the industry was influenced by the move toward reform that characterized the Progressive Era. The American piano industry was not operating in a vacuum. Nor was it the only industry at this time to organize trade associations, such as the National Piano Manufacturers Association and the Music Industries Chamber of Commerce, which could take better advantage of industry's growing national power and influence.[25] But the campaign against stencil pianos is another indication of the transformation of values from the Victorian producer ethic to the modern consumer culture that was taking place in American society.

Brand names were not new to Victorian Americans, who had been buying patent medicines, soaps, and cleaning powders since the Civil War period. But the rise of the nationally advertised trademark completely changed the consumer's consciousness to include brand loyalty toward products whose advertising promised consistent (and therefore superior) quality nationwide, in contrast to the unknown (and therefore inferior) quality of local or homemade products. The trend toward national trademarks was a significant part of the revolution in American business and industry that also included mass production, mass distribution, separation of ownership and management, and managerial expertise. By the First World War, Americans demanded national brands in watches, hats, chewing gum, breakfast food, razor blades—and pianos.[26]

The significance of the national trademark is also evident in legislative efforts to protect the manufacturer's brand name. The first federal trademark law was not passed until 1870, and was declared unconstitutional ten years later for restricting interstate commerce. In 1882 a new law passed, and served as the legal foundation behind the power and meaning that brand names came to enjoy both domestically and internationally. Not surprisingly, advertising became a respected profession. The American piano industry's role here is paradoxical. On the one hand, piano makers, rooted firmly in Victorian sensibilities, were very traditional in their philosophical beliefs and slow to adopt change. On the other hand, they were eager promoters of new advertising techniques and products of revolutionary consequence, such as the player piano. Conservative in their business organizations, piano makers were reluctant to adopting either the holding company type of merger or a system of administration that separated owner from manager. Yet they were also Progressive reformers eager to protect the integrity of their industry and its trademarks by actively lobbying Congress to pass a law forbidding the production of stencils in *all* industries.

It was not always so. In an address before the National Piano Manufacturers Association, William Tonk expressed doubt that a proposed resolution against stencils could be carried out when other industries accepted the practice as legitimate and when 70 percent of the piano trade itself manufactured products with names other than the maker's. Furthermore, many piano makers were not members of the NPMA and would not be affected by the resolution. Such a restriction upon association members without protection by federal statute also might endanger the very future of the NPMA, as those involved in stencil production might leave the organization rather than risk their business by complying with an antistencil resolution. Tonk insisted that the only sure way to improve existing conditions was to lobby Congress to enact a federal statute requiring all manufacturers in all kinds of industries to place their names upon the goods they sold that bore any name at all.[27]

The reform legislation inspired by the political movement known as Progressivism also gave impetus to those concerned about malpractice in the piano industry. Particularly important in the struggle to prevent the deception and fraud that the piano makers saw in stencils was William L. Bush, president of Bush & Gerts Piano Co. of Chicago. The founder of the Bush Temple of Music in Chicago (1902) and similar conservatories in Dallas and

Memphis, Bush mounted a campaign to bring into trade practice the fixed-price system[28] and the elimination of the illegitimate stencil whose manufacturer could not be traced. He founded and financed the National League for the Maker's Name to provide an effective tool with which to lobby Congress, but also to compel manufacturers to assume full responsibility toward the public for their products. According to Alfred Dolge, "it is the sole purpose of the 'National League for the Maker's Name' to sustain the agitation and active campaign until a proper law shall be placed on the statute books which will protect the purchaser against fraud."[29]

Bush became the acting secretary and treasurer of the League, and enlisted Dr. Harvey W. Wiley, father of the Pure Food and Drug Act, as president. Their efforts convinced Phil P. Campbell, a Republican congressman from the third district in Kansas, of the necessity of enacting a law preventing deceptive trade practices, a law resembling the Pure Food and Drug Act of 1906. After working on the problem for two years, Campbell introduced "a bill prohibiting fraud upon the public" in January 1912, with the provisions: "It shall be unlawful for any person, firm, company or corporation to place upon the market for interstate or foreign commerce any product of manufacture, without printing, embossing, or stenciling the name and addresss of the manufacturer upon such article or commodity."

The House debated the bill the following June, but the sixty-second Congress ended with no result. Campbell reintroduced his bill (with minor changes) to the sixty-third Congress. In April 1913 it came under the scrutiny of the House Committee on Interstate and Foreign Commerce. The congressman from Kansas declared before the House in January 1914 that no one had a right to "filch money from the public with a product that is not what it purports to be and is not worth the money that it costs." Campbell's certification bill did not prohibit the use of stencilled names by either the manufacturer or dealer, but it did require that every product bear the name of the original maker in a conspicuous place.

Although Campbell insisted that he had "from the beginning no particular manufacturer in mind," he informed the House that

many piano manufacturers were using poplar instead of hard-
wood. This resulted in "cheap, worthless" pianos and organs that
flooded the market and defrauded the public of millions of dollars
because the manufacturers were untraceable and could not be
held responsible. He underscored the extent of the problem by
pointing to similar practices in the shoe, clothing, buggy, and jewelry trades. The debate in the House centered on the feasibility of
a law requiring a manufacturer to list the components of his product in addition to his name and address, as the revised version of
Campbell's bill required. There was also doubt that any effective
government inspection would be possible to insure the accuracy
of the required labels.[30]

Legitimate piano makers and honest piano merchants praised
such Progressive reform, but Campbell's four-year effort to enact
a certification bill died in committee. Most congressmen did not
think that a bill requiring manufacturers to list materials used in
their products and government inspection to insure accuracy was
a workable solution. Furthermore, the Democrat-controlled Congress of 1913–14 was less likely to act upon a bill inspired by
Republicans. The need for reform seemed less urgent; President
Wilson was about to declare that Progressive reform had been
accomplished. The war in Europe would soon command attention.

The so-called "stencil menace" continued to be a problem for
the piano trade until after the Great War. By then, unfortunately,
the financial and cultural health of the industry was far more
severely imperiled by the transformation of values emerging full
force in the 1920s, the purported "prosperous" decade. Ironically,
the piano makers, in helping to bring about this cultural revolution toward consumerism through their promotion of the player
piano, national advertising, and trademark protection, also helped
to undermine the very cultural foundations on which their industry depended.

The stencil was hardly the sole cause for concern among legitimate piano makers or the only source of confusion for consumers. The classification of pianos by grade was used to distinguish
all uprights and grands, both player and what the trade called

"straight pianos." It was perhaps relatively easy to identify the low-grade piano, though most consumer guides assumed the average buyer to be wholly ignorant even at this level. "Few articles are offered for sale in such volume, concerning which so little is known by the average purchaser, as pianos," reported Byron H. Collins in *The Etude*. He revealed that millions of dollars were wasted each year by the American public in the purchase of inferior instruments.[31] Such purchases could ultimately be disastrous for the trade. A common result of buying a cheap piano, according to Frank L. Wing, was the "loss of all ambition to play, or desire to have anyone else play, the loss of all pride in the piano because it has become such an unmusical affair."[32]

But the difficulty of discriminating among grades was not limited to the public. William Tonk asserted that most experts, let alone most salesmen, were unable to point out the differences between pianos when the price did not vary more than 5 to 15 percent. "It is my opinion that, in most cases, the dealer would not realize the superior quality of the dearer piano were it not for the fact that it is dearer," Tonk declared. "It is this difference which prejudices him to think that the cheaper piano is as good, or, at least, *good enough*."[33]

Enterprising manufacturers and salesmen bewildered customers further in their common references to an upright piano's "grand" tone, or to the piano itself as an "upright grand." Such information was on occasion more legitimate than not, as the performance of many high-grade uprights with large soundboards equalled if not surpassed that of commercial-grade grand pianos. More often such a description was an exaggeration to effect a sale. Maud Nathan related an amusing incident which shows the extent to which such interchange of terminology confused even those in the industry. After transporting a Chickering concert grand piano to their new home in Green Bay, her mother called a local music store to put it in the house. She stressed that it would take three men because it was a grand piano: "Later on, two men called and said they thought they could manage it. However, when they saw the size and shape of the piano, they threw up their hands. My mother said: 'I told you it was a *grand* piano.' 'Yes,' they said, 'we know you did. We've handled many a grand piano, but never one of that *shape!*' They had supposed that my mother was merely boasting of the quality of the piano!"[34]

Grand pianos—those resting on three legs (or sets of legs), and having horizontal strings and the distinctive gull-wing topboard—also varied in both size and quality, from the so-called baby grand to the parlor grand to the concert instrument. Automatic pianos, which included both grand and upright styles, similarly were classified as either player, expression-player, or reproducing pianos, depending upon their mechanical sophistication. All were graded low, medium, or high. But such terminology was lost amid the dozens of popular tradenames and hundreds of stencil names christening each piano, from Aeolian's Pianola to Baldwin's Manualo, from Autopiano's Symphotone to George P. Bent's Repro-Phraso Personal Reproducing Player Piano. As if these conditions were not confusing enough, even a respected trademark was not necessarily a guarantee of legitimate parentage. As years passed, many well-known piano makers went out of business. Because these firms had well-established reputations with the public, they often sold their piano names—their trademarks—to other piano companies. This was a common feature of one of the most characteristic business trends of the time: the consolidation, or merger.

Discipline and Market Control through Merger

By 1890 the characteristic business structure in the United States had become the corporation, and the tendency toward bigness and concentration through merger was the basic change signifying modern industrial development. Beginning with the railroad industry, combination became standard not only in the manufacturing sector, but also among financial, insurance, and public utilities firms. A major reason businesses consolidated was to gain greater control of their market. Another was to achieve economy of scale by expanding unit production, a move intended to take advantage of the growing national market that was brought about in part by national advertising of trade-marked goods. One of the easiest ways to expand production was to merge with similar companies.

Historians have traced in great detail the two types of merger—horizontal and vertical—that brought about such market control. More recently, scholars have analyzed the "managerial revolution" that these new firms adopted to administer the giant businesses more efficiently—the creation of special departments to oversee the various parts of the whole: raw materials, manufacture, finance, marketing and sales. In other words, successful modern industry achieved what one historian calls "the integration of mass production with mass distribution."[35] The result was increased production and profits, and lower costs. This was achieved through the administration of expert managers, who oversaw the entire process of manufacture and distribution, from the gathering of raw materials to the sale of finished products to the consumer. This change created not only monopoly or oligopoly in the market, but also a public fear of this trend that engendered the Progressive reform movement in an effort to control the situation.

The piano supply industry made it fairly easy for new houses to enter the highly competitive piano trade with small amounts of capital. Unprecedented and seemingly unlimited prosperity also encouraged entrepreneurs. The result, much like that in the early automobile industry, was an increase of inexperienced, and sometimes dishonest, manufacturers who produced inferior pianos to sell to an eager but gullible public. There was also an increase in undercapitalized, ill-managed, and thus unstable businesses. These conditions in turn produced uncontrolled competition, a significant, though limited, mortality rate among firms, and the threat of demoralization of the industry. For many manufacturers, the answer to these problems seemed to be the industrial combination, which promised to restore order to the trade through monopolized control.

According to Alfred Dolge, the attempt to organize a piano trust began in the spring of 1892. "Such a development was not only logical and according to the laws of evolution," he asserted, "but in some instances the only salvation for an industry, which, because of too many rivaling establishments, suffered on the one hand from an unreasonable expense account, and on the other from over-competition, both of which reduced profits to a minimum. . . . the selling methods were anything but ethical [and] the greatest evil . . . was that the industry as a whole was suffering from lack of sufficient working capital."[36]

The proposed piano trust was to be capitalized at $50 million and managed by "the most experienced men engaged in the manufacture and sale of pianos and organs." The new organization, the American Piano and Organ Company, would begin as soon as a sufficient number of firms could be secured. A syndicate of New York bankers would use their influence to market securities of American Piano and Organ as soon as stocks were listed. Dolge, who played an active part in this trust movement, reported that the attempt failed because the majority of manufacturers understood "neither the scope nor aim of the proposition." Much protest also came, understandably, from the supply industries. Despite the continued support of the stronger firms, the piano makers abandoned the idea upon the outbreak of economic depression in 1893.

In September 1897 interested parties reintroduced the plan and organized the Columbia Investment Company, incorporated under New Jersey law with a capital of $1 million. Once more a syndicate of bankers, impressed with the increasing prosperity of the industry, agreed to finance the purchase of various firms. Despite the willingness of many large manufacturers to sell to Columbia Investment Company, the plan failed again "because of the state of the money market, which made the sale of new securities impossible for a long time to come," according to Dolge. *The Music Trades* revealed the alternate opinion that Dolge's plan, which was to maintain only eight to ten different piano makes and eliminate a reported 80 percent of the existing factories and 65 percent of the dealers, also threatened the trade press, a condition that the "anti-trust" piano makers and dealers could not tolerate.

The promoters attempted the trust scheme yet another time in early 1899, but on an entirely new basis. Rather than securing the financial backing of a bankers' syndicate, they invited only firms which were able to cover their own liabilities. Yet this plan failed too, because petty jealousy and distrust prevented even the leading manufacturers from working together. Unprecedented prosperity in all areas of the piano trade also encouraged satisfaction with existing conditions.[37]

This is not to suggest, however, that the piano industry remained outside the pattern of higher capitalization, integrated corporate structure, managerial expertise, and consolidation, all of which were necessary components of the emerging consumer culture. But an examination of the organizational structure of the piano industry as well as its corporate complexity is particularly difficult because company records, reports, and personal papers, with few exceptions, no longer exist for the period preceding the Second World War. Even the National Piano Manufacturers Association has disposed of its earlier records. Published memoirs, none of which exist from the titans of the industry, are very few. Trade publications are difficult to find, and are neither objective nor exhaustive in their reporting. Investment guides, such as *Moody's Industrials*, reported on only a few firms. The extremely confusing nature of the piano industry itself further inhibits accurate analysis. Mergers, holding companies, controlling corporations hidden from public view make it difficult if not impossible to identify the true ownership of a particular name, or actual production figures of a particular firm.

Hallet & Davis, for example, a very old and respected Boston piano company, is traceable to the 1835 formation of Brown & Hallet. Following the death of George H. Davis in 1879, the firm was incorporated in 1890 under the new management of G. Cook, W. D. Cook, and Edwin Nelson Kimball. The Conway Company, incorporated in 1905, took over Hallet & Davis that same year. E. E. and C. C. Conway, the sons of E. S. Conway, vice president of W. W. Kimball Piano Co. (Chicago), served as executive officers in both the Conway Company and Hallet & Davis. The Conway brothers also had worked with the Kimball firm. Obviously, Hallet & Davis enjoyed a close association with the W. W. Kimball Co. (The Conway firm also produced the Conway piano, and owned the Simplex Player Action Co. as well.) In 1916 Conway acquired the National Piano Manufacturing Co. of Boston, which in turn controlled Merrill Piano Mfg. Co., Norris & Hyde Piano Co., and Briggs Piano Co. Conway then turned over production of Briggs to Hallet & Davis.

Eventually the brothers purchased Sylvester Tower Co., an action and keys supplier, and also Wilcox & White, maker of the Angelus player piano. Hallet & Davis assumed production of the latter. Then after 1925, Jacob Doll & Sons of New York took control of the Hallet & Davis Co. In time, Winter & Co. acquired Hallet & Davis, and in 1959 Winter purchased the great Aeolian-American Corporation, and changed its corporate name to Aeolian, Inc. The new company resumed production of the Hallet & Davis piano in its Memphis factory. Thus, while one might refer to "the Hallet & Davis piano," neither production figures nor the piano itself have belonged to Hallet & Davis since 1890. Such transfers of names and control of companies were repeated endlessly in the history of the American piano industry.

Although the attempt to construct an industry-wide piano trust was a failure, the stronger firms were aware of the advantages offered in securing horizontal and vertical integration. By the late nineteenth century many American piano manufacturers had begun a move toward incorporation and high capital investment, although most businesses remained partnerships or proprietorships. An extremely conservative and highly competitive industry, the piano trade also was slow to implement the new managerial hierarchies, increasingly common in many other American corporations, in which the owners of a company had little to do with the its actual management. The piano corporation, when it existed at all, was usually managed by the owner, and the major stockholders were also the executive officers of the firm.

By the turn of the century far heavier capital expenditures were necessary to ensure success than had been required earlier, although the supply industry still made it possible for small firms to compete. The growing prosperity of the trade even during the depression of 1907 encouraged both entry into piano manufacturing and merger within it. To meet the increased competition, many of the older companies found it essential to increase their capitalization significantly. Bush & Gerts, for example, formed their Chicago partnership in 1885, with a total investment of $20,000. Five years later the firm was incorporated with $400,000 capital. By 1916 the capital stock amounted to $1 million. Jesse French, a pioneer in piano merchandizing through the control of chain stores directed from a main office, began business with a capital of hardly $3,000 in 1873. Twelve years later he organized the Jesse French Piano and Organ Co., incorporated with a capital of $500,000, which increased to $550,000 in 1902. Upon moving to St. Louis, French also became a director of the Missouri-Lincoln Trust Co., capitalized at $13 million, and president of the Mercantile Metal Milling Co., with a capital of $400,000. Similarly, Charles A. Sterling organized the Sterling Organ Co. in 1873 with a capital stock value of $30,000, which increased to $1 million by 1911.

The Baldwin Co. of Cincinnati also had come a long way since D. H. Baldwin had begun his retail proprietorship in 1862 with $2,000. Baldwin had formed a partnership with Lucien Wulsin in 1873 (D. H. Baldwin & Co.) and had increased capital to $50,000. By the time of the company's incorporation in 1901, total capital was $1.25 million, and the firm also controlled the Ellington and Valley Gem piano companies in Cincinnati, and the Hamilton Organ Co. in Chicago. In 1903 Baldwin's capitalization was changed to $1.8 million, and by 1916 the company's capital value was $2.8 million.[38] Wulsin's son, Lucien Wulsin II, indicated that the Baldwin management was well aware of the advantages in increased capital, "because this size capitalization gave us standing in the business world and it commands respect and attention and is a help in doing business."[39]

Some idea of the value of the piano trade in the United States and the trend toward large capitalization is evident in table 3.1, a compilation of companies whose capital worth was $100,000 or more in 1916. The list is representative of the more successful firms but is not exhaustive; nor does it take mergers into account. For example, Story & Clark owned Hobart M. Cable, and American Piano Co. controlled A. B. Chase and J. & C. Fischer. Aeolian Company belonged to Aeolian, Weber Piano & Pianola Co., which also controlled subsidiaries in Europe and Australia whose total capital stock amounted to an additional $4 million. Similarly, the Rudolph Wurlitzer Co. also owned the Rudolph Wurlitzer Manufacturing Co. in North Tonawanda, New York, which was capitalized at $1 million. The chart also does not reveal the extent to which large companies owned interests in other firms. Wurlitzer, for example, owned 40 percent of American Welte Co., 26 percent of American Piano Co., and significant holdings in Apollo Piano Co., Buescher Band Instrument Co., C. G. Conn, Martin Band Instrument Co., and Widney & Co. felt manufacturers.[40]

The general business trend toward incorporation and increased capitalization was therefore an important element in the modernization of the American piano industry. But just as significant was the trend toward combination. While no industry-wide piano trust developed, the great number of mergers that did take place made the name on a piano's fallboard almost meaningless, in that the name, while it denoted a trademark and often a respected history, did not necessarily denote the real maker—the controlling owner.

In the developing years of the American piano trade, the name on the fallboard represented the actual manufacturer and the true quality of the instrument, as well as the policies, responsibility, and experience of the firm. In time, however, the ownership of countless piano names changed hands through merger because of lucrative venture, insolvency, or death on the part of the original maker. In some cases, control of a name changed not merely once, but even three or more times. Although these changes did not necessarily affect the quality of the instrument, a brand named piano remained only as good as the policies, ideals, and experience of its *current* maker.

The reputable Boston firm of Mason & Hamlin typifies this practice. It achieved preeminence among the trade, becoming Steinway & Sons' chief competitor by 1910. Upon its combination with the massive Cable Company of Chicago in 1912, the management and factory operations continued as before, while the merger provided Mason & Hamlin with needed capital. Twelve years later the giant American Piano Company purchased the firm for $2 million cash to head a trinity of revered names, the others being Chickering & Sons and Wm. Knabe & Co., which it already controlled.

Table 3.1. Known Capital Stock Values of Representative American Piano Companies in 1916

Manufacturer	Location	Date Incorporated	Capital Stock
Firms Whose Capital Stock Value Was $2 Million or More			
American Piano Co.	New York	1908	$12,000,000
Aeolian, Weber Piano & Pianola Co.	New York	1903	10,000,000
The Cable Company	Chicago	1899?	5,000,000
The Rudolph Wurlitzer Co.	Cincinnati	1890	4,000,000
Grinnell Bros.	Detroit	1912	3,750,000
Conway Musical Industries	Boston	1905	3,500,000
Lyon & Healy Piano Co.	Chicago	1890	3,000,000
Story & Clark Co.	Grand Haven, Mich.	1895	3,000,000
The Baldwin Co.	Cincinnati	1901	2,800,000
W. W. Kimball Co.	Chicago	1882	2,750,000
Aeolian Company	New York	1887	2,000,000
Smith, Barnes & Strohber Piano Co.	Chicago	1884?	2,000,000
Steinway & Sons	New York	1876	2,000,000
Firms Whose Capital Stock Value Was $1 Million to $2 Million			
P. A. Stark	Chicago	1891?	$ 1,500,000
Autopiano Co.	New York	1903	1,000,000
Bush & Gerts Piano Co.	Chicago	1891	1,000,000
Haddorff Piano Co.	Rockford, Ill.	1902	1,000,000
Hardman, Peck & Co.	New York	1905	1,000,000
Hobart M. Cable	La Porte, Ind.	1890	1,000,000
Jacob Doll & Sons	New York	1904	1,000,000
Lester Piano Co.	Philadelphia	1888?	1,000,000
Melville Clark Piano Co.	Chicago	1900	1,000,000
The Sterling Co.	Derby, Conn.	1873	1,000,000
M. Welte & Sons	New York	1865?	1,000,000
Wissner & Sons	New York	1912?	1,000,000

Table 3.1 continued

Manufacturer	Location	Date Incorpo- rated	Capital Stock
Firms Whose Capital Stock Value Was $100,000 to $1 Million			
Ivers & Pond	Boston	1880	$ 878,000
Price & Teeple Piano Co.	Chicago	1903?	600,000
Jesse French & Sons Piano Co.	New Castle, Ind.	1902	550,000
A. B. Chase & Co.	Norwalk, Ohio	1875?	500,000
George P. Bent Co.	Chicago	1908	500,000
Krell Piano Co.	Cincinnati	1889	500,000
Wilcox & White Co.	Meriden, Conn.	1877	450,000
Bush & Lane	Holland, Mich.	1904	400,000
Kranich & Bach	New York	1890	400,000
Schiller Piano Co.	Oregon, Ill.	1891	400,000
Sohmer & Co.	New York	1872?	400,000
J. & C. Fischer & Co.	New York	1907	300,000
Vose & Sons Piano Co.	Boston	1889	300,000
Everett Piano Co.	Boston	1883?	100,000
National Piano Manufacturing Co.	Boston	1910	100,000
R. S. Howard Co.	New York	1902?	100,000
Winter & Co.	New York	1903	100,000

Source: Compiled from information in William Geppert, *The Official Guide to Piano Quality* (New York: Eilert Printing Co., 1916); Alfred Dolge, *Pianos and Their Makers*, 2 vols. (Covina, Calif.: Covina Publishing Co., 1911, 1913; vol. 1 reprinted, New York: Dover, 1972); *The Music Trades*.

The parent corporation marketed the Mason & Hamlin Ampico reproducing piano to compete with the Steinway Duo-Art Pianola reproducing piano[41] that the Aeolian Company was promoting. But financial difficulties forced American Piano to sell Mason & Hamlin to Aeolian in 1930, though the latter also was plagued with monetary problems. Salvaging what was left, the two mammoth companies merged into the Aeolian-American Corporation two years later, at which time the Boston Mason & Hamlin plant was closed and moved to East Rochester, New York.[42]

Thus, any comparison of pianos produced by the original Mason & Hamlin of Boston (1883–1910), the Mason & Hamlin combination with the Cable Company (1911–24), the Mason & Hamlin as absorbed into the American Piano Co. (1924–30), the Mason & Hamlin purchased by the Aeolian Company (1930–32), and the Mason & Hamlin as absorbed into the merger of Aeolian-American Corporation (after 1932), must take account of the fact that the name "Mason & Hamlin" denotes history, but not necessarily continuity. With production thus interrupted (especially following the closing of the Boston plant), performing artists loyal to the Mason & Hamlin as well as members of the piano trade itself came to doubt the constancy of the instrument's quality. The company never recovered its former reputation after the shuffle of 1930–32.

The complexity of the piano industry's practice of merger is evident in table A.1, which illustrates that among the plethora of piano trademarks in the United States from 1890 to the 1920s, a great number existed in name only. Three types of business mergers common to the piano trade are identified: combination (wherein a company's individuality, executive officers, and even factories are maintained), consolidation (in which a company is absorbed completely by an existing parent corporation), and amalgamation (wherein several companies form a new corporation). Often a single piano company controlled a variety of brand names, and this confusing situation was made even more bewildering because frequently a firm would manufacture two, three, or more piano brands in a single factory, and number the pianos—regardless of name—consecutively rather than independently.

The Baldwin Co., for example, owned Sargent, Schroeder & Sons, Winton, and Valley Gem trademarks, but all were part of the Howard Piano Co. (Cincinnati), a Baldwin subsidiary, and all pianos with those names were numbered consecutively with Howard pianos. In other words, they were Howard pianos despite their names. As if this were not complicated enough, Baldwin used consecutive numbers for its Monarch and St. Regis pianos, which were sold by the Monarch Piano Co. (Chicago), also a Baldwin subsidiary. Yet, there were no separate Monarch or Howard factories. Baldwin actually had only four factories: Baldwin, Valley Gem, and Ellington piano companies in Cincinnati, and Hamilton Piano Company in Chicago. All instruments were made in one of these facilities.

William Geppert decried the situation in his 1916 issue of *The Official Guide to Piano Quality*: "When one considers there are over sixteen hundred names of pianos and players in this edition of this book, it would be practically impossible for mistakes not to be made." Geppert's mission to enlighten the consumer was plagued not merely with the sheer existence of "over sixteen hundred names," but, as table A.1 illustrates, with the difficulty of tracing the actual ownership of those names as well—and then of determining continuity of quality. Similarly, the editors of annual trade listings, such as *The Piano and Organ Purchaser's Guide*, *Fox's Music Trade Directory*, and *Dealer's Handbook of Pianos and Their Makers*, tried to educate the retail dealer and his salesmen who were confused by the presence of old established names and unaware of a piano's actual parentage or ownership. Such publications intended to protect not only the purchasing public, but the reputation of the piano industry as well, by presenting the reputations and comparative merits of the various instruments for sale. In an effort to legitimate the trade, manufacturers and dealers used these guides as weapons against unscrupulous competitors. *The Piano and Organ Purchaser's Guide*, for example, was admitted as an authority by the courts in several states, and in 1905 it was used as expert testimony before the Canadian Tariff Commission.[43]

The sale of a piano trademark did not necessarily devalue the name. According to the *Dealer's Handbook*, "sometimes the new owner of a piano name, equally proud of his own good name, not only preserved but even enhanced the standards of quality that had made famous the name acquired." But this was not always so: "Other times, however, the new owner exploited the original name at the expense of the public by disguising his piano as a product of the original maker, when actually it was inferior, resembling the original in name only."[44]

Good trade practice allowed a piano manufacturer three options. First, he could place his own name on the fallboard and also cast it in the plate. This practice usually was reserved for a firm's first line of merchandise (the Baldwin piano, the Steinway piano, the Cable piano, etc.). Second, the manufacturer could place a purchased trademark or his own trademark on the fallboard, but cast his own name in the plate. Thus, piano name and piano maker were firmly identified, there being no attempt at concealment. This custom primarily denoted a firm's second or third line of instruments, made to sell at a lower price (the Ellington piano, built by Baldwin; the Whitney piano, built by Kimball, etc.). Finally, and much more commonly, a piano could bear an old, established name both on the fallboard and cast in the plate, but not identify the current maker. This was usually the result of a merger, often where the original manufacturer was an officer of the parent corporation and still in charge of his firm to some degree. In time, however, upon the death or retirement of the original maker, the firm's identity was absorbed completely by the parent corporation (Chickering & Sons, Wm. Knabe & Co., and Mason & Hamlin, all part of American Piano Co.). "The value of this piano," reported the *Dealer's Handbook*, "must be judged by the policies and reputation of its present maker and not those of the original owner of the name."[45] Table A.1 testifies to the complexity of such accepted trade practice, which characterized the piano industry.

To speak of Hallet & Davis without consideration of the Conway Company, or of Smith, Barnes & Strohber without Continental Piano Company—to speak of a piano maker without considering the real owner is to assume a continuity that just is not there. Nevertheless, intensive brand name advertising generally kept the public ignorant of real ownership and offered buyers the illusion of greater choice than really existed. The piano brand name supplied a crucial distinction to products that were physically similar in appearance, and perpetuated among consumers a sense of product history and stability. The name offered the purchaser an expression of individuality through purchase, while obscuring the extent of industrial merger and bureaucratic complexity. These were among the basic tenets of the developing consumer culture.

Table 3.2 (a condensed version of table A.1) demonstrates the importance of the combination in the piano industry. While the census listed 255 so-called separate firms in 1914, these twenty-five corporations and holding companies produced 74 percent of the total output of some 320,000 pianos. The basic problem with a strategy of combination, however, was the same problem that the automobile makers faced: no combination was able to include a sufficient number of leading producers to allow any control of the industry, and most were heavily invested in too many weak firms producing unknown or unpopular brand names. Those companies that had any real strength—Steinway & Sons, Baldwin, Kimball, Steger, Jacob Doll & Sons, Gulbransen-Dickinson, Schulz—were convinced of their ability to go it alone. The strong combinations—Aeolian, Kohler & Campbell, American, Cable, Wurlitzer, Conway, Continental—were already in control of most other major trademarks. The most likely remaining candidates for combination, therefore, were the companies weakest in capital, production and marketing capability, and stability.

The piano industry had already achieved success by producing good pianos in large volume at affordable prices. Mass production of standardized parts, the rise of independent supply industries, and the development of efficient factory organization under talented management contributed to this prosperity in the late nineteenth century. But prosperity also brought intense competition. While combination was helpful in combating this situation, it was not the complete solution. The leaders of the industry realized that the only real way to overcome these problems was to integrate forward and control the market itself. The real successes in the piano trade were the ones who were able to join "the managerial revolution."

Table 3.2. Major Piano Combinations and Corporations, ca. 1916

Manufacturer	Location	Date Incorporated	Production[d]
Holding Companies—Publicly Issued Stock[a]			
American Piano Company, Inc.	New York	1908	17,900
Aeolian, Weber Piano & Pianola Co., Inc.	New York	1903	9,800
Holding Companies—Closed Corporations[b]			
Kohler & Campbell Industries, Inc.	New York	1896	25,900
Conway Musical Industries, Inc.	Boston	1905	14,700
Continental Piano Co., Inc.	New Castle, Ind.	1912	14,700
Rice-Wuest Co., Inc.	Woodbury, N.J.	1913	10,000
The Cable Company, Inc.	Chicago	1899?	8,000
The Rudolph Wurlitzer Co., Inc.	Cincinnati	1890	?[e]
Closed Corporations[c]			
Steger Products Manufacturing Corp.	Chicago	1893?	13,800
W. W. Kimball Co., Inc.	Chicago	1882	13,400
The Baldwin Co., Inc.	Cincinnati	1901	12,800
Jacob Doll & Sons, Inc.	New York	1904	11,900
M. Schulz Co., Inc.	Chicago	1889	10,000
Gulbransen-Dickinson Co., Inc.	Chicago	1906	9,000
Starr Piano Co., Inc.	Richmond, Ind.	1884	7,000[f]
Hardman, Peck & Co., Inc.	New York	1905	6,100
Cable-Nelson Piano Co., Inc.	Chicago	1905	6,000
The Sterling Co., Inc.	Derby, Conn.	1873	6,000
Lester Piano Co., Inc.	Philadelphia	1888?	5,720
Haddorff Piano Co., Inc.	Rockford, Ill.	1902	5,000
C. Kurtzmann & Co., Inc.	Buffalo	1896	5,000
Steinway & Sons, Inc.	New York	1876	5,000
Story & Clark Co., Inc.	Grand Haven, Mich.	1895	4,300

Table 3.2 continued

Manufacturer	Location	Date Incor- porated	Pro- duction[d]
Department Store Corporations Manufacturing Pianos			
Wanamaker's, Inc.	Philadelphia	1909	7,400
Grinnell Bros., Inc.	Detroit	1912	1,800

[a]Combination led to formation of holding company, with the officers and managers of the merging companies directly concerned with total operating activities. Stocks were issued and sold on public stock exchange.

[b]Same as [a] except that issue of stock was restricted to family and others within the corporation.

[c]Private corporation whose central office (rather than a holding company) controlled the various subcompanies. Issue of stock restricted within family and corporation.

[d]Total production of all subsidiaries (see table A.1 for complete information). Estimates only, based on serial numbers; verification almost impossible. Treat with caution.

[e]Wurlitzer total production unknown. All authorities agree that Wurlitzer was the largest manufacturer of mechanical instruments, including player pianos. *Moody's Industrials* lists Wurlitzer sales for 1917 as $7,043,192. As a point of reference, American Piano Co. sales for the same year were $4,857,560.

[f]Alfred Dolge credits Starr Piano Co. with producing about 18,000 pianos annually (*Pianos and Their Makers*, 2 vols. [Covina, Calif.: Covina Publishing Co., 1911, 1913; vol. 1 reprinted, New York: Dover, 1972], vol. 1, p. 349).

The Baldwin Company— Model Organization

The industry-wide trust movement failed among piano manufacturers partly because of petty jealousy, because universal prosperity decreased the effects of intense competition, and because the piano trade, largely consisting of peripheral firms, was by its very nature unlikely to form a successful trust. But just as the Kaiser company was a center firm within the peripheral shipping industry, certain piano companies were able to achieve center status and successfully form powerful, vertically integrated trusts. They concurrently developed a sophisticated system of production, distribution, and sales capable of administering increasingly manipulative national advertising strategies and credit purchase plans. These were the necessary corporate components that together helped encourage the emergence of the consumer society.

Alfred Dolge recorded that the leaders of the trade had been developing the organization and management of the large, modern piano factory since the 1870s. The resulting increased efficiency and economy of scale achieved unprecedented production levels in an industry not traditionally given to mass production. Subsequently, large piano houses found it necessary to create, maintain, and increase the market for their products now being produced in record numbers. This was especially necessary in the wake of the intense competition from the many piano assembling companies, who were able to enter the field quite easily with little overhead and capitalization and produce thousands of instruments. But these assembling companies depended on the piano supply industry to manufacture their product and on the existing "jobber" (independent wholesaler) system of distribution to sell it. Hence, the leading corporations developed successful new methods of mass distribution, marketing, and advertising. They financed sales on credit and used franchised dealerships with limited sales territories to control distribution. As a natural consequence of increased production and marketing, the leaders of the industry found it necessary to employ expert financiers to help them achieve and maintain dominion through increased capitalization and combination. This trend accelerated in the twenty years following 1890.[46] Thus, the pursuit of a revolutionary musical democracy in America required of its patrons, if it would be successful, an equally revolutionary pursuit of emerging industrial and corporate patterns.

The largest trust in the industry was American Piano Company, the brainchild of George C. Foster. A graduate of a Boston business school (Harvard?), Foster started in the music business as a salesman for the Boston branch of Estey Organ Company. By 1894 he had formed a partnership with W. B. Armstrong (the Foster-Armstrong Company) and had begun manufacturing both Foster and Armstrong pianos in Rochester, New York. In order to bring into its business the prestige of a famous name, the firm acquired Marshall & Wendell from an Albany bank in 1899. Following a fire in 1902, Foster-Armstrong rebuilt its factories in the nearby village of Despatch through the financial backing of Philadelphia Trust Company. Completed in 1906, the new factory buildings were the first large-scale application in the United States of a new construction process, the Ransom-Smith reinforced concrete method. Subsequently, the town of Despatch changed its name to East Rochester.

Foster and Armstrong then acquired Chickering & Sons of Boston, Wm. Knabe & Co. of Baltimore, and a number of lesser known names, and incorporated their business in 1908 to form the American Piano Company. Initially capitalized at $12 million, American became the first music company listed on the New York Stock Exchange. The company-owned retail store, located at 39 Fifth Avenue, New York, required its salesmen to wear striped pants, swallowtail coats, and wing collars, a calculated complement to the artistic and social respectability already identified with the more prestigious piano lines.

After achieving a strong horizontal combination, Foster realized that in order to market the various lines that his company controlled, it would be necessary to assist retail piano merchants in both stocking and selling their merchandise. The establishment of Bankers Commercial Corporation in New York City brought into existence one of the earliest houses devoted exclusively to floor-planning of piano stock in retail stores and subsequent handling of retail piano contracts to the buying public. Foster maintained his devotion to the production of pianos until his death in 1953, although the banking firm took up most of his energies and far exceeded piano manufacturing in profits and financial strength. The American Piano Company continued to grow, developing the highly acclaimed Ampico reproducing mechanism in 1913, and acquiring the renowned Mason & Hamlin Company in 1922 for $2 million cash. The trust remained one of the strongest in the industry until the mid-to-late 1920s, at which time severe financial conditions forced American and most other firms into receivership.[47]

American Piano Company's chief rival was the Aeolian, Weber Piano & Pianola Co., which became the largest player piano manufacturer in the world. The company modestly began in 1883 when William B. Tremaine acquired the Aeolian Organ Co. and then the Automatic Music Paper Co. of Boston five years later. A veteran manufacturer of thousands of mechanical reed organs (he had organized the Mechanical Orguinette Co. in 1876), Tremaine then incorporated the Aeolian Organ and Music Co. under Connecticut law in 1897, making automatic organs and music rolls. He introduced the Aeriol self-playing piano in 1895 after acquiring the patents of Morgan Organ Reed Co. of Worcester, Massachusetts. In 1898 his son, Harry B. Tremaine, became the president of the Aeolian Company. Keen to the potential of Edwin S. Votey's Pianola piano-player, the Tremaines courted the inventor (with his patents) into their organization and proceeded to manufacture, promote, and distribute the invention.

Under Harry B. Tremaine's leadership the Aeolian Company assumed worldwide prominence. It acquired several popular piano and organ firms, including George Steck & Co. and the Wheelock Piano Co., which controlled Stuyvesant Piano Co. and Weber Piano Co., and in 1903 organized the Aeolian, Weber Piano & Pianola Co., capitalized at $10 million. This holding company also owned Universal Music Co., an American piano-roll manufacturer, and controlled the Orchestrelle Co. of London, the Choralion Co. of Berlin, the Aeolian Company of Paris, the Pianola Company Proprietary, Ltd of Melbourne and Sydney, in addition to a Steck factory in Gotha, Germany, and a Weber factory at Hayes in Middlesex, England. Together these companies employed about 5,000 people. Total capital under Tremaine's direction was $15.5 million, exceeding the capital that had been invested in the entire piano and organ industry in 1890. This influential corporation played a major role in the development of copyright legislation in both the United States and Great Britain, and it continued to develop player piano innovations, culminating in the Duo-Art Pianola Reproducing Piano. Tremaine also built Aeolian Hall, one of the landmark concert halls in New York City. In 1932 during the Great Depression, Aeolian eventually amalgamated with its rival, American Piano Co., forming the Aeolian-American Corporation.[48]

The Baldwin Company of Cincinnati, Ohio, achieved a powerful and well-respected position in the trade through efficient factory production and management, and pioneering methods of distribution, sales, and marketing. The company structure was so tight and well run that when Alfred Dolge compiled a second volume in his history of the piano trade (1913), he proclaimed that Baldwin had a "model organization" and was as important a pioneer in developing effective distribution and sales of pianos as Steinway & Sons was in improving production, mechanical operation, and marketing of the instrument. Indeed, Baldwin has managed the only consistently successful dealer consignment program in the music industry's history.[49]

Dwight Hamilton Baldwin was forty-one years old in 1862, when he became a retail dealer in pianos and organs in Cincinnati. For the previous twenty years he had been an itinerant Sunday school and music teacher in eastern Kentucky and the Ohio Valley. Though Baldwin taught violin and melodeon (reed organ), he became well known for his ability to lead community singing classes. When he settled in Cincinnati in the summer of 1857, his reputation in the public Singing School movement was already highly respected. That same year, Baldwin and Luther Whiting Mason compiled a *Book of Chants* for use in community singing, and in 1860 they prepared and published *The Young Singer Part I*, a music manual that was widely used in the Cincinnati schools. Mason was the son of Lowell Mason, founder of the Boston Academy of Music and one of the most important promoters of the Singing School system of music instruction in the public schools. Another son, Henry Mason, organized the Mason & Hamlin Organ and Piano Company. Baldwin continued to teach after his decision to enter the retail trade, and with $2,000 capital he became a dealer for Decker Bros. pianos.

In March 1866, twenty-one-year-old Lucien Wulsin, recently discharged from the Union Army, began working for Baldwin as a bookkeeper. The young man proved invaluable and Baldwin took him into partnership on June 2, 1873. Baldwin contributed $50,000 worth of stock and assets to the firm and Wulsin furnished $10,000 cash. The new business, D. H. Baldwin & Co., expanded quickly. During the next two decades, it developed into one of the largest wholesalers and retailers of eastern-made pianos and organs in the Middle West. In 1877 the firm opened a retail store in Louisville, under the management of Robert A. Johnston, and two years later a store in Indianapolis. Johnston, one of Baldwin's friends from the Singing School days, was made a partner in 1880. D. H. Baldwin & Co. became a sales agent for Steinway & Sons, Decker Bros., J. & C. Fischer, Haines Bros., Vose & Sons, Estey organs, and others. The eastern manufacturers restricted sales territories to protect their dealers from competition with each other. Baldwin, therefore, could not expand north of the Columbus River in Ohio, or sell in Pittsburgh, Cleveland, northern Indiana, Chicago, and St. Louis. To compensate for these restrictions, Baldwin contracted for the manufacture of pianos from Ohio Valley Piano Co., a small factory in nearby Ripley, Ohio, and stencilled these instruments, "Expressly Made for D. H. Baldwin & Co."

Baldwin and Wulsin recognized the value of the sewing machine trade's very effective method of distribution and sales—installment buying, or as its originator, Edward Clark of the Singer Manufacturing Co. called it, "hire purchase." Singer introduced the plan in 1856. It allowed a buyer lacking cash to sign a contract with a salesman for the purchase of a sewing machine, make a small down payment, and complete the purchase by small, regular payments until paid in full. The contract, however, kept the title to the machine in the possession of the manufacturer or wholesaler, so in case of default, the selling firm could recover the merchandise. Thus, a small retail dealer or traveling salesman could turn in cash or the buyer's contract to the manufacturer and avoid tying up money in stock of merchandise.

In 1872 Baldwin hired several men trained as sewing machine salesmen, some of whom would later become junior partners in the firm. Adopting the system of installment sales, the company soon became the dominant music business in the Ohio Valley.

Baldwin retailers often established themselves in county seats sending hundreds of deferred payments to the company each month, from which their commissions were paid. With this system the House of Baldwin was able to carry itself and its dealers through periods of slow sales or financial panics.

The firm suffered two setbacks in the spring of 1884. The manager of the Indianapolis branch unexpectedly locked the store and left town, and the third partner (the manager of the Louisville division) died quite suddenly. In addition, D. H. Baldwin, then sixty-three years old, was less and less active in the affairs of the partnership as he devoted most of his time to teaching Sunday school and working for the Presbyterian church. Wulsin was carrying the burden of the entire business. With the company expanding and in need of management, Baldwin and Wulsin created three new partners from the ranks: Clarence Wulsin (Lucien's younger brother, who was sent to Indianapolis), Albert Van Buren (who replaced Johnston in Louisville), and George W. Armstrong, Jr., (who remained in Cincinnati). Each new partner furnished $5,000 cash to the capital of the firm.

As D. H. Baldwin retired increasingly into church activities, Wulsin became more active in Cincinnati's musical life. He was a handsome man who sported a thick mustache; his energy and forceful personality commanded respect in the community. Together with Theodore Thomas, Colonel George Ward Nichols, and others, Wulsin helped launch the Cincinnati College of Music and the May Musical Festivals. He also served as president of the Cincinnati Music Club and later was elected to its board of directors. Wulsin helped organize the Cincinnati Philharmonic Orchestra, which provided the nucleus of musicians with which Mrs. William Howard Taft and her associates developed the Cincinnati Symphony Orchestra in 1895. Wulsin remained a principal adviser on the orchestra board until his death in 1912.[50]

In the late 1880s D. H. Baldwin & Co. was caught between the territorial restrictions that the eastern manufacturers imposed and the desire to sell merchandise over wider areas. In 1887 Baldwin was no longer allowed to represent Steinway, and the partners decided to manufacture their own pianos and organs.[51] They

established the Hamilton Organ Co. in Chicago and began production of Hamilton and Monarch reed organs in 1888 under the
direction of Clarence Wulsin. Two years later the partners ven-
tured into making pianos. The new firm, the Baldwin Piano Company, dedicated to manufacturing the best piano that could be
built, shipped the first "Baldwin" piano to the Cincinnati store in
1891. Lucien Wulsin became the director of the manufacturing
business. The Baldwin piano, however, was an expensive, high-
grade instrument. In order to cater to more moderate incomes,
the partners formed a new corporation, the Ellington Piano Co.[52]
in Cincinnati, and purchased the Ohio Valley Piano Co. in Ripley,
renaming it Valley Gem Piano Co. D. H. Baldwin & Co., which
remained the selling organization, thus controlled four manufacturing firms, producing the Hamilton and Monarch organs, and
the Baldwin, Ellington, Valley Gem, and Howard (made by Valley
Gem) pianos. By 1898 the firm reported a total capital of $537,000.

The partners enlarged their distribution organization and actively pushed their wholesale business into West Virginia, eastern
Kentucky and Tennessee, Indiana, Illinois, Alabama, and Mississippi. They established stores in New York, Philadelphia, and Boston. In addition to hire-purchase selling, Baldwin adopted a plan
that allowed dealers to sell on consignment, based on the model
developed by the W. W. Kimball Co. of Chicago, but improving on
the Kimball idea by making it virtually impossible to break contracts. A dealer supplied a knowledge of his sales territory, selling
ability, and place of business, while Baldwin supplied the necessary capital in the form of merchandise, business organization,
and credit control, and collected the customers' installment contracts. The dealer paid his local expenses, including freight from
the factory. In turn, he retained the down payment and shared in
the monthly payments from the customer. His commission was
the difference between the wholesale price for the instrument
and the total of the time-payment contract. This usually amounted
to 25 to 30 percent of the monthly payment. Since Baldwin collected payment directly from the customer, the dealer's commission was remitted to him by the manufacturer as it was collected.
Each dealer was required to sign a monthly report of the stock on

hand from consignment and was expected to increase his commission balance in the manufacturer's books. These safeguards were designed to protect both dealer and manufacturer from financial difficulties.[53]

Dwight Hamilton Baldwin died in the summer of 1899 and, according to his will, left the bulk of his estate, including five-sixths of the shares of D. H. Baldwin & Co., to the Board of Home and Foreign Missions of the Presbyterian Church. Not content to see their efforts end so abruptly, Wulsin and Armstrong negotiated with the church to buy Baldwin's share of the business. A settlement with the church was reached in 1901. The solution was to consolidate the various parts of the business into one corporation and issue nonvoting preferred stock, the sale of which would be used to buy Baldwin's share from the church.

The new parent corporation, the Baldwin Company, was capitalized at $1.25 million in 1901, and purchased all assets of the Baldwin Piano Co., maker of the Baldwin piano. The next year, the Ohio state legislature amended the corporation code to permit holding companies to own stock in other corporations. This enabled the Baldwin Company to buy control of Ellington Piano Co., Valley Gem Piano Co., Hamilton Organ and Piano Co., and D. H. Baldwin & Co., the wholesale-retail selling organization. Capital of the holding company was increased to $1.8 million. Lucien Wulsin became president and owned control of the business. George Armstrong was vice president and directed the expanding sales operation.[54] Thus, Baldwin joined the trend in the prosperous years of 1898 to 1903, when other combinations were organized: American Tin Plate, Otis Elevator, International Paper, Standard Oil, U.S. Steel, International Harvester, United Shoe Machinery, and many others.

Figure A.1. shows the complexity of the Baldwin organization in 1916. The Baldwin Company assumed ownership of all real estate, buildings, factories, patents, goodwill, and trademarks. Manufacturing and assembly of pianos and organs were allocated to the various subsidiary corporations: the Baldwin Piano Manufacturing Co. (formerly Baldwin Piano Co.), Ellington Piano Co., Hamilton Piano and Organ Co., Monarch Piano Co., and Valley Gem

(Howard) Piano Co. The Baldwin Supply Factories and William H. Perry Lumber Co. supplied the necessary lumber and manufactured cases, actions, hammers, strings, and other parts for the various subsidiary piano companies. The Baldwin Piano Company (formerly D. H. Baldwin & Co.), which was the selling organization of the business, administered wholesale-retail divisions in Cincinnati, Indianapolis, Louisville, Chicago, St. Louis, Denver, Dallas, New York, and San Francisco. These independently managed divisions in turn supplied franchised dealerships with Baldwin products on consignment contracts for distribution all over the United States. In 1905, Baldwin enjoyed an export business to twenty-eight countries, thirty-two by 1913. Baldwin production made Cincinnati the fourth largest producer of pianos in the United States, behind New York, Chicago, and Boston.[55]

Except for the discontinuation of reed organ production in 1913 and the change in name from Valley Gem to Howard Piano Co. in 1920, this corporate structure remained through the 1930s. The Baldwin Company remained a closed corporation, and the owners continued to be the chief executives and managers. Baldwin did make use of expert middle managers, however. John Warren Macy, the designer of the Baldwin scale (the unique string-plan of the piano: tensions, bearings, length, thickness, and also cast-iron plate design), headed the firm's research department and was superintendent of the Baldwin factory. Philip Wyman, who graduated from Harvard in 1910, joined the firm that same year and worked in advertising until he became executive vice president in charge of sales. Wyman and Lucien Wulsin II, who joined the company in 1912, the year of his father's death, would become the backbone of the second generation Baldwin leadership in the 1920s.

The success of the Baldwin Company did not escape the notice of the industry's historian. Alfred Dolge called it "one of the marvels of the trade. . . . one of the great manufacturing and selling organizations of this country, whose output is one of the largest and the character of the product the highest."[56] The house strategically designed the Ellington piano to meet competition from Kranich & Bach, Vose, Sohmer, Ivers & Pond, Mehlin, A. B. Chase,

Conover, and Weber. Similarly, Hamilton pianos offered customers an alternative to Hobart M. Cable, Story & Clark, Kimball, Cable, Schulz, Bush & Lane, Haddorff, and Kohler & Campbell.[57] The Baldwin piano, of course, was aimed at the exclusive market that Steinway & Sons and Mason & Hamlin enjoyed. The excellence of the Baldwin was recognized when the company received the Grand Prix at the 1900 International Exposition in Paris, the only American piano so honored. Baldwin repeated the feat in 1904 at St. Louis and 1914 in London.

The strength of the Baldwin organization is shown by its constant growth in production, assets, and capitalization from 1901 to the mid-1920s. The company increased its capital to $2.8 million by 1916. Total production increased from 8,313 units in 1901 to 12,776 in 1916, and following a brief downward trend following the Great War, to 21,932 units in 1925. Total assets climbed from $3,535,000 in 1906 to $6,061,000 in 1916 to $15,089,000 in 1927. In several financial panics—the summer of 1893 (manufacture ceased for several months), the Panic of 1907, the depressions of 1914 and of 1920–21—Baldwin sales and profits declined only slightly.[58] To deliver these record numbers of pianos, the company had to purchase an increasing number of trucks. In 1925, Chevrolet Motor Co. listed Baldwin as a National Fleet User and gave the piano firm a 12 percent discount from list price on vehicles f.o.b. Michigan.[59]

A major factor in this success was the accumulated surplus that Baldwin and Wulsin frugally built up in the business and the constant income generated from installment sales, both of which provided a buffer against immediate financial stress. Another factor was the conservative nature of the partners themselves. By keeping salaries far below those of most houses within the trade, and by never allowing assets to become overextended with liabilities (selling on consignment to dealers insured that no dealer was caught with stock on hand that endangered his business with the Cincinnati firm), they made sure the company could stay in business. The real loss would be only in potential sales and profits. A third factor was that the Wulsins, and later Wyman, were aggressive salesmen, who promoted higher quality instruments through effective, modern advertising techniques. This strategy captured for the house not only a larger share of the market, but also the best class of business. The careful selection of agents underscored Baldwin's sound sales principles. "It is against our policy to pay any large salary," wrote Lucien Wulsin to a prospective salesman in Indiana. "We stand on this principle—*that a man who can make money for us can make it for himself,* and if he cannot do that, we do not wish to be the ones to hold the bag."[60]

So impressive was the House of Baldwin's organization and management that "one of the most distinguished manufacturers of the United States" (Steinway?) was moved to remark, "The business of D. H. Baldwin & Co. is the model upon which the entire piano and organ trade of the country should be done."[61] The Cincinnati firm's growing success resulted from the combination of this model organization with an intensive merchandising campaign designed to familiarize the public with the Baldwin name. The pioneering efforts of the American piano trade to cultivate notions of brand name loyalty, to stress benefit of ownership as much as product, and to improve society assisted the rise of the consumer culture. Given Lucien Wulsin's devotion to both art and business, his company naturally became a leader in this transformation. But among the various companies that sought product recognition and consumer trust, one name became particularly celebrated. The name, of course, was Steinway. An appreciation of the avenue by which Baldwin and especially Steinway were able to capture brand name recognition and dominate the market, however, first requires an understanding of the historical development of piano merchandising, a development quite essential to the emergence of the consumer culture itself.

*1, 2. The Victorian pi-
ano embodied middle-
class ideals of domes-
ticity, the morality of*

*music and the work
ethic, social respect-
ability, and—as these
turn-of-the-century*

*postcards suggest—
romantic courtship.*

*1.
Try this on your piano
(author's collection)*

*2.
Practice this piece
with me (author's
collection)*

3.

Music hath charms. Folk beliefs in the moral power of music to inspire, enrich, and civilize are time-honored. Although this turn-of-the-century postcard misquotes William Congreve, its message in support of those beliefs, coupled with Victorian notions about the roles of women and the piano in assimilating the beliefs, is unmistakable. (author's collection)

4.
Victor Talking Machine advertisement. Although competition from the considerably less expensive phonograph caused little concern for the piano industry before the development of the high-fidelity, long-playing models of the 1920s (indeed many piano retailers also sold phonographs and later radios), the promotion campaigns of phonograph manufacturers, particularly the Victor Talking Machine Company, quickly extolled the invention as being a musical instrument "like a piano" but also "more than a piano" since it was able to play piano, orchestra, and voice recordings and since "it plays itself . . . not like an idle piano." (from McClure's Magazine, *1913; reproduced with permission)*

5, 6. E. S. Votey's push-up style piano-player, manufactured and marketed by the Aeolian Company of New York under the brand name "Pianola," revolutionized music making by allowing anyone to "play." Aeolian's pioneer advertising campaigns, which promised artistic results with minimal effort, so popularized the device that "pianola" became the generic name for all automatic players.

THE PRESENT OF A PIANOLA IS A PRESENT TO *EVERY* MEMBER OF THE FAMILY

A great factor in the Pianola's world-wide popularity is the fact that it brings pleasure, not merely to one or two members of the family, but to *all*. It appeals equally to the wife whose household and social duties have interfered with keeping up her piano practice, to the business man who needs some recreation after the day's worries, and the growing daughters and sons with a natural craving for some form of entertainment and who will seek it outside if it is not provided within the home.

So much has been said of the artistic possibilities of the Pianola in rendering the great classics of music that it is well to remember that it is also a humanly familiar instrument, capable of rendering popular selections—the latest light opera hits, dance music, favorite old songs, college glees, and the homely and lowly. In fact, it has instant response for all moods and needs.

When the Pianola is placed in a home it creates a new

Where there are growing children in the family, the Pianola is worth all that it costs from an educational standpoint alone. It fosters a taste for *the best* in music and teaches discrimination between the highest examples and the unworthy or trivial. Children who are too young to be taken regularly to the concert or the opera can acquire in the home, through the agency of a Pianola, that familiarity with the masterpieces of music which is just as essential in a well-rounded education as a knowledge of any of the other fine arts.

18   THE BOOKLOVERS MAGAZINE ADVERTISER

*5.
Votey's Pianola piano-player (from* The Booklovers Magazine Advertiser, *1904)*

THE PIANOLA—ITS MISSION

PIANOLA IN USE WITH UPRIGHT PIANO

THE AMOUNT of practice necessarily required to become a finished, artistic pianist is discouraging.

Before Paderewski could attain the high position which he occupies to-day in the musical world, and accomplish what now comes to him with ease, he was obliged to toil unceasingly day after day in practice. He is said to have spent six to eight hours out of every twenty-four at the piano. Even assured success is not sufficient incentive to tempt many to incur this drudgery.

Practice gives digital dexterity alone. It makes capable and obedient machines of the fingers. The artistic and esthetic is a matter of taste or temperament. Lacking this temperament, it is impossible to become a great musician, *although* one may learn to play acceptably.

With the soul full of music, a means of expressing it is still essential.

The Pianola supplies this means at once. The player can give his whole attention to the development of the artistic, and thereby *cultivate* a musical taste.

The Pianola is a substitute for the human fingers. The brain remains unfettered and is still the controlling influence.

To make the Pianola's felt-covered fingers strike the right notes no practice is necessary, no composition is too difficult, and the repertory is unlimited. Octaves are sounded with ease, and the rapid trills with a quickness envied even by the musician with the best-trained fingers in the world.

The Pianola saves labor and it saves time. This is its mission.

It enables those who have not had the time to devote to musical training to play the piano.

It increases the repertory of the most efficient. Even Paderewski's repertory must of necessity be limited, and it is a significant fact that he has a Pianola both in his Paris and his Switzerland residences.

The Pianola makes accessible the great masterpieces of the famous composers and enables every one to become familiar with the best music. It is therefore a developer of musical taste unparalleled in the history of music.

Paderewski says: "*Every one who wishes to hear absolutely faultless, free of any kind of nervousness, piano-playing should buy a Pianola. It is perfection.*"

Pianola, $250.
Aeolians, $75 to $750.
Aeolian Orchestrelles, $1,000 to $2,500.

The popularity of the Pianola is pronounced. It is not a matter of opinion. It is a fact, and there must be a reason for it. The suggestion that you send for our literature that you may better understand what the Pianola is and what it will do, is certainly in your own interest. Write for Special Pan-American catalogue W.

The Aeolian Company
New York, 18 West Twenty-third Street

Brooklyn, 500 Fulton St.; Cincinnati, 124 E. Fourth St.; Buffalo, H. Tracy Balcom, 694 Main St.; Chicago, Lyon & Healy, Wabash Ave. and Adams St.; Boston, The M. Steinert & Sons Co., 162 Boylston St.; Philadelphia, C. J. Heppe & Son, 1117 Chestnut St.

(Fleming & Carrick Press, New York)

When you write, please mention "The Cosmopolitan."

6.
The Pianola—its mission (from The Cosmopolitan, *1901)*

7–10. Victorian ideals of home and family life were powerful symbols in player piano advertising, which also promised easy access to the virtues of music for both women and men.

7.

Straube player piano advertisement (from The Saturday Evening Post, 1923)

VIRTUOLO

Her thrilling surprise

SUDDENLY, a future vibrantly happy with music is revealed to her. With a Virtuolo in her home the pent-up music of her soul is liberated. She can play with all the expressiveness of the long-practiced musician. Even better, for unwearied by the tedious finger exercises.

The Virtuolo is instantly responsive to all her moods; she can vary the tones to all shades of meaning, imbue each rendition with emotion. The playing is effortless.

Recreation for all

She will teach her children the quaint pieces her mother played to her. She will take rest from household cares in dreaming over the favorite melodies, those which have such a deep meaning to her.

Under the lamp-light she will pour forth to him who made possible such a home, all the tenderness that forever entwines itself in music.

There will be parties of friends, sparkling affairs because of the magical cheer of music. She will delight her guests with both pop-ular and classic music. Dances will swing merrily through her home. All will say: "Hers is the nicest place of all."

In thousands of homes

All over America the Virtuolo is bringing happiness and home contentment. A Virtuolo can be in your own home a few hours after you have talked with a dealer.

The eighty-year experience of Hallet & Davis Piano Company, and its unparalleled resources, have wrought a new-day triumph —a piano-player of soundless mechanism, so durable it lasts a life-time, and the easiest to play in every way.

An illustrated book

Write at once that we may send you this complete description of the Virtuolo Player-Piano in its three makes: in the incomparable Hallet & Davis at $750 and $685; in the Conway at $595 and $575; in the Lexington at $495—*the same price everywhere.*

Let us also direct you to a neighboring dealer where you can hear and play the Virtuolo.

Hallet & Davis
ESTABLISHED 1839
Piano Company
661 Boylston St. Boston, Mass.

8.
*Hallet & Davis
Virtuolo player piano
advertisement (from*
The Saturday Evening
Post, *1923)*

9.
Estey player piano ad-
vertisement (author's
collection)

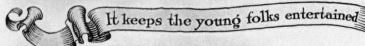

It keeps the young folks entertained

The
Manualo
The Player Piano that is all but human

is the one instrument upon which you can express your musical feeling through the pedaling.

You need not be a pianist—the **Manualo** will respond to your pedaling as the piano responds to the skilled touch of the accomplished player.

You *do not* operate the **Manualo**—you play it.

10.
*Baldwin Manualo
player piano adver-
tisement (author's col-
lection, courtesy of
Baldwin Piano and
Organ Co.)*

GULBRANSEN
(Pronounced Gul-BRAN-sen)
Player-Piano

Oh! Ride-a-Cock-Horse to Banbury Cross, th' Gulbransen Has Made a Boy of the Boss!

Look at the Joneses—Such Fun with their Gulbransen!

If you knew the Joneses you'd know why. The merry music of the Gulbransen—the delight each of them takes in playing it—here's a world of new fun for family and friends.

Listen—mechanically produced music is pretty tame compared with the human playing anyone can do on the Gulbransen. Listen—your ear tells you it is real; you warm up to it; you try it yourself—and you are amazed.

For the Gulbransen is not a "player-piano" as you have known them. It is more truthfully a piano you learn to play in two weeks instead of two years. Instruction rolls show you how to play with every form of musical expression. You'll find it an ever-growing, delightful recreation; an unequaled education in music.

Nationally Priced

Gulbransen Player-Pianos, three models all playable by hand or by roll, are sold at the same prices to everybody, everywhere in the United States, freight and war tax paid. Price, branded in the back of each instrument at the factory, includes set of Gulbransen instruction rolls and our authoritative book on home entertaining and music study with the Gulbransen.

White House Model $700 · Country Seat Model $600 · Suburban Model $495

GULBRANSEN-DICKINSON CO., CHICAGO
Canadian Distributors: Musical Merchandise Sales Co., 79 Wellington St., West, Toronto

Get Our New Book of Player Music—Free

The only book ever published showing the complete range of player-piano music of all kinds. This book is so classed and arranged that it is a guide to musical education for any player-piano owner. Sent free, if you mail us the coupon at the right.

Did you know the wonderful Gulbransen Player action can be installed in any piano (or old player-piano)? Upright, grand or upright. Check coupon for details.

To Gulbransen Owners: Keep your instrument in tune—at least two tunings a year. You'll enjoy it more.

Try the Gulbransen Only Ten Minutes

At our dealer's store you can prove to yourself in ten minutes that the Gulbransen is easy for you to play well —a marvelous instrument—positively fascinating. The coupon below brings you dealer's address and full information.

- Check here if you do not own any piano or player-piano. ☐
- Check here if you want information about having a new Gulbransen player action installed in your present piano (or player-piano). ☐
- Write your name and address in the margin below and mail this to Gulbransen-Dickinson Co., 3230 W. Chicago Ave., Chicago.

11.
Gulbransen player
piano advertisement
(from The Literary   Digest, 1921, courtesy
of Gulbransen Incor-
porated)

11, 12. *Gulbransen's extensive advertising provided America with a poignant symbol of "easy-to-play" technology—the Gulbransen Baby trademark—and was among the most powerful messengers of the emerging consumer ethic. The Chicago manufacturer's ad campaigns also illustrate the contradiction of promoting ease of playing while extolling the individual creativity associated with the producer ethic. Unlike many players of lesser quality, the Gulbransen was capable of producing an expressive performance.*

12.
Gulbransen Baby trademark (detail from preceding illustration)

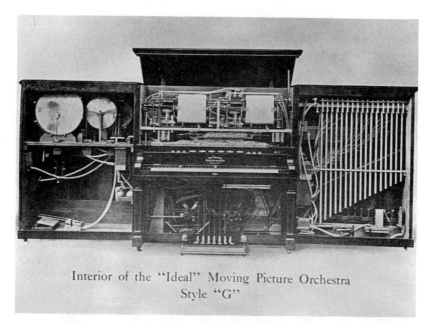

Interior of the "Ideal" Moving Picture Orchestra
Style "G"

13.

Sound for silent pictures: the Ideal photoplayer. The development of the movie industry gave rise to the business of providing sound to the silent celluloid through the photoplayer. These specialized player pianos were equipped with numerous sound effects devices and could play a variety of musical moods "at the touch of a button." Among the largest manufacturers of these machines were Wurlitzer, Seeburg, Link, American Photo Player, and—manufacturer of the photoplayer shown here— North Tonawanda Musical Instrument Works of New York. (from Harvey N. Roehl, Player Piano Treasury, *courtesy of the Vestal Press)*

14.
The first jukebox. Forerunner of the modern jukebox, the lucrative coin-operated player piano brought automatic music to the public for mere nickels. Wurlitzer and Seeburg, familiar names in the post– World War II jukebox culture, were among the largest firms manufacturing these machines, which often contained a variety of percussion instruments to complement the piano sound. Shown here is the Coinola brand player, built by Operators Piano Co. of Chicago, whose durable instruments are particularly sought by today's collectors. (author's collection)

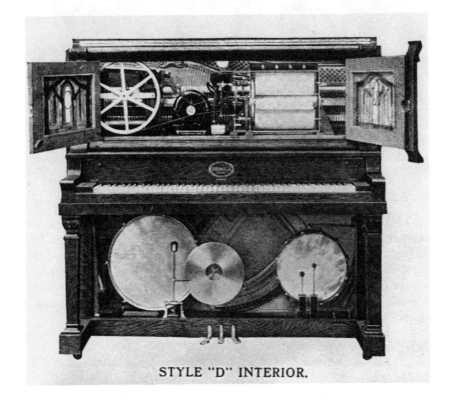

STYLE "D" INTERIOR.

120

International.

NATIONAL MUSIC WEEK REACHES ALL CLASSES AND AGES
Youngest Participants in a San Francisco Music Week

15.

National Music Week. Among the most successful campaigns to encourage music making and enjoyment for all Americans, espe- *cially children, was National Music Week, promoted in the 1920s and 1930s by the National Bureau for the Advancement of Music* and the music industry. (from National Bureau for the Advancement of Music, History of National Music Week)

16.
*Music will help you.
The musical awakening of the 1920s was not only stimulated by the piano industry with its sales campaigns; it was also en-* *couraged through associated organizations, such as the National Bureau for the Advancement of Music, which distributed messages like the* *one shown here. (from Harvey N. Roehl, Player Piano Treasury, courtesy of the Vestal Press)*

17.
Charles Milton
Tremaine. Tremaine
was founder of the Na-
tional Bureau for the
Advancement of Music
and organizer of Na-
tional Music Week and
the Music Memory
Contest. (from The
Musician, 1934)

18.
Henry E. Steinway.
Heinrich Engelhard
Steinweg, who upon
immigrating to the
United States changed
his name to Henry E.
Steinway, founded the
company whose in-
struments have en-
joyed preeminence in
the modern piano in-
dustry almost from
their first appearance.
(courtesy of Steinway
& Sons)

19.
D. H. Baldwin. Bal-
dwin was the founder
of D. H. Baldwin &
Co., Cincinnati, Ohio.
(author's collection)

20.
William Steinway. Fourth son of the founder, William Steinway transformed marketing techniques, in particular utilizing testimonials by eminent musicians and heads of state and publicizing awards won at international exhibitions. His efforts called attention to the technological innovations developed by his older brother, Theodore Steinway, and helped propel the piano to its early exalted status in American culture. (courtesy of Steinway & Sons)

21.

Charles H. Steinway. In 1900, during Steinway's presidency of Steinway & Sons, the company joined in partnership with the advertising firm of N. W. Ayer & Son to promote its renowned piano as "The Instrument of the Immortals." The collaboration between Steinway and Ayer lasted sixty-nine years, the longest in advertising history. (courtesy of Steinway & Sons)

22.
Lucien Wulsin I. Wulsin led D. H. Baldwin & Co. into artistic prominence with the Baldwin piano and organized one of the most powerful piano companies in the industry. (courtesy of The Cincinnati Historical Society)

23.
*Lucien Wulsin II.
Wulsin was head of
the Baldwin Co.
throughout the diffi-
cult years of the 1920s
and 1930s. He pro-
vided the industry*
*with leadership dur-
ing the Great Depres-
sion by serving four
terms as president of
the National Piano
Manufacturers Asso-
ciation as well as by*
*chairing the Piano
Code Authority under
the New Deal's Na-
tional Recovery Ad-
ministration. (courtesy
of the Cincinnati His-
torical Society)*

24.
William L. Bush. Bush, the progressive head of Bush & Gerts Piano Co. of Chicago, organized the National League for the Maker's Name as a trade and congressional lobby. In the years immediately preceding the First World War, the league sought to eliminate fraud in the stencil piano trade by enacting legislation that would force all industries to affix the true manufacturer's name to their products. (author's collection)

25.
Theodore E. Steinway. Steinway worked closely with Lucien Wulsin II to lead the industry through the dark days of 1927–37, while preserving the preeminence of Steinway & Sons. The modern image of the Steinway piano was essentially his creation. (courtesy of Steinway & Sons)

26.
C. N. Kimball. Curtis Nathaniel Kimball, conservative, independent head of the powerful Chicago piano house, W. W. Kimball Co., was opposed, like Henry Ford in the automobile industry, to allowing New Deal policy to regulate industrial life. He found himself unable to support Lucien Wulsin II's leadership in the NRA or the NPMA. (author's collection)

27, 28. Examples of Baldwin celebrity endorsements used to market the company's pianos. Note the use of the brand name placard attached to the instrument's side.

27.
Baldwin celebrity endorsements: Eddie Cantor (from The Baldwin Keynote, *au-* *thor's collection, courtesy of Baldwin Piano and Organ Co.)*

28.
Baldwin celebrity endorsements: Will Rogers (from The Baldwin Keynote, *au-* *thor's collection, courtesy of Baldwin Piano and Organ Co.)*

The Literary Digest for December 2, 1922   41

STEINWAY
The Instrument of the Immortals

Richard Wagner

"A Beethoven Sonata, a Bach Chromatic Fantasie, can only be fully appreciated when rendered upon a Steinway Grand," said Richard Wagner in 1879.

"Only upon a Steinway can the works of the masters be played with full artistic justice," said Sergei Rachmaninoff in 1921.

The price of happiness
—a thought for Christmas

It is the way with art that those who know and love the best can find no happiness in that which is other than the best. And therefore, to own a piano is one thing—to own the Instrument of the Immortals is another. For when you buy a piano you do not buy a thing of wood and steel, of wires and keys—it is music that you buy—the greatest of the arts.

Once your fingers touch the keyboard of a Steinway—once you know the eloquence of its response—once you drink the beauty of its tone—for you henceforth there can be no other piano.

Think! The Steinway is the piano over whose keyboard Richard Wagner dreamed his visions and enriched the world. It is the Voice with which Liszt, Gounod, Rubinstein and their immortal fellows spoke to mankind.

It is the piano of Paderewski and the piano on which Rachmaninoff and Hofmann are playing their way to immortality to-day. From the day of its coming it has been the chosen instrument of the masters and the lovers of great music.

You who find happiness in the music of the Immortals—surely you can find happiness only in the Instrument of the Immortals. And the price of this happiness is less than you may think. Steinway & Sons and their dealers strive constantly to make it so easy that there is no thought of burden. For it is the Steinway ideal to make the finest piano that can be made, and to sell it at the lowest cost and upon the most convenient terms that can be made.

Would you not be happier for possession of a Steinway? And could there be a time more fitting for its coming than this Yuletide of the year?

There is a Steinway dealer in your community or near you through whom you may purchase a new Steinway piano with a cash deposit of 10 per cent, and the balance will be extended over a period of two years. Used pianos accepted in partial exchange.

Prices: $875 and up—plus freight

There are several Steinway styles and sizes, but only one Steinway quality

STEINWAY & SONS, Steinway Hall, 109 E. Fourteenth Street, New York City

---

29.
The Steinway as art. The advertising firm of N. W. Ayer & Son presented the Steinway piano as art, featuring it as "The Instrument of the Immortals," the preferred piano of Wagner, Liszt, Rubinstein, Hofmann, Paderewski, Rachmaninoff, and other eminent musicians. Already well known in artistic circles, Steinway & Sons teamed with Ayer in 1900 to direct its advertising campaigns at consumers unfamiliar with what Steinway trade literature called "The Name." (from The Literary Digest, 1922, courtesy of Steinway & Sons)

30, 31. *The trade was particularly impressed by Baldwin's "Choose Your Piano as the Artists Do" campaign of the late 1920s and 1930s, which featured such prominent artists* as those pictured. Artistic endorsement was an essential part of piano merchandising. That the performer was not a pianist mattered little, for the piano also accompanied other musicians, singers, and symphonies. What was important was the endorsement itself and the popularity of the artist.

30.
Baldwin artist endorsements: Feodor Chaliapin (author's collection, courtesy of Baldwin Piano and Organ Co.)

CHOOSE YOUR PIANO AS THE ARTISTS DO

Gieseking plays only the Baldwin

ONLY the Baldwin piano itself can reveal the reasons why it is the choice of the world's great pianists, both for the concert stage and their homes. ¶ Gieseking, Bachaus, DePachmann, Carreras and scores of others find in the purity and finer resonance of Baldwin tone, the perfect expression of their art. The intimate response of Baldwin action fulfills every desire. ¶ The Baldwin is a revelation to all who play it. Grands, uprights, players and Welte-Mignon (licensee) reproducing models. Prices, $850 up. Convenient payments may be arranged with any Baldwin dealer.

THE BALDWIN PIANO CO., CINCINNATI

Baldwin

31.
Baldwin artist endorsements: Walter Gieseking (author's collection, courtesy of Baldwin Piano and Organ Co.)

32, 33. Contrasting piano styles. The towering Victorian upright piano, when fitted with a player mechanism allowing anyone to "play" it, brought the piano industry unprecedented sales; but the large, boxy design did not appeal to modern tastes, which came to prefer the more stylish (and less expensive) radio. The piano industry, however, appealed to people's creative instinct to "make" rather than just listen to music, and in the mid-1930s successfully marketed the modern console piano in a variety of styles and finishes.

32.
Upright player piano
(author's collection,
courtesy of Baldwin
Piano and Organ Co.)

33.
*Modern console piano
(author's collection,
courtesy of Baldwin
Piano and Organ Co.)*

34.
The Steinway as tradition. On the eve of the Great Depression, Steinway advertising made appeals to parents through their children, seeking to establish Steinway & Sons as the caretaker of traditional values as well as the guardian of an artistic legacy. This advertisement was one in a series featuring photographs by Anton Bruehl that won a Harvard Advertising Award in 1930. (from The Literary Digest, 1931, courtesy of Steinway & Sons)

CHAPTER FOUR

Strategies of
Piano Merchandising

It's a Steinway.
Nothing More Need
Be Said.
—Steinway &
Sons

Choose Your Piano
as the Artists Do.
—The Baldwin
Co.

The Costliest Piano
in the World.
—Mason &
Hamlin

All the Fun Without
Long Practice.
—Gulbransen-
Dickinson Co.

"Advertising is basically a form of education," President Calvin Coolidge told the International Advertising Association in 1926. "It informs its readers of the existence and nature of commodities by explaining the advantages to be derived from their use and creates for them a wider demand. It makes new thoughts, new desires, new actions. By changing the attitude of the mind, it changes the material condition of the people."[1] The idea that advertising could create need where none existed is characteristic of the consumer culture. It was well established by the mid-1920s by the pioneering efforts of men such as Walter Dill Scott, Edward Bernays, and Bruce Barton, who had made advertising into a legitimate and big business. It was a new science in a new age. President Coolidge's observation that "the advertisers are moulding the human mind" could scarcely have been made before the turn of the century.

Advertising during the Victorian age was primarily informative and was focused on the product. It explained a product's use or how it worked, and gave its price to purchasers that were assumed to be already in the market. Even where advertisers sought to attract attention amid the increasing clamor of printed claims, their goal was simple brand name publicity, their ads were still concerned with communicating information about products. Some manufacturers, such as Walter Chrysler, were even opposed to advertising, insisting that a product built properly and priced fairly should sell itself. By the first decade of the new century, however, the perceived purpose of advertising underwent a profound change. As the new science of psychology influenced advertising strategy, men like Chrysler embraced the idea that advertising could not only lead to immediate sales, but could educate the public to want things it would otherwise do without. Consumption could lead to a better life. Advertising the benefit of owning the product became more important than advertising the product itself. Advertising strategies became, in one historian's phrase, therapeutic rather than informative, vicariously offering through products such intangibles as excitement, style, status, and escape.[2] Joseph H. Appel, advertising manager of Wanamaker's during the 1920s, made this point succinctly: "Advertising . . . literally creates demand for the things of life that raise the standard of living, elevate the taste, changing luxuries into necessities."[3]

Leading manufacturers in the piano trade developed and adopted merchandising techniques that became characteristic of the emerging culture of consumerism. Cultivating brand loyalty, creating desire for a product, educating consumer consciousness, and presenting persistent and consistent sales messages were all part of the trade's campaign to stimulate public interest in music as one of life's greatest sources of enjoyment and inspiration. The trend was not universal. The local ads of piano dealers, with their incessant emphasis on price and bargains, were singled out especially by progressive manufacturers as inflicting immeasurable harm upon the industry. Even as late as 1930, A. G. Gulbransen of Gulbransen-Dickinson Co. issued a "Call to Arms" in the *The Music Trades* against those dealers who still were not "selling the things a piano will do for the home [but were] merely selling so much wood, felt, strings, duco [glue], and metal at a price."[4] But the absence of universal or even wide acceptance of persuasive advertising techniques within the piano trade is beside the point. What remains significant is that the industry's leaders developed and adopted strategies of selling that reflected the transformation of American society into a consumer culture.

The Fight to Establish Brand Loyalty

The piano industry has played a significant but unrecognized role in bringing about business practices that are associated with the consumer society. In the nineteenth century the industry developed laborsaving machinery and methods of specialization (division of function) in manufacture to produce greater numbers of instruments for a growing market. More efficient and fruitful techniques of management, financing, marketing, and distribution necessarily followed. Piano manufacturers—particularly the Kimball and Baldwin firms—helped develop the profitable science of consignment sales to dealerships. Together with the sewing machine and furniture trades, the piano industry perfected the technique of retail installment-sales to make easier the purchase of their relatively expensive products. The piano trade also pioneered the notion of brand name loyalty and the use of testimonials in advertising. Decades before nationally advertised brand names were preferred over generic or locally made items, the success of a piano firm depended largely on the familiarity and reputation of its name. Indeed, the main asset of any creditable company was the name and individuality of the owner.

"One of the remarkable peculiarities of the piano industry is the great value of an established name," wrote Alfred Dolge in 1911. "His name is the piano maker's trade-mark, and that concern is fortunate that controls a name which is impressive, euphonious, easy to spell, easy to pronounce, easy to remember—in short, of such a character that it cannot be easily confounded and always will make a lasting impression."[5] The chauvinism that this philosophy produced no doubt explains the great conservatism among piano makers, the reluctance to change any methods of production that made possible their individuality. The esoteric quality of a Steinway, Baldwin, Chickering, or Mason & Hamlin tone or touch has always been the essence of the piano. It is the real distinction among instruments that otherwise might *appear* identical.

"The reputation of the instrument which a piano maker produces follows him beyond his grave, often for generations," wrote Dolge.[6] This helps explain why the true ownership of a firm became clouded in mystery, giving the carefully guarded impression to the public that each piano maker was independent, each having its own executives, advertising, and factories, each maintaining its own individuality. It also explains beyond mere profit motives why certain stencil pianos were christened "Baldin" or "Steinvey": to effect illegitimate sales, indeed; but also to infuse the product with that most slippery of tangible assets—the reputation. Furthermore, the concurrent increase in brand name advertising directly resulted from the growing production of stencilled pianos, as manufacturers sought to protect the reputation of legitimate houses.

Piano makers, especially the leaders, pursued an artistic purpose as well as profit. As a result, they pioneered strategies of promotion that were characterized by a sense of cultural mission to counsel and uplift, strategies that imbued their products with notions of therapeutic fulfillment. Specifically, such strategies impressed upon the public the efforts of the piano trade to extend the virtues of music to the people by making the art generally available. These efforts included building performing halls and concert instruments, subsidizing and promoting the recitals of artists, and manufacturing pianos—especially the mechanical player—for the home in order to extend those virtues into families directly. "The name of Albert Weber will live, as long as pianos are built in America," declared Alfred Dolge, "as one of the great leaders who believed in the artistic mission of the instrument and impressed this belief upon the mind of the public."[7] Weber's individual contributions notwithstanding, Dolge is describing here the distinction between the piano trade and virtually any other business manufacturing products for sale. The piano was distinguished from other brand name items by its peculiar connection with the arts and notions of Victorian morality, home, and family life.

The piano trade's characteristic relationship with the arts (and the resulting cultivation of brand name loyalty) is at least as old as Mozart's open preference for Johann Andreas Stein's fortepianos.[8] But it was during Beethoven's lifetime that piano makers actively sought artists' endorsements by supplying them with pianos. Nannette Streicher (Stein's daughter) presented Beethoven with one of her instruments in 1796. Likewise, Sebastian Erard sent one of his Paris-built pianos to the composer as an unsolicited gift in 1803. Graf and Broadwood courted Beethoven's favor as well, knowing that the resulting publicity was as important as the artistic contribution. In time, it became customary for European piano makers to seek out the testimonial of virtually every major composer and performer.

As the nineteenth century progressed, American manufacturers also pursued this kind of publicity. They often financed a performer's entire concert tour to the United States, supplied a piano wherever needed, and even guaranteed an agreed sum. The musician, knowing the value of reputation in his own career, most likely would refuse the backing of a firm making a piano not up to his standard. No matter the financial consideration, the result might be ruin. Art and business were partners. The value of an artist's testimonial always was an incentive to "progressive piano makers," Dolge commented, to produce the best possible instruments "so that the greatest virtuoso cannot well refuse to play upon them."[9] And the favorable endorsement of "the immortals," itself an advertisement of the most persuasive kind in a piano culture, was featured proudly and very prominently in the manufacturer's various publicity campaigns. These ranged from concert playbills and programs to postcards, bookmarks, and magazine and newspapers advertisements.

The practice was old and honorable among piano makers, and it represented art as much as business. To have a piano preferred by the artists was more than a mark of distinction. It meant the company had arrived. It confirmed the quality of the product and the integrity of the business, and it contributed immeasurable publicity. The war among the elite piano makers to attract artists was an accepted necessity in this promotional game. In 1889 Kimball considered winning the testimonial of opera star Adelina Patti, long considered a Steinway artist, quite a coup. That Patti was a singer and not a pianist mattered little. It was common practice for performers other than pianists to favor one keyboard instrument as their "official accompanist." The Patti endorsement caused a stir in the music world. *Piano Trade Magazine* noted that artists "began to sit up and take notice of the Kimball piano," much to the chagrin of some eastern manufacturers. (The *Musical Courier*, based in New York, even doubted the validity of "the so-called Patti letter" of endorsement.)[10] Although piano manufacturers eagerly sponsored relatively unfamiliar names during concert seasons, they catered by necessity to the titans. Artur Rubinstein failed to get a renewed contract with the Knabe firm following his New York debut because "my tour was an experiment, so now they need an artist of international fame."[11]

This practice continued into the twentieth century. The professional pianist "is nothing more than an itinerant advertising medium for the manufacturer whose piano he plays," asserted William E. Walter in "The Industry of Music-Making," which appeared in *The Atlantic Monthly* for January 1908. Piano manufacturers not only contracted with a musician to play a specific piano in return for a concert tour and a prearranged sum, but often subsidized tours of orchestras, violinists, conductors, and singers as well. Such expenses were part of the firm's advertising budget. As Walter stressed, this subsidization was recognized on the concert program regardless of whether a pianist was featured: " 'The piano is a ———,' *even when no piano appears on stage.*" But were it not for the intense competition among piano manufacturers to sell their instruments, he reminded his readers, music making in the United States "would easily be cut in half."[12]

Thus, members of the young American piano trade vied not only with the older European makers but among themselves for the privilege of bringing music to this country and for the coveted testimonials of capable performers. Chickering and Steinway stole Rafael Joseffy's heart, Teresa Carena found the Weber, Steinway, Mason & Hamlin, and Everett pianos pleasurable. De Pachmann used the Baldwin, Liszt praised the Chickering, the Hallet & Davis, and the Steinway, "and so forth *ad infinitum!*" Dolge wrote appropriately. The sponsoring firms tended to get possessive, however. "The American piano makers hire us for their publicity," Raoul Pugno remarked comfortingly to young Artur Rubinstein, "since each of us plays a different piano they keep us isolated. The best proof is that I played the Baldwin, Lhévinne the Steinway, you the Knabe, and in spite of the fact that we all toured the same country at the same time, only now do we meet!" Josef Lhévinne agreed, adding, "There is such a competition among them that they consider us like boxing champions who have to fight it out for them."[13]

Piano companies did not limit the endorsement of their instruments to performing artists, however. Acknowledged use or even mere ownership by members of the First Family, particularly the president, were also valuable advertising copy. Lucy Hayes, who instituted the tradition of White House musicales, entertained guests upon the Chickering, although her husband "officially" owned a Knabe grand and a Bradbury upright. Bradbury's calculated campaign to become the official administration piano was set back during Garfield's term, when Hallet & Davis was given the distinction. President Harrison's choice was the Bradbury piano, but he also owned a J. & C. Fischer upright, ordered from D. H. Baldwin & Co. by his son Russell as a Christmas present to the First Lady. Vice President Levi P. Morton agreed that the Fischer "has given entire satisfaction in every respect," a compliment frequently quoted in Baldwin's advertising. William McKinley bought an A. B. Chase piano for his home in Canton when he was governor of Ohio, and ordered another (made from "specially prepared designs") for the White House parlor in 1897. It became, as A. B. Chase ads informed the public, the First Lady's "most constant companion." Steinway & Sons sought more worldwide endorsement, becoming the "appointed manufacturer" to the Kings of England, Sweden & Norway, Italy, and Saxony; the Queen of Spain; the Emperors of Germany, Russia, and Austria; and the Shah of Persia. The New York manufacturer had already received the endorsement of the American marvel, Thomas A. Edison.[14]

Nineteenth-century piano advertisements readily quoted the testimonial praise of the various artists and celebrities. As prominently featured in the ads were the awards and citations won in numerous world expositions. Recognition in international fairs demonstrated technological leadership in an increasingly competitive, industrial marketplace. The fairs were, as Edwin M. Good points out, "the nineteenth-century equivalent of mass media, an important means by which technological development was communicated throughout the world."[15]

Such display of manufacturing technology became an important aspect of brand name merchandising. In 1851 (two years before the establishment of Steinway & Sons) the pianos of Chickering & Sons, Timothy Gilbert & Co., Nunns & Clark, and Conrad Meyer attracted the attention of European makers and were awarded distinctions at the first World's Exhibition, in London. "The beginning of the piano industry in America, as an industry, can historically be dated from [the London exhibition]," Alfred Dolge ob-

served.[16] The Paris Exposition of 1867, however, proved to be even
more a turning point: American piano technology conquered Europe and became the model for the future. Chickering and Steinway both reportedly spent $80,000 to promote their pianos, both
claimed highest honors, and both carried the battle home to fight
it out in the trade press and the Boston and New York newspapers.
Obviously, both firms benefited from the increased publicity, whatever their mutual antagonism.[17]

Despite the international importance of the European exhibitions, Dolge cites the Centennial Exposition held in Philadelphia
in 1876 as the beginning of the modern American piano industry.
Hundreds of pianos of different makes were displayed, all incorporating the revolutionary innovations called collectively the
"American system" (overstringing the bass and using high-tension
wires and other construction to produce powerful tone). These
products showed visitors that "the piano industry was equal in
importance to that of any other American industry, and, of course,
far in advance of that of any other nation." Dolge also emphasized
that the exposition "established once for all the superiority of the
American piano as an *industrial* product, in comparision with
similar products of other countries." In other words, previous
world fairs had demonstrated American growth and superiority in
the *art* of piano building, but there had been only a few firms
showing instruments. The Centennial Exposition revealed the
magnitude of the American piano trade's "'industrial' proportions," showing that art and industry not only could be allies, but
that together each could reach its zenith.[18]

Although no radical changes or improvements in design were
shown at the Chicago World's Columbian Exposition in 1893, the
growth of the American piano industry was noticeable in three
ways. Extensive displays of actions, plates, hammers, sounding
boards, and other parts by the supply industries revealed a widening market for affordable instruments. Second, it was clear that
the expanding western manufacturers, particularly those in Chicago and Cincinnati, were appealing for recognition and offering
viable competition with the east. Finally, the factory organizer and

the piano distributor (what Dolge called "the industrial magnate of pianodom") received recognition for the first time. Efficient production, management, and distribution techniques were seen as vital to the industry's growth.[19]

The Chicago Exposition illustrates the advertising value of world's fair awards. Eastern manufacturers such as Chickering & Sons, Steinway & Sons, Weber Piano Co., Geo. Steck & Co., Decker & Sons, and Wm. Knabe & Co. boycotted the fair, most likely because of the suspicion (reportedly generated by the "blackmailing" editor of the *Musical Courier*) that the awards jury was slanted to favor Chicago piano firms. W. W. Kimball Co. was the predicted favorite. Although the majority of exhibitors deplored the withdrawals (George Steck served as a judge despite the boycott by his own company), a full-scale war ensued and was fought in the pages of Chicago and New York newspapers.

"Loyal Exhibitors" sought to ban the use of all boycotting piano brands in any concert at the fair. But the immensely popular Ignacy Paderewski, a Steinway artist, was scheduled to open the Exposition. Finding himself the center of the crisis, the pianist announced he was going to visit the fair whether he played or not. The Piano Committee of the National Commission, an investigative body set up by the Congress, declared that no "disloyal" piano would be allowed on the fairgrounds, or it would be removed "at point of a bayonet if necessary." A compromise was reached, however. The Council of Administers insisted that Paderewski rehearse on "loyal" instruments; but they allowed him to play a Steinway piano for the opening concerts in Music Hall by "disconnecting" the building from the Exposition.

The war between east and west raged in newspapers for months following the concert. The W. W. Kimball Co. of Chicago took highest awards despite a federal injunction brought by Chase Bros. to restrain the judges from making public their decisions. And for days people crowded into the showroom of the local Steinway dealer to view the piano Paderewski had played. The cover illustration for the World's Fair edition of *Puck* depicted a multi-armed, vigorously animated caricature of the pianist surrounded by various instruments. The caption read, "A Peaceful Solution—at the next World's Fair Paderewski will play on all the pianos at once."[20]

The publicity generated by world's fairs, celebrity endorsements, and subsidized concert tours had the combined effect of etching the names of pianos on the conscience of a nineteenth-century public not yet accustomed to a brand name culture. Should someone wander into Aeolian, Steinway, Steck, Chickering, Knabe, or Kimball Hall, read the concert program, and still miss the connection between piano brand and performing artist, he need only view the piano on stage. It was a customary advertising technique to hang on the side of the instrument facing the audience a large placard emblazoned with the piano's name. Bold letters informed even those in the back rows that the musician played or accompanied the "CHICKERING & SONS," the "MASON & HAMLIN," or the "WEBER," "And so forth *ad infinitum!*"

Cultivating a Mythology of Consumerism

This network of piano publicity and art promotion was firmly in place by the late nineteenth century. America's piano makers were proud of their industry, their art, and their product, and constantly reminded the public of these accomplishments. Their efforts both reinforced and promoted the importance of the piano in Victorian culture. The firms specializing in concert work generated sales for the entire industry, while the piano trade in general promoted a musical America and sought to preserve a certain way of life. "Mothers, increase your sons' and daughters' love of home by refining influences," stressed D. H. Baldwin & Co. in 1890. "The love of music is a strong factor in welding the affections of your children to all that is good, pure and noble, and to increase their love for home attractions. As soon as the children are old enough, give them music lessons."[21]

Most piano firms were not simply selling musical instruments. They were promoting home, family, motherhood, and the morality of music. Their advertisements, like most others of the period, spoke to an audience assumed to be already in the market for a product already familiar. The ad message was informative, not persuasive. Unlike most nineteenth-century retail advertising, however, which had only a minimal need for brand recognition, piano marketing necessarily required familiar brand names.[22] Hence, a Victorian piano ad used testimonials to establish impressive credentials and then boasted its product to be "the best piano manufactured," or the "standard of the world." Or it emphasized price. Either strategy assumed that no one needed to be convinced to buy a piano. Rather, advertisements merely informed the buyer which piano was the best instrument or the best deal. Such strategy had helped the American piano industry become a big business by the late-nineteenth century.

By the 1890s, however, piano advertisements had become stolid, generating criticism from the trade press. "Advertising is the most perplexing branch of the piano manufacturers business," *The Music Trades* advised its readers in 1892. The "average manufacturer" frequently wastes his publicity dollars on "uninteresting announcement[s]." "As a rule, the advertisements amount to the name and address of the firm, with possibly some stereotyped reference to the 'solidity' of construction, the 'improved' action, and 'elaborate' case design. Once inserted," the journal continued, "this advertisement is never changed, but stands there week in and week out, remindful of a tombstone proclaiming the virtues of some departed saint."[23]

The revolutionary impact of the player piano as a means of creating a musical democracy changed the advertising methods of the piano industry. The "technology of repeatable experience" (as Daniel Boorstin calls it), which, in addition to the player piano, produced the phonograph and the Kodak camera, brought with it a new advertising strategy as well. Since ads portray and reinforce values already in the culture, the recreational, consumer-oriented mentality of some turn-of-the-century advertising is an indication of the cultural change away from Victorian ways of thinking.

Public acceptance of the idea that recreation is one of life's necessities resulted in part from changes wrought by the industrial revolution itself: shorter work weeks, increased leisure time, more production by machine (which decreased fatigue), the steady decline of child labor after 1900 (especially after 1920). Industrialization also destroyed notions that hard work brought success or that scarcity of goods was permanent. Factory work became anonymous, monotonous, and unfulfilling. The sheer volume of goods produced undermined the Victorian economic philosophy based on production (and therefore the work ethic), and created another based on consumption. In addition to the greater numbers of goods, new inventions and activities competed for the consumer's increased leisure time: movies, phonographs, motor cars, sports, amateur photography, player pianos. By the 1920s recreation was no longer considered a sinful waste of time, but a positive good in itself. People generally had a sense of more choice in their lives. The moral value of work was undermined, even though the rhetoric of the work ethic prevailed. A fragile veneer was left upon a decayed frame.[24]

An important factor in the emergence of an advertising-oriented consumer culture was the promotion of nationally branded goods by innovative manufacturers concerned with uplifting, satisfying, or manipulating society. These national advertisers considered advertising as only one aspect of their marketing effort, however, and not by any means the most important feature. Mass marketing was not made possible so much by advertising as by revolutionary changes in corporate organization and product distribution. Recent scholarship shows that product quality, distribution, and price affected sales far more significantly than did (or does) advertising.[25] Thus, advertising was but one component in the competition among manufacturers of similar products, a strategy that also included forward integration into wholesaling and (considerably less often) retailing in an effort to reach the consumer more directly.

Moreover, although advertising does play some role in promoting new habits or use of new products, it really responds to, rather than creates, change in patterns of consumption. Thus, the power of advertising to sell goods is limited. Most authorities still agree with Neil Bordon's 1942 study, *The Economic Effects of Advertising,* that advertising can expand demand when underlying conditions support a trend, but cannot overcome weak demand when conditions are poor or unfavorable. The heavily advertised piano industry continued to decline during the "prosperous" 1920s, for example, and women began smoking in the same decade before a single ad was directed to them. Rather than creating a nation of female smokers, tobacco trade advertisements catered to (and perhaps reinforced) the trend. Since ad men increasingly believed that "woman is the buyer of everything," this strategy was also part of the developing notion that appeals should be directed toward women generally.[26]

The debatable capacity of advertising to sell goods says nothing of its general role in shaping public consciousness, however. Nor does it speak to questions regarding advertisers' concepts of the consumer consciousness. Advertising contributed the mythology of the consumer culture. The creations of ad men not only informed the consumer, they tried to persuade Americans to prefer national brands and offered an invitation to join the consumer society. As national advertisers turned from informative to persuasive techniques, they favored nonrational, even irrational appeals depicting consumers who were emotional, reactive, suggestible, impulsive, and susceptible to manipulation.[27]

But recent scholarship shows this philosophy was inconsistent. Apparently, American advertisers believed the consumer to be rational at times, emotional and impulsive at others; often status-minded, but often individualistic; traditional, but also a seeker after novelty. Nevertheless, theorists in the first decades of the twentieth century insisted that ads must attract attention (with illustrations and large type), must offer the consumer justification for preferring a national brand, and then should create in him the desire to buy it. Successful ads had to be grounded in the familiar, in common experience. And while ad men of the 1920s claimed the ability to manufacture tastes, they also knew that they had to cater to preferences because they could not alter them at will. The mythology of advertising is important not only because it reflects and reinforces the values of society, but because it is also a measure of cultural change.[28]

The mythology of the piano (that is, its recurring reliance on the icons of home and family life, art, and morality that appeal to our cultural consciousness) was a product of the Victorian age and was established long before the advent of modern persuasive advertising techniques. Public preference for (or at least awareness of) brand name pianos was also Victorian in origin. Whatever the extent that actual practice mirrored this mythology, the sheer number of used and new piano sold indicates the believability, and thus the reality, of this tradition. The limitation, of course, was that music making and the piano culture were confined to those able to learn to play. By the turn of the century, piano men began to use the developing techniques of persuasive advertising to exploit this established and familiar mythology in their efforts to increase sales of the revolutionary player piano. Significantly, piano advertising emphasized the supposed benefit of owning the player as much as the technology of the machine itself.

The strategy of promoting the automatic piano as easy to play was an accepted philosophy by 1902, a result of the Aeolian Company's very successful pioneering efforts to market its "Pianola" after 1897.[29] Capitalizing upon the novelty of the repeatable musical experience, the piano trade sold record numbers of instruments and appealed to consumers through Victorian notions of home, family life, and the benefits of music education. Testimonials from artists and celebrities, as well as appeals to aspirations for social mobility and "social security," remained important features of piano advertising. Thus, promotions for the player piano made the same appeals as did ads for straight pianos, with the crucial difference that automation made the mythology easily accessible. The musically untrained, especially men, who traditionally had been excluded, or at least discouraged, from an active role in what was essentially part of woman's domain, now were able to participate in the musical experience and more intimately share the accompanying mythology.

In the first decade of the new century, several manufacturers attempted to educate the public to use the automatic player in an artistic fashion and to cultivate an appreciation of music. As music education courses developed in the public schools, educators adopted these ideas. But by 1917, according to "an Eastern dealer," the attempt was a failure because "the player-piano never has been well played by the people and never will be satisfactory to them as long as they have to work [pump] it themselves." The development of the electric player piano removed this "bother." The dealer concluded that most people were not musical and did not wish to be musically educated. "They want to be amused and that is all. . . . and [they] want it without trouble."[30]

Without realizing the fundamental change taking place in American culture, this dealer was describing the gradual replacement of the Victorian work ethic with the leisure-oriented consumer ethic. Piano ad men almost effortlessly continued to sell player pianos until 1924. Fifty-six percent of the industry's production and sales eventually was built upon the potent combination of the repeatable experience and the Victorian virtues of music, work ethic, home and family, which were in fact being undermined by the very consumer culture so responsible for the piano trade's unprecedented success.

Playing the piano had never been so easy. Advertisements encouraged the notion that playing music was more thrilling than merely listening, and the player piano provided the means "to literally roll away the cares of the day, to refresh the spirit, mind, and body." Anyone could immediately produce music and bring happiness and contentment into any home. "If you have any talent whatever for music," and the Gulbransen ad assures that everyone has more than he knows, "this remarkable instrument will discover it."[31] As a Cable Piano Company ad emphasized, to operate its electric player was "as simple as turning on a light": "You have merely to insert the music roll of your choice and to press a lever. Then you may dance, you may sing, converse or listen as often as you choose. For it will play every composition ever written for the piano as perfectly as the most accomplished musician. And when it has finished it will automatically re-roll the music sheet and shut off the motor without a finger's touch from you."[32] When fitted with electric motors (which freed the "musician" even from the need to pump), these automatons became perfect entertainers. With "artistic perfection" and "almost unbelievable versatility," the electric Duo-Art "entertains your guests" by appealing "to the most cosmopolitan tastes—it can be dramatic or gay—thrilling or frivolous as occasion warrants."[33]

Piano advertisements by the 1920s depict a complex mythology. Cheaply made, low-priced, noticeably inferior pianos rarely appeared in ad campaigns, which were overwhelmingly aimed at a middle-class audience and which encouraged its preoccupation with upward social mobilty. Throughout the decade ads concentrated on stylish grand pianos and automatic instruments. They emphasized the family, a fashionable home, a social life, and the piano as a symbol of respectablility and cultural refinement. Because this concept was really the basic principle of piano advertising, the examples are endless. "What kind of people own the Ampico [reproducing piano]? People of culture!" Or, "three fashionable small [Knabe] grands for the Easter Bride. . . . If her new home is to be smart, fashionable, and complete, its living room must of course have its properly placed small grand."[34] The Duo-Art reproducing piano was found "in the palaces of Europe." Mason & Hamlin, "the costliest piano in the world," was portrayed in the same blue-chip league as Cox and Stevens yachts, Hispano Suiza motor cars, and Black, Starr and Frost jewelry.[35] The people shown gathered about or playing a piano are usually dressed either formally (dinner jackets, fox fur scarves, and evening gowns abound), or in their "Sunday best." Capitalizing on this traditional symbolic appeal of the piano, other businesses, especially clothing firms, used the instrument in their ads also, to convey the same aura of privilege, respectability, and artistic taste.

It was in their effort to cultivate a musical democracy through the mechanical player, however, that piano men most effectively promoted the new mythology of consumerism. An eager public was bombarded with advertisements that emphasized how little effort it took to play automatic pianos. A symbol of this was the famous "Gulbransen Baby" trademark of the Gulbransen-Dickinson Company (Chicago), a major manufacturer and promoter of player pianos under the leadership of A. G. Gulbransen. Arresting full-page ads, appearing frequently in such popular magazines as the *Saturday Evening Post,* used this image to draw upon fundamental Victorian values: the Gulbransen would "hold the home together" because family life "centers" around it. "Can you imagine anything that holds for you and yours such endless possibilities for downright enjoyment, entertainment and fun?" one ad asks. But with its slogan, "Easy to Play," the Gulbransen Baby also tapped the emerging recreational, consumer culture. "There's a thrill in *playing* music you cannot get from listening," and with the Gulbransen, "all the family will quickly become expert ... without long practice! All the joy without hard work!"[36] In an instant consumers were transformed from audience into "artists."

Gulbransen advertising poignantly illustrates the contradictory ideology of promoting ease of play while espousing the individual creativity traditionally associated with the producer ethic. "We would like to feel the thrill and satisfaction of putting *ourselves* into the creation of something fine." "There is rapture in listening to the playing of others; but in playing yourself there's the thrill of personal creation, the hush of ineffable sweetness, and the flight of joy to the heights no other music can attain. It is here you find your supreme inspiration." And with the Gulbransen Registering Piano ("You need no musical training to play it"), "... *you* control its playing.... You can ... do anything that you could do if *you* played by hand." The piano makes it "simple and easy" and "registers *your* touch exactly." "The Gulbransen ... is responsive, personal, human. It gives you all the enjoyment of hand playing. Its music cannot be told from hand playing." Now "you can play better by roll than many who play by hand," and "you can play ALL pieces while they can play but a few." You play "not 'mechanical' music, but human music, with human expression."[37]

Such an appeal not only promoted the emerging "gospel of relaxation" characteristic of the new leisure industry; it offered a remedy for the general sense of lost personal autonomy that accompanied industrialization and consumerism. Beyond selling a product, piano makers claimed to offer self-realization through the power of music. Patented expression levers appeared to retain the individualism and creativity lost in the automation of the perforated roll, while the roll allowed everyone access to music. Now universally available, music would uplift society, enrich the culture, and assuage the negative effects of industrial society. "A new word has been born to our language. 'MELOTHERAPY,'" proclaimed the *Standard Player Monthly*. "Music has peculiar curative powers. It works on the body through the mind, the soul, the delicate, responsive membranes of the mind. It effects the nerves. It will not cure all human complaints but it most assuredly will relieve a great many popular conditions, which often baffle physicians. According to the facts in the case, every home should have a Playerpiano, just as one would have a family physician." These "popular conditions" varied from "insomnia" and "hysteria" to "dyspepsia" and "neurasthenia." "The next time you have an attack of indigestion, make yourself comfortable and have a friend play something on your Playerpiano," because "Music Means Health."[38]

The advantages of the player piano in cultivating both a musical democracy and increased sales were common knowledge within the industry. The automatic instrument was attractive to almost everyone because of its novelty. Even after becoming relatively familiar to the public, it still attracted crowds when demonstrated in show windows and public places. It would play for everybody: the talented musician, the musically inclined but not educated, and those devoid of musical talent. It developed an appreciation of music, leaving the pianist (or more accurately, the "pianolist") with something to aspire to. And in this way music could work its magic to remove the stress of the workaday world and inspire idealism.[39] As Theodore T. Levy recorded in his "Ode to a Player Piano":

> There's a joy that's found each day, with a Player home to
>   play,
>   You can scarcely find a greater recompense.
> When from work you come home, weary, music always
>   makes you cheery
>   And the pleasure to be gained is—well—IMMENSE!
>
> If that "straight" piano's soundless and your thirst for music
>   boundless,

Why not make a change and get one that will PLAY.
Then—ah then, a home of gladness, where it once was silent
    sadness,
And you'll see th' old-time grouches fade away.

There's no need to fret and pine (tho' you may not read a
    line
Of the music that is written on the page).
For the roll brings syncopation, when you have that
    inclination,
It's the biggest joy-producer of the AGE.[40]

It is ironic that the piano industry concentrated on the mechanical player and persuasive advertising techniques to promote Victorian culture in an age rapidly replacing those values with consumerism. "The American home is the foundation of our nation's life—it is where character is molded, where education and refinement are influenced and where the enjoyment of life is realized in the rest hours," read a Baldwin Manualo ad poster in 1921. "Music is the greatest contribution to universal enjoyment. It is ever a source of wholesome pleasure. With the advent of the Manualo, *The Player Piano that is all but human*, every family can now have access to the entire world of music. If you would have your home all that it should be, tie the circle closer together with music—with a Manualo."[41]

Whatever its similarity to the traditional piano, the mechanical player was a product not of the Victorian age, but of the machine age of immediate gratification. As such, it had much more in common with the motor car, the phonograph, and the radio than with its manual predecessors. By 1929, Professor John Maurise Clark of the University of Chicago could even assert that pianos, radios, and phonographs all had the same appeal.[42] Likewise, they all had the same fragility. They were all objects to consume, all easily replaced by newer models, all in competition with endless numbers and kinds of other products. Permanence found no place in the philosophy of consumption, and the annual model could never have been the product of the Victorian age.

The player-piano era (approximately 1900 to 1925) offered

an alternative but precarious path to success for American piano manufacturers. The extent to which an individual company manufactured automatic instruments and advertised them as easy to play was but one factor in realizing success; managerial and sales talent, effectiveness of product distribution and payment collection, product quality and reputation, and capital strength also played roles. But there is no question that for the industry as a whole, the appeal to the consumer's laziness was a very profitable but eventually disastrous path. The two firms that best withstood this destruction characteristically did not abandon the so-called "silent" instrument. For Baldwin and especially Steinway, the primary emphasis remained centered around the promotion of art and the benefits of music played by *human* hands. The original ideal prevailed.

Baldwin—Pursuing the Ideal

"The history of Baldwin is the history of an ideal," claimed *The Baldwin Keynote* in 1929: "to build the piano that provides the perfect medium for self-expression. . . . Only the best enters into the making of a Baldwin Piano—the best material, the best engineering skill, the best craftsmen. There is no question of costs." Echoing this sentiment in an address before the American Newcomen Society in 1953, Lucien Wulsin II told his audience that his father had become the director of manufacturing for D. H. Baldwin & Co. when the firm decided to manufacture pianos in 1890. The new instrument would be "the best piano that could be built," and was named "Baldwin" in honor of the founder.[43]

In 1953 Wulsin could look back on the Baldwin Company as one of the most successful of all American businesses. By the late 1920s Baldwin offered the only serious challenge to Steinway & Sons, whose prestige had withstood the rivalry of Chickering & Sons, Wm. Knabe & Co., Everett, Conover-Cable, Weber, and Mason & Hamlin. Much of Baldwin's achievement was a product of relentless marketing and advertising, lending support to the contention that advertising, in Calvin Coolidge's words, "creates and changes the foundation of all popular action, public sentiment or public opinion."[44] But advertising was only a part of the Baldwin challenge. Other components contributing to this success were an excellent product, a talented leadership determined to take the Baldwin piano to greatness, and an impressively efficient distribution and sales system, which tied the national business of the Cincinnati office tightly to the regional activities of each division, and even to those of each local dealer.

Lucien Wulsin sought the professional concert spotlight for the Baldwin piano, in addition to the home market. In the autumn of 1899 (only eight years after the first Baldwin piano had been shipped to the Cincinnati store), the company submitted an application for space at the upcoming Paris International Exposition of 1900. In an important rules change, the International Music Jury abandoned the long-established French custom of awarding a Grand Prix only to those contestants who had already exhibited twice. It adopted instead a rule to make awards based on actual worth as judged at the exposition. The Baldwin piano received the Grand Prix, the first American piano to be so honored, and Wulsin was made a chevalier of the French Legion of Honor. After the Paris Exposition, Wulsin actively entered the concert field, seeking a part of the market then dominated by Steinway & Sons, Wm. Knabe & Co., and Mason & Hamlin. "The final proving ground for an artistic piano is the concert stage," wrote Lucien Wulsin II about his father's efforts. "This is its trial by battle." The concert piano must please both artist and audience, and "is the final measure of the standard of excellence of the manufacturer."[45]

By 1903 the Baldwin Co. had expanded its Cincinnati and Chicago factories, increased its output, and extended its sales outlets to penetrate every part of the United States. The Baldwin piano took the Grand Prize at the St. Louis International Exposition in 1904, and the Grand Prize again at the Anglo-American Exposition in London in 1914. By the time Wulsin's son entered the company upon his father's death in 1912, Baldwin's Artist Department was well established. The piano "is ... used in concert by the greatest artists," Alfred Dolge wrote at the time, "and is recognized as one of the artistic pianos of the world." "The Baldwin piano is an art product, made by artists who are living and working in an artistic atmosphere, because the man who created the Baldwin institution [Lucien Wulsin] is an idealist."[46]

The advertising value of a famous artist had to be carefully cultivated. In the spring of 1909 for example, Wulsin was advised by his Artists' Department that Raoul Pugno, the French pianist, was "a poor investment," although he was a fine pianist. Why? "There is no demand for him anywhere in the United States. . . . and in his recitals in New York, Boston, Chicago and Cincinnati he has failed to draw enough people to pay the local expenses of hall rent and advertising, not to say anything about his fee." But Pugno himself cancelled negotiations with Baldwin. As a consequence Baldwin had to secure another "big card, whose success will be assured." For the season of 1910–11 this was no easy task, since the firm had declined an arrangement with Ferruccio Busoni and also Sergei Rachmaninoff, thinking Pugno would accept. After all, he had long been associated with the Baldwin piano. In the meantime, however, Wm. Knabe & Co. secured the Italian pianist and Mason & Hamlin the popular Russian.[47]

For the most part, however, Baldwin's campaign to use artists was extraordinarily successful, though admittedly Baldwin did not possess the Olympian roster of names that Steinway & Sons proudly boasted. Under the guidance of G. W. Armstrong, Jr. (who became president following the death of Lucien Wulsin in 1912), and Lucien Wulsin II (who succeeded Armstrong in 1926), the firm underwrote hundreds of concert performers, including José Iturbi, Béla Bartók, Vladimir de Pachmann, Wilhelm Bachaus, Walter Gieseking, and Claudio Arrau. The contracts with these musicians reveal the extent to which concert promotion by piano companies was as much the merchandising of the piano as it was the encouragement of art. Baldwin paid artists' fees only for engagements for which admission was charged and for which the artists received a percentage for their services. The Baldwin Artists' Department was not allowed to pay fees for vaudeville and theatrical appearances, nor for appearances at banquets, dinners, musicales in private houses, or recitals in schools at which the musician was teaching. By contract an artist could not perform on any instrument other than the Baldwin. (Steinway & Sons preferred an unwritten "gentlemen's agreement," which unofficially held Steinway artists to the same thing.)[48]

Piano companies engaged in this concert warfare customarily pampered eminent artists. When Lucien Wulsin II sponsored Bartók and Iturbi on their first American tours in the late 1920s, their contracts were similar. Baldwin paid first-class traveling expenses, most if not all advertising expenses for music journals and newspapers, posters, circulars, "and any other necessary publicity," including managerial fees incurred in connection with the tour. A salary was included (Bartók received $300 a week for the entire time he was in the United States). Baldwin received the total proceeds from the concerts, but returned to the performers any surplus above the expenses of the tours. The piano firm agreed to supply Baldwin concert grands for recital appearances (tuner-technician included), and small Baldwin grands on which the artists could practice in their hotel apartments. In return, Bartók and Iturbi agreed to use and endorse the Baldwin piano exclusively not only for the introductory tour, but for four successive ones as well. In addition, all publicity and advertising undertaken by the concert managers required the line " 'Baldwin Piano Used Exclusively' or words to this effect." In all programs "The Piano is a Baldwin" had to appear.[49]

Personal endorsements from the musicians naturally followed. "It has given me great pleasure to make the acquaintance of your super-excellent piano," wrote Bartók. "A perfect action, a beautiful, full and rich tone combine to rank this instrument pre-eminent among the pianos of our time, and it therefore gives me joy to be able to play the Baldwin on this, my first American tour."[50] Such pronouncements, though understandably laudatory, were sincere. As Alfred Dolge asserted in 1911, a virtuoso could not afford to use a poor piano in concert or give testimonials of praise about an instrument with which he was not satisfied. His reputation was also at stake.[51] This did not necessarily eliminate fraud. In the fall of 1907, *The Etude* magazine undertook a campaign of protest against the "dishonest," "deceptive," and "contemptible" practice by some manufacturers "of importing pianists to play their pianos and paying them vast sums for this service in order to gain a sort of advertising." While Baldwin management heartily agreed with *The Etude*'s position, they also charged that such a pianist was being "dishonest, when for a money consideration, he praises or plays a piano which has not his approval and which does not enable him to properly present his art ideals. For such artists, we, as manufacturers, have no use." Fraudulent endorsements would be eliminated when musicians themselves adopted the same ideals that manufacturers like Baldwin were following to produce the "proper vehicle" for artistic expression.[52]

Lucien Wulsin II continued to enlarge Baldwin's concert program throughout the twenties in a conscious attempt to challenge the virtual monopoly of Steinway & Sons. His very determined and very successful campaign was a testament both to the power of persuasive advertising and to the effectiveness of a consistent plan in pursuit of an ideal. At a time when most of the industry was suffering declining production and bankruptcy, Baldwin set out on the most intensive promotion in its history. The campaign would use the latest persuasive techniques, as well as the latest medium—the radio.

Each month *The Baldwin Keynote* magazine informed Baldwin dealers of the various artists—solo pianists, but also violinists, singers, conductors, dancers, even orchestras—appearing each season who claimed the Baldwin as their piano. Historic events were also heralded. For his first appearance in America, George Antheil chose Baldwin instruments for the premier Carnegie Hall performance in April 1927 of his *Ballet mécanique*, scored for sixteen pianos. Igor Stravinsky's ballet *Les Noces* was performed in Aeolian Hall, New York, not upon Aeolian-built pianos, but upon Baldwin grands. Written for four pianos, the work was premiered in the United States in February 1926, with Leopold Stokowski conducting. In 1928 the League of Composers, which devoted itself to providing a hearing for significant contemporary music, especially that of American composers, adopted the Baldwin piano as its official instrument.[53]

Wulsin continuously stressed the significance of the Baldwin on the concert stage to his dealers: it would maintain pride and respect among both dealers and owners of the piano, and encourage prospective Baldwin customers. "Be Familiar with Music Appreciation," stressed *The Keynote* to dealers. Read music appreciation literature. Attend all musicales and concerts—"make yourself conspicuous by constant attendance." Visit schools and colleges having music departments—cultivate both teachers and pupils. "IMPRESS YOURSELF UPON YOUR COMMUNITY AS A MUSIC MERCHANT." Dealers familiar with the history, art, and practice of music, and knowing the correct pronunciation of artists' names displayed a sympathetic interest in the professional aspirations of teachers, pupils, and musicians—and created favorable feelings that often led to piano sales.[54]

Some advertising men outside the Baldwin organization suggested to Wulsin that he overemphasized the names of "long haired geezers" such as de Pachmann, Gieseking, and Bachaus. The public "would be much more interested in Rudy Vallee playing the Baldwin, or Mary Pickford getting her inspiration from it," wrote Fritz Forchheimer of Chatfield and Woods Co., Pittsburgh. But the suggestions of outside ad men with their "nebulous ideas" utterly failed to interest the firm's sales executive, Philip Wyman.[55]

Nevertheless, Wyman's Publicity Department promoted the endorsement and sale of the Baldwin to celebrities other than musicians. Writer-humorist Will Rogers, who achieved additional fame as a stage performer with the de Reszke Singers, declared that "the Baldwin is the best piano I ever leaned on." In 1919 the United States government endorsed the Baldwin after testing the ability of other brands to withstand tropical conditions, and purchased ten instruments for the Canal Zone in Panama. Evangelist Billy Sunday used Baldwin pianos in all his campaigns.[56] "It is getting so I feel these grand pianos are as much a part of my organization as Bob and the others who play them," Sunday wrote. *The Keynote* reported that the large "BALDWIN" sign attached to the side of the piano was seen by thousands, and the evangelist himself "mentioned the Baldwin pianos several times from the pulpit." More to the point, the campaign was "directly responsible for quite a few sales."[57]

Other celebrities lent their names to the Baldwin product. Mrs. William Howard Taft bought a specially designed piano for her private use in the Green Room of the White House. Fellow Cincinnatians, President Taft and Lucien Wulsin were cordial acquaintances. Later, Mrs. Warren G. Harding purchased a Baldwin grand in red mahogany for her personal use in the White House as well. An accomplished pianist (she was trained in Wulsin's own territory at the Cincinnati Conservatory of Music, which used Baldwin pianos exclusively), Mrs. Harding announced her intention to practice an hour each day on her new Baldwin, of which she said: "There is something about the tone, that I have never heard in any other instrument." Wulsin's pianos also attracted Mrs. Calvin Coolidge. "Another Baldwin in the White House," boasted *The Keynote* in 1924. Placed in the Lincoln Room, the dull brown mahogany grand reportedly afforded enjoyment to the First Family's intimate circle, "where the President and Mrs. Coolidge [could] be 'just home folks.'"[58] Baldwin's Publicity Department wasted no time in making available to dealers a 7″ × 11″ display card reading:

> This is a duplicate of the
> Baldwin Grand Piano
> which
> Mrs. CALVIN COOLIDGE
> has selected for her personal use in
> the White House.
> The Baldwin Piano was also the personal choice of
> Mrs. Warren G. Harding and Mrs. William H. Taft.[59]

"Boy, you ain't heard nothin' yet until you hear the Baldwin—the perfect piano," proclaimed Al Jolson, star of the first "talkie," *The Jazz Singer*. The film was produced in combination with the Vitaphone, a device synchronizing sound with action, which was produced by Western Electric Company, Vitaphone Corporation, Bell Telephone Laboratories, and Warner Brothers. Vitaphone engineers made exhaustive tests (unknown to the Baldwin Company)

of the five leading makes of pianos and found the recording ca-
pabilities of the Baldwin to be superior. Thus, Wulsin's piano
became the offical piano for Vitaphone productions. *The Keynote*
advised local dealers when Vitaphone pictures featuring the Baldwin were appearing in their cities so they could make the most of
the publicity.[60]

Baldwin's fame also grew following the purchase of its pianos
by motion-picture theaters and radio stations. Publix Theatres
Corporation of New York, one of the largest metropolitan chains
of vaudeville and motion-picture houses, chose Baldwin grands
for both stage and lobby. The Publix chain of approximately 1,300
theaters included Lubliner & Trinz Theatres, Balaban and Katz,
Famous-Players-Lasky, Keith Vaudeville Circuit, the Blanc Circuit,
and the Southern and Western theater enterprises. Patrons witnessed increasingly familiar words flashed upon the screen: "This
establishment uses the Baldwin piano exclusively."[61] Radio generated even greater publicity. Armstrong and Wulsin had been there
at the beginning. Station WLW, Cincinnati, which went on the air
March 2, 1922, used only the Baldwin. By 1929, 222 radio stations
nationwide preferred Baldwin's tone quality in broadcasting, and
announcers testified to that fact every day and night during programs. As *The Keynote* announced, "The Air is Full of Baldwin
Every Night." The publicity that the firm received through radio
broadcasts using its pianos made Baldwin a distinguishable if not
familiar name. And in many cases local dealers could trace piano
sales directly to theater promotions, concert performances, and
radio broadcasts.[62]

The Baldwin Co. carefully linked all these things to its national
advertising. Unlike Steinway & Sons, who used the respected N.
W. Ayer & Son ad agency exclusively, most of Baldwin advertising
was developed in-house through the talents of Philip Wyman. The
Cincinnati office would provide dealers free booklets containing
advertisements. On specified dates the ads were to be run in local papers to appear in conjunction with the national advertising.
Baldwin subsidized 50 percent of the dealers' advertising costs,
provided store and window posters of national ads, and provided
fliers imprinted with dealers' names and featuring Baldwin art-

ists. (The company also mailed these fliers directly to potential consumers upon receiving mail-in coupons that they had clipped from Baldwin ads appearing in national magazines and notified local dealers to follow up on this interest.) The goal was to produce "not only persistent but consistent advertising," a policy tightly uniting all divisions and their dealers with national headquarters. A piano was not purchased on impulse. Dealer's-help booklets reminded Baldwin salesmen that the average piano prospect considered his purchase for many weeks, often many months, before actually buying. Thus, the customer was in a receptive frame of mind for a long time and was susceptible to varying arguments and impressions. "It is the continual drip of the water that makes an impression on the stone," Baldwin literature advised. "This leads to the conclusion that 'all the time' is the best time to advertise."[63]

The rise in sales of high-grade Baldwin pianos throughout the late 1920s testifies to a successful campaign of "Getting the Quality Business." The Cincinnati leadership stressed that "national advertising is in reality local advertising" since sales must come from the follow-up of local dealers. The success of the "Choose Your Piano as the Artists Do" campaign exemplifies this cooperation. Baldwin advertising, "with well-planned regularity, goes into more than a half-million homes" of those interested in music and those "whose social position dictates that they purchase only a piano possessing the social prestige of the Baldwin." "Once you sell the Baldwin to the 'best people,'—the leaders in your community," *The Keynote* stressed to dealers, "many other people, following their example will demand it."[64]

Wulsin and Wyman chose the most important publications of the period to spread the Baldwin message: the *Musical Courier, The Etude, The Musician, Music Digest, Music News, Singing,* the *Bulletin of the National Federation of Music Clubs, Vogue, Century Magazine, Harper's Magazine, Scribner's Magazine, The Atlantic Monthly, Redbook, The American Magazine, House and Garden, The Spur,* and *National Geographic.* Ellington and Hamilton piano advertising was directed to the more general and less elite audience reached by *Saturday Evening Post, Good Housekeeping* and *Ladies' Home Journal*. In addition, Baldwin products were advertised in almost twenty farm journals and papers. The ads were directed largely to women, because "women have confidence in the advertising in these publications and believe what they read."[65] In the growing culture of consumption, women were the recognized consumers. Moreover, women traditionally were at the center of the piano culture so important in the Victorian households to which piano advertising still paid homage.

Lucien Wulsin II, who was a believer in the "keep constantly at it" philosophy of persuasive advertising,[66] was also well aware that advertising was not the most important thing in securing piano sales. That distinction went to the individual salesman. "In selling pianos no man is really successful unless he does create and develop business on the outside," Wulsin wrote. This meant "calling on prospects [and using] an awful lot of shoe leather gaining the experience."[67] All publicity messages had to be followed up by personal calls. "This is the most important factor . . . in the sale of a piano."[68] The appearance of Baldwin men was important as well: "In order to get the maximum results from house-to-house salesmen, they [must] be raised above the 'agent' class, against whom many women have a strong prejudice." "Be neat and clean in your appearance," stressed *The Keynote*. Shoes should be shined, fingernails trimmed, hair brushed, "and do not chew gum . . . [for if] you expect to sell high class people, you must deliver high class service as these things are very noticeable to the better class of people." Finally, "Talk quality and believe quality; believe in The Baldwin Piano Company, . . . Keep smiling," and "Do not take 'No' for an answer."[69] Recognizing those salesmen successfully following the Baldwin code, *The Baldwin Keynote* regularly featured "The Roll of Honor," listing the sales of the various divisions, and revealing the "success recipes" of star salesmen. The company also held regular national sales contests based on the quotas established for each dealer.

Baldwin considered at least six sources for prospective sales: music teachers, old customers and friends, selective telephone canvasses, classified ads, schoolteachers' class lists (especially of third-grade classes), and first-class mailings to music teachers, pupils, customers with charge accounts, and people on real estate lists or lists of car ownership. Salesmen were expected to exploit these sources in a regular, systematic way.[70] Indeed, the Baldwin dealership contract required the dealer to stock not only a "representative selection of Baldwin and Baldwin-built pianos" at all times, but to "produce a volume and quality of piano business that is commensurate with the importance of the territory [assigned]." The dealer also agreed "to cooperate fully" with Baldwin policy, plans, and activities designed to further sales, and to respect interdealer relationships. Finally, the dealer was required to maintain an adequate tuning and servicing department. "Your goal is an organization which will just bring you out of the black in the worst months and give you big results in the good months," Wulsin stressed, or the dealership would be revoked and given to someone who could.[71]

Although the piano sales resulting from such efforts determined the volume of Baldwin business, collections of payments on pianos sold determined the margin of profit. Wulsin realized that many potential piano payments were used instead to buy cars or other large purchases. To hold onto the sales that were so carefully cultivated, Baldwin relied on its proven collections system and on the experience of automobile companies. The National Association of Finance Companies had gathered statistics on motor cars bought on the installment plan. This research showed that larger down payments clearly made fewer repossessions necessary. Citing this information, *The Keynote* encouraged Baldwin dealers to "get a large enough down payment to make the customer feel that he has a real equity in the piano and is not just a renter." Dealers also were urged to secure larger monthly payments, arrange shorter terms, sell better instruments, keep all accounts up to date, and obtain payments on time. "Collections are the Life Blood of Business," stressed T. C. McGilliard of the Cincinnati collection department. The conservative Baldwin way of selling prevented the "$1.00 down, $1.00 a week plan" to which so many others fell victim.[72]

Wulsin used the latest technology to promote the Baldwin piano in addition to more traditional methods. Local dealers could purchase lantern slides featuring the piano along with their name and address for display on movie screens. Countless numbers of people were thus exposed to ads for: "Baldwin—The Official Piano for the Artists of the Chicago Grand Opera," or "Baldwin—The Dominant Instrument in the Concert World." Reaching even more people, Baldwin also used the radio extensively by underwriting recital programs, such as "At the Baldwin," which the whole trade proclaimed as an unqualified success. Indeed, the Baldwin radio campaign proved the most effective means of carrying the firm's message into millions of homes, demonstrating the piano's excellent tone, strengthening ties with music teachers and conservatories—and producing immediate piano sales.[73]

What is extraordinary about Wulsin's publicity campaigns is that efforts and budgets were increased during the lean years following 1925, when most of the industry suffered shrinking player piano sales. The trade press was particularly impressed with the "Choose Your Piano as the Artists Do" campaign of 1929.[74] The Baldwin Company was affected by the economic crisis plaguing the piano trade in the 1920s, but like Steinway—and unlike most of the remaining trade—the Cincinnati firm not only weathered the crisis, but emerged more powerful and influential than ever.

In 1927 Philip Wyman identified two reasons for the decrease in Baldwin's business: the belief among dealers that Baldwin sales "will take care of themselves, and as a consequence ... the let-up in propaganda and follow-up of our national work on the part of the Divisions due to the desire to make a showing this year." Wyman recommended that to improve wholesale business, Baldwin dealers "must be reached constantly" by marketing travelers, division heads, and advertising representatives to improve coordination of local and national promotions. In addition, the Cincinnati office encouraged dealers to provide concert grands when Baldwin artists were in their cities and to place pianos on loan for other local musical development as well. Then, dealers would "far more intensively" follow up these events with local sales efforts. Wyman thought it absolutely necessary to make the Baldwin franchise financially attractive by arranging necessary sales territory and providing pricing incentives and fifty-fifty aid to local advertising, all geared to *"enable them* [Baldwin dealers] *to make money."*[75]

Wyman suggested similar efforts to aid Baldwin retail sales. He endorsed the development of a systematic plan for the cultivation of music in schools and colleges and for the support of local music teachers and artists to make them "active producers of sales." This would include, for example, lending pianos to prominent teachers in exchange for sales on commission. (Using this strategy, both Baldwin and Steinway & Sons provided leadership for the campaign of the National Piano Manufacturers Association to encourage class piano instruction in the public schools.) These activities would be reported to Cincinnati, which would in turn send word of the events to all parts of the country. Wyman put the responsibility squarely upon the local dealers, but stressed that the Cincinnati office would supervise all efforts directly "to insure that the necessary work is done and carried on consistently and uniformly."[76] Cultivating the good will of music teachers and local artists was an especially important link in the Baldwin sales scheme. "Always deal fairly with them," advised *The Baldwin Keynote*. "Give them no cause for becoming unfriendly," for in addition to goodwill, dealers would receive consistent word-of-mouth endorsement of their business and product, "which is the most valuable advertising you can get. Money cannot buy such advertising."[77]

Despite Baldwin's intense promotional and sales efforts, total piano sales declined after 1927 (though, significantly, Baldwin grands continued to enjoy unprecedented sales until late 1929). "Conditions having changed in the piano industry due to the practical elimination of the player piano, the market is going to be more selective," wrote G. W. Armstrong, Jr., to all divisions in the summer of 1929. "Legitimate merchandise at national prices will be the order of the day and those manufacturers and dealers not equipped to cater to this new market must drop out of the picture." Of course Wulsin, Wyman, and Armstrong fully intended that the Baldwin Company would emerge strong and victorious. "We stand alone among piano manufacturers today as being *ideally* equipped to meet existing conditions," Armstrong continued.

An efficient industrial organization, quality pianos in various price classes, carefully trained personnel, extensive laboratory research producing improved products, a nationwide, intensive distribution and collection organization, ample financial reserves, a growing concert business, and one of the largest advertising budgets in the industry testified to Baldwin's strength. But Armstrong made it clear that for Baldwin's success to continue, the network of dealers must remain united, dedicated, and productive: "What Alexander [the Great] did [in defeating Darius of Persia] we must do—get rid of superfluous baggage, unproductive dealers, weak and inefficient salesmen. Eliminate camp followers in the field, in the store and office; spend money only for activities which will bring returns. You'll either be Alexander or—you'll be Darius."[78]

The Steinway as Art in the Age of Mechanical Reproduction

However abstract or visionary was Lucien Wulsin's pursuit of the ideal for his company, in practice this meant competing successfully with the long-established New York firm of Steinway & Sons. Indeed, to pursue Steinway's coveted reputation *was* to pursue the "ideal." A 1919 advertisement illustrates the company's conscious cultivation and reinforcement of this notion: "In the fabric of language, the word STEINWAY has come to mean the utmost in perfection. . . . Is it any wonder then that the word STEINWAY so breathes quality and supremacy as to be universally so unconsciously chosen as the symbol of perfection?"[79] Such an authoritative claim by its very nature set Steinway apart from any other manufacturer. And when backed by the testimonials of most of the great performing artists, the result was a formidable standard almost unapproachable by most other firms.

Steinway & Sons dominated the artistic piano market. Therefore, the Steinway was distinguished by considerably more than price. "No manufacturer has ever made a continued success in the piano industry by concentrating his major efforts on the Price

Market," Philip Wyman of Baldwin asserted. Nevertheless, Baldwin management was very much aware that if Baldwin prices were lowered, the company would "lose caste to our strongest competitor." Therefore, "Steinway prices determine Baldwin prices." Wulsin's conscious desire to put the Baldwin in direct competition with Steinway involved more than a clash of instruments; it required laying siege to a legacy firmly entrenched in piano mythology that identified the Steinway as the ideal piano.[80]

Scholars have identified the technological innovations of Steinway & Sons that contributed to its leadership in the industry.[81] But the prepotent mythology surrounding the firm was a product of merchandising rather than technology, and this aspect historians have not explored. The specialized salesmanship that was to distinguish the New York manufacturer was developed under the talented direction of William Steinway (1835–96), the fourth son of the founder. His first step in building up prestige was to get leading artists to use the Steinway piano. In the nineteenth century this required the firm to subsidize the American tours of European virtuosos. "It was without doubt the most effective of all advertising methods we employed," wrote Charles H. Steinway in 1912, "since it not only made the piano and its maker widely known, but assisted in laying the foundation for a broad national culture."[82]

The promotion of community musical enterprises formed the second most important element in Steinway's distribution scheme. Both steps required a loyal and active network of retail dealers. Further cultivation of what Steinway trade literature called "The Name" led William Steinway to seek the patronage of royalty, to establish Steinway Hall in 1866, and to exhibit in world expositions. The communication of Steinway patronage, endorsement, and honors to its major market—musical amateurs—flowered in the literature of consistent national advertising, a move that reportedly "shocked" other piano makers.[83]

Beginning in 1855, Steinway was the only piano manufacturer to advertise daily in the *New York Times*. From that time on, the firm never once offered sales or bargains, but only high quality, endorsement by artists, and cultural enrichment. By the 1870s and

1880s, Steinway & Sons and a few other manufacturers, including Kodak, Royal baking powder, Singer, and Sapolio laundry soap, were the only firms advertising extensively in national publications.[84]

The exchange of pianos for valuable advertising space in such reputable publications as *The Atlantic Monthly, Collier's Weekly,* and *The Globe* was also a strategy Steinway used at least into the 1920s.[85] Until 1900, however, Steinway advertising copy was generated in-house, and the firm's primary merchandising technique was supplying pianos at concerts and recitals to keep the name before music lovers. In that year, N. W. Ayer & Son, the oldest full-service ad agency in the country, approached Steinway & Sons with an innovative strategy. Ayer, whose respectable clientele included John Wanamaker, Montgomery Ward, Ferry Seeds, Singer Sewing Machines, and Procter & Gamble, argued that Steinway's existing promotion technique was influencing only those already interested in music and neglecting the millions who had not yet developed a taste for it. The ad agency offered to tap this source. Charles H. Steinway, who had become head of the firm in 1896, agreed to let Ayer advertise his pianos, providing it did not damage the Steinway prestige so carefully developed in the nineteenth century under William Steinway's guidance. The result was a successful partnership that lasted until 1969, the longest in advertising history.[86]

The Steinway organization enhanced its growing worldwide reputation through the combination of Ayer's national advertising and the piano firm's already existing concert service, which had been built up in the nineteenth century at a time when concerts were *the* popular entertainment. Unlike Baldwin, the Steinway concert service department used no written contract to secure artists' agreements. Instead, the New York firm developed the gentlemen's agreement, which became a successful experiment in loyalty. The Steinway marketing department contained four elements: salesmen, concert artists, advertising, and public relations. The firm's advertising, sales, and retail managers worked closely with N. W. Ayer & Son to hammer out what became Steinway ads. Final approval came from a committee made up of the sales department, the engineering departments, and the agency, though the result inevitably reflected the wishes of the Steinway president. As John H. Steinway, retired chairman of the board, remarked, "An ad *evolves* after a lot of input before a consensus is reached." To tie local dealers into this framework, travelers' kits supplied retailers with new artwork, which was then adapted to fit the locality. Unlike Baldwin, however, there was no fifty-fifty financial cooperation for advertising. (Also unlike Baldwin, Steinway did not sell its pianos to dealers on consignment; they had to purchase the instruments outright.)[87]

The mythology—that is, the image and cultural appeal—of the Steinway piano as seen in advertisements of the 1920s provides a portrait that differs substantially from that generally offered by the piano industry, which was obsessed with the production and sale of player pianos. American piano manufacturers, in their quest for a musical democracy through the player piano, used most advertising space to promote the latest automatic improvements in their instruments. Unfortunately, this attempt to exploit the emerging consumer culture was doomed to failure. Steinway & Sons, however, successfully met the challenge of the new era. This is not to say that Steinway did not lose business, or suffer production cutbacks and loss of profits. But Steinway did manage to preserve its market and its image, and it served as an example of successful promotion to what was left of the industry after the devastating 1920s and the Great Depression.

Steinway & Sons long cultivated its own uniqueness, identifying its product as not only synonymous with the term "piano," but as the perfect piano as well. While other names remain obscure to all but a select few, of Steinway there is no question. A famous 1923 product study found that Steinway was mentioned in a survey by more than twice as many persons as the next brand, with over 141 brands of pianos mentioned in all. Ford held this same distinction in the automobile industry, while in phonographs, Victor and Edison shared leadership. Steinway & Sons resembled other leaders of advertised brands: its product had been trademarked for a long time; it advertised extensively and continuously; it was the pioneer large advertiser in its field and offered a product of high quality with a good reputation; and advertising and use of the product were the two greatest factors influencing familiarity with its name.[88]

The specific avenue by which Steinway & Sons escaped the devastation that affected so many other piano companies began in 1919, when N. W. Ayer & Son created the slogan, "The instrument of the immortals." Unlike the nameless hundreds that chose to manufacture player pianos or emphasize price or effortless mastery in their generally sporadic advertising, Steinway remained content with its long-cultivated traditional piano market. Yet beyond this, Steinway advertising promoted its product not merely as a piano, but as a work of art. Indeed, these ads only occasionally stressed *playing* the piano (though playing was always implied); rather, the emphasis was on *owning* it.

More than any other piano, the Steinway has been associated with and endorsed by the great artists of the time. It is, in the truest sense, the "instrument of the immortals," from Liszt and Wagner to Paderewski and Rachmaninoff. While other companies could offer only Paderewski's recorded rolls, Steinway could boast that the real Paderewski "plays Steinway exclusively." "He who owns a Steinway," one ad read, "is in company with the great [and] possesses an unmistakable token of musical culture and distinction, recognized the world over." Just as art has always enjoyed royal patronage, Steinway relished a virtual monopoly in palaces of nobility and in great conservatories of music. Ads stressed that the Steinway was to be found "in those homes where the art of the piano is loved and the music of the masters is kept living." The Steinway was billed as "the best in the piano maker's art"; indeed, Wagner called it "a noble work of art."[89] Those purchasing a Steinway thus were not buying merely a piano, but something akin to great painting or sculpture. References to touch and tone —that is, the piano's *useful* functions—were nothing compared to the basic *uselessness* that allowed the Steinway to thrive in the consumer's imagination.

The association of Steinway and art was emphasized constantly in ads: the testimonials of the great performers; the piano pictured in a modern interior designed by Allen Saalburg; an interpretation of Wagner's "Entrance of the Gods into Valhalla" painted for the "Steinway Collection" by Rockwell Kent. In 1927 a painting of Tristan and Isolde by Harvey Dunn for Steinway was the first four-color spread ever published in the *Saturday Evening Post.*[90] Other painters whose work was commissioned for use in Steinway advertising include N. C. Wyeth, Ignacio Zuloaga, Miguel Covarrubias, F. Luis Mora (President Harding's portrait artist), Boris Anisfeld, Everett Henry, and Pierre Brissaud. The paintings, which were hung in Steinway Hall, depicted great pianists or composers who used the Steinway, or illustrated interpretations of musical compositions closely associated with these artists. N. W. Ayer & Son transformed the paintings into effective sales messages.[91]

The commission and use of modern art in Steinway ads of the 1920s was an extension of the advertising style that the New York firm had employed for decades. Warner S. Shelly, retired president of N. W. Ayer & Son, credits Gerold M. Lauck, also a former Ayer president, with the idea of using modern art in Steinway advertising.[92] Other companies also practiced the Steinway technique to enhance their own products with an aura of prestige—Maxwell House Coffee, Gruen Watches, Post Grape-Nuts.[93] But with Steinway the association was natural. However much another product's image was improved by its proximity to art, it remained a mere product. The Steinway itself became art.

Like fine sculpture or painting, the Steinway was described as "an eminently sound investment," which appreciated in value. The piano was known for its "durability," its "permanence," its aesthetic "beauty," its "superiority." While sounding like puffery, these ad lines could be proven true at the nearest retail store. Ads informed consumers that it took five years and eleven months of "painstaking preparation and workmanship" to produce the Steinway, and that the piano was still made under the supervision of the founding family, faithfully maintaining "STEINWAY IDEALS." As with any work of art, "the materials which go into a Steinway are available to the whole world, but the genius which transmutes them into a Steinway tone begins and ends with Steinway."[94]

Furthermore, although other firms offered pianos of various qualities and prices, Steinway advertising emphasized that "there are several Steinway styles and sizes, but only one Steinway quality." Similarly, "The name 'Steinway' on a piano means more than the word 'Sterling' on silver, because there are different grades of sterling and different weights, but there is only one Steinway, and that is the best."[95] Even the Steinway grand ("Old 100,000") presented to the nation in 1903 and accepted by President Theodore Roosevelt for the East Room of the White House was "in no way superior to any of the 99,999 pianos which had gone before, or of those which have been made since." This ornate piano, designed by Richard H. Hunt, was adorned with acanthus scrolls framing shields bearing the arms of the original thirteen states, and provided a mahogany canvas upon which Thomas W. Dewing painted the nine muses inspiring the young American Republic. The instrument's entire case was gilded and was supported upon legs carved as golden eagles. Yet beneath the ornate exterior, "A Steinway is a Steinway. . . . There is no such thing as a 'better' Steinway. Each and every Steinway is *the best Steinway.*"[96]

In this way Steinway & Sons cultivated its own mythology so successfully that its product became the much copied but never duplicated ideal. For artists, consumers, and even the rest of the industry, the Steinway became *the* piano. As Alfred Dolge remarked in 1913, "No other piano has almost from its very first appearance enjoyed the endorsement of its competitors to the extent that the expression 'as good as a Steinway' has became proverbial in the piano trade."[97] Only Steinway could boast without sounding artificial or shallow that "to own a piano is one thing—to own the Instrument of the Immortals is another."[98]

Nevertheless, Steinway & Sons maintained its business sense as well. Unlike Mason & Hamlin, which was advertised as "the costliest piano in the world," Steinway insisted that its price was "always as low as possible, as a matter of principle." "The reputation of the Steinway," one ad explained, "has caused many people to believe that it must necessarily be beyond their means." By offering "remarkably convenient" terms, and insisting it was a piano "primarily for the home," however, ads encouraged the "really careful and logical" buyer to "*invest*" in the Steinway. In this way Steinway & Sons emphasized "the logic of thrift," in that buying the best would be the cheapest in the end, because it afforded so much satisfaction and advantage to the buyer.[99]

In a real sense all traditional straight pianos are Victorians out of their time. That is, they are artifacts of an age preceding mass society, in which the home and family rather than business interests and consumerism governed society. Here lies the piano's critical link with the demise of the home as a production center and the erosion of the home as the center of social life. Almost without exception, however, piano manufacturers in the first decades of the twentieth century promoted (at the expense of the traditional instrument) the player piano, which was an easily replaced artifact not of the Victorian age, but of the modern one. By contrast, Steinway & Sons detached itself from this trend. Steinway ads necessarily were (and are) devoted to maintaining an appeal to a minority audience of high culture that has not been swept into mass society. Hence the promotion of Steinway as art. No Steinway was ever presented as a self-playing gadget. Quite the contrary, Steinway offered to build character and art appreciation—"the good life"—through "personally performed" music. No Steinway product was advertised as easy to play. Steinway did not make shallow promises to bring into your home a Paderewski or Rachmaninoff as did ads for mechanical pianos. Rather than cheat its customers out of what it promised, Steinway played upon their dreams ("If Paderewski or Rachmaninoff or Hofmann came to your house you would have an instrument worthy of their touch"), and did so honestly, for these artists themselves endorsed the Steinway.[100]

By the late twenties, Steinway began to cultivate another image in addition to that of the piano-as-art. While other manufacturers were necessarily committed to selling player pianos as entertaining gadgets (by 1925 pianolas were stockpiling unsold, victims of increased radio sales), Steinway—a successful Victorian in mass society—chose to cultivate an image of the piano similar to that of a concerned, demanding, moralistic Victorian parent or schoolmaster. The Steinway would provide the means to rear children in the cultured tradition, to guarantee their popularity and success in the world. Only a "first rate environment" will produce a "first rate person," one ad explained. Like a schoolmaster or Victorian parent, the Steinway "leaves the impressionable young talent unhandicapped ... by the distortive influences of practice on less perfect instruments." It "assists your children through their most difficult times to a sane and beautiful life." It will "help them make friends." The Steinway will "subtly connect them with a glorious tradition" by its "mere presence."[101] In this way Steinway & Sons identified itself and *handplayed* music with the waning Victorian tradition of the home as the center of social life and cultural development, with values which were considered lasting and true. This would appeal to those consumers searching for the stability that such a tradition would offer in a rapidly changing world. With this remarkable advertising strategy, Steinway seemed to protect threatened values, and yet it participated successfully in the emerging trend of business domination in family life. Such appeals secured for Steinway the 1930 Harvard Advertising Award for an ad conveying high artistic value through effective use of headline, text, and "practical visualization of the product in use."[102]

It is the Steinway legacy to support tradition in a world of change, to celebrate age in a world of youth, to honor creative skills and master craftsmanship in a world of shallow reproduction and machine operation, to portray itself as art in an age of mass production. This legacy, along with a superior product, sound financial policies, and expert management, preserved Steinway intact in mass society and contributed to its unapproachable position within the industry. The strategically important position of "Steinway's largest competitor" has been held by Chickering & Sons, Mason & Hamlin, and Baldwin, among others; but the challenge remains among the competition. Actually, there is no challenge to Steinway, and therein lies its success. "Larger houses are coming into the field, but they have had little effect on us except to stimulate and help us," Charles H. Steinway astutely observed in 1912. "Anything that increases the volume or sphere of musical appreciation increases our share of the business."[103]

When consumers speak of the mythology of the piano, they must necessarily focus on the Steinway, for it remains *the* piano.

All others appear to be mere reproductions of varying (and Steinway would insist inferior) quality. "Just as a most masterful copy of a Raphael or Correggio will ever be only a copy and far from the original," wrote Alfred Dolge in 1913, "so it has proved impossible to produce a piano equal to the Steinway piano, even though the Steinway were copied to the minutest detail. No art product can be duplicated by copying."[104] Although other piano manufacturers have been inspired by Steinway's piano-as-art campaigns, it is the Steinway that remains the coveted original. Steinway was the first to promote itself successfully as art in the age of mechanical reproduction. It is the Steinway legacy.

If the foregoing references to a severe decline in the American piano trade in the 1920s have raised questions about the nature and cause of such a downturn in business, especially when all seemed to be going so well, they will serve as an effective reminder of a similar confusion that plagued even seasoned piano men as the industry faced its greatest challenge. The United States was undergoing a revolution from the producer ethic to the consumer culture. It was a change in which the piano makers profited with the player piano, but a change that was undermining the very foundation of the industry itself. In the new era that followed the Great War, piano men found themselves, ironically, going bankrupt in an age of unprecedented appreciation of music.

CHAPTER FIVE

Industrial Bankruptcy in a Musical Age

The radio democratized art and educated the nation to a true appreciation of the highest standard.
—Walter Damrosch

In this age of victrolas and radios the piano is fast becoming a rare article in the ordinary home.
—The Antiquarian

It was said that someone had sold a piano in June, but the rumor had not been positively confirmed.
—Charles H. Parsons to George P. Bent

In April 1923 the American Piano Company celebrated the opening of the new Chickering Hall at 27–29 West 57th Street, New York, and the centennial anniversary of the founding of Chickering & Sons, Boston. The prominent names of those serving on the Centennial Committee underscored the importance of the event: Mrs. Calvin Coolidge, *New York Times* music critic Olin Downes, Senator Henry Cabot Lodge, and William Cardinal O'Connell, Archbishop of Boston. Vice President Coolidge chaired the National Honorary Committee, whose membership was equally notable, including Governor Channing Cox of Massachusetts, Mayor James Curley of Boston, New York Symphony conductor Walter Damrosch, Metropolitan Opera conductor Artur Bodanzky, violinist Fritz Kreisler, Philadelphia Orchestra conductor Leopold Stokowski, Senator Reed Smoot, U.S. Commissioner of Education John J. Tigert, Mrs. John F. Lyons, president of the National Federation of Music Clubs, and Richard Lawrence, president of the Music Industries Chamber of Commerce. The Chickering centennial would focus national recognition on an American piano maker and on the seemingly irreplaceable role of the piano in musical culture.

Newspapers reporting the celebration reminded readers that Jonas Chickering, the founder (1798–1853), was described in his own time as resembling his product in being "square, upright and grand." They also reported the honor bestowed upon the piano maker fifty years after his death. A colonnade was designed for the Industries Building at the St. Louis World's Fair in 1904, which contained ten statues of heroic size representing the ten greatest inventors in history. Those chosen were Elias Howe, Robert Fulton, Henry Bessemer, John Ericsson, James Watt, Alvan Clark, Robert Hoe, Samuel Colt, Charles Goodyear—and Jonas Chickering. "This distinction was a signal tribute to the position that the piano, the greatest and most eloquent of all musical instruments, holds in the history of civilization," reported the Columbus, Ohio, *Dispatch* in 1923. The Cincinnati *Commercial Tribune* agreed, adding, "when we say 'music' we think immediately of piano. That mysterious combination of wood, metal and ivory has awakened something in most human hearts that lifted them above the dull routine of business and household worries."

The climax of the Chickering celebration was a dinner at the Copley-Plaza Hotel on April 21. Vice President Coolidge was the principal speaker. He reportedly received "a thunderous outburst of wild and sustained applause," and his speech was broadcast as if by magic by the new radio "to every nook and corner of the United States." The vice president told America that Jonas Chickering "became a national figure because he filled a national need. He ministered to a national desire. He gave the people additional power to rise above the contemplation of material things to the contemplation of spiritual things. He brought increased strength for the expression of the aspirations of the soul. Such achievements entitle him to rank high as a national benefactor." The vice president then discussed the contribution of the piano, the fact that it enabled good music to become familiar and popular. "The children of our American families have mostly been brought up within reach of the keyboard," he said. "We cannot imagine a model New England home without the family Bible on the table and the family piano in the corner."[1]

Such thinking had made music a big business in the United States and had made the piano industry the most important single component within that business. American expenditures on music in 1913 reached $593.5 million. Of this, 27 percent was spent on pianos, reed organs, music rolls and sheet music, and 37 percent went toward piano lessons and music courses. Americans spent only $60 million in 1913 on talking machines and records, which produced a fascinating but not yet satisfactory musical experience.[2] That same year, a survey of every public school in Hartford, Connecticut, revealed that in grammar school, 29 percent of all girls studied piano through private lessons outside of school, and 11 percent of all boys, or 20 percent of all students. Piano continued to be the first choice among high school students: 57 percent studied music privately, and of these pupils, 78 percent chose to study piano. The survey concluded that this phenomenon was not limited to any one class, nationality, or income level, and that all had a high regard for music as an educational asset.[3]

Another survey of "a typical New England town" revealed similar findings about the popularity of the piano among adolescents. The 1919 survey reported that 43 percent of junior high and 49 percent of high school students studied piano through private lessons. Furthermore, 73 percent of the homes of all junior high school students had pianos, as did 66 percent of homes of the high school group. These figures seemed to verify the music industry's confidence in a sound future. But the survey also reported that 61 percent of the high school students dropped their music studies for reasons varying from school studies to dislike. The analyst, however, emphasized the positive aspects—the widespread study of music, especially the piano, among young people. The future seemed secure.[4]

Even the war in Europe, into which the United States was pulled in 1917, seemed to offer additional evidence that America was entering a musical renaissance in which the piano industry would offer its usual leadership. The war stimulated an interest in American music (as well as a prejudice against German music and musicians). Music appreciation courses became popular in colleges, and there was a significant increase in public school and community music. In 1917 John C. Freund, editor of *Musical America* and *The Music Trades*, formed the Musical Alliance of the United States, with the aim of establishing a secretary of fine arts in the president's cabinet. Such an appointment would "unite all interested in music and in musical industries" in an effort to strengthen the nation for war.[5] Though the House Education Committee was considering such a bill as early as October 1917, the government authorized no new cabinet post during the war years. Nevertheless, the music industries and various music groups continued to press for a Fine Arts Department as well as a national conservatory.[6]

The American Yearbook for 1918 reported that the war made the United States the new leading power in music, as American compositions proliferated, especially through the War Camp Community Service (a division of the War Department's Committee on Training Camp Activities). The most striking manifestation of an awakening civic consciousness of music was the phenomenon of community singing. "A singing nation has kept pace with a singing army," proclaimed the *Yearbook*, as people organized "liberty sings" and community choruses.[7]

Given the Victorian emphasis on the moral value of music, the newly formed Music Industries Chamber of Commerce (MICC) was confident that the government of the United States would declare the music trades to be an essential war industry. What could be better for moral, spiritual, and patriotic rejuvenation? Music is "one of the important factors in winning the war ... uniting and unifying people to the common purpose," declared C. M. Tremaine before the Music Supervisors National Conference in 1918.[8] The U.S. Navy and Army seemed to agree. Each bought many pianos and player pianos to use in training camps, in YMCA huts behind the lines, and on ships, such as the U.S.S. *Delaware*, which had six Autopiano players on board during the war.[9] Senator William M. Calder of New York also believed that music must be allowed its rightful place in the current crisis. As a guest speaker at the piano dealers' and manufacturers' 1918 convention, Senator Calder told his audience that he strongly disagreed with those who considered the musical instrument industry as a "nonessential." James W. Gerard, the former ambassador to Germany, told the convention that he hoped that the expensive practice of sending American young women to Germany to study music would now stop, since equally qualified teachers could be found here.[10] Indeed, much of the impetus behind the drive to establish a national conservatory was to declare American musical independence from European influence.[11]

Although the War Department declared music to be "vital ammunition" and crucial to the American war effort, the War Industries' Board originally designated the music trades to be a nonessential. This decision threatened the curtailment of raw materials and supplies. After much prodding, however, the Music Industries Chamber of Commerce (which the piano manufacturers, dealers, and travelers had organized only in 1916) succeeded in convincing the War Industries' Board that the products of the music trades were of "absolute indispensability" in winning the war. The government then put its stamp of approval on American piano manufacturing during the war by letting it continue "practically undisturbed as an essential." Not only was piano manufacturing exempted from the War Revenue Tax bill passed by the House Ways and Means Committee, it was reclassified in the fall of 1917 by the Council of National Defense as "essential to the national welfare."[12]

This decision resulted in part because the piano trade competed with the war industries for neither materials nor labor. Piano building was a skilled craft practiced generally by older men, who were unaffected by the draft. Furthermore, the only war materials used in piano making were foundry iron, copper, and steel, of which the industry used only 27,000 tons annually. Of that amount, 25,000 tons were of foundry iron, the least needed of the three metals. Piano manufacture was really an asset to the United States government as well. Since there was an active demand for American pianos in South America and Australia, the instruments could be exchanged for much needed wool and nitrate.[13]

These fortunate circumstances simply made a necessity somewhat more convenient, in the view of those who went to war to make the world safe for democracy. Was not music essential to the war effort? Did not music support virtues that were the foundation of American society? Did not the American piano industry play a major role in that society? Indeed, in the summer of 1918 Charles S. Whitman, governor of New York, congratulated the music industries for their efforts to get music "over there" to the boys. "There is no one doing more for the comfort and happiness of the land than those who are supplying the means and instruments for the expression of music of the human heart."[14] The nation's president supported this position enthusiastically. "The man who disparages music as a luxury and non-essential is doing the nation an injury," Woodrow Wilson admonished. "Music now more than ever before, is a national need. There is no better way to express patriotism than through music."[15]

The policy of allowing the American piano trade to continue "practically undisturbed as an essential" had worldwide repercussions. The United States became the new leader in the production and sale of pianos. Before the war Germany held 90 percent of the world piano trade. The Music Industries Chamber of Commerce estimated in 1918 that the United States had captured at least 75 percent of the trade. Because England, France, Germany, and Canada had curtailed production during the war, American piano manufacturers filled the demand for music in both foreign and domestic markets. The player piano was especially important in this trade. The total production in England, France, Germany, Italy, Sweden, and Canada amounted to only 65,000 pianos in 1917, whereas American production exceeded 300,000. The United States replaced Germany in the lucrative markets of Chile, Brazil, Argentina, and Australia, which amounted to about $18 million gained in total piano trade. The American piano industry now was exporting to sixty-seven countries, with Australia the primary customer, Spain the second, and Cuba, Argentina, Mexico, Peru, and England next.[16]

Because of the new worldwide popularity of American pianos, and especially of players and perforated rolls, a National Piano Manufacturers Association bulletin announced that the industry had to operate at "full capacity" to keep up with the demand. Fifty-three percent of the instruments sold by 1919 were player pianos. Europeans especially liked the automatic instrument because it helped spread American dance music. So important was the piano trade that the U.S. Labor Department Training Service developed a training course of instruction in piano making, with a concentration on players and pneumatic actions.[17] It was apparent to almost anyone in the business that America was on the verge of an era of unprecedented music appreciation.

An American Musical Renaissance

The Great War was instrumental in developing music as a unifying experience in the United States, and in securing a change of attitude toward the use of music in public education. The Music Supervisors National Conference, founded in 1907, was especially effective in promoting music study in

American public schools. During the war, the supervisors established an Educational Council, which spent three years studying the prospects for musical instruction. Cooperating with the Music Teachers National Association, their 1921 report presented outlines for a standard music course in the schools and for training public educators. This was important, according to the 1920–22 *Biennial Survey of Education*, because most conservatories were "woefully weak in educational content."[18] The report not only indicated the growing prestige of music as an educational subject, but fostered a move to give high school credit for "outside" (private) music lessons as well. Successful experiments were carried out in Pennsylvania, Ohio, Maryland, New York, and Texas. In addition to orchestral and band instruments, piano became the subject for class instruction in many schools, frequently at school expense. The 1921 investigation noted that such instruction had "now passed the experimental stage" and was being recognized as "a valid feature of public instruction in music."[19]

These changes also resulted from the efforts of the American piano manufacturers. In 1917 *The Outlook* magazine praised them as "pioneers in introducing the American public to good music." For decades, piano companies had been building and maintaining concert halls, securing performances by the finest artists, and arranging "excellent free programmes" for the benefit of anyone interested in the piano. Such free demonstrations directly helped piano students hear and be inspired by the best music. "This work has greatly encouraged the general use of the piano in the home," *The Outlook* maintained.[20] The Music Industries Chamber of Commerce—the conglomerate organization representing the entire music trade—having achieved government recognition of the industry as an essential during the recent war, set for itself a new purpose: to broaden the influence of music in work and play. Specifically, this meant encouraging the teaching of music appreciation in American public schools. The efforts of these industrial leaders were fueled when Secretary of Labor James J. Davis stated that he totally agreed with such a program. "There should be a musical instrument in every school room," said the secretary in an interview with *The Music Trades* in 1923. "[N]o education can really be considered complete without music training."[21]

The efforts of the Music Industries Chamber of Commerce and the music supervisors' and teachers' associations notwithstanding, the organization crucial to developing musical appreciation in the United States was the National Bureau for the Advancement of Music.[22] Historians and musicologists have ignored this multi-dimensional organization almost completely. Founded as a non-profit institution in 1916, the bureau was the brainchild of Charles Milton Tremaine, who sought to establish a central office from which to direct the spread of music at a time when Progressive reform and the threat of war underscored the moral and unifying value of music. Tremaine had entered the piano business as a young man with William E. Wheelock & Co., New York piano manufacturers. While with the Wheelock firm, Tremaine also became the president of the Bacon Piano Company (New York) in 1904. Tremaine left the piano manufacturing business to become the director of the National Bureau for the Advancement of Music, which he had organized in New York in September 1916. His efforts were subsidized by the musical instruments manufacturing industries (collectively organized as the MICC), particularly the piano trade, who saw in Tremaine an important ally in their effort to create a musical democracy in America.[23]

Addressing the Music Supervisors National Conference in 1918, Tremaine said that he had designed the National Bureau for the Advancement of Music to overcome "the present limitation in the musical culture of the United States [which] is due to the methods of the past." Furthermore, it was vital to spread music to the masses because of the pressing war situation. Therefore, the bureau must appeal to both children and adults. Central to this appeal was the development of the Music Memory Contest and National Music Week.

Tremaine told the supervisors that the idea for the memory contest had resulted from his playing a game with his children on the family player piano. This had aroused their curiosity about music. His children had gone on to take lessons and had even asked to attend concerts. Tremaine had then planned a wider application of the game. The first public "Music Guessing Contest" had been held in October 1916 in the public schools of Westfield, New Jersey, with the aid of player pianos, phonographs, and mothers playing the chosen pieces on school pianos. The bureau had given prizes to the winning students able to guess correctly the various titles and composers. The experiment had been a complete success and had rapidly become popular. Within five years the Music Memory Contest had swept over the entire country. Tremaine proudly noted that by 1927, about 1,500 cities and towns were holding the contests, some of which were conducted under the auspices of state departments of education. "No single project has received more hearty endorsement than has been given the music memory contest on the part of school music teachers," wrote Edward Bailey Birge, professor of music at Indiana University, in 1928. "The music memory contest has the distinctive merit, when well administered, of enlisting the participation of a greater number of persons, including children and parents, than any project promoted by the public schools." With its community appeal, the contest "brings the school and the home together in a single musical interest."[24]

The war situation and the "missionary service" (in Tremaine's words) of the National Bureau for the Advancement of Music "to bring about a wider understanding of the value of music" built another institution in American cultural life that would last for decades: National Music Week. "Music Week is a suggestion, as contrasted with an imposed project," wrote Tremaine, "and its spread has been due far more to public responsiveness to the idea than to any campaign." The bureau promoted Music Week not only for the general benefits an appreciation of music would bring, but also for music's more specific "missionary service"— assistance in industrial production, therapeutic use in hospitals and clinics, and contribution to social unity. "All three have something in common, for all are based ultimately upon the demonstrated powers of music over the nervous system—soothing, stimulating or steadying as the need may be. . . . and they have implications of the greatest importance for the statesman, the teacher, and the parent."[25]

The first public mention of National Music Week had appeared in an editorial in the February 17, 1917, issue of the *Music Trade Review*. Tremaine had announced that the newly formed National Bureau for the Advancement of Music was planning to inaugurate the event in New York; but there had been no immediate response. "I felt that the National Bureau was too new an organization at that time to take the initiative," Tremaine wrote later. The idea remained dormant for two and a half years.[26]

The first recorded observance of a music week was in Boise, Idaho, in May 1919. But the daily press and music trade journals gave the publicity to an apparently very successful Music Day in Dallas, Texas, on September 30, a celebration initiated by a local music teacher and the Dallas Music Trade Association. St. Louis and Sharon, Pennsylvania, observed a Music Week in November, but the catalyst for a national observance of Music Week was the celebration held in New York later the same year. As secretary of the National Music Week Committee, Tremaine directed the program to be a demonstration to the rest of the country. The committee's records showed that ninety-two cities and thirty-seven states received news items and information, in addition to the 4,300 inches of publicity given in New York City papers. The newly elected president, Warren G. Harding, endorsed New York's event in 1921.[27]

By 1923 fifty-six cities were holding Music Week celebrations, and the following year the National Music Week Committee reported that 847 cities participated. President Calvin Coolidge accepted the chair of the Honorary Committee of National Music Week (which also included forty state and territorial governors) in 1924, the year marking the first synchronized national observance. Local advisory boards and committees consisting of musicians, city officials, businessmen, club women, clergy, social workers, educators, movie house directors, concert managers, and even the Girl Scouts and Boys Scouts worked with the National Music Week Committee and the National Bureau for the

Advancement of Music to promote and organize the event beginning each year on the first Sunday in May. Public schools conducted essay contests on music, and school orchestras and bands competed for prizes. Over forty organizations, including the National Federation of Women's Clubs, the Federation of Temple Sisterhoods, the Rotary Club, the Inter-Racial Council, the Caruso Foundation, and the Music Industries Chamber of Commerce promoted or staged musical events ranging from major concerts in armories to small recitals in private home and programs in settlement houses. Lectures, contests, factory "sings," and open-air concerts all were part of National Music Week's attempt to uplift the music appreciation of the masses. The movement underscored the belief that art, especially music, inspired civic betterment and served as a deterrent to crime as it inspired youth to beauty and morality. "It is not high-brow stuff," reported the *New York Times*.[28]

Understandably, the Music Memory Contest became an integral part of National Music Week. Peter W. Dykema, a University of Wisconsin professor of music, reported a number of national efforts to the Music Teachers National Association in 1924. Music critic Sigmund Spaeth was director of the contest for American Piano Co., using the famous Ampico reproducing piano as the medium. Similarly, Franklin Dunham was in charge of Aeolian's program, using of course its own Duo-Art reproducing piano. Tremaine directed the contest using a newer, farther reaching, revolutionary technology—the radio.[29]

By 1927 C. M. Tremaine's National Bureau for the Advancement of Music could boast a long list of accomplishments. National Music Week was observed in 1,400 cities and towns, the Music Memory Contests in 1,500, outdoor Christmas carol services in 2,030. In addition, the bureau had published 3,624 news stories reporting musical activities. Furthermore, Tremaine had written 16,849 letters to music supervisors, music clubs, boards of education and school superintendents, chambers of commerce, women's clubs, parent-teacher associations, music teachers, colleges, universities, conservatories, libraries, orchestras, bands, community service organizations, playground and recreation organizations, churches and clergy, organists, mayors, governors, civic music associations, and music merchants.[30]

Tremaine emphasized that his organization worked for the promotion of music for public benefit in a manner similar to the way the Agriculture Department fostered agriculture for public benefit. (Massachusetts congressman George Holden Tinkham had submitted a bill in the House "to create a Department of Fine Arts," in January 1924, but this move to sanctify Tremaine's work with official recognition was for the time being locked in the House Committee on Education.[31]) "Picture to yourself what you think a government department of music should do, and you will not come very far from a mental conception of what we are trying to do," Tremaine told the music supervisors.[32] To this end the National Bureau for the Advancement of Music helped schools secure the appointment of music supervisors, aided the local or state organization of music teachers' associations, assisted in developing community music programs, and provided materials for lectures and presentations on musical subjects. It promoted musical opportunities among Boy Scouts and in hospitals, labor unions, prisons, and other institutions. It established public concerts under municipal auspices and distributed 125 different pamphlets prepared in response to the needs of music teachers and supervisors. The bureau promoted college credit for music taken at the secondary level, and encouraged the formation of school bands and orchestras by working with the Committee on Instrumental Affairs of the Music Supervisors National Conference. "We provide the means to procure ... a hearing to those anxious to promote music in any locality," Tremaine declared.[33]

In addition to the important work of the bureau to foster music appreciation among children and adults through the Music Memory Contest and National Music Week, Tremaine joined with the piano manufacturers[34] to convince administrators of the need to institute class piano instruction in the public schools. Here, the bureau was building upon the progress already made by the National Federation of Women's Clubs, the National Federation of Music Clubs, and the Music Supervisors National Conference. These groups, and especially the piano manufacturers, encouraged the creation of a democracy of music lovers in America to replace the select group of cultured, middle-class young ladies or proficient virtuosos, who had survived the severe Klavier Schule, which was still the standard among private teachers. Such a philosophy was new, however, and was certainly a product of the age of mechanical reproduction. As recently as 1903, the Department of Music of the National Education Association had reportedly been "shocked" when Samuel W. Cole, professor of music at the New England Conservatory, had supported teaching music in public schools, with the goal of creating a musical atmosphere in America, in every home. Cole had suggested that teachers should teach children to love music, not to become experts.[35]

By 1914 the means to create a musical democracy were widely popular: the player piano, phonograph, and movie theater. More than ever before, music was in the air, and concerned groups sought to extend the benefits of music to everyone. That year, U.S. Commissioner of Education Philander P. Claxton wrote: "Music should be democratic in the truest and best sense. This it can never be until it becomes an integral part of the education given in the schools of all grades, . . . [and] after the beginnings of reading, writing, and arithmetic, music has greater practical value than any other school subject."[36] The fundamental importance given to music by government, corporate, private, and civic organizations in winning the World War accelerated this trend. "The reacting effect educationally," wrote Professor of Music Edward Bailey Birge in 1928, "was the unqualified acceptance of music as a major subject on the part of both school authorities and the taxpayers of the nation."[37]

Much of this concern with music education was rooted in the combination of traditional beliefs about the moral value of music and distress over the social changes accompanying modern life. This was the basis, for example, of *The Etude* magazine's "Golden Hour Plan," which received such widespread support in the 1920s, including Commissioner Claxton's endorsement. *The Etude* offered the plan "as a remedy for our country's greatest peril, the lack of training in character-building," which had resulted because " . . . American ideals, industry, steadfast honor and love of right have faded before the noxious cheap cigarette, hip pocket flask, sensuous dances, putrid magazines, and sensational moving pictures." Public school and music teachers "all have a grave responsibility" to stimulate nobler traits, to prevent moral chaos and combat rising American crime, by using music as the binding and essential background for inspirational talks, readings, and programs. "The American home of yesterday has been auctioned off at the block for an orgie of golf, gasoline, dancing and moving pictures—all valuable and important diversions when not carried to excess," *The Etude* commented. "There is no way in which the music worker can render higher service to our country at this time than by working to inaugurate this ideal [the Golden Hour Plan] in his own community."[38]

Although the development of school bands and national music contests was also an important component of this phenomenon, class piano instruction was especially significant. Many families already owned a piano, and a 1922 survey revealed that one-fourth of all children above the third grade were taking private piano lessons. But private teachers were expensive, and therefore exclusive. "What would it mean to our city, to our schools, if all these children were trained to play the piano!" exclaimed Charles H. Miller in the January 1924 issue of *School Music*. "Here is a means for making a city musical that is within the power of any supervisor to use if she has the determination, the initiative and the will to organize. It need not cost the city anything."[39]

In 1928 the Subcommittee on Class Piano Instruction of the Music Supervisors National Conference issued a report declaring that every American had a "Right to a Musical Education" through class piano in the public schools.[40] Working closely with the music supervisors' and teachers' national associations, Tremaine issued booklets to assist the cause. Among them were *Piano Class and the Private Teacher, Piano Class Instruction*, and *National Survey of Piano Classes*. Bureau statistics show that nationwide requests from individual school supervisors for piano class information soared from 2,180 in 1928 to 13,281 in 1930. And while 358 schools reported piano classes in operation in 1928, the figure had jumped to 2,004 by 1930. The national piano dealers' association endorsed the piano class movement and sent Tremaine the names of local teachers to enable the bureau to enlarge correspondence and participation.[41] Newspapers reflected the popularity of the piano by publishing long lists of students in local piano contests. Some papers (especially in New York, Toledo, Seattle, Dallas, and Cincinnati) also provided readers with a series of instruction articles to accompany piano lessons broadcast over the radio.[42]

The decade following the World War was unprecedented in the cultivation of music for the masses. The period was, according to pianist Josef Hofmann, "a musical educational renaissance."[43] The national hunger for music led to the growth of civic orchestras, choral societies, music appreciation and class piano courses in schools, and of course, the Music Memory Contest, National Music Week, and other festivals. Harry Edward Freund, director of Music Research Bureau and editor of *Freund's Musical Weekly*, estimated that Americans had increased their spending on music education to $900 million annually by 1930.[44] Adult piano instruction in public libraries, YMCA, and YWCA facilities, as well as through the music division of the National Federation of Settlements, offered musical opportunity to those already beyond public school.[45] The establishment of a musical democracy seemed closer at hand than ever before.

The mood among educators and musical instrument manufacturers and dealers was one of confidence and optimism. "I believe the piano industry is on the threshold of its greatest era of prosperity," Corley Gibson wrote in *The Music Trades* in October 1929. With over two million children studying piano in the public schools, he urged the industry, "Let us appeal to children."[46] But by 1929, the American piano industry was already far into the most damaging economic crisis of its history.

The Decline of the American Piano Industry

The decade known as the "roaring twenties" ruined the American piano industry.[47] For most Americans, however, the 1920s were the "decade of prosperity," despite a short-lived depression following the Great War. For the first time in American history a significant percentage of the population was making more money and enjoying more leisure time than had any previous generation. With the help of the emerging advertising business, the production of consumer goods boomed as never before. Americans rushed to buy new products: wristwatches, cigarette lighters, hand cameras, linoleum. With electricity more widely available, American families could enjoy cheaper lighting, refrigerators, toasters, vacuum cleaners, and electric sewing and washing machines. Beyond comfort and convenience lay pleasure, and Americans largely filled this need by frequenting film palaces and by purchasing radios and motor cars. Mass production and installment buying helped the automobile become a national institution in the twenties, while the radio became an increasingly common addition to the American home. President Harding set the mode by installing a radio in the White House in 1922.

The president also owned another electrical gadget, one just as conspicuous and just as symbolic of the age: an A. B. Chase electric player piano.[48] Player pianos composed 53 percent of the pianos produced in 1919, and 56 percent by 1923. But unlike the motor car and radio industries, the piano trade did not continue to prosper; indeed, 1923 was a peak year. For the A. B. Chase Company—"an honored name . . . closely associated with the love and development of music in the home"—and hundreds of companies like it, the decade of the 1920s was an "age of excess" and a "new era" only in a very negative way. Annual production of player pianos alone fell almost 86 percent from 1923 to 1929, while the total number of pianos manufactured in 1929 was only 35 percent of the 1923 figure. This amounted to a $67.3 million loss in value for the industry. There were 191 piano makers in 1919, but only 81 by 1929—and then came the devastating depression of the 1930s.[49]

Even as late as January 1926, however, *The Music Trades* still agreed with Secretary of Commerce Herbert Hoover's report that prosperity was the name of the day. Yet that same year, the Music

Industries Chamber of Commerce and its component organizations[50] held serious business conventions to analyze worsening trade conditions. For the first time since their founding, the annual trade conventions ceased to be merely social functions, as piano makers and dealers put most of their energy into questions of business.[51]

The change had been gradual. In 1922 the *Harvard Business Review* advised that, "Since the player piano apparently has a future," then despite the considerable cost, the hypothetical "Procter Piano Company" should undertake player piano manufacture in order to capitalize on the great popularity of the mechanical instrument.[52] Like most other American businesses, unfortunately, the music industry—especially the piano trade—was in a slump during the postwar recession of 1921–1922. Industry leaders were uncertain of the causes.

The National Piano Manufacturers Association (NPMA) dismissed the theory that the market had reached a saturation point, for "according to the best available figures," there was only one "usable" piano per ninety people or eighteen families. Neither could price be the problem, since prices had fallen generally, and piano companies were using long installment terms with a low down payment (ten dollars), spreading small payments over three to four years. In addition, the piano trade had contributed significantly to the National Bureau for the Advancement of Music, which was awakening a very strong interest in music across the United States. Yet, the piano business was worse off, despite "liberal and progressive" newspaper advertising of about two million lines annually. Confusing the matter further, the wartime boom in the phonograph industry also had fallen flat, but sales of band instruments, harmonicas, and ukuleles were growing. The NPMA formed a special committee to investigate "What Is the Matter with the Piano Business?" and to promote a cooperative national advertising campaign among manufacturers. Its "not over-ambitious" goal was to double the sales of 1922 (which still would only equal those of 1913).[53]

In an effort to stimulate player piano sales in 1923, manufacturers and dealers launched a joint, industry-wide promotion.

With the help of local dealers, instruments were placed in select households on a trial basis during Player Piano Week. In another celebration, Aeolian honored its president of twenty-five years, Harry B. Tremaine, by staging International Duo-Art Week in November 1922. Duo-Art concerts were held worldwide. Walter Damrosch chaired the Tremaine Tribute Committee of 100 distinguished musicians to arrange the event, which included performances of Paderewski's "Minuet," marking the Polish pianist's return to the concert stage.[54]

The National Association of Music Merchants (formerly, Piano Dealers) was happy to report that with the aid of such promotions and consistent advertising, 1923 was a very successful year. "Instead of the usual slump during the months of December, January, and February, the sale of all musical instruments continued firm every month in the year . . . [and] it is noticeable that in 1923 there was a distinct absence of the former dry months." Indeed, the National Piano Manufacturers Association reported that over 343, 000 pianos were shipped, making 1923 the second most productive year in the industry's history, and the most successful for player piano sales. Fifty-six percent of the pianos manufactured were automatics (although expensive reproducing pianos comprised only ten percent of sales). "It is very gratifying," said NAMM secretary M. J. Kennedy. "It puts the music industry on a basis similar to banking or any other stable industry that does business 365 days a year."[55]

And yet, more and more piano manufacturers were in financial difficulty, closing up, or being taken over by the larger corporations. The music industry had always been "a good business for a few," according to the trade epigram. But as the decade progressed, even those few found themselves fighting for survival. "The Piano Trade Is Now on Trial!" declared *The Music Trades* in late 1926. The journal scolded its readers that except for the national advertising of a few manufacturers, no one was doing anything to stop the two-year downward spiral. "The piano business today stands at the cross roads of its long and notable career. . . . Action is the watchword now! It was never so plainly needed as it is at this time."[56]

The National Piano Manufacturers Association devised a hopeful solution: the Piano Promotion Plan, which was presented in the December 11, 1926, issue of *The Music Trades*. The goal was to educate the public to the importance of having an *active* piano in the home, and to promote group piano instruction in the public schools, as group instruction was "one of the most forceful means ever devised to promote sales in the history of American business." Thus, leading manufacturers, though not abandoning the player piano (automatic instruments were still valuable tools for spreading music to the masses and developing music appreciation), undertook a campaign to emphasize the rewards of playing music oneself. They did not, however, encourage the traditional Klavier Schule method still honored among the majority of private teachers. Music industry leaders, ever innovative, instead promoted the new philosophy of group instruction emerging in the public schools, which stressed the joys of music rather than the discipline of technique.

The Piano Promotion Plan required the cooperation of the National Bureau for the Advancement of Music with the piano manufacturers', music merchants', piano travelers', piano tuners', and music publishers' associations. Together they would underwrite a vigorous magazine and newspaper advertising campaign. Piano-playing contests and extensive assistance from retail dealers were also essential components of the program. NPMA's Piano Promotion Committee would work closely with piano teachers, women's clubs, and parent-teacher associations to generate or increase the demand among children and their parents for group piano instruction in the schools. With additional influence from the Music Supervisors National Conference, which already had a close relationship with the National Bureau for the Advancement of Music, music educators and school superintendents could be convinced to begin or improve a group instruction program.[57]

Although T. M. Pletcher (of the famous perforated-roll manufacturer, Q.R.S Music Co.) had been urging some step of this kind for the past five years, the NPMA had devised and adopted the piano promotion plan only in the past summer. Fortunately, the financial condition of the NPMA was healthy, which allowed the promotion committee an annual budget of $200,000 for the next three years. NPMA president Max de Rochemont stressed to the 1926 convention that the piano trade had to follow the promotional examples of other industries, such as the "Say it with flowers" campaign that the florists had designed so successfully. Too many needed piano salesmen were being won away to other industries by such extensive publicity, Rochemont warned. Something had to be done.[58]

Reflecting their Victorian values, the designers of the Piano Promotion Plan approved advertising focused on four ideas: the home, mother, the child, and the piano itself. They also enlisted the aid of music notables, such as Walter Damrosch, who agreed to make statements about the piano's necessary place in American society. Beginning in December 1926, the promotion committee ran national advertisements in nine magazines: *Good Housekeeping, Ladies' Home Journal, Better Homes & Gardens, The American Magazine, Children, The Etude, Parents' Magazine, McCall's,* and *Modern Priscilla.* Each ad included a coupon requesting information about group instruction in public school. By June 1927, NPMA president E. R. Jacobson happily reported that almost 3,000 people had responded, and that 9 million messages on the piano had been circulated. The committee planned 9 million more for the next six months.[59]

Music merchants and piano dealers throughout the country endorsed the activities of the Piano Promotion Committee of the NPMA. The piano manufacturers in turn praised the work of the National Bureau for the Advancement of Music and the help of the Music Supervisors National Conference in encouraging group instruction of music in the schools. So successful were the committee's efforts in reaching public attention that in early 1928 the NPMA also formed the Committee for the Advancement of Piano Study, whose membership included conductor Walter Damrosch, Mme Schumann-Heink, Harvard professor Walter R. Spalding, and Syracuse dean H. L. Butler. It would take the same approach as the promotion committee: using extensive magazine and newspaper advertising and editorials, and enlisting the aid of music dealers and teachers, piano tuners, music clubs, women's clubs,

Rotary and Kiwanis clubs, and piano playing contests. By urging piano instruction in colleges as well as in public schools, and promoting simpler, more *enjoyable* piano instruction, the Committee for the Advancement of Piano Study hoped to sustain the massive music appreciation movement already underway. Yet despite the efforts of the music trades, even C. M. Tremaine was forced to acknowledge a "gap between [the study of] music in schools and music in homes."[60]

Contemporary business leaders correctly recognized that the American piano industry lost trade and prestige during the 1920s because of alternative forms of entertainment, especially radio, movies, high-fidelity phonographs, and motor cars, but also because of the endless new variety of housewares, appliances, and furnishings, clothing, toiletries and cosmetics, sporting goods, jewelry, and other products offered for sale. They failed (as have historians) to attach these developments to larger changes in the culture, however. As the traditional function of the home was transformed from production to consumption following the rise of industrialization and urbanization, tension developed between the reality of the home and its ideal. Thus, the home ceased to be a refuge. Furthermore, by loosening the bonds of family life, business was able to dominate this sphere. Architecture reflected this change: by the 1920s homes grew smaller as the productive capacity of the family decreased. Rather than make products at home, families went out and bought them.[61] The demise of the piano, long considered the center of the productive home, was inevitable as this transformation occurred. Moreover, since piano manufacturers and dealers chose to emphasize automatic pianos rather than traditional ones, they accepted the values of an industrial world that was denying the importance of creative skills, a world paying lip service to old preferences but stressing their uselessness in the modern age. Again and again piano ads of the 1920s offered liberal trade-in allowances for "outdated," "silent" pianos in exchange for modern automatic ones.

This move was unfortunate, for it reduced the appeal of the piano to the level of its next great rival, the radio. In mass society, one cultural artifact is easily replaced by another: a consumer culture quickly abandons the last technological marvel when a newer one offering the same vicarious experience appears. The rise of the radio (and to a lesser extent the improvements in the phonograph) doomed the piano trade in ways it never understood. Radio beat the player piano at its own game: it was billed as a "miracle of science," it provided unlimited entertainment, it was available in fashionable ("piano-finished") cabinets, it was very easy to use. But in addition, it was cheap—far less in price than even the least expensive player piano. So, the piano industry lost the canned music market.

This suggests that the piano trade, however ignorant of the destructive quality of consumerism or impotent to withstand its assault, was in some way responsible for its own predicament. Scholars have given little attention to possible failings within the industry itself. Their analyses, which see the slump as a product of outside forces, ignore the serious flaws in the manner in which the industry conducted its day-to-day business. While it is doubtful that reform within the piano business would have prevented its decline in the wake of the consumer culture, certainly the descent could have been slowed, and perhaps even halted.

The person who most affects sales of musical instruments was and remains the retail dealer. With few exceptions, musical products have always been sold face to face, one at a time. Dealers, however, largely neglected to stress the benefits of music and the quality of their products (the elements that manufacturers stressed most intensely in their national advertising), preferring instead the short-term strategy of price-cutting. "The word 'sale' in the music industry is the weakest attraction in our vocabulary," admonished *The Music Trades*. Anniversary sales, inventory sales, seasonal sales, damaged-merchandise sales, all accompanied by clichéd slogans, peddle merely a product at a price. "The dealer who can offer only pianos offers the general public NOTHING."[62]

The retail piano business had also been plagued since the nineteenth century with unethical sales methods and bait-and-switch advertising, and had acquired a reputation similar to the time-worn caricature of the used-car salesman. In the intense competition for sales, customers were told that the piano case was made from timber cut from "our own forests," that synthetic ivorine keys were genuine ivory from "our own elephant farms" in Africa or "ranches" in India, that the sounding board was made of "Stradivarius violin spruce," the hammers of "camel's hair," the stringplate of "bell-metal steel," and the strings of "silver." "It was for the buyer to decide which of the ... stories was nearest to the truth," reproached one manufacturer.[63]

When such sales methods were coupled with the inferior quality of many stencil pianos or low-grade, mass-produced "thump boxes," the result was that the average buyer, who generally was ignorant about pianos in the first place, was misled easily and frequently by glib salesmen. "Do not listen to the honeyed words of the salesman," advised *The Etude* magazine, which often ran articles informing its readers of ways to purchase a *reliable* piano. "Do not be fooled by snide advertisements of conscienceless dealers." *The Etude*'s solution? Buy the best well-known, brand name piano one could afford from the most reputable dealer.[64]

Nor were music teachers and musicians a safe source of information, since "there are those ... who are subsidized by dealers whose recommendations are guided by sordidness rather than a sincere desire to assist the buyer in securing the best piano he can afford." Indeed, many teachers (dubbed "commission hounds" by dealers) supplemented their incomes by taking their customers not to the best affordable piano, but to the store offering the biggest commission—which was commonly the result of a fictitious inflated price in the first place.[65] Teachers further contributed to the decline of the industry with their adherence to poor and outdated teaching techniques descended from the Klavier Schule. The sad result was that 54 percent of all piano students stopped within three months, and 94 percent quit before they attained a third-grade proficiency. Publishers' statistics reflected this trend: 80 percent of all music sold was of first-grade difficulty. Educator Otto W. Miessner interpreted this to mean that the industry was killing off 80 percent of its customers each year, and was moved to cry, "The profession has been infested with parasites, quacks and charlatans."[66]

In addition, for decades progressive manufacturers had argued that encouraging music lessons would increase instrument sales. Such was the basis for the NPMA's Piano Promotion Plan. Yet, the majority of retailers scorned any personal effort to offer piano lessons through their own stores, took little or no personal interest in the musical activities of their communities, and considered teachers as competition for profits rather than as allies in the promotion of culture. Real profits came from selling stencil pianos, which could be marked up 100 percent, then often repossessed on the slightest technical violation of the contract. Much of this excessive emphasis on price rather than music stemmed from ignorance. Frank L. Wing of Wing & Son deplored the dealers' limited knowledge of music and pianos, which consisted of "the few desultory and misleading notions which they are able to pick up in the course of their business."[67] But until the late 1920s and 1930s, the trade associations offered little help in educating salesmen to sell music rather than pianos at a price.

This general ignorance was even more widespread in player piano sales. *The Music Trades* estimated that 90 percent of all dealers did not know enough about the mechanical player. "They dump it in the houses as a grocery deliveryman dumps sugar or coffee," with no instruction and no follow-up. All the salesmen did was put in a roll, get the customer to pump the pedals, and say, " 'That's fine—wonderful tone; Just sign here—you're a real musician!' "[68] The trade press continually admonished dealers to sell players on the basis of producing fine music and cultivating a democracy of music lovers; but few salesmen took the trouble to learn these techniques. Most were content to stress how easy the machine was to play and let the novelty of automation sell itself, rather than to educate themselves to their market by learning about music and composers, building a profitable library of perforated rolls or even acquiring the proper technique of operating the expression devices in order to make the piano sound less mechanical.[69]

Piano tuners often told dealers that their customers marvelled at how "real" the mechanical player could sound when played correctly. Alfred Dolge warned as early as 1909 that proper execution at the player piano required "not only practice, but earnest and intelligent study to learn the use of expression and accentuating devices, and more especially to master pedalling." Ten years later Robert Haven Schauffler, writing in *The Delineator*, sadly related, "There are more than a million player-pianos in America, and less than five hundred persons who can play them well. This means that 1,999 of every 2,000 . . . are played badly. Such mistreated instruments are a menace both to the art of music and to the business of selling mechanical pianos."[70] Indeed, potential sales in a neighborhood were often killed by someone who was not taught or did not care to learn the methods to do justice to the potential of the player piano. "No wonder people want something that will take real music from the air," F. A. Hurd lamented in *The Music Trades* in 1929.[71]

Like retail dealers, most manufacturers of player pianos were guilty of stressing the automatic nature of the instrument at the expense of its musical possibilities. Roy E. Waite, editor of *Piano Trade Magazine*, noted in 1933 that the profession had been "set back almost a generation in that specialized form of piano-selling which creates amateur musicians." Manufacturers and especially dealers destroyed the incentive to learn to play, which had formed the whole basis for the traditional market. The trade offered the mechanical player to the public as a means to create music *in spite of* the unpopularity and high failure rate associated with traditional piano lessons; and in this it succeeded—until the high-fidelity phonograph and the radio furnished virtually the same vicarious experience in a smaller, more attractive cabinet at a much cheaper price. "Your daughter is learning the piano?" asked a cartoon character appearing in *Life* magazine in 1927. "No, the phonograph—it makes less noise and is easier to move to the country."[72]

In addition to unscrupulous sales techniques, indifference to music appreciation, manufacture of poor quality instruments, and an unhealthy concentration on the player piano, the industry hurt itself further in its failure to provide the public with new product designs compatible with changes in furniture fashion and home architecture. Furthermore, by offering its product as a lifetime investment, the trade saturated its market, unlike the automobile business, which thrived on the annual model. This naturally led to a huge business in used pianos, which helped undercut the new piano market, especially given the disposition of most dealers to stress price. "What a mistake it is for dealers to educate the public down to cheap prices and make them believe that they can get a really first-class instrument for $300 or less," *The Music Trades* criticized as early as 1894.[73] The economic health of the trade was also jeopardized by the common but unhealthy policy of accepting ridiculously low down payments and monthly payments extended over long periods of time, and liberal trade-in allowances on piano purchases. In 1924 the trade press called the "trade-in problem" the "worst evil in the music industry," which cost an estimated seven to ten million dollars a year in lost revenues. With approximately ten million pianos in use by 1926 throughout the United States, the secondhand piano represented a significantly greater hazard to new instrument sales than the radio ever did.[74]

Nevertheless, radio remained the acknowledged culprit in the decline of the American piano industry. The meteoric rise in popularity of this most symbolic phenomenon of the emerging consumer culture also unsettled many private music teachers, who were convinced that such easy access to music would undercut any desire to learn to play. The marvel of the radio was irresistible "once one starts to radioize," reported *The Etude* in February 1923. The whole country was going "radio mad."[75]

Radio Music for Everybody

Few observers could have been as prophetic as David Sarnoff, when in 1916, the future president of Radio Corporation of America urged American Marconi Company to market "a simple 'Radio Music Box,'" a plan that "would make radio a 'household utility' in the same sense as the piano or phonograph."[76] By the time President Herbert Hoover called upon his Research Committee on Social Trends in 1929 to provide a review of recent national developments and "epoch-making events," the effects of the radio were very familiar. The president's study nevertheless listed 150 such effects, from "the penetration of the musical and artistic city culture into villages and country," to "widens gap between the famous and the near-famous." "It hardly seems necessary to try to prove such statements about the effect of the radio as that 'a new recreation has been provided for the home' or 'music has been popularized,'" the report affirmed. "These statements are obvious."[77] It was also obvious to many that radio's success apparently was undermining the phonograph, sheet music, and piano industries.

The music trade did not always view the radio as an adversary, however. Just as dealers had held no fear about the mechanical player supplanting the straight piano, many in the piano industry saw the radio as another means of stimulating musical knowledge. When the music trades held their 1925 Silver Jubilee convention in Chicago, they featured a conspicuous radio exhibit, but most salesmen considered the device just another musical instrument. Indeed, a survey of seven hundred music stores revealed that six out of ten dealers in the United States sold radio sets in addition to musical instruments. In the spirit of the Jubilee's slogan of "Make America Musical," the piano industry embraced the radio in its effort to create an American musical democracy, with the hope of stimulating sales of musical instruments.[78]

"The radio and phonograph should not be regarded as rivals of the piano but rather regarded as a means of increasing its popularity," proclaimed a Cable Company spokesman in 1928. These devices, together with the reproducing piano "should have the effect of making people want to produce their own music—to play for themselves."[79] George C. Foster, president of the mammoth American Piano Company, agreed. If the radio could awaken an interest in many who formerly were indifferent, the inevitable result would be a desire to make music. Quite naturally, the instrument choice would be the piano.[80] To aid this awakening, American Piano urged radio listeners to tune in to the "Ampico Hour" Thursday evenings on station WJZ to hear great artists "play" the Ampico reproducing piano.[81]

Aeolian's famous concert hall and office building at 29 West 42d Street, New York, was headquarters for RCA and Brunswick radios, which were displayed on showroom floors together with the pianos. The building also housed stations WJY and WJZ, and on February 12, 1924, premiered *Rhapsody in Blue*, with George Gershwin playing the piano with Paul Whiteman's orchestra. The concert, which Whiteman called "an experiment in Modern Music," was supported by Leopold Stokowski, Walter Damrosch, Sergei Rachmaninoff, Jascha Heifetz, and Fritz Kreisler, and brought much attention to Aeolian and RCA. The "Panatrope," a music-reproducing machine that could "compete with living artists" (developed through the combined efforts of RCA, General Electric, Westinghouse, and Brunswick-Balke-Collender) made its 1925 debut in Aeolian Hall as well. In 1927 the piano company sponsored a national music essay contest in connection with recitals broadcast over the WEAF network each Wednesday night. The prizes included an expensive Weber Duo-Art reproducing grand, a Steck grand, a Stroud upright, and cash awards of fifty dollars each.[82]

Steinway & Sons sponsored concerts broadcast through RCA over stations WJZ, WRC, and WGY, featuring conductors Walter Damrosch and Willem Mengelberg, and recitals by Josef Hofmann and Mme Schumann-Heink, among others. And in 1925, when the Steinways moved their hall uptown to 109 West 57th Street, they celebrated with reportedly "one of the finest radio concerts ever given in America," with Hofmann the principal artist. By 1929 Steinway Hall housed radio station WABC, complete with the Steinway piano specially voiced for broadcasts.[83]

Like the Aeolian and American Piano companies, the House of Baldwin sold most major brands of radios (and phonographs) through its many dealers. By late 1929, however, Lucien Wulsin II decided to retain only four "standard well advertised lines," including RCA, Atwater Kent, and Victor, in order to make room for the expensive new Baldwin-made Hamilton radio. But merely selling and manufacturing radios would not help the ailing piano trade. "The more we can impress the steady increase in the use of the piano and the serious study of the piano on the general public, the quicker we will overcome the feeling among many people that the piano is something of the past," Wulsin wrote. To this end, the

Baldwin Company used the new medium to inspire the public to a greater appreciation of the piano as essential in the home. Each Sunday evening (beginning in February 1929 over WJZ and the National Broadcasting Co. network) a distinguished musician was featured on a half-hour program in an effort to remind those listening of how the piano enriches life, of its importance in the family circle. Using a novel approach, the announcer appeared as a host welcoming "friends and neighbors [to] an informal home musicale. The featured artists were guests of honor in the home." Schedules and program information appeared in the radio program column of local newspapers throughout the country. The Baldwin Publicity Department furnished local dealers with advertising copy coordinated with the firm's intensive national campaign. The "At the Baldwin" program became the most popular of its type on the air, and Wulsin soon extended the program to an hour's length. In a few months the company received enough letters of response, all of them positive, to fill six folders fully. The radio press "generally agreed" that Baldwin's success was "unprecedented," and that it "took from the start" without any elaborate campaigning. "If there is a radio heaven, I was in it during your wonderful hour last night," wrote one listener. "We wished our 'Steinway' was a 'Baldwin.' "[84]

In the June 1, 1930, issue of the *Musical Courier*, "veteran musical editor" William Geppert, acknowledged national authority on the piano business and author of the series *The Official Guide to Piano Quality*, analyzed Wulsin's triumph. The Baldwin piano's tone was unexpectedly "carried over the air with a purity, receiving sets considered, to a degree that was unapproachable. So the Baldwin time was accepted with eagerness by the people all over the country." The promotional technique was not unlike the "old-fashioned way of placing a piano 'on trial in the home,' " or using the medium of concert auditoriums. Combining time-honored piano publicity methods with modern radio technology "was a bold stroke in music," Geppert stressed. "That beautiful Baldwin tone now is heard by millions in the homes where pianos are or should be."[85]

Although an increase in Baldwin sales was a direct result, the program also helped the entire industry. "The policy of the Baldwin concerts is in keeping with the general object of 'Music Week,'" expressed the *Christian Science Monitor*, "since it is intended to encourage by audible example the practice of playing at home instead of merely listening." Indeed, an "At the Baldwin" program was designated for the official closing of National Music Week, which in 1929 was observed in more cities and towns than ever before.[86]

When Henry C. Lomb reviewed the school music program for *The Music Trades* in 1929, he asserted of the radio and musical instrument industries that "far from being rivals for the public's affection, they are natural allies in every sense" for the purpose of transmitting music. (Indeed, at least one enterprising piano manufacturer offered a "Radi-O-Player," a player piano with built-in radio.) Together, they were elevating American musical sensibilities. Radio audiences increasingly requested classical music (by the mid-twenties only 5 percent preferred jazz, according to two surveys), symphony societies grew in number, and music publishers like G. Schirmer reported unprecedented sales of classical music in 1925.[87] The radio seemed to be working wonders.

Music educators throughout the country praised Walter Damrosch's lecture-concert radio series, broadcast each Friday morning to high school and college classrooms over the WJZ network through RCA's Music Education Bureau. Beginning in October 1928 and running for fourteen years, the program became one of the most popular on the air. Tens of millions of school children and young adults were encouraged to a greater appreciation of music as a regular part of their school week. Rescuing (in Damrosch's opinion) "at least ninety-eight percent of our school population" from an unbalanced life without a proper music appreciation in such a materialistic world, the conductor declared, "The radio has proved itself as the great democratic leveller and uplifter. . . . its entry into our schools marks a new era in the dissemination of education." But, he warned, the programs "were not to be a substitute for local instruction, but primarily to stimulate the love and interest in music and thus to encourage the children in self-expression through their own school singing and orchestras."[88] By 1931 Olin Downes, music critic for the *New York Times*, was moved to proclaim that the radio had brought to America "a new musical era," in which music was no longer the exclusive privilege of a few but the common property of all. And everyone would be elevated because of it.[89]

But the radio, despite its magic, its proven success in furthering music appreciation, and its promise in aiding the creation an American musical democracy, was increasingly blamed for the souring conditions in the music industry. "The Ragtime Queen Has Abdicated," was the headline of a story in the *New York Times Magazine*; the infectious piano music had been killed by the radio. E. C. Mills, chairman of the board of the Music Publishers' Protective Association, reported that sheet-music sales of popular tunes were down by one-third in 1924. Formerly, a sheet-music hit would sell for months, as fascination with it slowly swept across the country. The radio, although stimulating sheet-music sales for a time, familiarized the public with a hit song in only a few weeks, by which time most had grown tired of the ever-present strains. "It's that Gal in Kalamazoo don't buy sheet music," Mills said. " 'Try this over your piano' is a dead slogan."[90]

Figure 5.1 illustrates the sad fate of the piano industry in the "prosperous" 1920s. Total production had reached record levels even during the World War, and despite a critical falling-off period during the postwar recession, a peak was again achieved in 1923. Upright piano production was greatest in 1909, while player manufacture crested in 1923. The decline thereafter was rapid, although the development of the baby grand offered some promise. Throughout the 1920s many manufacturers reduced the size and price of grands, and produced baby grands in fashionable furniture styles. As figure 5.2 shows, these pianos dominated the grand trade. Roy E. Waite, editor of *Piano Trade Magazine*, contended that in this market pianos were bought as furniture rather than as musical instruments, especially given that baby grands were musically inferior to parlor grands or even high-grade uprights. And despite their attractive styling, these small grands still cost consid-

Figure 5.1. American Piano Production, 1909–1929

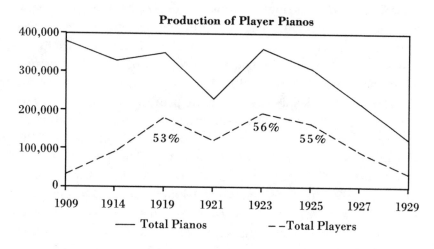

Production of Player Pianos

—— Total Pianos   – –Total Players

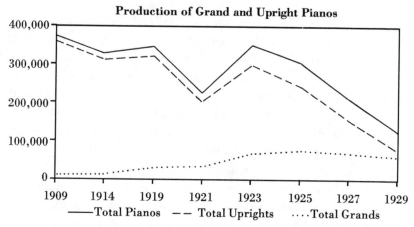

Production of Grand and Upright Pianos

——Total Pianos   – – Total Uprights   ····Total Grands

erably more and occupied much larger space than the upright, which unfortunately remained stylistically similar to its towering Victorian predecessor.[91]

Nevertheless, industry leaders took courage as quality instruments, especially full-size grand pianos, continued to sell, perhaps as a result of the industry's increased music appreciation campaigns, such as the NPMA's Piano Promotion Plan and the radio concerts sponsored by Steinway and Baldwin. Steinway & Sons enjoyed tremendous sales in the Christmas seasons of 1927

Figure 5.2. Upright and Grand Piano Production by Type,
1919–1929

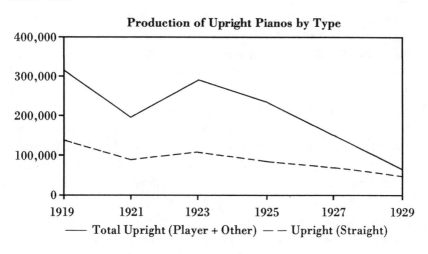

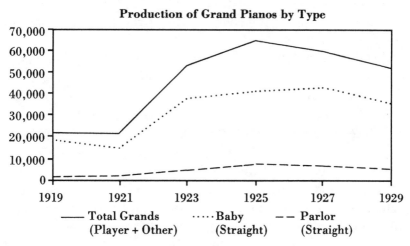

and 1928, although 1926 remained the year that shattered all
records. Baldwin shipped more high-grade grand pianos in the
last four years of the decade than in any other period of its history.
Despite this success in grand piano sales, however, Baldwin's total
sales had declined steadily since 1926. In 1929 the company found
itself operating in the red for the first time. This spiral continued
downward until 1935, forcing the company to survive on the pre-

cious reserves that D. H. Baldwin and Lucien Wulsin had so carefully had built up.[92]

The last three years of the twenties proved even more damaging
to the giant American Piano Company. Piano men attending the
firm's annual theater party and supper dance at the Casa Vincent
Lopez during the summer trade conventions of 1926 hardly could
have envisioned their impending financial despair. As the largest
manufacturers and distributors of pianos in the world, the company enjoyed enormous sales of mechanical players. Indeed,
American Piano stock was so attractive that the Rudolph Wurlitzer
Company acquired about 26 percent of the holdings—an investment which brought the Wurlitzers a dividend of $45,717 in 1923
alone.[93] Adverse conditions attributed to the radio, however,
caused American's player piano business to collapse. By 1928 the
company showed an operating deficit of $235,000, and its no-par
common stock dropped to 12¾ from its 1927 value of 43¼. The
last dividend paid on the common stock was in October 1927, on
the preferred in April the next year.[94]

Chronic financial reverses forced American Piano into voluntary receivership in 1929 (negotiations with Wall Street syndicates
for control of the company had been underway since late 1927).
Though American Piano was solvent, Irving Trust Company was
appointed receiver in equity for lack of ready cash to meet obliga-
tions of $1.2 million.[95] In an effort to reduce expenses, the new
president, George Urquhart, radically changed company policy.
He closed eight of the twelve factory retail stores, and combined
into a single dealership the sale of American's three great pianos:
Mason & Hamlin, Chickering & Sons, and Knabe. This automatically eliminated two dealers in each community, caused much
anguish, and led to the loss of advertising dollars. To the further
dismay of the piano trade, Urquhart combined some of the manufacturing plants, which then no longer kept the time-honored
names distinct. The luster of the old names were diminished further when the new management concentrated on prices in its
advertising. These efforts did reduce American Piano's expenses
by about $2 million by January 1930. But *The Music Trades* decried

the methods. "The piano business is one peculiarly based upon reputation," the journal declared. The injury resulting from Urquhart's consolidation plan was "incalculable." Bankers, ignorant of such nuances, should leave the piano industry to its own business.[96]

To that end American Piano Company was reorganized in the spring of 1930. The holders of preferred stock purchased the company from Irving Trust, issued new stock, and formed the American Piano Corporation under Delaware law. The holding company's founder, George G. Foster, became the new president. One of his first moves was to sell Mason & Hamlin to Aeolian, Weber Piano & Pianola Co., which no doubt saw "old M & H" as possible salvation for its own deteriorating condition. Aeolian had been operating in the red since 1929 as well. The prestige of the Mason & Hamlin piano, once Steinway & Sons' biggest competition, irreversibly withered among musicians, however, as Aeolian proceeded to manufacture the piano in its George Steck & Co. factory (which was really the original Hallet & Davis plant). That summer American Piano Corporation was able to pay its creditors fifty cents on the dollar, although production steadily decreased. Like the other manufacturers still surviving in the trade, the company continued to operate at a loss as it lumbered into the Great Depression.[97]

From 1923 to 1929 the industry as a whole suffered a production loss of $67.3 million at manufacturers' prices (retail value would be about double this figure), of which $49.8 million represented player and reproducing pianos.[98] The National Lumber Manufacturers' Association reported in 1928 that although piano production was down by 60 percent, the loss was absorbed "several times over" by the demand for radios.[99] Indeed, radio production and sales skyrocketed from 190,000 units in 1923 to almost five million in 1929. *Radio Retailing* affirmed that 6,500,000 receiving sets were in use by 1927, and that the radio audience had quadrupled when the speaker replaced the earphone. As J. Andrew White prophetically observed in *The Etude* in 1922, there would soon be "radio music for everybody."[100]

The 1920s had begun promisingly enough for the piano trade. With a product essential to the war effort, American makers had continued production uninterrupted and had captured the world markets. Manufacturers and dealers had concentrated on the mechanical player. They had seen it not only as the logical means to a musical democracy, but also as salvation for a market they considered saturated with conventional pianos—automatic pianos would appeal to both new and old customers. The returning clientele common in the motor car and furniture trades was rare in the piano business because a family hardly ever bought more than one instrument in a generation. The industry had promoted permanence, not obsolescence. The player, then, was considered a boon to the piano retail trade. It would give dealers the opportunity to keep selling merchandise: music rolls, player actions to convert traditional pianos already owned, and electric pumping units to modernize old foot-operated instruments. The piano roll industry helped sustain sales by offering wide varieties of music marketed for adults, fraternal and religious organizations, teenagers, and even toddlers.[101] The sale of mechanized pianos would disseminate the art of music, make it available to far greater numbers of people than ever before. This would encourage a musical appreciation that the piano industry hoped would benefit society through the virtues of music, as well as benefit their business.

With the possible exception of the coin-operated trade, however,[102] the market for the player piano was stagnant by 1925. The premiere of sound movies in 1927 quickly destroyed the photoplayer business as well. And because most firms concentrated on player manufacture—some did so exclusively—the entire piano industry was on the verge of collapse when the market for players dropped. Unlike the general economic trends of the decade, piano prices, production, and employment declined, especially after 1923. The piano trade thus joined coal mining, railroads, shipbuilding, cotton textiles, the shoe and leather business, and especially agriculture as a stagnant or declining industry in an age commonly remembered as prosperous.

The twenties witnessed an acceleration of the trend toward consumerism. While society still preached traditional canons, honoring the work ethic and the moral value of hand-played music, it was following quite another set of canons. It was an age of unprecedented exposure to music via the radio, phonograph, public schools, National Music Week, music clubs, the National Bureau for the Advancement of Music, and the piano industry itself. Music was increasingly used in hospitals, prisons, schools, and industry to rehabilitate, to develop character, and to encourage good work habits. Writers in the popular press still professed the Victorian necessity of having a piano in the home, but the public was buying fewer and fewer instruments. Acknowledging this irony before the 1930 conference of the Music Teachers National Association, Peter W. Dykema concluded that people were *"consuming* rather than *producing* music."[103]

Inspectors in the tenements of New York reported in 1930 that radios were so popular among families that they viewed their pianos as "white elephants," and left them behind rather than move them. These abandoned pianos were shoved into hallways, blocking fire exits and creating what the inspectors called a "piano menace." Only fifteen years had passed since Thomas Tapper had written about a settlement house mother who had refused to sell her piano even though the money would have paid overdue bills, because the instrument kept her family together and out of trouble.[104] The "basic musical instrument" seemed lost in the new age.

CHAPTER SIX

Depression, Reform, and Recovery

*Rising Piano Sales
Point to Renaissance
of Music.*
—Business Week

THE PIANO IS
COMING BACK!
—The Baldwin Co.

*Our goal must be to
make America not
only a musical
nation but a playing
nation.*
—National
Association of
Music Merchants

In May 1929 the music division of the National Federation of Settlements reported the results of its survey to determine the musical condition of the United States. It proclaimed a "music renaissance," citing the largest National Music Week to date, the growing numbers of music clubs, music schools, and high school orchestras nationwide, and the increased participation of young people in music contests. Similar results were reported the following May, when a national poll asked participants, "Do you feel that the degree of participating in music, as distinguished from listening, by the people of your community has increased or decreased in the last five years?" The overwhelming majority—86 percent—thought that participatory music had increased. This renaissance was attributed to the National Music Week, the growth of public school music and music clubs, and the radio, which was "causing more people to talk about music."[1]

Yet, the American piano industry was still in a severe downward economic spiral; bankruptcies continued, production declined. Ironically, much of the country's new musical awareness resulted from the efforts of industry leaders to sell their pianos in a culture now attuned to listening rather than to making music. These efforts included sponsorship of concerts and recitals on the radio, and more importantly, support and development of National Music Week, of radio instruction in music, and of class piano in public school. The crucial support for this movement came from the National Bureau for the Advancement of Music (subsidized almost entirely by the industry until 1930), the Music Industries Chamber of Commerce, the Piano Promotion Plan of the National Piano Manufacturers Association, and of course, the extensive national advertising of individual firms.

Because radio had apparently replaced the player piano, the task was clear to trade leaders: to convince their market of the need to perpetuate the producer ethic in a consumer culture by encouraging active music making. "Our goal must be to make America not only a musical nation but a playing nation, because music appreciation derived from listening to music alone is not enough," admonished the National Association of Music Merchants in 1931. "True and complete music appreciation requires actual participation by the individual in the playing of a musical instrument."[2]

As the surveys revealed, the efforts of the industry had some success. America seemed to be becoming more musically productive. An increased musical awareness developed in many an urge to play. Some firms even reported that the downward slide had leveled off as sales of straight pianos continued to rise. Huge stockpiles of unsold player pianos, however, reminded manufacturers and dealers alike of how treacherous fad and obsolescence could be in a consumer culture. Yet, there appeared to be salvation in the traditional piano market. While the radio, phonograph, and automatic piano could develop an appreciation of music and even inspire the desire to make music, each was also an agent of consumption, not an instrument of expression. "I look upon the increase in demand for 'straight pianos' during a period of overwhelming preponderance of ready-made music as an unmistakably healthy sign," proclaimed Hermann Irion of Steinway & Sons in 1929. "The piano is no longer regarded merely as a desirable piece of furniture nor as a necessary adjunct to comparative social prestige. It symbolizes the cultural aspirations of the home and with the widespread introduction of piano instruction in our public schools ... no American home will remain long without its piano."[3]

The presidents of the Music Industries Chamber of Commerce and the National Association of Music Merchants agreed. Pianos and sheet music now were more in demand nationwide, and there were more music students than ever before. The combination of the effects of radio and the efforts of the music trades and music educators was clearly developing among the public a taste for music, stimulating a need for an appreciation of music, and creating a desire for self-expression. Still, the piano industry was suffering a ruinous decline, primarily from the collapse of the player-piano market, although sales of straight pianos were also declining (Figure 5.2.). The paradox confounded industry leaders. But whatever trend may have been developing, in 1930 the piano industry saw its business collapse still further as a depression began to affect the economy much more seriously than did the stock market crash the year before.

Toward the Slough of Despond

The disheartening business conditions within the music industry during the "prosperous" 1920s provided the impetus for leaders to share successful sales plans and unite in their support for piano instruction in the public schools. In the spring of 1929, the National Association of Music Merchants officially committed itself to obtaining government recognition of the fine arts in America, forming a committee chaired by Frederick P. Stieff, head of the Charles M. Stieff Piano Co., Baltimore.[4] This was only the latest effort of the trade to promote music in the United States, however. The Music Industries Chamber of Commerce and the National Bureau for the Advancement of Music had been among the first supporters of the movement to establish a national conservatory and a Department of Fine Arts by act of Congress.

Though the movement had been stuck in committee since 1917, the music industry and fellow supporters[5] continued to press the government to help "make the United States independent of the other nations in music and art, and to make the United States a great center for music in this hemisphere."[6] Originally a patriotic extension of the effort to exert international influence during the Great War, this move to obtain government recognition of the arts—to establish music's necessity to the nation's welfare— served the music industry equally well as a stimulus to business. After all, the rationale for the bill to establish a national conservatory was to produce "a broader rather than a higher culture in music, more lovers of music rather than more musicians, more understanding rather than more technique."[7] Was this not also the basis for the trade's venture to establish a musical democracy through the player piano?

While the player reigned as the primary disseminator of musical culture, the industry grew fat and overly confident in its future, and neglectful of its traditional market. But as radio became the most important piece of furniture in the living room, the trade found itself coping with bewildering cultural and economic changes that had reduced the number of firms to eighty-one by 1929. Industry leaders, trusting that salvation lay in cultivating the amateur musician, embarked on one of the most carefully planned and elaborate promotions of their history. The trade press encouraged all "wide awake dealers" to use a specially produced National Music Week stamp on all correspondence. Leading manufacturers sponsored radio concerts and lent pianos to public schools to help educators promote group teaching methods. National advertisers sought to inspire a greater appreciation of the piano as essential in the home and family circle, and as an enrichment of life in general.[8] Significantly, the Piano Promotion Committee of the National Piano Manufacturers Association redoubled its three-year intensive campaign to bolster piano study and sales.

Launched in 1927, the NPMA's Piano Promotion Committee, together with the Music Industries Chamber of Commerce and the National Bureau for the Advancement of Music, urged unification within the trade and among dealers. The collaborators recognized radio as an important ally, but stressed through advertisements and publicity articles in almost every major American magazine and in more than 2,000 newspapers that people must *use* the piano to reap the real benefits of music. By 1930, fifteen of the largest U.S. magazines freely gave editorial support, and class piano instruction was given a decided boost in national popularity. "The piano manufacturers and the Music Industries Chamber of Commerce are doing their utmost," stressed Edward C. Boykin, executive secretary of the NPMA's Piano Promotion Committee. "It remains for the dealer to drive the point home."[9]

Furthermore the Chamber, whose purpose was to promote music as well as develop and protect the commercial interests of the industry, combined with U.S. Fidelity and Guaranty Co. to institute a collection department to collect outstanding debts on members' accounts. For fiscal year June 1930 to May 1931, 111 claims were filed by 35 companies in the amount of $25,000, and $9,978, or 39.8 percent, was collected. The organization helped raise needed funds for the NPMA, the National Association of Music Merchants (NAMM), and the National Bureau for the Advancement of Music by issuing a 50¢ piano stamp on grands and uprights and a 75¢ stamp on reproducing grands. Such efforts supplied 78 percent of the $45,000 the National Bureau spent from June 1930 to May 1931, the remainder being contributed by the Carnegie Foundation. So successful were MICC fund raising efforts that RCA asked the group to help finance public awareness programs for piano on the radio.[10]

Berthold Neuer, vice president of Wm. Knabe & Co. (part of American Piano Co.), told the music merchants' association in 1930 that the industry had grown spoiled by the period of easy sales during and following the Great War. Dealers had stressed price, decoration, pride of possession, and social status to the point that "we've lost sight of the piano's strongest appeal—as a musical instrument." Ironically, the industry's new sales campaigns *did* succeed in making America more musically productive; but the public overwhelmingly chose *secondhand* pianos to express themselves. The sales of used pianos were impossible to document, though they were estimated to exceed new piano sales by three to one, with perhaps 300,000 to 400,000 sold in 1929 alone. Although some of this activity represented the forced sale of possessions among hard-hit families, it still offered tangible proof that a constant market existed and that the public was responding to promotions by the music trade that stressed the benefits of making music. While this may have produced a more musical America (given the nature and varying quality of used pianos, any conclusions should at best be cautious), the trend did nothing to help manufacturers of new instruments. Still, the public seemed willing to accept the music industry's new focus on producing rather than merely consuming music.

But given the immensity of choice in the emerging marketplace, with so many other amusements, products, and experiences offered, the public apparently was interested in only a minimal investment in the creative musical experience. Secondhand pianos, whose boxy, towering Victorian designs were virtually identical to new ones, would suffice. Thus, there seems considerable justification for assuming that the used piano rather than the radio was now the trade's real competition. Both the NPMA and the NAMM urged local dealers and shops to destroy all used pianos that could not be sold for more than $100, but many chose to ignore this suggestion in favor of immediate sales. Thus, production continued to decline and firms went bankrupt until merely fifty establishments manufactured only 51,370 pianos in 1931.[11]

In an effort toward improved efficiency and increased funding, the National Bureau for the Advancement of Music—the most significant agency stimulating music interest in the United States—was reorganized in 1930. C. M. Tremaine, the founder, remained director; but the organization was no longer to be a subsidiary of the Music Industries Chamber of Commerce. Now it fell under the direction of a committee of nine: three representatives of the music industry (Lucien Wulsin of Baldwin, Hermann Irion of Steinway & Sons, and Alfred L. Smith of Conn Instrument Co.), three representatives of the Music Supervisors National Conference, and three from the philanthropic foundations aiding music: the Juilliard Musical Foundation, the Eastman School of Music, and the Carnegie Foundation. Ever industrious, Tremaine continued to push love of music as a vital part of social life and to cultivate a desire to give this love expression through class piano, choral instruction, and band.[12]

Gordon G. Campbell, president of the piano manufacturers' association, tried to remain optimistic in the wake of worsening economic conditions. He asserted that the banking end of the piano business was more secure in its collateral than were New York real estate mortgages. In reality, however, the anxiety to force sales led to an indiscriminate issuing of credit and a lowering of retail prices and monthly payments to the extent that many people who were induced to buy instruments were unable to afford the purchase at all. The result was innumerable repossessions, extensions of payments over four or even five years, and increased bankruptcies by companies finding themselves short of capital. This economic unhealthiness was already common enough by

1927 for *Life* magazine to publish a cartoon in which a wife tells her husband, "The piano man was here to collect to-day and he said unless he got the payment to-morrow they would take the piano." "How much is it?" her husband asks. "Eight Dollars," is the reply. "Let him take it. We can Get a new one for five dollars down." Campbell even tried to see benefit in this tragedy, noting that undesirable manufacturers and dealers who "have been progressing without the guidance of a profit sense so necessary to good business activity" have been eliminated. And with a good market for straight pianos developing, plenty of skilled workers, reasonably priced materials, and good dealer organization, the "future of [the] piano business is secure."[13]

But that security was questionable, as the Music Publishers' Protective Association dropped the price of sheet music from forty cents to twenty-five cents a copy to induce sales, as some dealers began to accept wheat payments for pianos, as sales of used instruments threatened to undermine the potential new piano market, and as the strongest firms in the trade continued to operate in the red.[14] Baldwin's sales continued to fall, and its losses in 1931 reached a record $1.56 million. Theodore E. Steinway was forced to shut down the Steinway & Sons factory in 1931, with 2,100 unsold pianos in stock. It remained closed for two years. The temptation to diversify must have been great, but the firm's president twice refused one-million dollar offers to lend the Steinway name to radios and refrigerators. In 1932 he even was forced to sue a Bronx organ company for using "Steinway" as its brand name.[15]

Similar dilemmas did force most other companies into outside diversification. Kimball, for example, began to sell appliances, radios, phonographs, laboratory and office furniture, and "merchandise and personal property of every kind and description." Wurlitzer tried to compete in the furniture and refrigerator business to obtain fresh revenue.[16] Other houses made clock cases, coat racks, toys, and tennis racket frames. Reportedly, some companies even turned to the manufacture of boats, toilet seats, and caskets. Almost without exception, however, these ventures were unsuccessful, causing firms to suffer losses into the millions of dollars.[17]

The music trade joined other manufacturers in a plea to Presi-

dent Hoover to aid the country's industries with a two-year postponement of government prosecution under the Sherman and
Clayton antitrust acts. Such a move would enable the trade to
formulate agreements and redress improper credit sales and inadequate prices. But Hoover on "general principles" feared to
leave the public unprotected, though he was open to suggestion.
He also believed that radical changes might result in unwanted
government regulation of industry. He remained inclined to do
little.[18] This image of passivity convinced many of the need for
change and led to the election in 1932 of an apparent man of
action, who promised the music industry and the rest of depression America a "new deal."

Under the Blue Eagle

The National Industrial Recovery Act, one
of the major pieces of national economic legislation passed during the Franklin Roosevelt administration's Hundred Days, was
authorized to establish an industrial code system to restore economic prosperity. The National Recovery Administration, or NRA
(June 1933–January 1936), was the federal agency in charge of
administering the codes, which were to control pricing, production, trade practices, and labor relations. As enacted, the bill sus-
pended antitrust laws for two years and authorized industrial organizations, usually trade associations, to formulate codes that
would secure for each industry fair competitive behavior and labor practices. Under the leadership of General Hugh S. Johnson,
formerly a member of the War Industries' Board, the NRA Blue
Eagle emblem became the familiar sign of patriotism and loyalty
to the New Deal policies of recovery. Practices for most major
industries were codified by the end of 1933, and more than 540
codes were eventually written and approved.[19]

The Code of Fair Competition for the Piano Manufacturing Industry was the ninety-first such code and was among the larger
ones that Franklin Roosevelt approved on November 4, 1933. En-
forced by the NPMA Piano Code Authority, it covered approxi-

mately 3,800 employees, a work force that had decreased 85 percent since 1923. It did not serve as an umbrella code for the entire music industry. The musical merchandise, band instrument, pipe organ, and music publishing industries each had their own codes of fair competition, and covered another 6,500 employees. In addition the retail code authorities oversaw the distribution of instruments and merchandise to consumers, the most influential being those of the NPMA and NAMM.[20] Historians have demonstrated that many of the individual codes were as controversial as the NRA itself. The code for the piano trade, which hitherto has received no attention among scholars, was certainly so. Arguably it was a failure, yet contributed positive benefit. It reputedly improved conditions, though apparently instituted little change. Like all others it was declared unconstitutional and abolished January 1, 1936, but trade leaders fought to continue its programs.

The effort to establish a code authority was not the first attempt in the music trade to organize for relief during the hard times. In the fall of 1931 Aeolian president W. H. Alfring created five work groups to solicit relief funds throughout the industry, from the piano manufacturers to the music publishers. But such efforts hardly surmounted the problems of unfair trade practices and overextension of credit, which by 1933 had reduced the number of piano manufacturers to thirty-six. Equally alarming, the mammoth American Piano Corporation, which had been reborn from its own ashes in 1930, was again in the red despite having paid all the debts formerly incurred and showing a profit its first year. Aeolian, which had become a subsidiary of International Holding Co. (Garwood, New Jersey) also lumbered along, and continued to operate at a loss despite its reorganization and closing of factory retail branches.

The two giant piano conglomerates merged in 1932 because Aeolian was heavily invested in American Piano stock and the consolidation eliminated costly parallels. Although the new Aeolian-American Corporation maintained separate sales organizations, factory operations were combined. The former president of American Piano, George C. Foster, had already found it necessary in 1930 to standardize the parts of his seven major companies, thus removing any "essence of individuality" that had distinguished the various brands. Upon the merger of Aeolian and American, President William H. Alfring consolidated the manufacture of all twenty brands now under his control into the East Rochester factory. Nevertheless, Aeolian-American continued to operate at a loss until 1934.[21]

"The Mighty Wurlitzer" Company also found itself in trouble because of a lack of liquid capital. In addition to the destruction of the player piano market (in which it was heavily invested), Wurlitzer had suffered the loss of substantial photoplayer and theater-organ sales upon the emergence of "talkies" after 1927. Unsound sales policies and heavy investments in real estate and other companies had also burdened the firm's working capital. In 1927 corporate reserves had been depleted further when Rudolph H. Wurlitzer, a son of the founder, was forced to order the company to buy $4.2 million in stocks from his brother Howard, who had insisted on withdrawing from the firm after an uneasy relationship between the men had become unbearable. By mid-1934 the giant Rudolph Wurlitzer Co. was owned by six different banks, the largest of which sent R. C. Rolfing to reorganize the faltering corporation. Rolfing already enjoyed a reputation in the radio and agriculture trades for successfully salvaging businesses. In this latest effort he consolidated piano manufacture into one factory, closed all but ten factory retail stores, liquidated many investments (including a great deal of real estate and the Wurlitzer radio, furniture, and refrigerator manufacturing businesses), and with Farny Wurlitzer,[22] concentrated on production of the coin-operated phonograph. The company eventually achieved success once more, but the House of Wurlitzer ceased to be essentially a family business after 1934.[23]

The two men destined to carry the piano industry through the trials of the depression headed perhaps the strongest firms left in the trade. Leading promoters of music appreciation, Lucien Wulsin II and Theodore E. Steinway had already used the strength and reputations of their companies to provide invaluable benefit to the entire music industry during the difficult 1920s. With the onslaught of the depression, they were determined not to let their beloved trade perish—or their preeminence within it. Given what was at stake, they naturally assumed the leadership role.

Lucien Wulsin, a Harvard engineer, had joined Baldwin upon the death of his father in 1912. Serving as treasurer and later vice president, he had become president of the firm in 1926. A meticulous person, a perfectionist, he was a strong businessman, very autocratic, very proper. He and his wife enjoyed riding to hounds with the Camargo Hunt, of which the Wulsins were charter members. "To me, to get on a horse is a complete relaxation," he told his Harvard fiftieth class reunion. "If I am tired or worried, the best cure is to go out for a ride." He smoked cigars, cared little for pleasantries (though he enjoyed the chance of playing chef or host), and was opinionated and outspoken. "Theodore," he would bellow to his good friend, the president of Steinway & Sons, "tonight we will go to the Carleton for dinner."

In addition to running the Baldwin Co., Wulsin became one of the three representatives of the piano industry serving on the newly reorganized National Bureau for the Advancement of Music in 1930. The following year he became first vice president of the National Piano Manufacturers Association, and he assumed the presidency in 1932. He centered his program on preserving the overburdened organization, "if only in the shape of a name, office, address, telephone number and stationery testifying to the fact of its continued existence." In 1933 he was elected chairman of the NPMA Piano Code Authority and was one of the three members of the Code Drafting Committee established under the Roosevelt administration's NRA Code of Fair Competition for the Piano Industry. In addition, Wulsin was appointed as representative of the piano trade on Roosevelt's Council of the Durable Goods Industry.[24]

Theodore E. Steinway was a music lover first and a businessman second, though he was the kind of president who could build a piano himself if he were put to the test. He was musically informed, and when not guiding Steinway policy he was acting in amateur theatricals or poring over his extensive stamp collection. Steinway was a man of exquisite taste, but of a very American rather than European refinement. A soft-spoken man, he paid attention to both business and art in a sensitive manner. Proud and sentimental, he chose as his home after his marriage the apartment house built on the site of the first Steinway factory.

The new president worked under a double burden. He had the misfortune to take charge of Steinway & Sons just at the moment of business decline in 1927. Secondly, his father was the exemplary William Steinway (1835–96)—the man responsible for cultivating the aura of the Steinway name. The pressure of living up to his beloved father's reputation and having to deal with adverse business conditions tormented him severely. Nevertheless, the modern look of Steinway & Sons was essentially Theodore E. Steinway's handiwork, reflecting his own particular elegance, style, and artistic taste.

He was able to inject "the Steinway logic" into the NPMA's Piano Promotion Committee and the reorganized National Bureau for the Advancement of Music through Hermann Irion, the Steinway representative in both organizations. In 1933 Theodore Steinway joined Lucien Wulsin and NPMA secretary Harry Meixell as a member of the NRA Piano Manufacturing Code Drafting Committee and also the NPMA Piano Code Authority. In addition, he served as chairman of the NPMA's Code Authority for the Retail Code (which oversaw the distribution of pianos to the consumer), serving with W. H. Alfring (Aeolian Company) and Harry Sohmer (Sohmer & Co.).[25]

The piano trade associations, primarily the NPMA and especially the NAMM, had long promoted solidarity and fought abuses within the industry, such as unfair retail pricing, fraudulent and bait advertising, and more recently, the sale of used pianos that could not bring at least $100. In this sense the industry had anticipated the NRA by adopting its own code even before the New Deal. The Code of Fair Competition submitted by the NPMA (which claimed to represent 90 percent of the industry) was essentially the code by which the trade association already operated in order to control the disastrous economic crisis of the 1920s. During the June 1933 trade conventions, some members argued that the pending NRA code was unnecessary if only the industry as a whole would adhere to its trade practice rules and just "act fairly to each other." The NPMA, however, pledged to cooperate "in every way" with the NRA board and Gen. Hugh Johnson, and with Secretary of Commerce Daniel F. Roper.[26]

The NPMA Piano Code Authority members were elected on August 21, 1933, illegally so, in the opinion of Deputy Administrator Robert M. Davis, since they were chosen three months before the actual approval of the code itself. Nevertheless, on January 30, 1934, the NRA approved the piano manufacturers' code authority: Lucien Wulsin, chairman (president of NPMA and the Baldwin Co.), Theodore E. Steinway (Steinway & Sons), W. G. Heller (Winter & Co.), Charles H. Wood (Wood & Brooks), Eugene A. Schmitt (Hardman, Peck & Co.), and Harry Meixell (secretary of the NPMA and Music Industries Chamber of Commerce). Four were NPMA members, two were not, but each had been with his company all his business life. The only appointee was Major R. B. Paddock, the NRA deputy administrator, who was in charge of the music industries until he resigned in March 1934.[27]

After hearings in September 1933 the Piano Manufacturing Code that Wulsin, Steinway, and Meixell drafted received President Roosevelt's signature practically in the form originally submitted. "This Industry has cooperated in a most satisfactory manner with the Administration," Hugh S. Johnson informed the President. Wulsin asserted that the code passed so quickly because it was "truly representative of the whole industry."[28] The most belabored objection involved the basic wage. The NRA's minimum wage was forty cents an hour. Even though almost 78 percent of wage earners already were making that or more, many makers advertising their pianos as "the product of artisans" were employing workers at thirty cents an hour. *The Music Trades*, long the voice of the industry, asked dealers not to handle the pianos of such manufacturers, but instead, to "sell a piano worthy of your retail reputation."[29] The new document empowered the code authority to "require and receive sworn or unsworn reports" of wages, hours of labor, conditions of employment, and number of employees, as well as production, shipments, sales, stocks, and prices of pianos on a weekly basis. There was no provision of confidentiality.[30]

Secretary Meixell admonished the trade that the code "will not *ipso facto* give . . . markets and profits," which come largely from "hard and conscientous endeavor." Likewise, Lucien Wulsin, who by now had become a commuter from Cincinnati to New York to Washington, D.C., asserted that the code would not produce increased sales. For that "we must fight hard collectively to create a greater market, and fight equally hard individually for [our] entitled share of this market." The manufacturing code and the retail trade code would provide the needed incentive and "clean house of many unfair and uneconomic practices" as well. He urged that breaches of both codes be reported conscientiously.[31]

Despite this apparent unity in support of the NRA, the regional director of the Compliance Office and the deputy administrator were quick to inform Roosevelt that all was not well. Just as the automobile industry's adherence to NRA policy was impaired by the feisty independence of Henry Ford (who refused to sign the automobile manufacturing code or even talk to President Roosevelt), so did the piano trade have its maverick. Like Ford Motor Co., the W. W. Kimball Piano and Organ Co., Chicago, was one of the largest and most powerful firms in the industry. And like Henry Ford, C. N. Kimball refused to cooperate with his code authority—but particularly with Lucien Wulsin.[32]

A favorite with his uncle, W. W. Kimball (founder of the company), Curtis Nathaniel Kimball was for many years the firm's top salesman and was made a vice president in 1898. He became president in 1905 upon the death of his uncle. Although responsible for such innovations as the Kimball phonograph (1915–25), he was much influenced by his uncle's conservative, old guard executive staff that insisted the company follow long-established patterns of business. C. N. Kimball was widely known both within and outside the trade. *Piano Trade Magazine* called him one of the "most conspicuously successful figures" in the trade, a man "revered and respected . . . [but] in no sense a mixer." Throughout his thirty-one years as president of reportedly the largest manufacturer of affordable pianos in the world (he would die in 1936), he was a renowned conservative. The piano-trade paper *Presto-Times* asserted that his conviction sometimes caused him to be "misunderstood." Indeed, Kimball's cautious conservatism was often criticized for holding the company back or for being slow to respond to changing demands.[33]

A fair, sensitive, yet brooding man, C. N. Kimball, like Theodore E. Steinway and Lucien Wulsin, had inherited the family responsibility of carrying on the work that had made his company a leader in the trade. (Indeed, W. W. Kimball Co. advertised that "more Kimball pianos are in use in American homes than pianos of any other name in the world.") Likewise, all had the misfortune to watch their industry decline in the wake of radio sales and desperate economic times. Unlike the presidents of Baldwin and Steinway & Sons, however, Kimball had little use for the National Piano Manufacturers Association or Franklin Roosevelt's New Deal, especially the National Industrial Recovery Act.

A lifelong Republican, C. N. Kimball regarded the NRA Code as anathema. He could not go along with the Roosevelt administration, whose tenet was, he said, "tax and tax—spend and spend and elect and elect." He was incensed enough on at least one occasion to tear up an income tax form handed him by an accountant, roaring, "Send 'em last year's almanac and tell 'em to go to hell!"[34] Since Lucien Wulsin appeared to be siding with Roosevelt policy, Kimball firmly resisted the code authority. Such animosity shows how very controversial the New Deal was at the time and how divided any community could become.

Beneath this political polarity, however, lay personal reasons for Kimball's estrangement from the National Piano Manufacturers Association. Wulsin, as stubbornly independent and forceful as the president of Kimball, supposedly insulted the Chicago manufacturer in a dispute over NRA protocol. Kimball left the NPMA (the firm would not rejoin the association until the 1950s) and refused to cooperate with anything Wulsin did. While the details of this feud are lost except through secondhand oral accounts, it was a major factor in Kimball's refusal to comply with NRA policy, nevertheless.[35] "Undoubtedly there was a great deal of friction between the various elements in the industry which was aggravated by the hostile attitude towards NRA by one of the largest members, namely W. W. Kimball, of Chicago," reported Deputy

Administrator Robert O. Dawson in June 1935. Dawson was apparently unaware of the reasons for or degree of this hostility. But he placed complete blame for the failure and unsatisfactory results of the piano code squarely on Lucien Wulsin, whom he saw as weak and ineffectual.[36]

From the government's point of view, the operation of the piano code probably was a failure. Kimball protested the "amount of work and expense" required to file the weekly reports of employment, production, and sales statistics that the code authority requested. He insisted that no "reasonable excuse" was given for requiring such frequent reports. As a result he refused to cooperate either in sending Wulsin reports of wages and hours or in complying with the hour and wage provisions of the code.[37] The regional director of the NRA Compliance Office reported that Kimball had a "justifiable complaint" since the early report forms were so involved. But the director added that this conflict was "merely indicative of other differences which had developed" between the code authority and Kimball.[38]

The NPMA Piano Code Authority established no compliance or statistical agencies and no local offices, and did not hold meetings for several months because of a general attitude that they would be useless while such blatant violations continued. Because the original document addressed only wages and hours—and clearly abuse of credit sales was a greater problem—Wulsin appointed a committee of three (Wood, Steinway, and Meixell), which drafted six amendments to the piano code to cover trade practices as well. They were approved in April 1934 but still required Washington's ratification. The proposed six amendments dealt with a variety of trade iniquities: lack of sound credit terms, inaccurate or bait advertising, false billing, inaccurate references to competitors, bribing of competitors' employees, uncontrolled production, the stencil piano, absence of minimum standards of piano quality, and fraudulent retail price gouging.[39]

After a month-long postponement, a public hearing on the modification of the piano code convened on September 3, 1934, in the Willard Hotel, Washington, D.C. The proposed amendments seemed "beneficial" and "excellent" to the NRA administration.

But the larger manufacturers of quality pianos felt no need to incorporate into the code practices they already adhered to, and unless Kimball was forced into compliance, they argued, any attempt to introduce provisions affecting trade practices would be a "useless gesture." Quantity manufacturers of low-priced pianos (against whom most of the provisions were aimed) "vigorously opposed" the amendments because these additions would restrict many of their selling methods. There also developed some disagreement within the code authority itself. As a result the hearing lasted less than an hour, the code authority withdrew its request for amendments and the subject was dropped.[40]

The first conference of the NPMA Piano Code Authority was not held until September 20, 1934, in New York City. Wulsin discussed with the other members Kimball's failure to send reports, and a representative was selected to try to persuade Kimball to cooperate. Acting on Kimball's complaints, the code authority adopted a new, simplified report form. Kimball still did not comply. A second meeting of the code authority took place on November 15. At that time Wulsin cited W. W. Kimball Co., Schiller Piano Co., and Jesse French Corp. to Deputy Admnistrator R. B. Paddock for failure to furnish reports, a violation of Section 2, Article VI of the code. Thus, Kimball's strength within the industry and refractory independence was able to attract others to adopt a similar position. Realizing this, the NPMA and particularly its code authority agreed that there was "no justification in going to the expense of Code Authority meetings so long as this member of the Industry was able to block any progress or attempt to cooperate with the N.R.A."[41]

This "complete failure to secure compliance" from Kimball, coupled with the unsuccessful attempt to adopt trade practice amendments and the admittedly futile meetings of the code authority gave the NRA deputy administrators enough cause to declare the piano code a failure. "The work of this Code Authority has been generally unsatisfactory," wrote Robert O. Dawson to his NRA supervisors in June 1935. He reported that, while W. W. Kimball Co. never reported wages and hours, "their general attitude would indicate the considerable probability" that they did violate code provisions (a minimum wage of forty cents per hour for a maximum of forty hours per week, eight per day). Furthermore, the conflicting elements of the piano industry (the makers of high-quality instruments, good commercial grade pianos, and quantity pianos "made to sell at a price") were never brought together. Dawson and Robert M. Davis both exonerated Harry Meixell for these failures, but placed the blame firmly upon what Davis considered "a poor choice of Code Authority members, and especially the Chairman," Lucien Wulsin. "A strong and aggressive Chairman might have accomplished a great deal for this industry," Dawson wrote. Concurring, Davis emphasized, "There is no reason to believe that these difficulties could not have been overcome if the Administration had insisted on a more competent Code Authority." Davis concluded that "the benefits to the Industry resulting from the slipshod efforts of the Code Authority to get compliance with the Code were very few, if any."[42]

Quite a different picture emerges from the piano trade's point of view. Lucien Wulsin is credited with rebuilding the National Piano Manufacturers Association under the NRA, and uniting most of the industry during very trying times. Despite the incomplete support given the NPMA Piano Code Authority, Wulsin and Theodore Steinway worked hard on the piano code.[43] In addition, the two presidents consistently and extensively advertised the general benefits of music as well as their own products. By sponsoring radio programs, stressing the need for musical self-expression, and supporting the NPMA's Piano Promotion Committee and the National Bureau for the Advancement of Music in their efforts to develop class piano in the public schools, Steinway and Wulsin buttressed the entire industry and stirred up a musical public, thereby laying the necessary groundwork for the success of the WPA's Federal Music Project.

"No matter what you think about the N.R.A., or the price of gold in London, business IS better," heralded *The Baldwin Keynote* (adorned with the Blue Eagle) in the winter of 1933. "All doubts as to the future of the piano have cleared away. You have emerged from the 'fire that tests men's souls,' with a fine, keen temper to your activities. . . . People have always wanted pianos, . . . NOW you are able to sell them." In his 1934 annual report as president of NPMA, Wulsin stressed that the NRA code had helped the piano trade considerably. "The piano manufacturers are satisfied with our code. It has brought uniform wages, erased some of the evils of our trade and has meant a betterment of our industry." Pulling together meant surviving together. The piano code was practical and therefore usable—not idealistic, he reminded members. Compared to other codes, this one was "very simple," "limited to bare essentials." Wulsin announced that with few exceptions piano manufacturers were filing their monthly shipment figures with the code authority, a reported 32,000 units in 1932, and 34,300 the following year.[44] Things looked better.

Obviously the Baldwin president was sidestepping the problems with Kimball and NRA officials. But there were positive elements to the piano industry's NRA experience. Unlike many other industries under the Blue Eagle, there was no evidence of discrimination between large and small firms by the piano code authority. Wulsin's superb abilities as seen in his success with the Baldwin Co. and the NPMA clearly demonstrate his capability as chairman of the code authority. The NPMA, apparently satisfied with his guidance, reelected him to four consecutive terms as president. Considering the talented leadership of Lucien Wulsin and also Theodore E. Steinway, who was successfully maintaining the preeminence of Steinway & Sons and infusing the NPMA with his considerable insight, it is doubtful that a more competent code authority could have been possible. NRA administrators expected compliance in an industry traditionally independent and extremely competitive.

Some idea of the real feelings about NRA policy in the music industry is evident in the early 1935 congressional hearings on the possible extension of the National Recovery Administration. The National Association of Music Merchants supported hundreds of other retail dealers in praise of the NRA, particularly the retail code authorities, and submitted a petition in favor of continuing the emergency legislation for a period of not more than two years. Francis X. Regan of Arthur Jordan Piano Co., Washington, D.C., more specifically addressed the benefits of the NRA program. He stated that the code's provisions for minimum wage and hours had improved conditions and that bait advertising had been "to a great degree" discontinued throughout the country. The NRA had been no inconvenience, but instead had given "the public and us" the opportunity to buy legitimately priced pianos at fair profit to both dealer and manufacturer.[45] Thus the NRA, while not bringing about recovery in the piano trade, offered hope and reinforced the industry's efforts to recover itself from a decade of economic backsliding. It revealed unsound business policies and provided the means to rebuild a faltering trade association.

Additional evidence supporting the positive impact of the National Recovery Administration may be taken from the industry's reaction to the Supreme Court's 1935 declaration that the NRA and its component codes were unconstitutional. By 1935 conditions looked decidedly better. No more firms had suffered bankruptcy, and the thirty-six remaining makers shipped more than 65,000 pianos—an increase of 27 percent over the previous year, 51 percent over 1933. (C. N. Kimball, in the last annual report before his death, acknowledged a recovery in progress in spite of Roosevelt.) The summer music trades convention conducted seminars ranging from "The NRA—Its Future Effect on the Music Business" to "Combatting Adverse Legislation" and "What the Motion Picture Industry Has Done for the Music Business." The NAMM hosted the largest trade show to date, and everywhere there was optimism and enthusiasm.[46]

Significantly, *The Music Trades* encouraged the entire industry to continue NRA code practices, despite the Supreme Court decision. The music publishers, band instrument makers, and sheet music dealers adopted *The Music Trades* position, as did a majority of the piano manufacturers. In fact, 80 percent of the piano makers agreed that the NRA provisions found to be "advantageous to the trade" should be maintained in their entirety. A "skeletonized" NRA report sent to *The Music Trades* indicated that the provisions of the outlawed NRA piano code were "to a considerable extent being maintained by common agreement."[47]

Whatever its failing, the Code of Fair Competition for the Piano Manfacturing Industry did succeed in bringing the diverse elements of the trade closer together, in at least revealing unfair or uneconomic trade practices, and in renewing the incentive to understand and correct the problems that had plagued the industry since 1925. Wulsin recognized that the principal cause of so many bankruptcies was "lack of sound credit control" and general ignorance of the market. The piano trade had pioneered installment buying, but ironically (and with the exception of firms such as Kimball and Baldwin), it had developed few rules governing the sound extension of credit. Lessons had to be learned from the automobile and home appliance industries in order to help eliminate repossessions and to produce profits above the cost of carrying the notes. "We need to learn when credit becomes dangerous," Wulsin told the NPMA. "As an industry we are very backward in our lack of correct knowledge as to the real size of the retail piano market and its variation." Therefore, the trade must gather statistics, conduct market surveys, and sell to a select constituency.[48]

Such were the goals for the trade that the head of Baldwin, the piano manufacturers' association, and the piano code authorities knew to be necessary for the continued success of the piano industry as a whole. Such was the basis for the ill-fated trade practice amendments to the piano code. Significantly, before the end of the decade many of these goals would become reality.

Regardless of the NRA's influence on the recovery of the music industry, however, there were two much more important factors in the upturn of events: an increase in music appreciation and music making in the United States, and the production of a new, smaller, stylish upright piano. Both represent not only the continued influence of the piano industry on American culture, but also the determination of an industry rooted in Victorian philosophy to triumph in the consumer culture.

Music and the Depression

In the eight years after his triumphant return to the concert stage in 1923 following his service as Poland's prime minister, Ignacy Paderewski happily detected a growing number of young people attending concerts. The unparalleled showman noted that they had rarely been seen in the recital halls when he first visited the country. Conductor Leopold Stokowski echoed this observation following his 1936 American tour, when he discovered larger audiences and warmer responses than in the past. "Everywhere there appears to be a thirst for music," he commented; a vast evolution in musical awareness had occurred. And he credited the radio and the depression for the phenomenon.[49]

This apparent "thirst for music" (actually a continuation of the trend that so characterized the previous decade) was not just evident in the concert halls. In an address to the Music Teachers National Association in 1931, Peter Dykema reported increasing musical participation in the community nationwide. The National Bureau for the Advancement of Music, National Music Week, the National Federation of Music Clubs, the music division of the National Federation of Settlements, and Harold Bauer's new Guild of Musical Amateurs all had been expanding their activities. Adult piano classes, which were administered through public libraries, the YMCA, and the YWCA were becoming increasingly popular, as was piano instruction on the radio. In connection with National Music Week in 1934, Irl Allison, president of the newly formed National Music Guild, held the first national piano-playing contest in New York at Steinway Hall under the auspices of his National Guild of Piano Teachers. This "tournament," as he called it, was open to students of elementary, high school, and college age, who were studying with members of the Guild. Students did not compete against each other but against a standard. Turnout was strong; reaction was very positive and encouraging. The National Piano Playing Auditions became an annual event nationwide, a splendid, still highly successful cultivation of the amateur spirit.[50]

The significance of music in the Great Depression was even more apparent in the growth of National Music Week, whose theme in 1932 was that music could relieve the present stress. The event was celebrated in more than 2,000 cities and towns and invited everyone's participation. The festival's slogan showed its democratic essence: "music of the people, for the people and by the people." President Roosevelt was head of the Honorary Com-

mittee (a position held by every president since Harding). "Discord vanishes with music," the president wrote. Music aids in "in-
culcating the spirit of good will," is "enobling," and "should be
encouraged as a controlling force in the lives of men." Music is
especially valued during the present trauma, for it "makes us
happy, better able to see values and problems in true perspective,
[and gives a] saner view of life."[51]

There were other signs of music's considerable value in hard
times. In 1934 C. M. Tremaine disclosed the results of a survey by
the National Bureau for the Advancement of Music which showed
that the economic crisis had not caused music education in the
public schools to suffer. Fifty-one percent indicated no change in
music education courses. An example of the support for music in
the schools is a public concert hosted by the Music Educators
(formerly Supervisors) National Conference in 1936 for a New
York audience of more than 18,000, including Mrs. Eleanor Roosevelt and the mayor, Fiorello LaGuardia. More than 3,500 children
from elementary and high schools performed a program of choral
and symphonic music, with Walter Damrosch as a guest conductor. Reports hailed the event as evidence of America's musical
awakening, and the mayor proclaimed that music, though once a
luxury for the few, was now a "necessary of life" to be enjoyed by
all. Ambitious radio programs complemented this increasing activity as cigarette, soap, coffee, and auto manufacturers followed
the leadership of American Piano Co., Aeolian Company, the Baldwin Co., and Steinway & Sons to sponsor symphony concerts on
the air. (The music industry's contribution to the development of
sponsored programs "in the public interest," which used radio as
a means for general cultural uplift, has not been properly appreciated.) Advertisers were learning what the public wanted, music
critic Olin Downes reported. This blossoming of musical energy
in the United States was specially recognized at the First International Congress for Musical Education at Prague, Czechoslovakia,
in April 1936.[52]

The climax of this musical awakening was the Federal Music
Project of the Works Progress Administration. Before the Great
Depression, radio and sound movies had forced thousands of mu-

sicians into unemployment. The onset of economic collapse intensified their situation, causing a 60 percent displacement (an estimated twenty to seventy thousand people) by 1934, compared to a national unemployment rate of 25 percent. Early relief was administered inefficiently under the New Deal's Civil Works Administration and Federal Emergency Relief Administration, which led to the organization in mid-1935 of the Federal Music Project as an agency of the WPA. Directed by Dr. Nikolai Sokoloff, the FMP sought to employ professional musicians, to give free concerts, and to educate the public about music. Soon musicians were taken from manual labor and reassigned to work better suited for their talents.[53]

The Federal Music Project (1936–41) could claim not only that it employed more people than any other WPA cultural program, but that it reached the most Americans as well. An extension of American nationalism, it concentrated on giving American music a long overdue hearing, and sponsored an intensive music appreciation effort in the public schools.[54] With the aid of local chapters of the National Federation of Women's Clubs and the National Federation of Music Clubs, the education division of the project brought group music instruction to two-thirds of the rural schools that had not had music education. The FMP blended well with National Music Week in the effort to bring music to everyone, to raise the culture of the United States in the same manner as had public libraries and museums and public education. Understandably, however, the Music Teachers National Association as well as unaffiliated private music teachers criticized the FMP for offering free music instruction to pupils able to pay, arguing that the government was competing with private enterprise. The Music Teachers Defense Committee gave this movement an additional critical voice.[55] Nevertheless, observers then and since have declared that the government projects rejuvenated American culture.

The musical awakening that scholars have credited to the radio, the Federal Music Project, and the intensity of the depression drew strength, as did most of the New Deal, from previous experience rather than radical innovation. The "vast new musical awakening" (Sokoloff's phrase) so apparent by the time of Roosevelt had been stimulated systematically as far back as the turn of the century by the American piano trade's early promotion of a musical democracy through the player piano. During the Great War and the 1920s, the National Bureau for the Advancement of Music and the Music Industries Chamber of Commerce had emphasized that music was essential and encouraged community participation and self-expression in music. The continuous work of the NPMA's Piano Promotion Committee, the NAMM, and such firms as Baldwin and Steinway & Sons to make America a playing nation rather than merely a listening one nourished these efforts.

The awakening was also an outgrowth of Progressive reform through the Music Settlement House, the music-in-industry movement, and the use of music as psychological therapy. Taking up the cry of "America First," it took on a nationalistic emphasis as a means of "Americanization" following the World War. The awakening benefited from the successful labor of the Music Supervisors National Conference, the National Bureau for the Advancement of Music, and the piano industry to make music a necessary part of public school curriculum. And it did respond indeed to the needs of a depression-wearied nation.

To credit the Great Depression or the New Deal with generating a musically productive America without acknowledging the efforts of the industry that had made this its business and cultural goal since the late nineteenth century is simply wrong. The cultivation of a musical democracy—however enhanced by the radio and federal music programs—was a fundamental tenet of business philosophy that was buttressed with age-old beliefs in the social, cultural, and moral benefit of music. The Tremaines, Steinways, Wulsins, Wurlitzers, Gulbransens, Kimballs, and their colleagues in the trade were patrons of culture as well as business. They cultivated sales, but concurrently sought to uplift society through their product and its characteristic bond with art. In so doing, they encouraged their society's appreciation of music. And as that society became more consumption oriented, they fought to regenerate the importance of making music and of self-expression. In this, because the consumer culture can never be wholly absorbing, they were successful.

Music for the Fun of It

The commercial activities of the piano industry had been the most powerful single source of American interest in music. The campaigns to reeducate the public to the true purpose of the piano—as an instrument of music and not just a piece of furniture or a gadget—had been successful to the extent that record numbers of children and adults were taking music lessons, and dealers were doing an enormous business in used pianos. Countless families had been forced to sell their pianos to purchase necessities during the depression; thousands of others had failed to keep up payments on instruments and suffered the humiliation of repossession. Manufacturers of new pianos were still operating in the red, but each year (following the abysmal 1932 reports) showed increasing sales. In 1933, according to Roy E. Waite of *Piano Trade Magazine*, dealers in all parts of the country seemed to agree that they had "never had the names of so many people who say they wish to buy pianos."[56]

However successful the music trade's campaign to promote the benefits of music and the satisfaction of making music, the inevitable link between the consumer's inspiration to buy a piano and the ability to play it lay not with the industry at all, but with the music teacher. As Richard McClanahan insightfully acknowledged in the popular magazine, *The Musician*, "The salvation of the piano lies with those who teach it." Otto B. Heaton of the National Association of Music Merchants expressed the similar opinion that the music teacher was "the most constructive factor in creating piano sales." *New York Times* music critic Olin Downes also believed that "sincere and progressive teaching [in] due course ... will reinstate the piano, or do much toward that end, at least for the amateur, who represents the largest and the best class of music lover." The importance of the amateur in sales of musical instrument remained in clear focus among the music industry, for it was the amateur that provided the volume market and business profits. As music educator Otto W. Miessner affirmed, "The *amateur makes the market.*"[57]

But American music educators were bitterly divided over the proper method of creating a playing public. Moreover, there was much anger among private teachers over the rise of class piano instruction in the public schools and over the free (or minimally priced) music lessons of the Federal Music Project. There was disagreement as well with the use of the radio for music education. Many private teachers approved of using radio to elevate the nation's appreciation of music through concerts, though a large number were quite opposed to broadcast music lessons. Still others saw themselves as the last bastion against the nation's "spiritual paralysis," the encroaching "back-sitting, dial-turning, let-the-other-fellow-do-it, paralyzing attitude" (in Hans Kindler's emotionally charged words to the Music Teachers National Association) that mechanization had inflicted upon American society.[58] This point of view was nothing less than an effort to preserve the producer ethic in an increasingly recreational consumer culture. Music education, like the music industry, was caught in the conflicting movements of cultural change.

In the Victorian age when the home piano was most responsible for the spread of music appreciation, simultaneously adding to the home's prestige, daughters were taught to play by the strict and demanding rules and technique of the Klavier Schule, which exemplified the work ethic so characteristic of the time.[59] From the vantage point of 1933, Olin Downes commented that "in most cases it required severe discipline or exceptional talent to survive [the experience]. A child was singled out by its parents to be the victim of piano teachers." Conductor Walter Damrosch remembered, "The most exciting and welcome news to me at the time [of the Great War] was that my piano teacher had been drafted and I had high hopes of not having to continue to undergo the dreary necessity of daily finger exercises."[60]

The work ethic prescribed that means were more important than ends. Hard work built character; music contributed to moral and spiritual improvement, especially in the hands of women. The two together would uplift society. But the work ethic tended to reduce music education to a sort of grammar, full of rules and regulations, and to exalt the virtuoso at the expense of the musical amateur, a situation increasingly coming under criticism in the 1920s and 1930s. "Does Miss Jones raise her fingers according to the method of Prof. Slamboni, or does she keep them glued to the keys, as practiced by Prof. Pressinsky?" Clarence G. Hamilton acridly remarked to the Music Teachers National Association in 1931. Such questions often became the basis of serious criticism, rather than, "Does Miss Jones play with sincerity, intelligence, and artistry?" The result was a "94 percent mortality rate" among beginning piano students and ironically, the creation of a strong aversion to music.[61] Nevertheless, most private music teachers adhered strictly to concepts derived from the Klavier Schule, seeking the virtuoso, repelling the amateur.

The American piano industry, though intimately bound up with this Victorian attitude, had revolutionized the amateur music market with the player piano. But many teachers argued that, while Americans might be more musically conscious, they were *consuming* music, not producing it. Moreover, player pianos were destroying self-expression and contributing to laziness. This dilemma was compounded by the widespread sale of the radio and the improved phonograph. Music was becoming too easy, too commonplace, and hence diminished in its impact. To counteract this subversive trend, the descendants of the Klavier Schule were stubbornly determined to hold their ground. Similarly reacting to the radio, the piano trade—itself now displaced by the box of dials and tubes—sought to reestablish the value of self-expression in an age of mechanical reproduction.

The answer for the piano industry, however, had not been to support the system of music instruction from which the automatic player had emancipated the culture. Rather, the trade had seen the salvation of its business in class piano in the public schools. As Lucien Wulsin II affirmed, "the keynote of the future of music in this country . . . is an increasing public who loves to do its own performing for the joy of the performance with no thought of the professional or the virtuoso."[62] The basis of the public school music program was to appeal to children on their own terms, and represented evidence for the growing interest in child psychology. Furthermore, class instruction testified to a fundamental change in attitude toward work that was becoming characteristic of the developing recreational mentality. In the larger culture, reformers became increasingly aware that in an age of modern factory production, work could be harmful when it stifled creativity and independence with endless monotony. Work could actually undermine rather than underpin morality. A shift occurred toward an appreciation of the benefits of recreation and leisure as remedy for these modern ills. Play was not idleness, however. As the work week shortened, Americans turned to bicycling, sports, motoring, going to movies, vaudeville, and amusement parks, picnicking, "playing" the player piano—in a word, *consuming*. And in time, consuming the products of industry rather than producing with determined industry became the basic tenet of the new culture.

This new respect for leisure enabled modern music educators to assert that strenuous lessons and hard work were not educational at all. Rather, the drudgery of old-fashioned piano practice often produced minimal results. Music should be a social enterprise, an avocation for most rather than a vocation. Teachers should train amateurs who love music, not try to produce artists, because the emphasis on virtuosity meant most students dropped out before ever learning to play even simple tunes. Adults as well as children, men as well as women could learn to *enjoy* making music. After the interest and enthusiasm developed, then the teacher could work on the technical aspects. As Olin Downes voiced the new philosophy: so we bumble, so we use too much pedal, so we hit wrong notes—so what? "What a delight the piano is for those of us who play badly!"[63]

The strongest devotion to this new ideology was found in American public schools. According to Ella Mason of the National Bureau for the Advancement of Music, group piano instruction in public school music had begun about 1909, pioneered by Osbourne McConathy, Otto Miessner, and Mrs. E. K. Evans, among others. With the aid of the bureau and the Music Supervisors National Conference, it spread rapidly across the United States in the years following the World War. From 1924 to 1929 the movement accelerated, aided by the feverish activity of the National Piano Manufacturers Association—notably the Piano Promotion Plan—and certain individual manufacturers distraught over declining player piano sales. Because it originated in the public schools (which were themselves undergoing the philosophical evolution toward a child-centered curriculum that was central to the New Education of John Dewey), school music instruction followed more progressive educational lines than did private teaching. The low cost and emphasis on pleasure of the piano class popularized taking lessons even among boys, and indicated that past methods of teaching were inadequate to children's needs and wants. Progressive piano teachers were also hopeful that the new curriculum would counteract the tendency toward passive listening.[64]

The aim of public school music, as pursued by the Music Supervisors National Conference, was "to cause children to know, to love and to appreciate music . . . to bring added joy into their lives and added culture and refinement into their natures."[65] The National Bureau for the Advancement of Music published a pamphlet that further expressed the philosophy: "Every person in the world is born with some degree of music potentiality. . . . [and] it is the inherent right of everyone, and not the special privilege of a few, to have this gift, to whatever degree the individual possesses it, developed and allowed expression in musical study. [Music should be] part of the general education of everyone."[66]

This philosophy of "music for the fun of it" and music making being an "inherent right of everyone" had been, of course, the fundamental principle behind the piano industry's promotion of a musical democracy through the player piano. Once this market became saturated and the machine was replaced by the radio, the piano trade naturally supported a movement that not only echoed its own beliefs, but offered the possibility of encouraging the sale of straight pianos. The child inspired through modern, enjoyable music appreciation methods would want an instrument in the home. The trade's new sales technique was to reach the parents through the children.

Radio, the apparent bane of the piano industry, also figured prominently in the cultivation of "music for the fun of it." Walter Damrosch, whose own music appreciation courses had keenly interested an estimated five million children, told the 1930 music industries' convention that the radio was the musical instrument's "best ally," and together they could counteract the harmful disruptions of the family caused by the automobile. "May the new slogan be, 'That which the motor car has destroyed, the radio and the piano will again build up.'"[67]

Particularly innovative was the National Broadcasting Company's use of the medium to broadcast piano lessons. The entire music industry, from piano manufacturers and dealers to music publishers, was quick to endorse "Keys to Happiness" and "Music in the Air," which were broadcast on the NBC network in early 1931. Students inspired to participate actively were encouraged to enroll by mail. By April enrollment had reached 50,000 and reportedly was increasing at four to five thousand a day (more than 60 percent of the applicants were women). In addition to conducting basic lessons following the "Look and Play" method (which the NPMA had helped develop), the semiweekly series also featured "amateurs at the piano" to help "rekindle the interest in piano playing in the home." These amateurs included the aviator Casey Jones, head of the Juilliard Musical Foundation Dr. John Erskine, architect Kenneth Murchison, cartoonist Peter Arno, Mrs. Calvin Coolidge, and Edna St. Vincent Millay. Each series consisted of six lessons and required only a keyboard chart to enable the student to find the proper keys and play simple tunes. The program was meant merely to introduce music, however. Listeners were encouraged to seek lessons thereafter, and John Mills, creator of the piano-radio series, suggested that private teachers offer a free lesson to aid in the transition.[68]

Such progressive impulses disconcerted many traditional thinkers. A majority of private teachers were resentful of radio and suspicious of the new piano pedagogy. Many others (one estimate claimed 99 percent) were simply incompetent and felt threatened.[69] The Associated Music Teachers' League was formed to combat the radio and other phenomena of "our restless and speedened age," arguing that such devices endangered the self-expression of children because they easily became bored in an age "rampant with the spirit of wild abandon." The League did encourage teachers to adopt newer methods, however, and urged that class piano could supplement private instruction.[70] A 1930 Music Teachers National Association survey among retail music dealers in a dozen major cities disclosed that most private teachers were hostile toward public school piano classes, or at least were unconvinced that such classes would help them, even though the MTNA endorsed the method. The teachers claimed that parents were being beguiled into thinking that twenty-five cent lessons in public schools were equal to private lessons at proper fees. (Significantly, the study revealed that the retail dealers themselves endorsed class piano as salvation for their industry.) The MTNA survey report concluded that the majority of private teachers were poorly trained and used obsolete methods, though the number of these teachers was decreasing.[71]

Thus, the circle was complete. The radio, which had taken people away from self-expression and helped devastate the piano industry, was now stimulating both. "We have good reason to believe that in the last analysis," admitted L. P. ("Perk") Bull, president of Story & Clark Piano Co. and Wulsin's successor as NPMA president, "instead of stultifying individual effort in music, the devices of recording and transmitting sound encourage it." Indeed, an estimated 15 million Americans could play some musical instrument, according to the NPMA, with 9 million being amateur pianists. Furthermore, a later study by the Institute of Musical Art of the Juilliard School of Music confirmed that over the seven years from 1934 to 1941, piano study in the United States increased 82.5 percent. The welcome evidence was apparent in increasing sales of new pianos. Shipments in November 1935 broke all records since January 1931, a 34 percent increase over the previous year and 186 percent over 1932.[72]

The depression undoubtedly contributed to the widening cultural acceptance of "music for the fun of it" and to the rebirth of the piano in the home. Economic devastation and severe unemployment prompted many music teachers to encourage only the most gifted to seek professional careers in music, while most other students were taught merely to love music as amateurs. Furthermore, the hard times brought a revival of Victorian values and provoked a new interest in the importance of home and family life. Movies and much of the literature glorified traditional American moral values, seeking to establish a sense of security, an identity with a somewhat mythical age of cooperation, justice, and moral economics. Iron deer reappeared on lawns, old-style wallpaper became popular, the waltz replaced the Charleston, and the flapper was urged home again. Even fashion once again emphasized what the Sears catalog called the "definitely indented waistline, long tapering hips and the molded bust," achievable through the "smart, new corsets," symbolic of Victorian attitudes.[73]

The depression reinforced the traditional division of male and female roles—the man as breadwinner, the woman running the household. Domesticity was again idealized. Women, especially wives and mothers, were "the inspirations of the homes, the persons for whom the men really work," as Eleanor Roosevelt put it in 1933. Or, as Mrs. Thomas A. Edison asserted on a radio talk show in 1930, "The woman who doesn't want to make a home is undermining our nation." The New York State Federation of Women's Clubs similarly proposed to get women "back to the home."[74]

Part of this ideology stemmed from the belief that working women took needed jobs away from husbands and fathers. But more important, the culture in general yearned for a return to what one writer called the "commonsense of the nineteenth century as a rest cure [from the] troubles and stupidities" of the present age.[75] The renewed interest in traditional values resulted in a wider recognition of marriage and homemaking as vital to social welfare, and there was a greater family realization of the need for each other, an interdependence to survive hard times. In addition, people were forced into entertaining themselves at home. Here the radio became crucial (the Supreme Court even declared it a necessity[76]), and the piano—long the center of family entertainment in the Victorian household—quite naturally returned to complete the home.[77]

Whatever the impact of these exogenous factors on the rejuvenation of the piano industry, trade leaders contributed to their own recovery through continued support of class piano instruction in the public schools, progressive piano pedogogy, and radio music appreciation programs. Equally important was the trade's internal reformation. For the first time, systematic consumer analyses were used to enable manufacturers and dealers to understand the idiosyncrasies of their market. Moreover, piano makers introduced the small, streamlined, fashionably-styled instrument they called the "console." The result was a triumph of marketing.

The Triumph of the Piano

The upright piano played havoc with interior decorators and housewives, who continually complained (to the deaf ears of piano manufacturers) that the instrument was a "vast black dot" that "threatened delicate walls and furnishings," or that it was "an inky pool, yards in circumference [and] is sure to bring discord into any color arrangement." Mrs. Somerset Maugham lamented, "How can we combat its ugliness?"[78] Prior to the Great War hundreds of piano companies had manufactured hundreds of thousands of towering uprights, all cut from almost identical patterns. Fashionable housewives chose to decorate the box-shaped instruments with red throws, heavily embroidered with chenille flowers, and trimmed with plush tassels. And what better place to display ordered rows of family portraits than atop the ubiquitous symbol of home and family life?

By the mid-1920s, however, eye appeal had replaced durability in the market place; "Model T" became a derogative label of ridicule. Women's magazines emphasized interior decorating around period and modern designs. Alert and competitive makers of an endless variety of products, from motor cars to bathroom towels, from clocks to women's cosmetics, intensely promoted style and color as an aid to sales, until it became standard practice.[79] Radio manufacturers, noting the success of other industries that incorporated beauty and style into their products, left behind the "'Model T' stage in radio design" in favor of miniature, streamlined models "at prices that will wake up the industry."[80] But piano manufacturers missed the cue. Decorators, horrified at the piano's faithful adherence to ancient design, eagerly replaced the eyesore with the new radio, which was available in period and modern styles—and still provided music.

In addition, as housing costs increased and apartment living became the vogue, living space decreased. Pianos were shoved into dark corners or removed entirely. "Where shall we put that piano?" asked the *Ladies' Home Journal* in 1928, summarizing the problem. "If I didn't have a big piano my room could look so smart!"[81] Most piano manufacturers tried to fill this demand with the production of baby grand pianos under five feet in length, in both period and modern styles and a variety of woods and finishes. These pianos became quite popular in the 1920s and helped many makers survive the rapid collapse of the player market (Figure 5.2). Yet, the stylish baby grand still took up the space of a dining table, cost considerably more than an upright, and was in many cases an inferior instrument.[82] In 1930 the National Association of Music Merchants and *The Music Trades* addressed a formal complaint to the American Institute of Architects, charging that the rooms in modern houses and apartments were too small to accomodate pianos. Such poor design obviously was hurting piano sales, and the architects had failed to respond to the piano industry's campaign (launched two years before) to create space for the instrument.[83] This stubborn adherence to old design in a world inundated with streamlined products from vacuum cleaners to pencil sharpeners is an ironic measure of the conservatism of an industry that had been innovative enough to produce the player piano and progressive enough to support class piano.

For the American piano industry, the world changed in May 1935. The Haddorff Piano Co. and Winter & Co. independently, but almost simultaneously, introduced a new upright piano, smaller and available in period and modern styles and finishes that were influenced by furniture fashion.[84] By the June music trades' convention other makers were producing these "consoles" or "flat tops," bringing into the language a plethora of new trademarks: Musette, Vertichord, Acrosonic, Spinette, Cabinet, Pianino, Mini-piano, Spinet, Pianette, and a dozen others. Their height averaged 3'9" and they cost 25 percent less than the average upright had fifteen years before. But the revolution was in styling rather than in cost or size. (Public demand had already forced piano makers to design a 3'9" frame soon after the World War, but the cabinet had remained box-like, stylistically just a shorter version of its predecessor.) Decorators admired the new piano's "gracious lines." They were impressed with chromium trimmings, mirror inlays, and zebrawood, chintz, blonde mahogany, and imitation leather finishes. And they advised consumers that nothing now prevented their bringing the piano home once more.[85] "No place for a piano? Nonesense!" encouraged *American Home.* "Gone are the 'Model T' styles of yesterday and in their place smaller, moderately priced types that will fit into any home."[86]

Business Week queried most of the piano companies to ascertain the economic effect of the console on the industry. Manufacturers overwhelmingly reported a massive revival in sales.[87] The NPMA announced that the first six months in 1936 were the best in fifteen years, total sales for the industry were 300 percent above 1933, total shipments surpassed 90,350 units, and unfilled orders had reached the highest point in more than a decade. The boom was not sectional, but nationwide. Many new piano stores opened, the number of manufacturers rose to thirty-seven, sheet music sales were up, more children reportedly were taking piano lessons than ever before, and the NAMM convention and trade show recorded the greatest dealer attendance in its history. It was a banner year.[88]

Three additional factors contributed to the industry's emergence from what Theodore E. Steinway called "an Era of Frustration and Bewilderment."[89] One was a general increase in consumer purchases. Dun and Bradstreet reported a 12 to 20 percent increase in 1936 over the previous year, with typewriter and radio manufacturers in addition to piano makers being months behind shipping dates despite weekly increases in schedules.[90] Another factor was the recovery of the secondhand piano market from the glut of 1925–35. This resulted partly because rural areas, particularly in the South, absorbed thousands of old pianos, but also because of a successful campaign among dealers to destroy thousands of "jalopies" in an attempt to clear the market.[91]

More important, however, was the piano trade's adoption of the modern marketing survey and improved merchandising strategies. Children had often appeared in player piano advertisements, but direct child appeal in piano merchandising developed concurrently with the emphasis on children in modern piano pedagogy. Pioneered by Steinway & Sons, Story & Clark, and Baldwin, among others, child appeal proved an effective avenue to sales. In the mid-1930s, the sizable Sherman, Clay & Co., which had been specializing in retail sales of musical instruments on the West Coast since 1870, conducted a two-year campaign to tap the lucrative child market. The company mailed a series of seven folders, each depicting an episode in the life of a little girl, to 5,000 families having an annual income of $2,500 to $5,000, and having a daughter from seven to ten years old but not having a piano. Courthouse records supplied the child's name, which was imprinted on each mailing. The folders depicted how making music encouraged good character, joy, and popularity in the life of the girl and young woman, how it will win love and admiration from her future husband, how she would pass along the same gift to her future child, and finally, how an anonymous elderly woman (this final mailing was not personalized) reflected on the way music had influenced her gracious beautiful life. The series was mailed in intervals of twenty-five days to allow salesmen to contact the recipients and give them a booklet of piano styles, prices, and terms, and a list of music teachers. Costing under ten thousand dollars, the campaign increased the company's pianos sales 30 percent above the national average, produced almost a half million dollars in total sales by 1937, and received national attention in the advertising trade journal *Printers' Ink*.[92]

In 1936 the Piano Promotion Committee of the National Piano Manufacturers Association turned over its publicity campaign to the Lawrence H. Selz Organization of Chicago. Formed ten years before as an emergency measure against declining piano sales, the NPMA committee had become one of the most effective elements in promoting class piano in the public schools and in making the public more piano-conscious. By 1937 Selz had succeeded in getting five leading advertisers (Lucky Strike, Squibb, Libby-Owen Glass, Coca Cola, and Anheuser-Busch) to feature pianos in their ads, which reached an estimated 100 million people.[93]

In his merchandising Selz mainly stressed children's education to his contacts in major national magazines; but he also emphasized the social and decorative value of the new console to architects, decorators, and home interest magazines. He praised National Music Week to major newspapers and coined the slogan: "Make your house a home—buy a piano." Furthermore, he informed business periodicals and newpapers of the increase in piano sales and even inspired Eleanor Roosevelt to discuss the rising popularity of the piano in her column, "My Day." He assembled sales clinics for piano retailers, where they were addressed by experts from the Studebaker Corp., Metropolitan Life Insurance, and other organizations skilled in specialty selling. "We feel safe in saying that the American public is more piano-conscious today than at any other period in the past decade," the organization reported in December 1938.[94]

However efficiently the Lawrence H. Selz Organization performed the Piano Promotion Committee's tasks, it merely capitalized on the intense publicity campaign already developed by the National Piano Manufacturers. Selz made his real contribution with his "Consumer Investigation," a survey sponsored by fifty-nine American piano makers and piano supply manufacturers and published by the NPMA in 1938. The sixty-page report summarized the results of 4,800 questionaires distributed among families of all income levels living in cities, towns, and villages. It was the first systematic survey ever made for the piano industry in an attempt to investigate consumer attitudes toward its product.[95]

The report supported the progressive merchandising of firms such as Steinway & Sons and Baldwin by revealing that the most profitable retailing method was that which regarded the piano as a cultural product. It defined the potential market as almost every self-supporting family—there was no direct relation between a purchaser's income and what he would pay for an instrument. But the survey did uncover unexploited markets among middle-income families with children. Reportedly 24 percent of all families not owning pianos were considering purchasing them, revealing a potential market of 768,859 families. Furthermore, more than half of the pianos in American homes were over fifteen years old, and 5,865,296 families owned pianos. Since an instrument over that age was not only worn out, but out of style, the replacement possibilities were enormous. "It is up to you to get these replaced," Selz advised dealers. "You must accelerate obsolescence." He asserted that to reach these potential markets, the industry would take almost six years at present capacity to fill the orders.[96]

Significantly, the survey revealed the folly of price advertising, again sustaining the promotion methods of trade leaders. The most important factors determining the consumer's piano purchase were tone, reputations of manufacturer and dealer, and style. Price considerations ranked a low fourth, though outweighing the influence of salesmen, friends, and previous experience. Advice of the piano teacher fell last. Selz discovered that two out of five people wanted to learn to play the piano, again pointing to tremendous market potential, and that 46.6 percent were enthusiastic about class piano in public school. Moreover, while there were 6,282,676 families in the U.S. in which one or more members already could play, the primary reason for disposing of pianos was "no use" or "don't play." "It is part of your problem to make sure that your customers find competent, modern teachers. You must evolve a general program of fostering appreciation of music in your community." Thus, the survey confirmed the work of the National Bureau for the Advancement of Music and the NPMA's Piano Promotion Committee to be accurate and effective. The Selz report also underscored the importance of advertising. Without making any judgments about the ability of ads to sell merchandise, the study revealed that 55 percent of the potential market was indeed reading piano advertising. Selz's advice: "Do more advertising."

The American Association of Advertising Agencies had already issued a report asserting that consistent advertisers had maintained a better average of business during the depression than those who had curtailed their efforts.[97] Certainly the leaders among the piano manufacturers were also the strongest advertisers, and in 1937–38 announced sharp increases in both national and retail advertising. By 1939 (when the new console comprised 80 percent of production), modern merchandising within the piano trade had created a second sales peak in the spring to complement the traditional fall season. It had increased total sales over 400 percent of the 1933 level and had sustained production despite a setback during the recession of 1938. By the American entry into the Second World War, the NPMA reported shipments of almost 160,000 pianos, the largest figure since 1927 (see figure 6.1).[98] Baldwin led the industry in production volume and in both gross and net sales. Kimball, Steinway & Sons, and Winter & Co. were not far behind in dollar volume, followed by Wurlitzer, Aeolian-American, Gulbransen, Story & Clark, Lester, and Hardman, Peck & Co. *Sales Management* summed it up succinctly: "'Dying' Music Industry Lives Anew as Millions Turn to Tune-Making."[99]

Sales prophets envisioned a Golden Age that would rival the years before the radio. *Advertising Age* announced that the music trades had finally reached the point of stability that all had desired. The piano industry, once a steadfast pillar of Victorian social philosophy, had emerged triumphant from the onslaught of alternative entertainment, recreational attitudes, mechanization, whimsical fashion, a frivolous public, and a devastating economic depression. The emerging culture of universal accessibility and instant gratification, which had so welcomed and then abandoned the player piano, could still be inspired to creativity and handicraft. But that creativity had to be enjoyable and the means had to be stylish. The piano industry had discovered the answer in the console instrument and modern

Figure 6.1. American Piano Production, 1929–1941

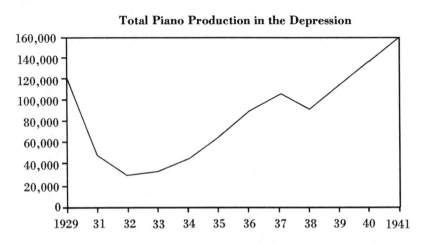

Total Piano Production in the Depression

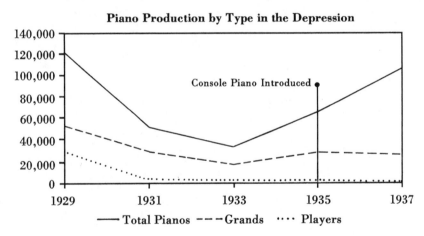

Piano Production by Type in the Depression

methods of piano teaching. They had also discovered that their product was particularly attractive during the Great Depression as the culture sought stability in traditional values, values that the trade had learned to promote effectively. "You are selling happiness," *The Music Trades* professed in 1938.[100] Ever resourceful, the piano industry had confronted the consumer culture, and prevailed.

The Piano—Symbol of a Past Age

The piano will ever continue to be the basic musical instrument.
—H. P. Knowles, editor, The Music Trades

The pianoforte more than any other single object will be looked upon in years to come as the emblem of the Victorian age.
—W. J. Turner, New York Times

The recovery of the American piano industry was interrupted in the spring of 1942 when the War Production Board ordered all production ceased. Unlike the experience of 1917–18, the role that the piano makers would play in the Second World War was much more directly linked to the manufacture of wartime equipment. Nevertheless, the National Piano Manufacturers Association still reported that 61,500 instruments were shipped in the first three months of the year alone, before the order took effect.[1]

The government lost little time in utilizing the industry's long-established woodworking expertise. Steinway & Sons manufactured wings, underbodies, and tail assemblies for the U.S. Army Air Force's troop-carrying glider, which would be used in the Allied invasion of France in 1944 and in other areas. Story & Clark made glider spar caps and landing skids for the Ford Motor Co. in a similar venture. Kimball built twenty-one different aircraft parts for Boeing, Lockheed, and Douglas airplane factories, parts such as landing gear doors, multiple seat assemblies for paratroopers (including devices that automatically opened the parachutes), bomb bay doors, bulkheads, and flare bomb protector shields. The Chicago manufacturer publicized that while its factories "once provided musical America with the instruments of discriminating choice [they] now supply a fighting America with products for victory!" The firm also made some of the equipment used in the secret Manhattan Project atomic bomb program.[2]

Baldwin had already been working with the State Department and War Department before Pearl Harbor. As early as September 1939 Secretary of State Cordell Hull had approached Lucien Wulsin indirectly through Senator Robert Taft and the director of the Cincinnati May Festival regarding the importance of maintaining close ties with Latin America through music. The State Department's newly created Division of Cultural Relations arranged a conference on Inter-American Relations in the Field of Music in Washington that October for the purpose of developing a "firm and friendly understanding between the American nations [which] has never been more important than it is today."[3]

More direct were Baldwin's contracts with the War Department. Because of a critically low supply of aluminum and other metals, wood became the crucial element in airplane design. The Cincinnati piano company manufactured wings, center sections, and fuselage fairings for the Aeronca PT-23 (later called the PT-19) training plane, and the Curtiss-Wright C-76 twin-engined cargo plane, which had an enormous forty-foot wingspan. Retooling from woodworking to metalworking once aluminum became more readily available in 1943, Baldwin produced the ailerons for the C-46 cargo plane, and ailerons and wing tips for the B-24 Liberator bomber and the B-29 Superfortress. The piano factory also made escape doors for bombers and gliders, and bomb racks for fighter planes. In addition, Baldwin research developed a discardable gasoline tank made of leakproof papier-mâché that increased the range of fighter planes, and produced for the Navy the top-secret proximity fuse.[4]

In the spring of 1944 the War Production Board authorized the piano trade to manufacture a small number of pianos for the "U.S. Armed Forces, War Shipping Administration, Maritime Commission and all other Governmental Agencies, war plants, hospitals, Red Cross, U.S.O. entertainment centers, religious organizations, education institutions and other essential users such as musicians, music teachers, music students, hotels and other places of public gatherings."[5] Steinway was able to supply more than 2,500 of these "GI pianos." Baldwin, Kimball, Wurlitzer, and others managed to finish the production of instruments that had been left uncompleted in 1942 and to manufacture a limited number of new pianos. But materials remained in short supply until after the war and the industry still was expected to devote most of its energy to war production, thus making for "difficulty in getting back into the piano business," as George W. Lawrence of Baldwin put it. Even after V-E Day, Story & Clark and other piano companies were not permitted to manufacture for the civilian market because the Army Air Force was anticipating a glider-borne invasion of Japan.[6]

Reconversion began almost immediately after the Japanese surrender. Dealer networks remained intact for the most part, surviving on the used piano trade, tuning, and repair work. Most piano companies had established some sort of postwar planning committee to speed the transition back to piano production. By 1946 the NPMA happily reported that 93,499 pianos were shipped. The number rose to 146,393 the following year and 165,107 in 1948.[7] Americans were still anxious to buy the new console piano and the new electronic organ as well. In the era of postwar prosperity, renewed consumer interest in making music and the resulting increased sales of stylish instruments demonstrated that the piano trade, for the time being, had successfully adapted to modernity and the culture of consumption.

The larger implications of this victory speak to general questions about the process and degree of rapid social change. The complexity of this change, however, suggests the need for a review of the particular circumstances that affected the destruction and recovery of the American piano industry. A majority of the business leaders who witnessed the decline in the American music industry and piano trade in the 1920s blamed radio, movies, and the motor car. Historians also have been content to assess the trend in terms of exogenous factors, giving little attention to possible failings within the industry itself.[8] The assault upon the prosperity of the trade seemed to have come from the outside.

Yet, there were serious flaws in the manner in which the piano industry conducted its day-to-day business. Retail dealers, the most important link between manufacturer and customer, generally counteracted much of the manufacturers' intense promotion of music, culture, and brand name distinctiveness with their emphasis on price and special sales. This tended to reduce the piano to just another product for sale in a market already flooded with an endless variety of merchandise competing for the attention of the new consumer. The retail piano business also suffered an unfortunate association with unethical sales methods and bait advertising, which destroyed trust, creating suspicion among the public. This association was reinforced when the piano sold was a low-grade stencil or "thump-box" produced by an equally unethical manufacturer, but misrepresented as a fine instrument. An age idolizing the brand name was equally disturbed by the piano industry's practice of making instruments bearing venerable names of companies no longer in existence. Though the quality of the instrument did not necessarily change, the practice was deceptive, inspiring trust in annual buying guides, not in old names.

The general indifference of many retailers to music appreciation or the technical aspects of their product encouraged a preoccupation with selling by price alone. It futher inclined dealers to stress the simplicity of the player piano rather than to educate customers or themselves to operate pedals and levers to produce a more enjoyable musical experience. The national advertising of most player piano manufacturers was equally damaging. By offering an invention capable of achieving a musical democracy despite the unpopularity and high failure rate of private piano lessons, the trade undermined traditional sales methods that encouraged the amateur musician, essentially destroying the incentive to learn to play by hand. The marvel of mechanization allowed the Victorian piano industry to produce a means enabling everyone to enjoy the virtues of music. Ignorant of the destructive nature of the emerging consumer culture, trade leaders both used and significantly aided this cultural change.

The novelty of automation itself sold player pianos until radio and improved phonographs provided a more rewarding, less expensive, but still automatic musical experience. The major mistakes within the industry were in the promotion of the player piano that reduced the instrument to the level of a machine, and in the neglect and even contempt for the conventional straight piano market. With almost 60 percent of its business built upon canned music by 1923 (many manufacturers and dealers were completely dependent on this trade), the piano industry could hardly avoid economic catastrophe when this clientele made the swift and sudden move to the radio. The radio was to blame, but so was the piano trade itself. The industry hurt itself further by offering its product as a lifetime investment, by failing to provide the public with modern designs, by encouraging unsound credit sales, and by not addressing the problem of trade-ins until used pianos became a bigger threat to new instrument sales than was the radio.

Private music teachers contributed in no small way to the decline as well. Their stubborn adherence to some form of the rigid and strenuous Klavier Schule in an age enjoying easy access to music through player pianos, phonographs, and radio, and at a time when most children were exposed to the friendlier, more encouraging music instruction offered in public schools, discouraged all but the most persistent amateurs. Most others remained content with turning knobs and dials to enjoy music. Though by the 1930s private teachers slowly began to adopt the modern philosophy stressing "music for the fun of it" that characterized school programs, far too many retained what music critic Olin Downes called the "stereotyped, unimaginative and uncreative attitude" of the old school.[9] They were perhaps the most persistent latter-day Victorians, the most resistant to the changes of modern society.

These self-inflicted injuries greatly diminished trade success. What made them particularly harmful is that they occurred during an era of radical social change over which the trade had no control and of which it had little understanding. The success of the motor car, motion picture, phonograph, radio, even the bicycle as alternative sources of entertainment certainly contributed to the descent of the piano in American society. The existing literature recognizes the piano industry's inability to compete with these new businesses, but it fails to attribute this dilemma to the fundamental changes then occurring in the culture. The entire music industry, from piano manufacturing and sheet-music publishing to teaching, was subjected to competition from new commodities that offered recreation, comfort, convenience, and social prestige, many of which were themselves purchased on credit. Automobiles, oil heaters, electric washing machines, refrigerators, irons, stylish furniture, bathroom accessories, radio, phonographs, the movies, and sports commanded an increasing share of the buyers' market. The combined effect of these new products was to shift recreation away from the home and to redefine social distinction, leisure time, and personal identity in terms of consumption.

The piano, however, remained a critical link with the traditional concept of the home. It was a Victorian artifact, representative of an age in which the home and family rather than business interests and consumerism ruled society. But accompanying the rise of industrialization and urbanization was the demise of the home as a production center, and the erosion of the home as the center of social life and cultural development. Values stressing the home, production, and the work ethic were rendered obsolete and were even considered harmful as recreation, leisure, and consumerism gradually became the ethos preferred.

Eleanor Roosevelt noted that this revolution from individual production in the home to mass production in factories had occurred in her lifetime. The new home demanded less of women and children, thus forcing them out and destroying family solidarity. As the home ceased to serve its traditional function, its symbols—especially the piano—fell from their exalted place within that tradition. The revolution was especially evident in the arts. The machine age discouraged amateur study, since at the turn of a dial, one could "have better music than mother used to make."[10] This explanation runs full circle, because it also accounts for the great popularity of the alternative sources of entertainment with which the piano industry could not compete. As James Truslow Adams observed, "restlessness has replaced restfullness." The trade's promotion of a musical democracy through the player piano enjoyed tremendous success in the first decades of what Adams called the "press-a-button-and-get-all-you-want" age because it appealed to and even promoted the new mentality. The player did make music "a more every-day possession of everybody," in one teacher's phrase. But it required no effort—and neither did the radio.[11]

The conflict erupting as one culture replaced another was manifest in the legal and moral debate over canned music, the fight between descendants of the Klavier Schule and advocates of progressive piano pedogogy, and in the struggle within the piano trade to sell its symbol-laden product in an age apparently taken with so many other interests. The real value in studying the American piano trade lies in realizing how a fundamentally Victorian industry ultimately took advantage of the developing consumer culture (which initially devastated its business) to bring about success. Trade leaders adopted the trappings of consumerism to appeal successfully to a select clientele. They cultivated self-expression and amateur music making "for the fun of it" through class piano, music contests, and National Music Week; they manufactured smaller, stylish grand and console pianos more appropriate for modern tastes; they used radio rather than criticizing it, and conducted market surveys, seminars in retail sales, and arresting publicity campaigns.

"Today, we KNOW what goes to make a successful sale," boasted Baldwin's sales handbook of 1931. "Today, it is even more necessary than ever before, to know exactly what plans produce Piano sales and which do not." For in addition to other music merchants, the salesman "has still more relentless competition with the automobile dealer, the refrigerator distributor, the oil-heater salesman and many others. The customer wants ALL of these things. And she wants a Piano too. But she buys the merchandise that is SOLD to her."[12]

Success returned to the industry in an irony of history. Not only did the market quicken and business revive during the worst economic depression yet recorded; the trade capitalized on the very Victorian values that the consumer culture seemed to have undermined. In an age fraught with appeals to self-improvement through products, leaders in the piano trade recognized that the days of selling their product as a badge of social standing, as furniture, or even as the basic musical instrument were largely past. Instead, as the Baldwin sales manual stressed in 1931, "the newer generation" will value the piano "for what it enables its owner to do and to become."[13]

To promote music, the trade drew upon traditional values and impressed upon consumers that piano study improved the mind, contributed self-discipline, prevented melancholy, bred contentment, and increased general culture. It gave the dignity of accomplishment, helped one make friends and meet a better class of people, and led to community leadership. Piano study also provided entertainment, added romance to life, and afforded pleasant diversions. Baldwin and other leaders stressed that an ability to play the piano contributed to religious advancement by giving the soul comfort and improving one's ability "to resist evil [and] the fruits of idleness."[14]

Moreover, the piano would make "the difference between a house and a home," encourage home entertainment, bring joy into the household, strengthen family ties and promote family harmony. Music study was particularly important for children, since the ability to play the piano would teach discipline, invite popularity, provide a safe, wholesome environment, develop ambition, open the door to a variety of careers, and stir "all of the nobler emotions." "Let the salesman go forth secure in the knowledge that every time he makes a sale, he also makes a valuable contribution to the mental and physical well-being of an untold number of people," affirmed the manual of the NAMM's Sales Training Committee. "Such is the power and glory of music."[15]

These appeals to a lost Victorian ethos were especially valuable selling points during the Great Depression, when the culture called modern values into question and embraced once again many of the rejected traditional beliefs. The music industry successfully exploited the very nature of the culture that had almost destroyed it. Trade leaders took advantage of the basic insecurities of the consumer culture: distrust of automation and impersonality, fear of inferiority, the need to belong to the group, and the desire to be individualistic—each of which could be resolved or fulfilled through purchase of a piano. They offered the benefits of home and family life—happiness, contentment, safety, wholesomeness—and also the virtues of the work ethic—perseverance, achievement, self-improvement, discipline, self-expression, self-respect, sociability, self-control, patience, endurance, character, fortitude—as commodities to be purchased and realized vicariously through the modern, smartly styled console or grand piano. The comforting notions of the Victorian age were not lost after all.

The significance of the American piano industry's confrontation with the consumer culture from 1890 to 1940 lies in its successful cultivation of the amateur spirit in music and its appreciation of productive values in a consumer age. The irony is that the trade accomplished this through promoting the values of the Victorian culture as a commodity, yet appealing at the same time to the values inherent in the consumer culture. Both the rise of the player piano and the ensuing decline of the piano business heralded a new age. W. J. Turner correctly affirmed in 1925 that "the pianoforte more than any other single object will be looked upon in years to come as the emblem of the Victorian age." Yet, it was precisely this imagery, once torn away from its context and made into an increasingly abstract ideal by the emergence of a new ethic, once packaged and merchandised as a product available in a variety of modern styles to be sold to a culture struggling to find reference points in a period of rapid social change, it was this imagery that ultimately sustained the American piano industry.

The larger implications of this victory allow a greater understanding of the ethos of the modern age. The experience of the piano trade underscores the precarious nature of a culture that has high regard for the benefit of technological advancement and places high value on style, therefore encouraging obsolescence. In addition, the effect of advertising and merchandising is but one factor in the successful promotion of a product. Much more important are the degree of control in manufacturing, distribution, sales, credit, and payment collection; the abilities of the managerial and sales staff; the quality of the product and the financial strength of the firm; and perhaps most important, the degree to which a given product is or is not a part of the current trend among consumers—the trend that advertisers would like to believe they manipulate, but to which, in reality, they must cater. Nevertheless, subtleties of choice can be manipulated among consumers within a given trend; the trend can be intensified. Here, merchandising is essential.

Furthermore, the piano trade's experience demonstrates that the encroachment of consumerism is probably impossible to date accurately. It was certainly evident by the mid-to-late nineteenth century, definite by the first decade of the present century, and comfortably recognizable by the 1920s. This development was gradual, allowing time for adjustment to change as well as opportunity for even traditional businesses to profit, though not without risk. Still, the piano industry demonstrated that it was not only possible to adjust to and even promote the new culture, but also to use it. Finally, the recovery of the piano industry shows that one culture seldom fully replaces another. The trade successfully promoted the producer ethic to win over (and alleviate the fears of) the new consumer. The culture of consumption was never completely overpowering; Victorian values were not completely lost, but were transformed.[16]

"There still remain some unchanging, fundamental things that serve to connect all generations ... within which parents and children develop a sustained relationship," said a Steinway advertisement that won the 1930 Harvard Advertising Award. Of course, the key was music, the medium was the piano. They offered the link between the changing world of modern children—with its "airplanes, fast motorcars, new theories of human relationships" —and "the vanished world of their fathers and mothers." They offered comfort and hope to such parents, who often found themselves caught in the "wide-eyed gaze" of their children seeming "to brand them as beings in an unknown and antique world."[17] The piano industry offered the solace of the Victorian age with all the convenience of the consumer culture. It was a profitable combination.

Appendix

Figure A.1. The Baldwin Company: Organizational Structure, ca. 1916

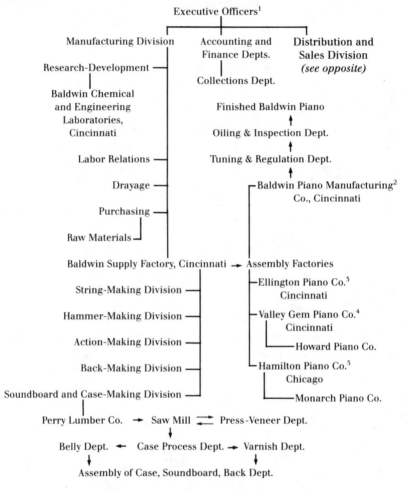

Source: Constructed from materials found in the D. H. Baldwin & Co. Archives, Cincinnati Historical Society, Eden Park, Cincinnati, Ohio.

[1]As in almost every piano company, the stockholders were also the major officers (owner-manager structure). In 1916 the officers were: G. W. Armstrong, President; H. S. Dickenson, Vice President; Lucien Wulsin, Treasurer; Frank A. McGee, Assistant Treasurer; Thomson DeSerisy, Secretary; J. P. Thornton, Assistant Secretary.

[2]Manufacturing the Baldwin piano—concert grands, grands, and uprights, and Baldwin Manualo player.

[3]Manufacturing the Ellington piano—grands and uprights, and Ellington Manualo player.

[4]Manufacturing the Howard upright piano, Howard Manualo, and Valley Gem upright.

Figure A.1 continued

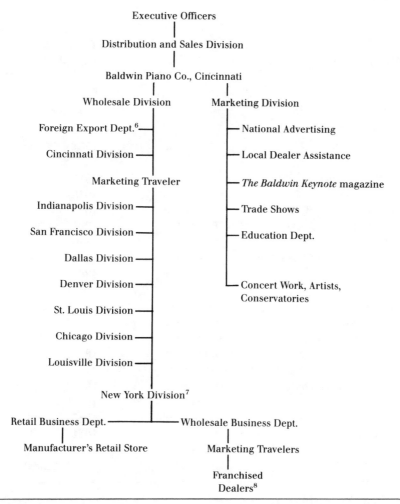

[5]Manufacturing the Hamilton piano—grands and uprights, and Hamilton Manualo piano; manufacturing also the Monarch upright piano, Monarch player, St. Regis upright, St. Regis player and the Modello player piano.

[6]Exporting to Mexico, Cuba, Puerto Rico, Jamaica, Barbados, Surinam, Demerara, Venezuela, Argentine Republic, Chile, Costa Rica, Mauritius, Queensland, East India, New South Wales, New Zealand, South Africa, Holland, Belgium, England, Denmark, France, Norway, Sweden, Italy, Russia, Turkey, and Spain.

[7]Each division is subdivided similarly. Marketing travelers were sales agents as well as collections agents at this time.

[8]The number of franchised dealerships varied per division. Sales were on consignment-contract.

Table A.1. Piano Combinations, Their Companies, and
Their Products, ca. 1916

Manufacturer	Location[e]	Date Estab- lished[f]	Produc- tion[g]
HOLDING COMPANIES—PUBLICLY ISSUED STOCK[a]			
American Piano Company, Inc.[1]	New York	1908	17,900 Total
Ampico Corporation[1'4]	New York	1915	*
Ampico[4]	New York	1916	*
Wm. Knabe & Co.[2]	Baltimore	1837	3,000
Chickering & Sons[2]	Boston	1823	1,500
J. & C. Fischer[2]	New York	1840	1,100
Foster, Armstrong & Co.[1'2]	Rochester	1894	3,000
Foster & Co.[3]	Rochester	1881	*
Ellsworth[4]	Rochester	?	*
Haines & Co.[3]	Rochester	?	*
Normandie[4]	Rochester	1902?	*
R. H. Waud[4]	Rochester	?	*
Armstrong Piano Co.[2]	Rochester	1884	2,400
J. B. Cook Piano Co.[3]	Rochester	?	*
Holmes & Sons[4]	Rochester	1906?	*
Stratford[4]	Rochester	190-?	*
Brewster Piano Co.[2]	Rochester	1883	3,000?
Haines Bros.[3]	Rochester	1851	900
Marshall & Wendell[2]	Rochester	1836	2,000
Primatone[4]	Rochester	1914?	1,000
Aeolian, Weber Piano & Pianola Co., Inc.[1]	New York	1903	9,800 Total
Aeolian Co., Inc.[2]	New York	1887	4,000
Pianola Co.[4]	New York	1897	*
Aeriol[4]	New York	1897?	*
Duo-Art[4]	New York	1913	*
Pianola[4]	New York	1897	*
Technola Piano Co.[3]	New York	1908?	*
Stroud Piano Co.[3]	New York	1911	*

Table A.1 continued

Manufacturer	Location[e]	Date Estab-lished[f]	Produc-tion[g]
Chilton Piano Co.[3]	New York	19-?	*
George Steck & Co.[2]	New York	1857	2,100
Wheelock Piano Co.[1'2]	New York	1877	700
Stuyvesant Piano Co.[4]	New York	1881	1,500
Weber Piano Co.[2]	New York	1851	1,500
Vocalion Organ Co.[2]	New York	—	†
Votey Organ Co.[2]	New York	—	†
Universal Music Co.[2] (perforated rolls)	New York	—	†
Orchestrelle Co.[1'4]	London	1903	†
Choralian Co.[1'4]	Berlin	1903	†
Pianola Co., LTD[1'4]	Melbourne	1903	†
Aeolian Co., LTD[1'4]	Paris	1903	†

HOLDING COMPANIES—CLOSED CORPORATIONS[b]

Kohler & Campbell Industries, Inc.[1]	New York	1896	25,900 Total
Kohler & Campbell[2]	New York	1896	11,000
Gordon & Sons[4]	New York	1909?	*
Preston[4]	New York	1897?	*
Conroy Piano Co.[4]	St. Louis	1900?	*
Milton Piano Co.[3]	New York	1892	*
Behr Bros. & Co. [2]	New York	1881	*
Waldorf Piano Co.[4]	New York	1896	*
Behr Bros.[4] (grand pianos)	New York	1881	2,000
Hazelton Bros.[2]	New York	1850	3,000
Francis Bacon Piano Co.[3]	New York	1856	1,500
Astor[3]	New York	1789	*
Davenport–Tracy Piano Co.[2]	New York	1873	1,100
Carter Piano Co.[4]	New York	1912	*
A. M. McPhail Piano Co.[2]	New York	1839	1,300

Table A.1 continued

Manufacturer	Location[e]	Date Estab-lished[f]	Produc-tion[g]
Autopiano Co.[2]	New York	1903	6,000
Pianista[4]	New York	1903	*
Symphotone[4]	New York	19-?	*
Auto-Pneumatic Action Co.[4]	New York	1900	†
Standard Pneumatic Action Co.[2]	New York	190-?	†
Republic Player Roll Corp.[2]	New York	19-?	†
Conway Musical Industries, Inc.[1]	Boston	1905	14,700 Total
Hallet & Davis Co.[2]	Boston	1835	4,000
Simplex Player Action Co.[2]	Worcester	—	†
Virtuola[4]	Boston	19-?	*
National Piano Manufacturing Co., Inc.[1'2]	Boston	1911	10,700 Subtotal
Air-O-Player[4]	Boston	1913	*
Briggs Piano Co.[3]	Boston	1868	3,500
Conway Piano Co.[2]	Boston	1906?	3,300
Lansing[4]	Boston	1906?	*
Lexington Piano Co.[4]	Boston	1906?	*
Merrill Piano Co.[2]	Boston	1885	1,900
Norris & Hyde Piano Co.[2]	Boston	1873	2,000?
Rice-Wuest Co., Inc.[1]	Woodbury, N.J.	1913	10,000 Total
Blasius & Sons[2]	Philadelphia	1855	10,000
Charles Albrecht Piano Co.[3]	Philadelphia	1789	*
Regent[4]	Philadelphia	1890?	*

Table A.1 continued

Manufacturer	Location[e]	Date Estab-lished[f]	Produc-tion[g]
Continental Piano Co., Inc.[1]	New Castle, Ind.	1912	14,700 Total
Jesse French & Sons Piano Co.[2]	New Castle, Ind.	1875	5,800
Krell-French Piano Co.[3]	New Castle, Ind.	1898	*
Lagonda Piano Co.[4]	New Castle, Ind.	1898	*
J. H. Browning[4]	New Castle, Ind.	?	*
Continental[4]	New Castle, Ind.	1912?	*
Euphonola[4]	New Castle, Ind.	?	*
Jefferson[4]	New Castle, Ind.	?	*
Ackerman & Lowe[4]	New Castle, Ind.	1907?	900
Kasselman[4]	New Castle, Ind.	?	*
Smith, Barnes & Strohber Piano Co.[2]	Chicago	1884	8,000
P. C. Hoffman[4]	Chicago	?	*
Lessing[4]	Chicago	1884?	*
Willard[4]	Chicago	?	*
Chicago Electric[4] (coin pianos)	Chicago	?	?
The Cable Company, Inc.[1]	Chicago	1899?	8,000 Total
Conover-Cable Piano Co., Inc.[1'2]	Chicago	1890	7,000
Conover Bros. Piano Co.[2]	New York	1881	*
Cable Piano Co.[2]	Chicago	1880	*
Carola Inner Player[4]	Chicago	1904	*
Euphona[4]	Chicago	1904	*
Kingsbury[4]	Chicago	1885	*
Wellington[4]	Chicago	1885	*
Western Cottage Piano & Organ Co.[2]	Ottaw, Ill.	1865	Disc. 1916
Merrifield[4]	Ottaw, Ill.	1900?	Disc. 1916
Mason & Hamlin Co.[2]	Boston	1854	1,000?

Table A.1 continued

Manufacturer	Location[e]	Date Estab- lished[f]	Produc- tion[g]
The Rudolph Wurlitzer Co., Inc.[1]	Cincinnati	1890	
Rudolph Wurlitzer Co.[2]	Cincinnati	1856	3,000[j] Total
Lyric Piano Co.[4]	Cincinnati	1909	*
Merriam[4]	Cincinnati	19-?	*
Underwood[4]	Cincinnati	19-?	*
Schaff Bros. Piano Co.[2]	Huntington, Ind.	1868	1,200
Rudolph Wurlitzer Manufacturing Co., Inc.[1'4]	N. Tonawanda, N.Y.	1909	?
Strad Piano Co.[3]	N. Tonawanda, N.Y.	1860	?
Farny[4]	N. Tonawanda, N.Y.	19-?	?
Kingston[4]	N. Tonawanda, N.Y.	19-?	?
Strad[4]	N. Tonawanda, N.Y.	1860	?
DeKleist Musical Instrument Mfg. Co.[3]	N. Tonawanda, N.Y.	18-?	?
Milner Musical Co.[2]	N. Tonawanda, N.Y.	?	†
R. L. Loud Music Co.[2]	N. Tonawanda, N.Y.	?	†
Tonophone Electric Player Co.[4]	N. Tonawanda, N.Y.	1899	?
Wurlitzer-Hope Jones Organ Co.[2]	N. Tonawanda, N.Y.	1910	†
Melville Clark Piano Co.[2,h]	Chicago	1900	2,200
Apollo[4]	Chicago	1901	*

CLOSED CORPORATIONS[c]

Steger Products Manufacturing Corp.[1]	Chicago	1893?	13,800 Total
Steger & Sons Piano Mfg. Co.[2]	Chicago	1879	1,800
Thompson Piano Co.[3]	Chicago	1870?	*
Artemis[4]	Chicago	18-?	*

Table A.1 continued

Manufacturer	Location[e]	Date Estab-lished[f]	Produc-tion[g]
Melostrello[4]	Chicago	1884	*
Singer Piano Co.[4]	Chicago	1893	12,000
Reed & Sons[3]	Chicago	1842	*
W. W. Kimball Co., Inc.[1]	Chicago	1882	13,400 Total
W. W. Kimball Piano Co.[2]	Chicago	1857	10,200
Whitney Piano Co.[4]	Chicago	1890?	2,000
Hinze[4]	Chicago	1885	1,200
The Baldwin Co., Inc.[1]	Cincinnati	1901[k]	12,800 Total
Manualo[4]	Cincinnati	19-?	*
Baldwin Piano Mfg. Co.[2]	Cincinnati	1862	2,300
Ellington Piano Co.[4']	Cincinnati	1890	1,500
Hamilton Piano Co.[4']	Chicago	1889	3,360
Monarch Piano Co.[4]	Chicago	1894	5,640
St. Regis[4]	Chicago	?	*
Modello[4]	Chicago	?	*
Schroeder & Sons[3]	Chicago	1888?	*
Howard Piano Co.[4]	Cincinnati	1895	*
Valley Gem Piano Co.[3]	Ripley, Ohio	1869	*
Sargent[4]	Ripley, Ohio	?	*
Jacob Doll & Sons, Inc.[1]	New York	1904	11,900 Total
Jacob Doll & Sons[2]	New York	1871	4,500
Doll & Son[4]	New York	18-?	*
Stodart[3]	New York	1819	*
Baus Piano Co.[3]	New York	1895	3,300
Mason[4]	New York	1908?	*?
Wellsmore Piano Co.[4]	New York	1908?	1,500
Hudson[4]	New York	19-?	*
Shattinger[4]	New York	19-?	*
Ernest Gabler & Bro.[2]	New York	1854	2,000
Faber[4]	New York	1912?	600

Table A.1 continued

Manufacturer	Location[e]	Date Estab-lished[f]	Produc-tion[g]
Electrova Co.[4] (coin pianos)	New York	1912?	?
The Gulbransen-Dickinson Co., Inc.[1]	Chicago	1906	9,000 Total
Gulbransen-Dickinson Co.[2]	Chicago	1906	9,000
Gulbransen[4]	Chicago	1915	*
Dickinson[4]	Chicago	1915?	*
M. Schulz Co., Inc.[1]	Chicago	1889	10,000 Total
M. Schulz Co.[2]	Chicago	1869	10,000
Brinkerhoff[4]	Chicago	1907?	*
Irving[4]	Chicago	1904?	*
Walworth Pianos[4]	Chicago	19-?	*
Schmoller & Mueller[4]	Omaha	19-?	*
Werner Piano Co.[2]	Chicago	1902	*
R. K. Maynard Piano Co.[3]	Chicago	1905	*
Bradford & Co.[4]	Chicago	19-?	*
Starr Piano Co., Inc.[1]	Richmond, Ind.	1884	7,000 Total[l]
Starr Piano Co.[2]	Richmond, Ind.	1872	7,000
Gennet & Son[4]	Richmond, Ind.	18-?	*
Remington[4]	Richmond, Ind.	1895	*
Richmond[4]	Richmond, Ind.	1895	*
Trayser Piano Co.[3]	Richmond, Ind.	1869	*
Hardman, Peck & Co., Inc.[1]	New York	1905	6,100 Total
Hardman, Peck & Co.[2]	New York	1842	2,100
Autotone[4]	New York	19-?	*

Table A.1 continued

Manufacturer	Location[e]	Date Estab- lished[f]	Produc- tion[g]
Playotone[4]	New York	1910?	*
E. G. Harrington & Co.[2]	New York	1886	4,000
Hensel[4]	New York	?	*
Standard[4]	New York	?	*
Cable-Nelson Piano Co., Inc.[1]	Chicago	1905	6,000 Total
Lakeside Piano Co.[3]	Chicago	1874	*
Sweetland[4]	Chicago	?	*
The Sterling Co., Inc.[1]	Derby, Conn.	1873	6,000 Total
Sterling Piano Co.[2]	Derby, Conn.	1866	3,000
Mendelssohn[4]	Derby, Conn.	1890?	1,000
Goetz & Co.[4]	Derby, Conn.	?	*
Lohmann[4]	Derby, Conn.	?	*
Huntington Piano Co.[2]	Shelton, Conn.	1894	2,000
Lester Piano Co., Inc.[1]	Philadelphia	1888?	5,720 Total
Lester Piano Co.[2]	Philadelphia	1888	3,000
Lawrence[4]	Philadelphia	1895?	*
Leonard & Co.[4]	Philadelphia	1900?	1,500
Channing[4]	Philadelphia	?	*
Schilling[4]	Philadelphia	?	*
Schubert Piano Co.[2]	New York	1882	1,220
Haddorff Piano Co.[1]	Rockford, Ill.	1902	5,000 Total
Clarendon[4]	Rockford, Ill.	1902?	*
Karl Zeck[4]	Rockford, Ill.	19-?	*
Temple[4]	Rockford, Ill.	1902?	*
Troubadour[4]	Rockford, Ill.	1912?	*

Table A.1 continued

Manufacturer	Location[e]	Date Estab- lished[f]	Produc- tion[g]
Zellner[4]	Rockford, Ill.	19-?	*
Brooks-Evans[4]	Minneapolis	1910?	*
C. Kurtzmann & Co., Inc.[1]	Buffalo	1896	5,000 Total
C. Kurtzmann & Co.[2]	Buffalo	1848	*
Louismann-Capen Co.[1'4]	Brockport, N.Y.	1912	*
Brockport Piano Mfrg. Co.[3]	Brockport, N.Y.	1893	*
Capen[4]	Brockport, N.Y.	1893	*
M. S. Phelps[4]	Brockport, N.Y.	1893	*
Witney & Co.[4]	Brockport, N.Y.	1893	*
Louismann[4]	Brockport, N.Y.	1912	*
Steinway & Sons, Inc.[1]	New York	1876	5,000 Total
Steinway & Sons[2]	New York	1853	5,000
Story & Clark, Co., Inc.[1]	Grand Haven, Mich.	1895	4,300 Total
Story & Clark Co.[2]	Grand Haven, Mich.	1857	*
Hampton[4]	Grand Haven, Mich.	1901?	*
Irvington[4]	Grand Haven, Mich.	1901	*
Repro-Phraso[4]	Grand Haven, Mich.	19-?	*

DEPARTMENT STORE CORPORATIONS MANUFACTURING PIANOS[d]

Manufacturer	Location[e]	Date Estab- lished[f]	Produc- tion[g]
Wanamaker's, Inc.[1]	Philadelphia	1909	7,400 Total
Schomacker Piano Co.[2]	Philadelphia	1838	880
Emerson Piano Co.[2]	Boston	1849	2,100
Lindeman & Sons Piano Co. (Henry & S. G. Lindeman affiliate)[2]	New York	1887	1,500
Melodigrand[4]	New York	1911?	3,000

Table A.1 continued

Manufacturer	Location[e]	Date Estab- lished[f]	Produc- tion[g]
Grinnell Bros.[1]	Detroit	1912	1,800 Total
Grinnell Bros.[2]	Detroit	1882	*
Clayton[4]	Detroit	—	*
Holly[4]	Detroit	—	*
Leonard[4]	Detroit	—	*
Playtona[4]	Detroit	—	*

Source: Information compiled from William Geppert, *The Official Guide to Piano Quality* (New York: Eilert Printing Co., 1916); *Presto Buyer's Guide to Pianos, Player-Pianos, and Reproducing Pianos* (Chicago: Presto, 1926); Alfred Dolge, *Pianos and Their Makers*, 2 vols. (Covina, Calif.: Covina Publishing Co., 1911, 1913; vol. 1 reprinted, New York: Dover, 1972); Bob Pierce, comp., *Pierce Piano Atlas* (Long Beach, Calif.: Bob Pierce, publisher, 7th ed., 1977).

Note: This table portrays those corporations with the largest production (5,000 pianos per year or more) in 1916, the exceptions being the well-known Story & Clark and Grinnell Bros. firms, which enjoyed a very high capitalization (see table 3.1, chapter 3), despite their lower production figures. Other popular firms manufacturing less than 5,000 units per year but not included in this appendix include: 1) *Werner Industries* (Cincinnati), a holding company controlling Auto-Grand Piano Co. (Connersville, Ind., est. 1905), which in 1905 had absorbed the (Albert) Krell Piano Co. (Cincinnati, 1889), manufacturing Krell, Auto-Grand, Auto-Player, Pian-Auto, and Royal pianos; 2) *Janssen Piano Co.* (Elkhart, Ind., 1901?), manufacturing Janssen and R. S. Howard pianos, the firm absorbed Franklin L. Raymond Piano Co. (Cleveland, 1856), manufacturing Raymond and Langdon Piano Co. pianos—Janssen eventually absorbed Horace Waters & Co. (New York, 1845), manufacturing Chester and Autola brands, and also absorbed Wissner & Sons (New York, 1878), manufacturing Wissner, Putnam, Reinhard & Co., and Leckerling & Co. (New York, 1886), which Wissner previously had absorbed; 3) *Waltham Piano Co.* (Milwaukee, 1885), manufacturing Waltham, Wilson, Warfield, Electratone, and others; and 4) *Wesser Bros.* (New York, 1879), manufacturing Wesser, Billings & Co., Marveola, ReRendo, Orpheola, and Winfield pianos.

[1]Parent corporation or holding company.
[1,2]Combination—Former parent corporation absorbed into [1] and retaining separate factories after merger.
[1,4]Trademark parent company—created by [1] and not acquired through merger.
[2]Combination—formerly an independent company, retaining its separate factory organization under [1] after merger or incorporation; original owner may be re-

Table A.1 continued

---

tired or deceased. (Note: In certain examples—Steinway & Sons, Gulbransen, Story & Clark—the [2] designates the original company rather than a combination, since only an incorporation rather than a merger occurred.)

[3]Consolidation—Formerly an independent company, completely absorbed into [1] or [2] and existing in trademark-name only after merger; no separate factory.

[4]Trademark name only—Product created by its parent company; did not exist previously; not acquired through merger; no separate factory (if separate factory organization known, denoted as [4']).

*Production of this trademark is included in and not distinguished from the production figure immediately above this entry. Usually indicates no separate factory.

[†]Table excludes figures for overseas piano production or for manufacture of actions, organs, perforated rolls, etc.

[a]Combination led to formation of holding company, with the officers and managers of the merging companies directly concerned with total operating activities. Stocks were issued and sold on public stock exchange.

[b]Same as [a] except that issue of stock was restricted to family and others within the corporation.

[c]Private corporation whose central office (rather than a holding company) controlled the various subcompanies. Issue of stock restricted within family and corporation.

[d]Department store corporation which controlled piano companies listed.

[e]Location in 1916.

[f]Year in which entry was established (if [1] then this is the year entry was incorporated; if [4] then this is the approximate year this brand name began to be manufactured).

[g]Estimates only, based on serial numbers; verification almost impossible. Treat with caution.

[h]Wurlitzer became the exclusive dealer for Melville Clark in 1914, and absorbed the firm completely in 1919.

[j]Wurlitzer total production unknown. Figures shown are only for pianos designed for home use; does not include coin-operated pianos or theater photoplayers and organs for commercial use. All authorities agree that Wurlitzer was the largest manufacturer of mechanical instruments, including player pianos.

[k]Formerly D. H. Baldwin & Co., est. 1873.

[l]Alfred Dolge credits Starr Piano Co. with producing about 18,000 pianos annually (*Pianos and Their Makers*, vol. 1, p. 349).

Table A.2. Number of Musicians and Teachers of Music, 1900–1940

Year	Number
1900	92,000
1910	139,000[a]
1920	130,000
1930	165,000
1940	167,000

Source: U.S. Department of Commerce. Bureau of the Census.

[a]61 percent were classified teachers of music, of which 82 percent were female. By contrast, only 29 percent of the remaining 55,000 classified as musicians were female. The census did not distinguish teachers of music from musicians for the other years.

Notes

PREFACE

1. Louis C. Elson, *History of American Music* (New York: Macmillan, 1904), p. 279.

2. Halévy quoted in "Days of Glory Revived for the Piano: New Teaching Modes Repopularizing the Instrument, Once a Social Asset," *New York Times Magazine*, May 31, 1931, p. 16.

3. Slang dictionaries are useful tools for discovering a culture's undercurrents or establishing popular trends. Among the best are Harold Wentworth and Stuart Berg Flexner, eds., *Dictionary of American Slang* (New York: Thomas Y. Crowell, 2d supplemented ed., 1975); Eric Partridge, ed., *A Dictionary of Slang and Unconventional English* (New York: Macmillan, 7th ed., 1970); and Lester V. Berrey and Melvin Van Den Bark, *The American Thesarus of Slang* (New York: Thomas Y. Crowell, 2d ed., 1953).

4. Julius Weinberger, "Economic Aspects of Recreation," *Harvard Business Review* 15 (Summer 1937): 450–51.

5. Robert Braine, "Canned Music," *The Etude* 50 (February 1932): 136.

6. Francis Toye quoted in *New York Times*, June 17, 1928, sec. 8, p. 7.

CHAPTER ONE

1. Daniel Walker Howe, "Victorian Culture in America," in *Victorian America*, ed. Daniel Walker Howe, pp. 3–28 (Philadelphia: University of Pennsylvania Press, 1976).

2. The term historians are assigning the nineteenth-century doctrine of separate spheres, or role division of the sexes, which found woman's place in the home, accompanied by an elaborate set of assumed stereotypical female characteristics, such as piety, purity, and domesticity. (Sometimes also called the cult of true womanhood.)

3. Daniel T. Rodgers, *The Work Ethic in Industrial America, 1850–1920* (Chicago: University of Chicago Press, 1978), pp. 7, 12, 14, 15, 16. See also Walter E. Houghton, *The Victorian Frame of Mind, 1830–1870* (New Haven: Yale University Press, 1957).

4. Review quoted in Arthur Loesser, *Men, Women and Pianos: A Social*

History (New York: Simon and Schuster, 1954), p. 502. On the phenomenon of the music virtuoso in Victorian America, see Loesser, pp. 483–90. 497–502, 527, 531–36; and H. Wiley Hitchcock, *Music in the United States: A Historical Introduction* (Englewood Cliffs, N.J.: Prentice-Hall, 2d ed., 1974), pp. 58–59. See also the accounts of various artists in America in Harold C. Schonberg, *The Great Pianists from Mozart to the Present* (New York: Simon and Schuster, 1963).

5. Loesser, *Men, Women and Pianos*, pp. 531–36; Schonberg, *Great Pianists*, pp. 289–91, 349.

6. Gerald Carson, "The Piano in the Parlor," *American Heritage* 17 (December 1965): 55.

7. "Old Fashioned Piano Teacher Gives Way to Studio and Radio," *New York Times* (hereafter *NYT*), June 28, 1925, sec. 9, p. 2.

8. Schonberg, *Great Pianists*, p. 234.

9. Quoted in *101 Best Songs* (Chicago: The Cable Piano Co., 1915). Beneath the songs are epigrams supporting the work ethic or the benefit of music.

10. Ernest R. Kroeger, "Changes in Piano Teaching in Fifty Years," *The Etude* 47 (December 1929): 885.

11. Ibid.

12. Amy Fay, ["Master Rules for Successful Piano Practice,"] in *Master Rules for Successful Piano Practice*, edited by James Francis Cooke, pp. 9–10 (Philadelphia: Theodore Presser Co., 1910).

13. Frederick E. Drinker and Jay Henry Mowbray, *Theodore Roosevelt: His Life and Works* (Washington, D.C.: National Publishing Co., 1919), p. 455; *101 Best Songs*, p. 54.

14. Gerald W. Johnson, "Excerpts from *A Little Night Music*," *American Home* 21 (December 1938): 22, 77.

15. Arthur L. Manchester, "The Status of Music Education in the United States," *U.S. Bureau of Education Bulletins*, 1908, no. 4: 78–79. See also Grace Helen Nash, "Modern Trends in Piano Teaching," *Music Teachers National Association Conference Proceedings* (hereafter *MTNA Proceedings*), 1930:158–66; and Olin Downes, "The Question of the Piano," *NYT*, June 4, 1933, sec. 9, p. 4.

16. R. F. Delderfield, *For My Own Amusement* (New York: Simon and Schuster, 1972), pp. 63–65.

17. Quoted in *101 Best Songs*, p. 69.

18. Alfred Dolge, *Pianos and Their Makers*, 2 vols. (Covina, Calif.: Covina Publishing Co., 1911, 1913; vol. 1 reprinted, New York: Dover, 1972), vol. 1, p. 347.

19. Charles M. Schwab, "Music, the Great Humanizer," *The Etude* 43 (December 1925): 839–40.

20. For the music in industry movement, see Virgel J. Grabel, "How

American Industries Are Utilizing Music," *The Etude* 41 (May 1923): 303–4, 351; Kenneth S. Clark, *Music in Industry* [two-year survey of the National Bureau for the Advancement of Music] (New York: National Bureau for the Advancement of Music, 1929); "Music as a Spur to Production," *Playground* 16 (January 1923): 461–62; *Music in Industry: A Manual on Music for Work and for Recreation in Business and Industry* (Chicago: Industrial Recreation Assn., 1944); "Music and Labor: Symposium," *The Etude* 41 (June 1923): 867–68; and the appropriate chapters in Dorothy M. Schullian and Max Schoen, eds., *Music and Medicine* (New York: Henry Schuman, 1948).

21. Rodgers, *Work Ethic*, pp. 231–32.

22. Houghton, *Victorian Frame of Mind*, pp. 341–48; Nancy F. Cott, *The Bonds of Womanhood* (New Haven: Yale University Press, 1977), pp. 64, 67–69.

23. *New York Times Magazine*, August 10, 1930, p. 2; *NYT*, July 8, 1930, p. 4.

24. Cott, *Bonds of Womanhood*, pp. 1–2, 11n, 64, 67–69, 71, 84, 92; Rodgers, *Work Ethic*, pp. 182–83, 208. See also Carl N. Degler, *At Odds: Women and the Family in America from the Revolution to the Present* (New York: Oxford University Press, 1980), especially pp. 8–9; Nancy Woloch, *Women and the American Experience* (New York: Knopf, 1984), pp. 113–20 passim.

25. Woloch, *Women and the American Experience*, pp. 113–25, especially pp. 119–20; Degler, *At Odds*, pp. 26, 27, 30, 31.

26. Harvey Green, *The Light of the Home: An Intimate View of the Lives of Women in Victorian America* (New York: Pantheon, 1983), pp. 93–94; Cott, *Bonds of Womanhood*, pp. 115, 117–19; E. Chester, *Girls and Women*, The Riverside Library for Young People, no. 8 (New York: Houghton, Mifflin, 1890), pp. 99, 101.

27. *The Habits of Good Society: A Handbook of Etiquette for Ladies and Gentlemen* (London: Virtue and Co., n.d. [1890?]), p. 237. Published also under titles *The Ladies' and Gentlemen's Etiquette Book* (New York, 1879), and *Sensible Etiquette and Good Manners of the Best Society* (New York, 1882), both "edited by Mrs. Jane Aster [pseud.]."

28. *The Habits of Good Society*, p. 231.

29. Chester, *Girls and Women*, pp. 45–46.

30. Justus M. Forman, "The Honor of St. Cere," *Everybody's Magazine* 18 (February 1908): 256.

31. Lilian Bell, *A Book of Girls* (Boston: L. C. Page, 1903), pp. 28–29.

32. Adolph Bernard Marx, *The Music of the Nineteenth Century and Its Culture* (London: Robert Cocks & Co., 1855), pp. 73, 75.

33. Letter, Oscar Wilde to Robert Ross, quoted in *The Wit and Humor of Oscar Wilde*, ed. Alvin Redman, p. 88 (New York: Dover, 1959).

34. Chester, *Girls and Women*, pp. 46, 100.

35. *Habits of Good Society*, pp. 232–33.

36. Loesser, *Men, Women and Pianos*, p. 65.

37. "Galloping Years in Musicdom," *The Etude* 47 (May 1929): 344.

38. Jane Austen's sentiments toward "James Benwick" were echoed over eighty years later by Elinor Glyn, who wrote of her character in *The Visits of Elizabeth* (1900), "The Marquis . . . looked thoroughly worn out and as *piano* as a beaten dog." On the feminization of music, see Satis N. Coleman, *Your Child's Music* (New York: John Day Co., 1939), pp. 80–81; "Is Music an Effeminate Art?" *Current Opinion* 75 (November 1923): 586–87; Harold Randolph, "The Femininization of Music," *MTNA Proceedings*, 1922:194–200; Thomas Whitney Surette, *Music and Life* (Boston: Houghton Mifflin Co., 1917), pp. xii, 27; and Herbert Witherspoon, "Music as a Vital Factor in Education," *MTNA Proceedings*, 1926:54–65.

39. "Music and Labor," p. 867.

40. Randolph, "Feminization of Music," pp. 194–200. See also Frank A. Scott, "A Survey of Home Music Study," *MTNA Proceedings*, 1919:171–77; and Ralph L. Baldwin, "An Unsuspected Popular Instinct for Musical Education," *MTNA Proceedings*, 1913:179–84.

41. The survey also showed that where males did play a musical instrument, it was the guitar; 65 percent of all guitarists were men. See 1978 Gallup Survey in "1977 A Banner Year for U.S. Music Industry," *The Music Trades* 126 (August 1978): 50.

42. Chittenden Turner, "Music and the Women's Crusade," *Arts and Decoration* 19 (September 1923): 29, 70.

43. *NYT*, November 9, 1922, p. 16.

44. Congreve quoted in *The Oxford Dictionary of Quotations*, 3d ed., (New York: Oxford University Press, 1980), p. 160.

45. Quoted in Trinity Lutheran Church, Victoria, Texas, *Bulletin*, March 1985: insert (author's collection).

46. Doyle quoted in *Oxford Dictionary of Quotations*, p. 192.

47. Quoted in Austin B. Caswell, "Social and Moral Music," in *Music in American Society, 1776–1976*, ed. George McCue, p. 51 (New Brunswick, N.J.: Transaction Books, 1977).

48. Charles L. Gary, *Vignettes of Music Education History* (Washington, D.C.: Music Educators National Conference, 1964), pp. 4–5.

49. Lloyd Frederick Sunderman, *Historical Foundations of Music Education in the United States* (Metuchen, N.J.: Scarecrow Press, 1971), pp. 206–7.

50. *Habits of Good Society*, pp. 215, 232.

51. A. Pupin, "Formation of Character through a Proper Study of Music," *The Musician* 14 (February 1909): 67; Surette, *Music and Life*, pp. 24–25, 250. Surette also asserted that though music is an end, not a means, and it

is not a moral force "in the Darwin-Spencerian sense," music neverthe-less supplies "the only means" of bringing children into "actual and inti-mate contact with beauty," and it is a powerful social force as well. Surette then readily acknowledged the moral value of beauty and socialization.

52. Walter R. Spalding, "Is Music a Non-Essential?" *The Outlook*, March 20, 1918, pp. 441–42; Walter R. Spalding, "Music a Necessary Part of the Soldier's Equipment," *The Outlook*, June 5, 1918, pp. 223–24. See also Leon R. Maxwell, "Music as War Ammunition," *MTNA Proceedings*, 1918: 68–77.

53. *NYT*, May 26, 1918, sec. 5, p. 8; *NYT*, June 2, 1918, p. 16.

54. Walter Damrosch quoted in Elliot Gabrielle, "Music at the Front," *The Outlook*, October 23, 1918, pp. 286–87. See also L. Waldo Fullerton, "Music and the War," *The Outlook*, January 19, 1916, pp. 151–52.

55. "The Golden Hour Plan: America's Most Serious Problem—A Possi-ble Solution in which You May Have a Vital Part," *The Etude* 39 (April 1921): 223; "The Golden Hour," *The Etude* 39 (May 1921): 294; "What about the Golden Hour," *The Etude* 40 (March 1922): 151; "America's Greatest Present Problem," *The Etude* 44 (January 1926): 8.

56. Witherspoon, "Music as a Vital Factor," pp. 58–59.

57. *Habits of Good Society*, p. 215.

58. Marx, *Music of the Nineteenth Century*, p. 133.

59. Thomas Tapper, *The Education of the Music Teacher* (Philadelphia: Theodore Presser Co., 1915), pp. 80, 83.

60. See, for example, Ronald Pearsall, *Victorian Popular Music* (Lon-don: David and Charles Publishers, 1973), pp. 111, 123.

61. Augustus D. Zanig, "Music Settlement Schools," *MTNA Proceedings*, 1922:62–66.

62. Tapper, *Education of the Music Teacher*, pp. 85–87.

63. Willem Van de Wall, "The Musician's Contribution to Modern Men-tal Health," *MTNA Proceedings*, 1924:145–59; MTNA Committee on Com-munity Music, "1925 Report," *MTNA Procedings*, 1925:264; *NYT*, June 6, 1922, p. 18; *NYT*, March 17, 1931, p. 28; James L. Mursell, *Human Values in Music Education* (New York: Silver, Burdett & Co., 1934), p. 130. See also the appropriate chapters in Schullian and Schoen, *Music and Medi-cine*.

64. Mursell, *Human Values in Music*, pp. 34–35, 141–43, 148–53, 160; A. Fellows, "Creative Music and the Bad Boy," *Progressive Education* 8 (April 1931): 348–49; Coleman, *Your Child's Music*, pp. 3–4.

65. Nancy Cott, for example, identifies the moral power of the Victorian woman in her ability to socially integrate men and restrain them from antisocial behavior; see *Bonds of Womanhood*, p. 69n.

66. Catharine E. Beecher and Harriet Beecher Stowe, *The American Woman's Home* (New York: J. B. Ford, 1869; reprint, Watkins Glen, N.Y.:

American Life Foundation Library of Victorian Culture, 1979), pp. 26, 296.

67. Chester, *Girls and Women*, pp. 123–24, 149–50.

68. Woloch, *Women and the American Experience*, pp. 116–17.

69. Siegfried Giedion, *Mechanization Takes Command* (New York: Norton, 1948), pp. 378, 623, 689. See also Gwendolyn Wright, *Moralism and the Model Home: Domestic Architecture and Cultural Conflict in Chicago, 1873–1913* (Chicago: University of Chicago Press, 1980), p. 34.

70. Ralph Dutton, *The Victorian Home: Some Aspects of 19th-Century Taste and Manners* (London: Batsford, 1954), p. 8; Dennis Chapman, *The Home and Social Status* (London: Routledge and Kegan Paul, Ltd., 1955), p. 42; David P. Handlin, *The American Home: Architecture and Society, 1815–1915* (Boston: Little, Brown, 1979), pp. 18–19; Woloch, *Women and the American Experience*, p. 116. See also P. W. Wilson, "Victorian Days that Beckon Us," *NYT Magazine*, April 30, 1933, pp. 10–11; and Wright, *Moralism and the Model Home*.

71. Loesser, *Men, Women and Pianos*, p. 54.

72. H. Wayne Morgan, *Unity and Culture: The United States, 1877–1900* (Baltimore: Penguin Books, 1971). p. 83. See also Loesser, *Men, Women and Pianos*, pp. 520–31.

73. James Parton, "The Piano in the United States," *The Atlantic Monthly* 20 (July 1867): 82.

74. William Braid White, "The Decline of the American Piano Industry," *The American Mercury* 28 (February 1933): 211. Historian Paul E. Johnson notes that pianos entered rural areas around Rochester, New York, even before the Civil War—see his *A Shopkeeper's Millennium* (New York: Hill and Wang, 1978), p. 19; and Loesser, *Men, Women and Pianos*, pp. 520–31.

75. The original reference to prudish American ladies' draping the "limbs" of their pianos with "modest little trousers" appears in Captain Frederick Marryat, *A Diary in America* (London, 1839): vol. 2, pp. 45, 246. Various writers have commented on this fantastically Victorian phenomenon, e.g. Lewis Mumford, *Sketches from Life: The Autobiography of Lewis Mumford, The Early Years* (New York: Dial Press, 1984), p. 11; Eric John Dingwall, *The American Woman* (New York: Rinehart & Co., 1957), pp. 83, 93; Carl N. Degler, "What Ought to Be and What Was: Women's Sexuality in the Nineteenth Century," *American Historical Review* 79 (December 1974): 468. Piano historian David Wainwright asserts that Victorians put frills on piano legs to protect from dust and damage, not because of prudery—see *The Piano Makers* (London: Hutchinson, 1975), p. 114. The most recent historical analysis appears in Peter Gay, *Education and the Senses* (New York: Oxford University Press, 1984), pp. 341, 495. Gay doubts the validity of the whole phenomenon, contending that "this peculiar bit of prudishness is either wholly fictitious, unique, or very rare." Wainwright and Gay both miss the complexity of the situation: the inter-

twining of domesticity, the moral value of music, and the role the piano played in Victorian society. Part of the reason Victorians dressed their pianos in skirts of Genovese velvet, Chinese brocade, silk, satin, India cotton prints, "a rare bit of tapestry, brocade, or an old Paisley shawl" was that it was fashionable to do so, even into the 1920s. Also, covering the massiveness and ugliness of Victorian furniture, as Harvey Green points out, was common—see *Light of the Home*, pp. 98–99. See also Helen Harford Baldwin, "The Piano—The Soul of the Studio," *The Musician* 31 (December 1926): 15, 36, and the articles by Mrs. Somerset Maugham and Helen Spracklin in note 94. Nevertheless, it makes little difference why Victorians dressed the piano, or even whether they did at all. The significance lies in the existence of the myth itself, not in whether it is to be believed. That such a story was circulated at all is just another example of the close relationship between woman and the home, domesticity, the moral value of music, and the role of the piano in tying all this together.

76. Green, *Light of the Home*, pp. 93–94.

77. Mary Gay Humphreys, *The House and Home, A Practical Book* (New York: Charles Scribner's Sons, 1896), vol. 2, p. 113.

78. See James Truslow Adams, "Our Way of Life Yesterday and Today: The Symbolic Evening at Home Has Been Annihilated in America by Mechanical Devices," *NYT Magazine*, August 3, 1930, pp. 4–5; Green, *Light of the Home*, pp. 93–94; and Chapman, *Home and Social Status*, pp. 21, 41–42, 115.

79. Adams, "Our Way of Life Yesterday and Today," pp. 4–5.

80. Julia B. Foraker, *I Would Live It Again: Memories of a Vivid Life* (New York: Harper and Brothers, 1932), pp. 69–70; Emily Apt Geer, *First Lady: The Life of Lucy Webb Hayes* (Kent, Ohio: Kent State University Press, 1984), p. 177. See also Elise K. Kirk, *Music at the White House: A History of the American Spirit* (Urbana: University of Illinois Press, 1986), pp. 113, 115, 124.

81. Dutton, *Victorian Home*, p. 137.

82. *Habits of Good Society*, pp. 233, 234; Daphne Dale, *Our Manners and Social Customs: A Practical Guide* (Chicago: Elliot and Beezley, 1892), pp. 234–35. See also Pearsall, *Victorian Popular Music*, p. 88; and Ronald Pearsall, *Edwardian Popular Music* (Cranbury, N.J.: Associated University Presses, 1975), pp. 119–23.

83. Janet Dunbar, *The Early Victorian Woman: Some Aspects of Her Life* (London: George G. Harrap and Co., 1953), p. 89; Chester, *Girls and Women*, pp. 149–50; Loesser, *Men, Women and Pianos*, pp. 503–4, 506–7, 508; Pearsall, *Victorian Popular Music*, pp. 81–82.

84. Loesser, *Men, Women and Pianos*, pp. 73, 291–92, 506–7, 508, 543–45; Pearsall, *Victorian Popular Music*, pp. 89, 94.

85. "Why Should a Young Girl Take Up the Study of Music?" *The Musician* 14 (February 1909): 72. See also Anne Bryan McCall, "Girl's Education in Music," *Woman's Home Companion*, March 12, 1912, p. 27.

86. Quoted in Carson, "Piano in the Parlor," p. 55.

87. Kathryn Kish Sklar, *Catharine Beecher: A Study in American Domesticity* (New York: Norton, 1976; first published by Yale University Press, 1973), p. 29.

88. George Payne Bent, *Tales of Travel, Life and Love: An Autobiography* (Los Angeles: The *Times-Mirror* Press, 1924), p. 165; De Forest quoted in Erik Barnouw, *A History of Broadcasting in the U.S.* (New York: Oxford University Press, 1966), vol. 1, p. 26.

89. Ernst Lubin, *The Piano Duet* (New York: Da Capo Press, 1970), p. 4.

90. *Habits of Good Society*, pp. 215–16.

91. Wright Morris, *A Cloak of Light: Writing My Life* (New York: Harper and Row, 1985), pp. 12–13.

92. For Phelps, see Ann Douglas, *The Feminization of American Culture* (New York: Knopf, 1977; reprinted, New York: Avon Books, 1978), p. 269.

93. Green, *Light of the Home*, p. 13; "Keep Your Foot on the Soft Pedal" song slide shown in John W. Ripley, "Romance and Joy, Tears and Heartache, and All for a Nickel," *Smithsonian* 12 (March 1982): 76, 77.

94. Mrs. Somerset Maugham, "Lighting the Piano: Some Suggestions for Dressing This Instrument So That It Becomes an Object of Decoration," *House and Garden* 47 (April 1925): 72; Helen Spracklin, "How to Determine Its Place in the Room," *House Beautiful* 63 (February 1928): 151; James Francis Cooke, "The Piano as a Home Investment," *The Etude* 47 (February 1929): 91.

CHAPTER TWO

1. *New York Times* (hereafter *NYT*), June 4, 1911, p. 1.

2. Arthur Loesser, *Men, Women and Pianos: A Social History* (New York: Simon and Schuster, 1954), pp. 548–49.

3. George M. Otto, Executive Director, National Piano Manufacturers Association, letter to author, November 11, 1980; C. Albert Jacobs, Jr., "The Piano Industry: Its Past, Present and Future," *National Retail Dry Goods Association Bulletin* 22 (May 1940): 35; Alfred Dolge, *Pianos and Their Makers*, 2 vols. (Covina, Calif.: Covina, 1911, 1913; vol. 1 reprinted, New York: Dover, 1972), vol. 1, pp. 459–66.

4. *NYT*, August 17, 1924, sec. 8, p. 10.

5. Rudi Blesh and Harriet Janis, *They All Played Ragtime* (New York: Oak Publications, rev. ed., 1971), p. 135; Edward A. Berlin, *Ragtime: A*

Musical and Cultural History (Berkeley and Los Angeles: University of California Press, 1980), p. 41; Rudi Blesh, "Scott Joplin," *American Heritage* 26 (June 1975): 87.

6. Quoted in Peter Gammond, *Scott Joplin and the Ragtime Era* (New York: St. Martin's Press, 1975), p. 179.

7. Leo Oehmler, " 'Ragtime': A Pernicious Evil and Enemy of True Art," *Musical Observer* 11 (September 1914): 15.

8. Quoted in Gammond, *Scott Joplin and the Ragtime Era*, pp. 7–8.

9. Neil Leonard, "The Reaction to Ragtime," in *Ragtime: Its History, Composers and Music*, ed. John Edward Hasse, pp. 102–13 (New York: Schirmer Books, 1985); William J. Schafer and Johannes Riedel, *The Art of Ragtime: Form and Meaning of an Original Black American Art* (Baton Rouge: Louisana State University Press, 1973), pp. 103–4, 128; Berlin, *Ragtime*, pp. 123, 128. See "Ragtime's Popularity," in Berlin, *Ragtime*, pp. 45–46, and Blesh, "Scott Joplin," *American Heritage*, p. 87.

10. K. Peter Etzkorn, "Popular Music: The Sounds of the Many," in *Music in American Life*, ed. George McCue, p. 129 (New Brunswick, N.J.: Transaction Books, 1977).

11. Michael Montgomery, Trebor Jay Tichenor, and John Edward Hasse, "Ragtime on Piano Rolls," in *Ragtime: Its History, Composers and Music*, ed. John Edward Hasse, p. 95 (New York: Schirmer's Books, 1985). This insightful, scholarly treatment of the phenomenon of ragtime is especially useful for its splendid bibliography.

12. Rudi Blesh, "Scott Joplin: Black-American Classicist," in *The Collected Works of Scott Joplin*, ed. Vera Brodsky Lawrence, vol. 1, pp. xxiii (New York: New York Public Library, 1972); James Haskins, with Kathleen Benson, *Scott Joplin: The Man Who Made Ragtime* (New York: Stein and Day/Scarborough House, 1980; originally published in 1978 by Doubleday), pp. 101–5, 109, 111, 131–32; Berlin, *Ragtime*, pp. 74–75; Blesh, "Scott Joplin," *American Heritage*, pp. 28, 87; "Scott Joplin: From Rags to Opera," *Time*, September 15, 1975, p. 86; Rudi Blesh, "Scott Joplin," LP booklet in *Scott Joplin: The Complete Works for Piano*, played by Dick Hyman, p. 1 (New York: RCA Records, 1975). In their award-winning biography of the composer, Haskins and Benson challenge the legend that the "Maple Leaf Rag" sold 75,000 copies in the first six months, though they acknowledge its phenomenal if eventual success—see *Scott Joplin*, pp. 102, 131–32, 217n35, 220n21. David A. Jasen and Trebor Jay Tichenor cite publisher John Stark's personal ledger for the figure of 500,000 copies of the rag sold by the end of 1909—see *Rags and Ragtime: A Musical History* (New York: Seabury, 1978), p. 78. Blesh affirms that the rag was the first sheet music piece to reach a million sales, but does not give a date, except in the RCA booklet, where he states the year 1904.

13. Scott Joplin, *School of Ragtime: Exercises for Piano* (New York: Scott Joplin, publisher, 1908), reprinted in Lawrence, ed., *The Collected Works of Scott Joplin*, vol. 1, p. 284.

14. Schafer and Riedel, *Art of Ragtime*, p. 90. On the notion of Theodore Roosevelt as celebrity, see Lewis L. Gould, "The Price of Fame: Theodore Roosevelt as a Celebrity, 1909–1919," *Lamar Journal of the Humanities* 10 (Fall 1984): 7–18.

15. Schafer and Riedel, *Art of Ragtime*, pp. 34, 37; Jasen and Tichenor, *Rags and Ragtime*, p. 7. Edward A. Berlin notes that "however artless the Tin Pan Alley product may be," it was hardly a late arrival. By the 1880s, New York publishers already were issuing compositions resembling the rag idiom, and such pieces were well established by the time "Maple Leaf Rag" was published in 1899—see *Ragtime*, p. 195. David Ewen treats the subject more fully in *The Life and Death of Tin Pan Alley: The Golden Age of American Popular Music* (New York: Funk and Wagnalls, 1964).

16. David Ewen, *American Popular Songs from the Revolutionary War to the Present* (New York: Random House, 1966), pp. 8–9; Schafer and Riedel, *Art of Ragtime*, p. 94; Berlin, *Ragtime*, p. 185.

17. Scott Joplin, *School of Ragtime*, reprinted in Lawrence, ed., *Collected Works of Scott Joplin*, vol. 1, p. 284.

18. Chorus from "I'm Certainly Living a Rag-Time Life," by Robert S. Roberts and Gene Johnson (1900), quoted in *The Ragtime Songbook*, Ann Charters, compiler (New York: Oak Publications, 1965), pp. 108–9. Also quoted in Schafer and Riedel, *Art of Ragtime*, p. 111.

19. Blesh and Janis, *They All Played Ragtime*, pp. 130, 139.

20. "Pianofortissimo: In 1935 the Piano Industry Discovered Style," *Fortune* 20 (August 1939): 46.

21. "Music Ex Machina," *The Atlantic Monthly* 112 (November 1913): 714.

22. See, for example, E. Chester, *Girls and Women* (New York: Houghton, Mifflin, 1890), p. 46; Jacob Eisenberg, "Apathy toward Piano Study: Causes and Remedies," *The Musician* 27 (November 1922): 17, 30; John C. Bostelmann, Jr., "A New Approach to Piano Study," *The Musician* 32 (October 1927): 13, 34; Thomas Whitney Surette, "Music for Children," *The Atlantic Monthly* 117 (March 1916): 356–65; B. H. Haggin, "A Pretty Mess," *The Nation*, July 18, 1928, pp. 66–67; Archibald T. Davidson, *Music Education in America* (New York: Harper and Bros., 1928); and David S. Grover, *The Piano: Its Story from Zither to Grand* (London: Robert Hale, 1976), pp. 171–72.

23. Letter quoted in J. Lawrence Erb, "The Problems of the Music Teacher," *Music Teachers National Association Conference Proceedings* (hereafter *MTNA Proceedings*), 1917:9–10.

24. R. F. Delderfield, *For My Own Amusement* (New York: Simon and Schuster, 1972), p. 65.

25. Wilde quoted in *The Wit and Humor of Oscar Wilde*, ed. Alvin Redman, p. 89 (New York: Dover, 1959). Shaw quoted in *The Oxford Dictionary of Quotations*, 3d ed. (New York: Oxford University Press, 1980), p. 497.

26. Carroll Brent Chilton, "A Musical Caliban," *The Independent*, April 11, 1907, pp. 838–44; Rice quoted in Chilton, p. 840; Edward B. Birge, "Music-Appreciation in Public Schools," *MTNA Proceedings*, 1909:142–44.

27. Yolanda Mero, "Musical Democracy vs. Pianism," *The Musician* 22 (June 1917): 494.

28. "Music and the American Home," *The Outlook*, October 3, 1917, pp. 180–81, 182–83; Aeolian advertisement, *NYT*, December 30, 1908, p. 2; H. Wiley Hitchcock, *Music in the United States: A Historical Introduction* (Englewood Cliffs, N.J.: Prentice-Hall, 2d ed., 1974), pp. 53–60, 65.

29. Votey presented the original Pianola to the Smithsonian Institution in the 1920s. For the development of the push-up piano-player and the self-contained player piano, see Arthur W. J. G. Ord-Hume, *Pianola: The History of the Self-Playing Piano* (London: George Allen and Unwin, 1984), pp. 24–27; Arthur W. J. G. Ord-Hume, *Player Piano: The History of the Mechanical Piano and How to Repair It* (London: George Allen and Unwin, 1970), pp. 32–33; Harvey N. Roehl, *Player Piano Treasury: The Scrapbook History of the Mechanical Piano in America as Told in Story, Pictures, Trade Journal Articles and Advertising* (Vestal, N.Y.: The Vestal Press, 1961; 2d ed. 1973), pp. 1–10; and *The New Grove Dictionary of Music and Musicians*, 1980 ed., s.v. "Player piano," by Frank W. Holland. Ord-Hume's volumes are illustrated and have a useful annotated list of principal makers, patentees and agents; Roehl's is marvelously illustrated as well.

30. George Payne Bent, *Tales of Travel, Life and Love: An Autobiography* (Los Angeles: The *Times-Mirror* Press, 1924), p. 306.

31. Dolge, *Pianos and Their Makers*, vol. 1, pp. 328, 330.

32. Advertisement reproduced in Roehl, *Player Piano Treasury*, p. 7.

33. Arthur Whiting, "The Mechanical Player," *Yale Review* 8 (July 1919): 830.

34. These were product brand names and trademarks. The corresponding manufacturers were as follows: Pianola (Aeolian, New York); Angelus (Wilcox & White, Connecticut); Cecilian (Farrand Company, Detroit); Pianista (Kohler & Campbell, New York); Simplex (Theodore P. Brown Co., Worcester, Massachusetts); Maestro (Elbridge-Winter, Eldridge, New York), which at $125 was half the price of Pianola and Cecilian; and Paragon (Needham Piano & Organ Co., New York). See Roehl, *Player Piano*

Treasury, pp. 8–12; Ord-Hume, *Player Piano*, pp. 33, 88, and his annotated list of principal makers.

35. Lucien Wulsin I to Mr. Storer, November 29, 1902; E. E. Roberts to Lucien Wulsin I, December 1, 1902; E. E. Roberts, Memorandum, undated (1902), in Miscellaneous Art Piano folder, Correspondence with Mr. Storer, 1902, D. H. Baldwin & Co. Archives, Cincinnati Historical Society, Eden Park, Cincinnati, Ohio.

36. Dolge, *Pianos and Their Makers*, vol. 1, pp. 136–37; Ord-Hume, *Player Piano*, pp. 33–34; Ord-Hume, *Pianola*, pp. 27–28. Advertisement reproduced in Roehl, *Player Piano Treasury*, p. 13.

37. Paul Brown Klugh of the Cable Company, inventor of the Carola Inner Player, called together and chaired the joint meetings of the player and music roll manufacturers at the Buffalo convention. Dolge, *Pianos and Their Makers*, vol. 1, p. 378; Dolge, *Pianos and Their Makers*, vol. 2, p. 75; Roehl, *Player Piano Treasury*, pp. 12–17 passim; Ord-Hume, *Pianola*, pp. 112–16; Ord-Hume, *Player Piano*, pp. 40, 90.

38. *NYT*, January 14, 1909, p. 7; David L. Cohen, *The Good Old Days: A History of American Morals and Manners as Seen through the Sears, Roebuck Catalogs 1905 to the Present* (New York: Simon and Schuster, 1940), pp. 38–39; advertisements reproduced in Roehl, *Player Piano Treasury*, pp. 17, 31.

39. The Steinway Duo-Art Pianola was a unique hybrid among reproducing pianos—see chapter three, note 41. For the history of the reproducing piano, see Larry Givens, *Re-Enacting the Artist: The Story of the Ampico Reproducing Piano* (Vestal, N.Y.: The Vestal Press, 1970); Ord-Hume, *Player Piano*, pp. 94–97; Ord-Hume, *Pianola*, pp. 173–92 passim; Roehl, *Player Piano Treasury*, pp. 61–100 passim; and Edwin M. Good, *Giraffes, Black Dragons, and Other Pianos: A Technological History from Cristofori to the Modern Concert Grand* (Stanford, Calif.: Stanford University Press, 1982), pp. 232–35.

40. "Recording the Soul of Piano Playing," *Scientific American* 137 (November 1927): 422–23; Ampico advertisement reproduced in Roehl, *Player Piano Treasury*, p. 78.

41. "The Duo-Art Pianola Piano," *The Piano and Organ Purchaser's Guide for 1919*, and Welte-Mignon advertisement reproduced in Roehl, *Player Piano Treasury* (1st ed.), pp. 50–51, 71. Other reproducing piano actions developed in the United States include the ArtEcho, built by American Piano Co. for sale to independent piano manufacturers, and the Apollo, which the company sold to the Rudolph Wurlitzer Co.; the Angelus Artria, invented by Wilcox & White and used in the Hallet & Davis, Conway, and Merrill pianos manufactured by Conway Music Industries; the Aria Divina, used in M. Schulz pianos; the Cable Company's Carola

Solo Inner Player; and the Celco, which was fitted in A. B. Chase, Emerson, and Lindeman pianos. Welte-Mignon Licensee, Ampico, and Duo-Art, however, dominated the American market. See Ord-Hume, *Pianola*, chap. 7 passim.

42. *NYT*, June 5, 1918, p. 9

43. "Reproducing Versus Expression Piano," *The Piano and Organ Purchaser's Guide for 1919*, reprinted in Roehl, *Player Piano Treasury* (1st ed.), p. 70. For a list of artists who recorded exclusively for the various reproducing piano makes, see Ord-Hume, *Pianola*, pp. 242–43.

44. Daniel J. Boorstin's perceptive term, though now coming under criticism, is still valuable—see *The Americans: The Democratic Experience* (New York: Random House, 1973), pp. 89–166, passim; and Daniel Horowitz's valuable overview of the scholarly literature in *The Morality of Spending: Attitudes toward the Consumer Society in America, 1875–1940* (Baltimore: Johns Hopkins University Press, 1985), pp. 187–201.

45. This concept of community should not be taken to imply an absence of conflict. Such community was confounded by the conflict between a search for individualism and the desire to remain comfortably part of the group; an apparent domination of the masses by experts, who themselves were caught in the dilemma of social and cultural change; a blurring of distinction between false and real pleasure, accomplishment, and companionship; the questionable morality of a system that fosters a need to buy and creates a dependency on obsolescence. See, for example, Horowitz, *The Morality of Spending*; Roland Marchand, *Advertising the American Dream: Making Way for Modernity, 1920–1940* (Berkeley and Los Angeles: University of California Press, 1985); Richard Wightman Fox and T. J. Jackson Lears, eds., *The Culture of Consumption: Critical Essays in American History, 1880–1980* (New York: Pantheon Books, 1983).

46. Boorstin, *Americans: Democratic Experience*, p. 371.

47. Quoted ibid., p. 374.

48. Ibid., pp. 379–80.

49. Roland Gelatt, *The Fabulous Phonograph, 1877–1977* (New York: Collier, 2d rev. ed., 1977), pp. 39, 49, 88.

50. Ibid., p. 69.

51. Ibid., pp. 73, 117, 122, 136, 141.

52. Ibid., pp. 141–46, 148–49, 154, 157; Victor Talking Maching ads in author's collection.

53. Jasen and Tichenor, *Rags and Ragtime*, p. 138.

54. See David A. Jasen, *Recorded Ragtime, 1897–1958* (Hamden, Conn.: Archon Books, 1973).

55. *NYT*, June 16, 1913, p. 8; *NYT*, June 5, 1910, p. 10; vaudeville joke quoted in Boorstin, *Americans: Democratic Experience*, p. 384.

56. Ferruccio Busoni to his wife, November 20, 1919, quoted in Harold C. Schonberg, *The Great Pianists from Mozart to the Present* (New York: Simon and Schuster), p. 353.

57. George M. Otto, Executive Director, National Piano Manufacturers Association, to author, November 11, 1980; *Historical Statistics of the United States from Colonial Times to Present* (Washington, D.C.: U.S. Government Printing Office, 1975), pp. 696–97; Cyril Ehrlich, *The Piano: A History* (London: Dent, 1976), p. 186; Roehl, *Player Piano Treasury*, pp. 51, 53.

58. Gelatt, *Fabulous Phonograph*, p. 190.

59. William Geppert, *The Official Guide to Piano Quality* (New York: Eilert Printing Co., 1916), p. 19.

60. Dolge, *Pianos and Their Makers*, vol. 2, pp. 209–15; Q. David Bowers, *Put Another Nickel In: A History of Coin-Operated Pianos and Orchestrions* (Vestal, N.Y.: The Vestal Press, 1966), pp. 196–97; Ord-Hume, *Player Piano*, pp. 115, 276.

61. Many of these "makers" were really just assemblers of the machines. It was a common trade practice to purchase pianos from other firms, and then purchase and install player mechanisms, coin slots, and percussion and other instruments inside the piano cases. Bowers, *Put Another Nickel In*, p. 132; Roehl, *Player Piano Treasury* (1st ed.), pp. 96, 117.

62. The huge and expensive coin-music machines were called "orchestrions." They housed any number of instruments, including pipe organ, drums, triangle, cymbals, chimes, castanets, xylophone, mandolin, tambourine, and of course, piano. See Bowers, *Put Another Nickel In*, chap. 7, pp. 137–66. For illustrations of these marvelous machines, see Roehl, *Player Piano Treasury*, chap. 4, passim. Wurlitzer 1910 catalog noted in Roehl, *Player Piano Treasury* (1st ed.), pp. 97–98; Wurlitzer advertisement reproduced in Bowers, *Put Another Nickel In*, pp. 81, 100.

63. Wurlitzer advertisement reproduced in Bowers, *Put Another Nickel In*, pp. 93–94.

64. *The Coin Slot*, reproduced in Roehl, *Player Piano Treasury* (1st ed.), pp. 145, 163.

65. Bowers, *Put Another Nickel In*, pp. 61, 93–94.

66. Roehl, *Player Piano Treasury*, p. 102.

67. Wurlitzer advertisement reproduced in Bowers, *Put Another Nickel In*, p. 95.

68. Wyn Wachhorst, *Thomas Alva Edison: An American Myth* (Cambridge, Mass.: MIT Press, 1981), p. 98.

69. "Musical Opportunities in Motion Picture Theaters," *The Etude* 39 (April 1921): 267.

70. For an illustrated survey of the photoplayer, see Roehl, *Player Piano*

Treasury, pp. 213–30; Ord-Hume, *Player Piano*, pp. 118–19; Bowers, *Put Another Nickel In*, pp. 28–31; L. C. Turner, *How and What to Play for Moving Pictures* (San Francisco: N.p., 1914).

71. Steven Fay, "Pianist Hofmann Brings Stars of the Silent Screen to Life," [University of Texas at Austin *Daily Texan*] *Images*, April 11, 1983, pp. 8–9.

72. Link Piano Co. advertisement reproduced in Roehl, *Player Piano Treasury*, pp. 224–25. The piano manufacturer was originally the Automatic Musical Company, but upon bankruptcy in 1910 was reformed as the Link Piano Co. by Edwin A. Link, chairman of the creditors' committee. The firm produced about 300 coin-operated instruments a year. During and after the Second World War the company manufactured the pneumatically-operated Link Trainer used in flight schools nationwide.

73. N. S. Pardoza to J. P. Seeburg Piano Co., May 26, 1915, reprinted in Roehl, *Player Piano Treasury*, p. 218.

74. *NYT*, November 17, 1918, sec. 7, p. 9.

75. *NYT*, May 18, 1919, sec. 2, p. 10.

76. *NYT*, October 6, 1912, sec. 3, p. 16; Harvey Green, *The Light of the Home: An Intimate View of the Lives of Women in Victorian America* (New York: Pantheon, 1983), p. 85.

77. *NYT*, December 30, 1908, p. 8; *NYT*, June 10, 1908, p. 5.

78. The slang phrase "canned music," though coined for the resemblance of the phonograph cylinder to a can, was used to describe all forms of mechanically reproduced music—phonograph, player piano, even radio. Bandmaster John Philip Sousa seems to have been the first to give the term national recognition, and may have coined the phrase himself.

79. John Philip Sousa, "Sousa's Protest against 'Canned Music,'" *Current Literature* 41 (October 1906): 426, 427–28 (originally published as "The Menace of Mechanical Music," in *Appleton's Magazine* 8 [September 1906]: 7). The best work on Sousa's fascinating life is Paul E. Bierley, *John Philip Sousa: American Phenomenon* (New York: Appleton-Century-Crofts, 1973). See also Craig H. Roell, "John Philip Sousa," in *Great Lives from History: A Biographical Survey*, ed. Frank N. Magill, pp. 2122–28 (Pasadena, Calif.: Salem Press, 1987); Boorstin, *Americans: Democratic Experience*, pp. 382–83; and Gelatt, *Fabulous Phonograph*, pp. 146–47.

80. Quoted in Sousa, "Sousa's Protest against 'Canned Music,'" p. 428.

81. Gelatt, *Fabulous Phonograph*, p. 73.

82. Leo Rich Lewis, "Music-Education and 'Automatics,'" *The Atlantic Monthly* 101 (March 1908): 383–87.

83. "The Democracy of Music Achieved by Invention," *Current Literature* 42 (June 1907): 670–73.

84. Robert Haven Schauffler, "The Mission of Mechanical Music," *Cen-*

tury Magazine 89 (December 1914): 293–98.

85. Gustav Kobbe, *The Pianolist—A Guide for Pianola Players* (New York: Moffat, Yard & Co., 1907; 4th ed., 1912); William Braid White, *The Player Pianist* (New York: Edward L. Bill, 1910). Other books contemporaneous with these works include William Braid White, *The Player Piano Up to Date* (New York: Edward L. Bill, 1914); H. L. Atta, *The Piano Player* (Dayton, Ohio: Ohio Printing Co., 1914); Sydney Grew, *The Art of the Player Piano* (New York: E. P. Dutton, 1922); Sydney Grew, *The First Book of the Player-Pianist* (London: Musical Opinion, 1925); David Miller Wilson, *The Player Piano, Its Construction and How to Play* (New York: Pitman & Sons, 1923); and David Miller Wilson, *The Player Pianist* (London, 1911).

86. Gertrude Borchard, "The Player Piano as Teacher's Aid," *The Musician* 24 (January 1919): 18, 42.

87. Adolph Bernard Marx, *Music of the Nineteenth Century and Its Culture* (London: Robert Cocks & Co., 1855), pp. 73–74.

88. Delderfield, *For My Own Amusement*, pp. 65–66.

89. See Boorstin, *Americans: Democratic Experience*, pp. 384–89.

90. Whiting, "Mechanical Player," pp. 828–35.

91. "Music Ex Machina," pp. 714–16.

92. George Coleman Gow, "The Pros and Cons of the Mechanical Player," *MTNA Proceedings*, 1910:77–87; Helena Maguire, "Autopianos and Automobiles," *The Musician* 19 (December 1914): 809; "Piano-Players, Human and Mechanical," *The Literary Digest*, June 21, 1913, p. 1376; "Discriminating Player-Pianos," *The Literary Digest*, July 12, 1913, p. 52; and "Piano-Players and Player-Pianos," *The Literary Digest*, September 20, 1913, pp. 468–69.

93. Theodore Roosevelt, Message to Congress Regarding Copyright Revision, 59th Cong., 1st sess., December 5, 1905, *Congressional Record* 40:102.

94. U.S. Congress, Senate and House, conjointly, Committee on Patents, *To Amend and Consolidate the Acts Respecting Copyright, Hearings on S. 6330 and H.R. 19853*, 59th Cong., 1st sess., 1906, pp. 310, 332–33 (hereafter referred to as *Revision of Copyright Laws, Hearings*, 1906); U.S. Congress, Senate and House, conjointly, Committee on Patents, *To Amend and Consolidate the Acts Respecting Copyright, Hearings on S. 9440 and H.R. 28192*, 60th Cong., 1st sess., 1908, pp. 290–91 (hereafter referred to as *Revision of Copyright Laws, Hearings*, 1908).

95. Unless a quotation is cited specifically, the reader is advised that the following events were collected from these sources: *Revision of Copyright Laws, Hearings*, 1906; *Revision of Copyright Laws, Hearings*, 1908; U.S. Congress, House, Committee on Patents, *To Amend the Copyright Act of 1909, Hearings on H.R. 6250 and H.R. 9137*, 68th Cong., 1st sess., 1924

(hereafter referred to as *Revision of the Copyright Act of 1909, Hearings,* 1924); U.S. Congress, House, Committee on Patents, *Revision of Copyright Laws, Hearings, Revised Copy for Use of the Committee on Patents,* 74th Cong., 2d sess., 1936; U.S. Congress, Senate, Committee on Patents, *To Amend and Consolidate the Acts Respecting Copyright,* S. Rept. 1108, 60th Cong., 2d sess., 1909; U.S. Congress, House, Committee on Patents, *To Amend and Consolidate the Acts Respecting Copyright,* H. Rept. 2222, 60th Cong., 2d sess., 1909; U.S. Congress, House, A Bill to Authorize and Consolidate the Acts Respecting Copyright [1909 Copyright Act], H.R. 28192, 60th Cong., 2d sess., 1909, *Congressional Record* 43: 3744, 3747, 3765–68; "Kill Paragraph (G)," *Musical Courier,* June 30, 1906; "The Men Behind," *Musical Age,* February 29, 1908; "'The Men Behind' in This Country," *Musical Age,* March 7, 1908; *NYT,* January 13, 1908, p. 6; *NYT,* January 14, 1908, p. 7; *NYT,* March 4, 1908, p. 6; *NYT,* February 19, 1909, p. 9.

96. *Revision of Copyright Laws, Hearings,* 1908, p. 218.

97. A roll could contain more than a single composition. The 1905 Pianola catalog listed 7,260 available rolls in every musical category, the supplemental 1906 Pianola catalog of "Metrostyle marked music" listed an additional 2,421 titles. "The Metrostyle," read a 1904 ad for Aeolian's piano-player, "is a most important addition to the Pianola. It is a device which insures a musicianly rendition even on the part of a person possessing no previous knowledge of music whatever" (The Aeolian Company, *Catalog of Music for the Pianola and Pianola Piano* [New York: The Aeolian Company, 1905]; The Aeolian Company, *Catalog of Metrostyle & Themodist Music for the Pianola and Pianola Piano* [New York: The Aeolian Company, 1906]; Aeolian Pianola advertisement, 1904, author's possession).

98. Photographs of and quotations from these Aeolian contracts with both the publishers and dealers are included in the evidence submitted in the hearings of the joint House and Senate Committee on Patents. See *Revision of Copyright Laws, Hearings,* 1908, pp. 219–21, 311–13, 347, 356.

99. Albert H. Walker, *Revision of Copyright Laws, Hearings,* 1906, pp. 277, 305.

100. *Revision of Copyright Laws, Hearings,* 1906, p. 228.

101. On *White-Smith* v. *Apollo,* see *Revision of Copyright Laws, Hearings,* 1906, pp. 83, 271; *Revision of Copyright Laws, Hearings,* 1908, pp. 222, 251, 272.

102. Paul Cromelin, *Revision of Copyright Laws, Hearings,* 1908, p. 324. Cromelin was also a vice president of Columbia Phonograph Co.

103. *Revision of the Copyright Act of 1909, Hearings,* 1924, pp. 344–45.

104. F. W. Hedgeland for Kimball, *Revision of Copyright Laws, Hearings,* 1906, p. 28. Julius Winter, chairman of the Executive Committee of the Player Manufacturers' League, and president of Winter & Company, told

Congressman Currier that the Aeolian monopoly would completely destroy the player piano industry in America. (See pp. 335, 336.)

105. The remarks are worth quoting:

> George W. Pound (for Wurlitzer): "I assert that the Aeolian Company has spent $75,000 to get an exclusive monopoly, which they would get under the Kittredge bill [thus endangering 624 businesses]."
>
> Rep. Barchfeld: "You do not come before this committee with the statement that if we pass this bill there are 624 or 625 companies whose establishments are to be closed by the action of this committee?"
>
> Pound: "Yes, sir."
>
> Barchfeld: "You do not mean that?"
>
> Pound: "I do, most decidedly. Your bill would."
>
> Rep. Currier: "Mr. Pound is right."

(See *Revision of Copyright Laws, Hearings*, 1908, p. 352.)

106. Homer E. Capehart, vice president of the Automatic Musical Instrument Association, *Revision of the Copyright Act of 1909, Hearings*, 1936, p. 799.

107. John W. Daniels, remarks on the 1909 Copyright Act, H.R. 28192, 60th Cong., 2d sess., 1909, *Congressional Record* 43:3747.

CHAPTER THREE

1. Alfred Dolge, *Pianos and Their Makers*, 2 vols. (Covina, Calif.: Covina Publishing Co., 1911, 1913; vol. 1 reprinted, New York: Dover, 1972), vol. 1, pp. 410–11; John F. Majeski, "International Music and Sound Expo," *The Music Trades* 126 (July 1978): 24; James W. Johnson, "What NAMM Is All About," *PTM World of Music* 75 (June 1978): 30.

2. See, for example, *New York Times* (hereafter *NYT*), June 12, 1916, p. 9.

3. *NYT*, February 16, 1916, p. 15; *NYT*, February 17, 1916, p. 18.

4. *NYT*, June 12, 1916, p. 9; *NYT*, June 22, 1916, p. 11; *NYT*, June 23, 1916, p. 8; *NYT*, June 24, 1916, p. 16.

5. On the preparedness controversy, see Arthur S. Link, *Woodrow Wilson and the Progressive Era, 1910–1917* (New York: Harper, 1954), pp. 174–96.

6. Dolge, *Pianos and Their Makers*, vol. 2, p. 28.

7. "Center" firms, which formed successful trusts, characteristically had high productivity and profits, intensive use of capital, strong unionization, and a long-range perspective. "Peripheral" firms, by contrast,

were small, seasonal in product supply and demand, labor intensive, low in profit and productivity, had weak unionization and small capital, and lacked the assets, power, and size to take advantage of economies of scale, or spend large sums on research and development. Thus, market competition was intensive, and trusts usually failed. See Thomas K. McCraw, "Rethinking the Trust Question," in *Regulation in Perspective,* ed. Thomas K. McCraw, pp. 1–55 (Cambridge: Harvard University Press, 1981); Charles Tolbert, Patrick M. Horan, and E. M. Beck, "The Structure of Economic Segmentation: A Dual Economy Approach," *American Journal of Sociology* 85 (March 1980): 1095–1116; Tolbert, Horan, and Beck, "Stratification in a Dual Economy," *American Sociological Review* 43 (October 1978): 704–20.

8. Alfred D. Chandler, Jr., *The Visible Hand: The Managerial Revolution in American Business* (Cambridge: Harvard University Press, 1977).

9. Cyril Ehrlich's important book on the international piano industry acknowldeges this trend, but by his own admission, "understates the extent to which large firms came to dominate the American piano industry." Edwin M. Good, whose book represents the most recent scholarly literature on the piano and its industry, also acknowledges that marketing and distribution rather than technology determined success in the trade, but says "consideration of that matter lies beyond our scope here." There have been many studies of the technological development of the piano itself; but there has been a systematic study of neither the specific corporate, distribution, or marketing structure of the piano industry, nor of how that structure fits into the general industrial trends of the time—see Ehrlich, *The Piano: A History* (London: Dent, 1976): chap. 7 passim; Good, *Giraffes, Black Dragons, and Other Pianos* (Stanford, Calif.: Stanford University Press, 1982): chap. 7 passim.

10. Frank L. Wing, *The Book of Complete Information about Pianos* (New York: Wing & Son, 1897), pp. 15–16.

11. On the American automobile industry, see James J. Flink, *The Car Culture* (Cambridge: MIT Press, 1975); and James J. Flink, *America Adopts the Automobile, 1895–1910* (Cambridge: MIT Press, 1970).

12. Daniel Spillane, *History of the American Pianoforte: Its Technical Development, and the Trade* (New York: Daniel Spillane, 1890; reprinted, New York: Da Capo Press, 1969), p. 311.

13. Dolge, *Pianos and Their Makers,* vol. 1, p. 115.

14. Ibid., pp. 120, 464–65.

15. William Geppert, *The Official Guide to Piano Quality* (New York: Eilert Printing Co., 1916), p. 12.

16. Byron H. Collins, "What Should I Know to Purchase a Reliable Piano?" *The Etude* 40 (October 1922): 669.

17. Wing, *Book of Complete Information,* pp. 15–16.

18. Collins, "What Should I Know," p. 669; Wing, *Book of Complete Information*, pp. 15–16.

19. Geppert, *Official Guide to Piano Quality*, pp. 12–17.

20. Ibid., pp. 12–16.

21. The acknowledged entrepreneurial tycoon in the stencil trade was Joseph P. Hale, a pioneer as well in new methods of mass distribution. His contemporary reputation ranged from notorious (Spillane did not even mention him) to a reserved respect (Dolge praised his "genius an an organizer"). According to William Steinway's diary, Hale's election in January 1876 as president of a newly formed piano manufacturers' "protective society" (Steinway had attempted to establish a trade association for piano makers in December 1875) caused the new organization to split into factions. Disgruntled manufacturers formed a second association in February—see William Steinway, Diary, December 21, 1875, January 31, 1876, February 8, 1876, Steinway Family Archives, Steinway Hall, New York. For a current assessment of Hale and the stencil piano, see Ehrlich, *Piano*, pp. 90, 130, 137–38; Good, *Giraffes, Black Dragons, and Other Pianos*, p. 205; Arthur Loesser, *Men, Women and Pianos: A Social History* (New York: Simon & Schuster, 1954), pp. 526–31.

22. William Tonk, *Memoirs of a Manufacturer* (New York: Presto Publishing Co., 1926), pp. 171–72.

23. Geppert, *Official Guide to Piano Quality*, especially pp. 38, 132–33.

24. Dolge, *Pianos and Their Makers*, vol. 2, pp. 45–46.

25. An excellent starting place to examine the many dimensions of Progressive reform is Lewis L. Gould, ed., *The Progressive Era* (Syracuse, N.Y.: Syracuse University Press, 1974). See also Robert H. Wiebe, *The Search for Order* (New York: Hill and Wang, 1967); Samuel P. Hayes, *The Response to Industrialism* (Chicago: University of Chicago Press, 1957); William L. O'Neill, *The Progressive Years* (1975).

26. Daniel J. Boorstin, *The Americans: The Democratic Experience* (New York: Random House, 1973), pp. 146–48.

27. Tonk, *Memoirs*, p. 172.

28. Many manufacturers at the time were listing piano prices so high that the dealer could afford to cut prices by as much as 65 to 70 percent and still make a good profit. Originating with the National Association of Piano Dealers, and subsequently adopted by many manufacturers, the campaign to enact a "one price" or fixed price system was seen as a way to end many of the abuses associated with the retail piano trade—see "From Fighting Crooks to Staging Trade Shows: A Look at NAMM's Evolution and the Role of Trade Shows in the Music Industry," *The Music Trades* 131 (May 25, 1983): 76.

29. Dolge, *Pianos and Their Makers*, vol. 2, pp. 45–48, esp. 47.

30. U.S. Congress, House, Remarks on a Bill Prohibiting Fraud upon the Public by Requiring Manufacturers to Place Their Own Names upon Manufactured Articles, H.R. 16844, 62nd Cong., 2d sess., 1912, *Congressional Record* 48:677, 7740–42, and H.R. 2970, 63d Cong., 1st sess., *Congressional Record* 50:227; U.S. Congress, House, Extension of Remarks on H.R. 2970, a Bill Requiring Manufacturers to Certify to the Materials of and Place Their Names upon the Products They Produce, 63d Cong., 2d sess., January 21, 1914, *Congressional Record* 51: Appendix, pp. 79–82; Dolge, *Pianos and Their Makers*, vol. 2, pp. 45–48.

31. Collins, "What Should I Know," p. 669.

32. Wing, *Book of Complete Information*, p. 85.

33. Tonk, *Memoirs*, pp. 157–61.

34. Maud Nathan, *Once Upon a Time and Today* (New York: Putnam, 1933), p. 39.

35. Chandler, *The Visible Hand*, part 4, pp. 285–376 passim. See also Alfred D. Chandler, Jr., *Strategy and Structure: Chapter in the History of the Industrial Enterprise* (Cambridge: MIT Press, 1962).

36. Dolge, *Pianos and Their Makers*, vol. 1, p. 205.

37. Ibid., pp. 205–10; "90 Years Ago In Music Trades: Piano Trust Threatens Trade Press," *The Music Trades* 136 (January 10, 1988): 26. Quite possibly, the piano trade failed to construct an industry-wide trust because of the very nature of the piano business itself. Most firms were small, labor intensive, low in productivity, had small capital, weak unionization, did not have the means to establish economies of scale or departments of research and development, and were compelled to participate in intensive market competition. In other words, most piano firms were "peripheral," and such industries by nature were prone to unsuccessful trust efforts. See McCraw, "Rethinking the Trust Question," pp. 9–10, 22–23, 32–33.

38. On Bush & Gerts, Jesse French, Charles A. Sterling, and Baldwin piano companies, see Dolge, *Pianos and Their Makers*, vol. 2, pp. 48–49, 91–93; vol. 1, pp. 345–48, 356–57, 370–71; Geppert, *Official Guide to Piano Quality*; Lucien Wulsin, *Dwight Hamilton Baldwin (1821–1899) and the Baldwin Piano* (New York: Newcomen Society in North America and Princeton University Press, July 1953); Morley P. Thompson, "Financial History of the Baldwin Company since 1902," typewritten manuscript, pp. 2–12, Baldwin Co., Financial History 1902–1954, Morley P. Thompson folder, D. H. Baldwin & Co. Archives, Cincinnati Historical Society, Eden Park, Cincinnati, Ohio (hereafter Baldwin Archives).

39. Lucien Wulsin II to Fritz Wulsin, September 6, 1932, Baldwin Co., Correspondence Involving Baldwin and Its Financial Situation, etc., Lucien Wulsin II, 1930–1940 collection, Baldwin Archives.

40. Lloyd Graham, "The Story of the Rudolph Wurlitzer Family and Business," pp. 99–101, typewritten manuscript in the possession of Mrs. Janet Wurlitzer Stites, Cincinnati, Ohio.

41. The "Steinway Duo-Art Pianola Piano" was the product of a contract between Steinway, who manufactured the piano, and Aeolian, who manufactured and installed the Duo-Art reproducing mechanism. There was no connection between the two companies except in this agreement, which lasted from March 1909 to April 1933. Aeolian maintained exclusive control over the sales and promotion of Steinway Duo-Art pianos, but by contract had to "relegate their Weber Pianola Piano to second place under the Steinway Pianola Piano." Furthermore, Aeolian agreed to withdraw from the artistic concert field and to exploit their Weber in public "only through such minor pianists as Steinway & Sons may permit." See *NYT*, February 20, 1909, p. 14; Arthur W. J. G. Ord-Hume, *Pianola: The History of the Self-Playing Piano* (London: George Allen & Unwin, 1984), pp. 183–84.

42. E. F. Brooks, Jr., President, Aeolian American Division, "Aeolian American Division of Aeolian Corporation, East Rochester, New York," typed manuscript in possession of author; Dolge, *Pianos and Their Makers*, vol. 2, pp. 144–54.

43. *Purchaser's Guide to the Music Industries, 1983* (Englewood Cliffs, N.J.: The Music Trades Corporation, 1983), p. 4.

44. *Dealer's Handbook of Pianos and Their Makers* (Tulsa, Okla.: Robert G. Anderson, 1972), p. 3.

45. Ibid., p. 3.

46. Dolge, *Pianos and Their Makers*, vol. 2, p. 21.

47. Brooks, "Aeolian American Division," pp. 3–4.

48. Dolge, *Pianos and Their Makers*, vol. 1, pp. 327–33; Geppert, *Official Guide to Piano Quality*, pp. 29–30; Ord-Hume, *Pianola*, pp. 26, 270, 312; Brooks, "Aeolian American Division," p. 4.

49. Unless a specific citation is noted, the reader is advised that the following information on the Baldwin Company is derived from the following sources: Lucien Wulsin II, "A Piano Man Looks Back," *The Music Trades* 111 (February 1963): 38–44; Lucien Wulsin II, *Dwight Hamilton Baldwin*; Lucien Wulsin II, Monographs in Baldwin History folder, Baldwin Archives; Paul Erwin, "Preliminary Draft of Baldwin Early Years," typewritten manuscript, Baldwin Archives; Dolge, *Pianos and Their Makers*, vol. 1, pp. 345–48, and vol. 2, pp. 34–36.

50. Wulsin, "Piano Man Looks Back," p. 43; Sylvia Kleve Sheblessy, *100 Years of the Cincinnati May Festival* (Cincinnati: N.p., 1973).

51. Lucien Wulsin II wrote that the local prestige of D. H. Baldwin & Co. in the Ohio Valley "generally was worth more than the warranty of the eastern manufacturers," and "the Steinway piano had a fine reputation,

but it was an expensive piano, and did not by any menas [sic] sell itself."
Lucien Wulsin II to Countess de Chambrum, July 28, 1938, Baldwin Co.,
Correspondence, etc., Lucien Wulsin II, 1930–1940 folder, Baldwin Ar-
chives; Lucien Wulsin II, "Dwight Hamilton Baldwin" Newcomen Draft,
File 2, Business Papers—D. H. Baldwin Biography, Information, etc., Bal-
dwin Archives.

52. Baldwin's family name already was being used on the company's
premier instrument, and his middle name on Hamilton organs. The
name "Ellington" was chosen to honor one of Baldwin's Kentucky friends
from the music teaching days. The manufacturer's first name, Dwight,
was unacceptable because Baldwin was a strict Presbyterian unwilling to
have anything to do with liquor. It so happened that the town of Dwight,
Illinois, was the location of a very popular facility for curing alcoholics.
"Dwight," therefore, could not be used on any product of D. H. Baldwin &
Co.

53. D. H. Baldwin & Co., General Information, 1898–1912, Paul Erwin
folder, Baldwin Archives.

54. Clarence Wulsin died in 1897, and Albert Van Buren retired and sold
his shares to the remaining partners.

55. "Musical Instruments," in *Leading Industries of Cincinnati, Ohio*
(Cincinnati: *Cincinnati Enquirer*, 1900), pp. 19–21. Cincinnati, 1800–1900
folder, Paul Erwin box, Baldwin Archives.

56. Dolge, *Pianos and Their Makers*, vol. 2, p. 35.

57. Recommendations to the President for Increase in the Sale of Our
Standard Makes, May 14, 1925, Baldwin Co., Correspondence, etc., Lucien Wulsin II, 1925 folder, Baldwin Archives.

58. See Thompson, "Financial History of the Baldwin Company."

59. Intercompany Memorandum, the Baldwin Piano Co., January 29,
1925, Correspondence, etc. of Lucien Wulsin II, 1925 folder, Baldwin Archives.

60. Lucien Wulsin to an unidentified Evansville, Indiana, man, 1891,
quoted in Paul Erwin, "Preliminary Draft of Baldwin Early Years," chap. 4,
p. 12.

61. Quoted in *City of Cincinnati and Its Resources*, quoted in Paul Erwin,
"Preliminary Draft," chapter 4, p. 9.

CHAPTER FOUR

1. Coolidge is quoted in C. C. Givens, Jr., *Modern Advertising: Its Importance to the Retailer and His Community* (New York?: C. C. Givens, Jr.,
1928), p. 4.

2. Roland Marchand, *Advertising the American Dream: Making Way for*

Modernity, 1920–1940 (Berkeley and Los Angeles, Calif.: University of California Press, 1985), pp. 9–13; T. J. Jackson Lears, "From Salvation to Self-Regulation: Advertising and the Therapeutic Roots of the Consumer Culture, 1880–1930," in *The Culture of Consumption: Critical Essays in American History, 1880–1980*, pp. 17–30, ed. Richard Wightman Fox and T. J. Jackson Lears (New York: Pantheon Books, 1983). See also Daniel Horowitz, *The Morality of Spending: Attitudes toward the Consumer Society in America, 1875–1940* (Baltimore: The Johns Hopkins University Press, 1985), especially pp. xxi–xxix.

3. Joseph H. Appel quoted in Givens, *Modern Advertising*, p. 7.

4. Axel G. Gulbransen, "A. G. Gulbransen Issues Call to Arms," *The Music Trades* 78 (April 1930): 3.

5. Alfred Dolge, *Pianos and Their Makers*, 2 vols. (Covina, Calif.: Covina Publishing Co., 1911, 1913; vol. 1 reprinted, New York: Dover, 1972), vol. 1, p. 213.

6. Ibid., p. 214.

7. Ibid., p. 299.

8. Wolfgang Amadeus Mozart to his father, Leopold, October 17–18, 1777, quoted in *The Great Pianists from Mozart to the Present*, by Harold C. Schonberg, pp. 35–36 (New York: Simon and Schuster, 1963).

9. Dolge, *Pianos and Their Makers*, vol. 1, p. 401.

10. Van Allen Bradley, *Music for the Millions: The Kimball Piano and Organ Story* (Chicago: Henry Regnery Co., 1957), pp. 118–28.

11. Artur Rubenstein, *My Young Years* (New York: Alfred Knopf, 1973), p. 193.

12. William E. Walter, "The Industry of Music-Making," *The Atlantic Monthly* 101 (January 1908): 91–96.

13. Dolge, *Pianos and Their Makers*, vol. 1, p. 399; Artur Rubinstein gives a revealing account of his contract and premiere American tour with the Knabe piano firm in *My Young Years*, pp. 152, 173, 176–81, 188, 190–91.

14. *Pierce Piano Atlas* (Bob Pierce, comp., Long Beach, Calif.: Bob Pierce, publisher, 7th ed., 1977, pp. 4–5) lists (sometimes inaccurately) the presidential pianos from Washington to Carter. For an in-depth study of White House pianos and music appreciation, see Elise K. Kirk, *Music at the White House* (Urbana: University of Illinois Press, 1986). For Lucy Webb Hayes, see also Julia B. Foraker, *I Would Live It Again: Memories of a Vivid Life* (New York: Harper & Bros., 1932), pp. 69–70. For the Harrison and Morton endorsement of J. & C. Fischer, see "The 'Fischer Piano' at the White House," *Baldwin's Musical Review*, no. 20, 1890, p. 4 (author's collection). McKinley's testimonial quoted in an A. B. Chase advertisement illustrated in Judith Oringer, *Passion for the Piano* (Los Angeles: Jeremy P. Tarcher, 1983), p. 108. Steinway & Sons "appointments" taken

from a decal on a 1903 piano sounding board, letters from the Shah of Persia in 1899, and from Thomas A. Edison in 1890, pictured in Theodore E. Steinway, *People and Pianos* (New York: Steinway & Sons, 1953), pp. 51, 66, 67.

15. Edwin M. Good, *Giraffes, Black Dragons, and Other Pianos* (Stanford, Calif.: Stanford University Press, 1982), p. 176.

16. Alfred Dolge, *Pianos and Their Makers*, vol. 2, p. 25.

17. For the very entertaining story of the American piano manufacturers at the Paris Exposition of 1867, see Arthur Loesser, *Men, Women, and Pianos: A Social History* (New York: Simon and Schuster, 1954), pp. 512–13; Cyril Ehrlich, *The Piano: A History* (London: Dent, 1976), pp. 58–62; and Good, *Giraffes, Black Dragons, and Other Pianos*, pp. 181–83, 185–86. These authors treat other expositions, exhibitions, and industrial fairs as well.

18. Dolge, *Pianos and Their Makers*, vol. 2, pp. 26–27. For a detailed account of the Philadelphia Centennial Exposition, see Cynthia Adams Hoover, "Music and Musical Instruments," in *1876: A Centennial Exposition*, ed. Robert C. Post, pp. 138–43 (Washington, D.C.: Smithsonian Institution, 1976). The technical developments of the piano, including the "American System," are discussed and illustrated in Dolge, *Pianos and Their Makers*, vol. 1; Ehrlich, *Piano*; Good, *Giraffes, Black Dragons, and Other Pianos*; David S. Grover, *The Piano: Its Story from Zither to Grand* (London: Robert Hale, 1976, and New York: Charles Scribner's Sons, 1978); Rosamond E. M. Harding, *The Piano-Forte: Its History Traced to the Great Exhibition of 1851* (Cambridge, Eng., 1933; 2d ed., Old Woking, Eng., 1978); Cynthia Adams Hoover, *The Steinways and Their Pianos in the Nineteenth Century*, offprint from *Journal of the American Musical Instrument Society*, vol. 7, 1981; and Daniel Spillane, *History of the American Pianoforte: Its Technical Development and the Trade* (New York: Daniel Spillane, 1890; reprinted, New York: Da Capo Press, 1969). See also the scholarly overview articles in *Encyclopedia Britannica*, 11th ed., 1911, s.v. "Pianoforte," by Alfred J. Hipkins and Kathleen Schlesinger; and in *The New Grove Dictionary of Music and Musicians*, 1980 ed., s.v. "Pianoforte," by William J. Conner, Cyril Ehrlich, et al.

19. Dolge, *Pianos and Their Makers*, vol. 2, p. 28.

20. Notably, Dolge mentions none of this controversy in his chapter devoted to world's fairs in the second volume of *Pianos and Their Makers*. The two most informative (though at times conflicting) accounts of the piano trade's antics in the 1893 World's Columbian Exposition are Bradley, *Music for the Millions*, pp. 157–68; and Paul Hume and Ruth Hume, "The Great Chicago Piano War," *American Heritage* 21 (October 1970): 16–21.

21. D. H. Baldwin & Co. was then a dealer for Decker & Sons, J. & C.

Fischer, Haines Bros., and Schubert pianos, and Estey and Story & Clark organs. The firm began the manufacture of Baldwin pianos and Hamilton organs only that same year. (Message quoted in *Baldwin's Musical Review*, no. 20, 1890, p. 2, author's collection.)

22. For general advertising techniques, see Daniel Pope, *The Making of Modern Advertising* (New York: Basic Books, 1983), pp. 232–33. See also Stephen Fox, *The Mirror Makers: A History of American Advertising and Its Creators* (New York: Morrow, 1984).

23. "Advertising Difficulties in the Music Business," *The Music Trades*, 1892, quoted in "90 Years Ago," *The Music Trades* 130 (November 25, 1982): 16.

24. See Daniel T. Rodgers, *The Work Ethic in Industrial America, 1850–1920* (Chicago: University of Chicago Press), pp. 1–29 passim; J. Frederick Dewhurst and Associates, "Recreation," pp. 274–85, in *America's Needs and Resources* (New York: Twentieth Century Fund, 1947); and Foster Rhea Dulles, *America Learns to Play* (New York: D. Appleton-Century, 1940).

25. Michael Schudson, *Advertising, The Uneasy Persuasion: Its Dubious Impact on American Society* (New York: Basic Books, 1984), pp. 88, 94–99, 112–14, 166–67. See also Alfred D. Chandler, *The Visible Hand: The Managerial Revolution in American Business* (Cambridge: Harvard University Press, 1977).

26. Pope, *Making of Modern Advertising*, pp. 247–49.

27. The standard account of this change is Merle Curti, "The Changing Concept of 'Human Nature' in the Literature of American Advertising," *Business History Review* 41 (Winter 1967): 335–57. See also Pope, *Making of Modern Advertising*, especially chapter 6, for an excellent synthesis and bibliography.

28. The most balanced account examining the controversial qualities of advertising and its arguable ability to create desire and cause purchase, an account that also traces the historical growth of advertising philosophy, is Schudsen, *Advertising, The Uneasy Persuasion*. See also Pope, *Making of Modern Advertising*; Lears, "From Salvation to Self-Regulation"; and Marchand, *Advertising the American Dream*, the latter especially valuable for its bibliography.

29. See chapter two.

30. "The Day of the Electric," *Music Trades Review*, March 31, 1917, reproduced in Harvey Roehl, *Player Piano Treasury* (Vestal, N.Y.: Vestal Press, 2d ed., 1973), p. 47.

31. *Saturday Evening Post*, November 5, 1925, p. 190; *SEP*, November 21, 1925, p. 187.

32. Cable Company advertisement reproduced in Roehl, *Player Piano*

Treasury, p. 43. Also quoted in Lester A. Weinrott, "Play That Player Piano," *Chicago History* 4 (Summer 1975): 79.

33. *NYT*, December 11, 1923, p. 17.

34. *NYT*, April 10, 1928, p. 14; *NYT*, April 4, 1928, p. 26.

35. *NYT*, December 9, 1923, sec. 5, p. 8; *NYT*, December 11, 1929, p. 20.

36. Axel G. Gulbransen developed the Gulbransen Baby from an actual incident: "a tiny baby did play the Gulbransen," said one ad. "Thousands of babies have since." The Gulbransen Baby was frequently seen in ads in the *Saturday Evening Post* throughout the 1920s, and the company even supplied its dealers with a papier mâché toddler to use as a window display. Quotes are from: *SEP*, December 12, 1925, p. 223; *SEP*, November 17, 1923, p. 95; *SEP*, January 13, 1923, p. 115; *SEP*, December 18, 1920, p. 98.

37. Gulbransen ads in *Saturday Evening Post*, July 10, 1926, p. 107; and *SEP*, October 17, 1925.

38. "Music Means Health," *Standard Player Monthly*, undated reproduction in Roehl, *Player Piano Treasury*, p. 46.

39. William Tonk outlined most of these advantages for the National Piano Manufacturers Association. See *Memoirs of a Manufacturer* (New York: Presto, 1926), pp. 161–63.

40. Theodore T. Levy, "Ode to a Player Piano," is from Roehl, *Player Piano Treasury*, p. 291. Used with permission of The Vestal Press.

41. "Make the Home Ties Stronger with Music," 1921 Baldwin Manualo advertising poster in possession of the author.

42. John Maurise Clark, "How Many Appeals Sell Merchandise?" *The Music Trades* 77 (January 5, 1929): 16.

43. "The History of Baldwin is the History of an Ideal," *The Baldwin Keynote*, vol. 9, no. 2, 1929, p. 2; Lucien Wulsin II, *Dwight Hamilton Baldwin (1821–1899) and the Baldwin Piano* (New York: Newcomen Society in North America and Princeton University Press, 1953), p. 16.

44. Calvin Coolidge quoted in Givens, *Modern Advertising*, p. 4.

45. Wulsin, *Dwight Hamilton Baldwin*, pp. 20–23.

46. Dolge, *Pianos and Their Makers*, vol. 2, pp. 35–36, and vol. 1, p. 348.

47. Arnold Sombyo? to Lucien Wulsin, May 5, 1909, Correspondence Regarding Artist Promotion: 1900–1910, D. H. Baldwin & Co. Archives, Cincinnati Historical Society, Eden Park, Cincinnati, Ohio (hereafter Baldwin Archives).

48. Lucien Wulsin II to W. B. Murray, March 29, 1926, Artists' Department, 1920–30, Scrapbook-Artist Contracts, Baldwin Co., General Sales Promotions, 1920–30, Baldwin Archives.

49. Contract with José Iturbi, December 7, 1928, and contract with Béla Bartók, January 28, 1927, Artists' Dept. 1920–30, Scrapbook—Artist Con-

tracts, Baldwin Co., General Sales Promotions, 1920–30, Baldwin Archives.

50. Bartók's remarks found in Scrapbook—Artist Contracts, Baldwin Co., General Sales Promotions, 1920–30, Baldwin Archives.

51. Dolge, *Pianos and Their Makers*, vol. 1, pp. 397, 400.

52. James Francis Cooke, editor of *The Etude*, to the Baldwin Piano Co., October 16, 1907, and the Baldwin Co. to The Etude Publishing Co., October 18, 1907, Advertising/Sales Promotion 1900–1910, Magazine Articles folder, Baldwin Archives.

53. "Sixteen Baldwin Pianos for Antheil—American Premiere," *The Baldwin Keynote*, vol. 7, no. 3, 1927, p. 5; "Four Baldwin Pianos are Featured at New York Premiere of Stravinsky's Famous Ballet," *The Baldwin Keynote*, vol. 6. no. 2, 1926, p. 9; "Baldwin Adopted by League of Composers," *The Baldwin Keynote*, vol. 8, no. 1, 1928, p. 17.

54. "Business Getting Suggestions," *The Baldwin Keynote*, vol. 6, no. 1, 1926, p. 2; "Be Familiar with Music Appreciation," *The Baldwin Keynote*, vol. 6, no. 1, 1926, p. 7.

55. Fritz Forchheimer to Lucien Wulsin II, August 9, 1930, Miscellaneous Correspondence Regarding Art and Artists, 1930 folder, Correspondence of Lucien Wulsin II, Baldwin Archives; A. W. Diller to Philip Wyman, October 5, 1934, folder A, 1934, Baldwin Co., Correspondence of Philip Wyman, 1934, Baldwin Archives.

56. On his office wall Wulsin kept a large framed photograph of Rogers leaning on a Baldwin grand, the picture captioned in the humorist's own handwriting. See "Will Rogers," *The Baldwin Keynote*, vol. 6, no. 6, 1926, pp. 4–5; "United States Government Endorses Baldwin," *The Baldwin Keynote*, vol. 5, no. 2, 1925, p. 25.

57. W. A. Sunday to the Baldwin Piano Co., December 1922, reproduced in *The Baldwin Keynote*, vol. 3, no. 1, 1923, p. 9; W. S. Jenks, " 'Billy' Sunday and the Baldwin Piano," ibid., p. 9.

58. Harding White House Piano, ca. 1921 folder, Baldwin Archives; "Another Baldwin in the White House," *The Baldwin Keynote*, vol. 4, no. 1, 1924, p. 3.

59. "Display Card for Style K Baldwin Grand," *The Baldwin Keynote*, vol. 4, no. 5, 1924, p. 9.

60. "Al Jolson Discovers 'The Perfect Piano,' " *The Baldwin Keynote*, vol. 8, no. 2, 1928, p. 20; "Baldwin Official Piano for Vitaphone Productions," *The Baldwin Keynote*, vol. 7, no. 7, 1927, pp. 11–13.

61. "Baldwin for 1300 Theatres," *The Baldwin Keynote*, vol. 7, no. 2, 1927, p. 18; "Lubliner & Trinz Theatres Purchase Baldwin Pianos," *The Baldwin Keynote*, vol. 6, no. 6, 1926, p. 11.

62. Milton Weiner (of Radio Station WLW) to Roy Riegler (of Baldwin

Piano Co.), July 12, 1949, reprinted in "WLW, The Nation's Station," *The Baldwin Keynote*, September 1949, p. 4; "222 Radio Stations Testify to Baldwin's Tone Quality," *The Baldwin Keynote*, vol. 9, no. 2, 1929, pp. 24–27; "Accomplishments of Baldwin Radio Campaign," *The Baldwin Keynote*, vol. 9, no. 2, 1929, p. 5; "Radio and Artist Concerts Lead to Sales of Baldwins," *The Baldwin Keynote*, vol. 9, no. 2, 1929, pp. 12–13; "The Air is Full of Baldwin Every Night," *The Baldwin Keynote*, vol. 6, no. 5, 1926, p. 21.

63. "The Baldwin Piano Co. on Advertising," *The Baldwin Keynote*, vol. 3, no. 3, 1923, inside front cover (reprint from *The Music Trades*, September 22, 1923.)

64. "Getting the Quality Business," *The Baldwin Keynote*, vol. 7, no. 1, 1927, pp. 5–6; *The Baldwin Keynote*, vol. 4, no. 5, 1924, p. 2.

65. "Getting the Quality Business," pp. 5–6.

66. Wulsin followed the writings of C. C. Givens, Jr., author of *Modern Advertising* (1928), and was impressed with Carl Byoir's "A Master Advertiser Tells How to Get Results," in *Forbes* magazine, November 15, 1927, p. 9.

67. Lucien Wulsin II to Mrs. Robert Hotz, November 3, 1936, Baldwin Co., Correspondence, etc., Lucien Wulsin II, 1936, Baldwin Archives.

68. "Each Month More Than 335,000 Baldwin Sales Messages Are Read by Your Best Prospects," *The Baldwin Keynote*, vol. 6, no. 5, 1926, p. 5.

69. "Ten Things to Remember When You Write an Ad," *The Baldwin Keynote*, vol. 4, no. 4, 1924, p. 9; "Canvass Hints!" *The Baldwin Keynote*, vol. 5, no. 3, 1925, p. 24.

70. Baldwin Co., Memoranda, Financial Working Papers, etc., Lucien Wulsin II, 1931 folder, Lucien Wulsin II correspondence, 1931–43, Baldwin Archives.

71. Baldwin Dealer Contracts, Advertising/Sales Promotions, 1940–50, Correspondence with Various Dealers, 1944–45, Geo. W. Lawrence file, Baldwin Archives; Lucien Wulsin II to W. T. Abel, September 20, 1924, Baldwin Co. Selling Division, St. Louis Special File, 1924–28, Baldwin Archives.

72. T. C. McGilliard, "Collections are the Life Blood of Business," *The Baldwin Keynote*, vol. 3, no. 1, 1923, p. 7; Jno. B. Vesey, "Keep Collections Standards High," *The Baldwin Keynote*, vol. 3, no. 2, 1923, p. 19 (see also p. 31); Floyd E. Stearnes, "Stick to the Baldwin Policies," *The Baldwin Keynote*, vol. 4, no. 1, 1924, p. 21; "Larger Cash Payments and Shorter Terms," *The Baldwin Keynote*, vol. 6, no. 6, 1926, p. 32.

73. "New Baldwin Lantern Slides," *The Baldwin Keynote*, vol. 3, no. 2, 1923, p. 19; "'At the Baldwin': Radio Presentations of The Baldwin Piano Company Prove Most Effective Method of Promoting the Piano in History

of the Industry," *The Baldwin Keynote*, vol. 9, no. 2, 1929, pp. 3–8; "Radio and Artist Concerts Lead to Sales of Baldwins," *The Baldwin Keynote*, vol. 9, no. 2, 1929, pp. 12–13

74. See "Baldwin Portfolio Opens Big Campaign," *The Music Trades* 78 (January 19, 1929): 7.

75. Philip Wyman to Lucien Wulsin II, November 19, 1927, Baldwin Co., Correspondence, Lucien Wulsin II folder, Baldwin Archives.

76. Ibid.

77. "Suggestions on Cultivating the Good Will of Music Teachers and Local Artists," *The Baldwin Keynote*, vol. 7, no. 6, 1927, p. 2.

78. Memorandum written to all division heads from G. W. Armstrong, Jr., June 28, 1929, Baldwin Co., Memoranda, Financial Working Papers, etc., Lucien Wulsin II 1929–1930 folder, Baldwin Co., Correspondence of Lucien Wulsin II, 1910–1931, Baldwin Archives.

79. Steinway & Sons advertisement, *New York Times Index*, Statements of Record section, January–March 1919.

80. Memorandum by Philip Wyman, October 20, 1931, Baldwin Co., Memoranda, Financial Working Papers, etc., Lucien Wulsin II, 1931 folder, Baldwin Archives.

81. See Hoover, *Steinways and Their Pianos*; Ehrlich, *Piano: A History*, pp. 47–67; Good, *Giraffes, Black Dragons, and Other Pianos*, pp. 174–85. See also the additional sources list in note 18.

82. Charles H. Steinway, "Building Up Prestige and What It Entails," offprint of *Printers' Ink*, November 7, 1912 (reprinted in pamphlet form by Steinway & Sons, New York, 1912), p. 4, Unprocessed Publications and Advertising Box, Steinway Factory Archives, Fiorello H. LaGuardia Community College, City University of New York, Long Island City, New York (hereafter, Steinway Factory Archives).

83. Lawrence M. Hughes, "A Century of Salesmanship Helps Build Steinway Name," offprint from *Sales Management*, April 15, 1953, p. 5, Unprocessed Publications and Advertising Box, Steinway Factory Archives.

84. John F. Majeski, "Steinway: 125 Years of Service to Music Worldwide," *The Music Trades* 126 (April 1978): 62; Victor Margolin, Ira Brichta, and Vivian Brichta, *The Promise and the Product: 200 Years of American Advertising Posters* (New York: Macmillan, 1979), p. 30.

85. Julius Klausner, *New York Trade Review*, to Steinway & Sons, January 19, 1906; Walter C. Kimball, *The Atlantic Monthly*, to F. Reidemeister, Steinway & Sons, February 10, 1910; P. F. Collier & Son to Steinway & Sons, January 13, 1912; The Globe, Inc. to Steinway & Sons, May 23, 1923, Advertising Correspondence Book, Steinway Factory Archives.

86. Barbara Johnson, "Ayer-Steinway 69-Year History Resulted in 'Immortal' Ads," *Advertising Age*, August 25, 1969, p. 255.

87. Interview with John H. Steinway and Henry Z. Steinway, March 18–19, 1984, Steinway Hall, New York City.

88. George Burton Hotchkiss and Richard B. Franken, *The Leadership of Advertised Brands* (New York: Doubleday, Page & Co., for Associated Advertising Clubs of the World, 1923), pp. 42–44, 116, 117, 119.

89. Steinway ads in *The Literary Digest*, October 17, 1925, p. 57; *The Literary Digest*, October 1, 1921, p. 35; *The Literary Digest*, November 5, 1921, p. 34; *The Literary Digest*, December 16, 1922, back cover; *The Literary Digest*, November 25, 1922, inside front cover; *Saturday Evening Post*, November 9, 1929, p. 50.

90. Johnson, "Ayer-Steinway 69-Year History," p. 255.

91. Charles T. Coiner, "How Steinway Uses Modern Art," *Advertising Arts* (supplement to *Advertising and Selling*), April 2, 1930, p. 17.

92. Warner S. Shelly to Henry Z. Steinway, January 22, 1984, copy to author; Henry Z. Steinway to author, December 10, 1985.

93. Marchand, *Advertising the American Dream*, pp. 140–43.

94. *Saturday Evening Post*, November 10, 1928, pp. 88–89; *Saturday Evening Post*, November 9, 1929, pp. 50–51; *The Literary Digest*, October 1, 1921, p. 35; *Saturday Evening Post*, December 7, 1929, pp. 116–17; *The Literary Digest*, November 19, 1927, p. 55; *The Literary Digest*, October 17, 1925, p. 57; *The Literary Digest*, December 16, 1922, back cover; *The Literary Digest*, November 5, 1921, p. 34.

95. Steinway & Sons, *The Steinways of Today* (New York: Wm. Bradford Press, n.d., ca. 1920s), p. 11.

96. In 1938 Theodore E. Steinway replaced this piano with the concert grand now in the White House. Steinway & Sons, *The Steinway in the White House*, advertising pamphlet, n.d., ca. 1910, Steinway Factory Archives; "All about 'That Gold Piano in the White House,'" Washington *Sunday Star*, August 21, 1966, sec. E, p. 1; Henry Junge, Steinway & Sons, to Franklin D. Roosevelt, December 12, 1936, Steinway Family Archives, Steinway Hall, New York City. See also Kirk, *Music at the White House*.

97. Dolge, *Pianos and Their Makers*, vol. 2, p. 174.

98. *The Literary Digest*, December 2, 1922, p. 41.

99. *The Literary Digest*, December 11, 1926, p. 71; *Saturday Evening Post*, November 9, 1929, pp. 50–51; *The Literary Digest*, November 19, 1927, p. 55; *The Literary Digest*, October 17, 1925, p. 57; *NYT*, March 2, 1924, Rotogravure Picture Section. See also, for example, *Saturday Evening Post*, December 8, 1928, pp. 76–77.

100. *Saturday Evening Post*, November 9, 1929, pp. 50–51; *The Literary Digest*, November 25, 1922, inside front cover.

101. *The Literary Digest*, November 15, 1930, p. 41; *The Literary Digest*, October 18, 1930, p. 47; *The Literary Digest*, December 13, 1930, p. 41.

102. *Harvard Advertising Awards, 1930*, published for the Graduate

School of Business Administration, Harvard University (New York: McGraw-Hill, 1931).
103. Charles H. Steinway, "Building Up Prestige," p. 16.
104. Dolge, *Pianos and Their Makers*, vol. 2, p. 174.

CHAPTER FIVE

1. The Columbus, Ohio, *Dispatch*, the Cincinnati *Commercial Tribune*, and Calvin Coolidge quoted in *The Jonas Chickering Centennial Celebration* (New York: Cheltenham for Chickering & Sons, Boston, 1924), pp. 17–18, 33–37, 49–50.
2. John C. Freund, editor of *Musical America* and *The Music Trades*, compiled these figures for American expenditures on music in 1913:

Teachers, conservatories, schools	$220,000,000
Pianos	135,000,000
Organs (church & reed)	10,000,000
Sheet music	10,500,000
Music rolls	5,000,000
Musical merchandise, violins, etc.	9,500,000
Talking machines & records	60,000,000
Church organists, choirs	40,000,000
Brass & military bands	30,000,000
Movie, theater, vaudville orchestras	25,000,000
Concerts	25,000,000
Opera	8,000,000
Students abroad	7,500,000
Conventions, festivals	2,500,000
Musical papers, critics, writers	3,500,000
Artist royalties	2,000,000
Total expenditures	$593,500,000

See Arthur Farwell, "Music," in *The American Yearbook, 1913*, edited by Francis G. Wickware, p. 781 (New York: D. Appleton & Co., 1914).
3. Ralph L. Baldwin, "An Unsuspected Popular Instinct for Musical Education," *Music Teachers National Association Conference Proceedings*, (hereafter *MTNA Proceedings*) 1913:179–84.
4. Frank A. Scott, "A Survey of Home Music Study," *MTNA Proceedings*, 1919:171–77.
5. Frederick H. Martens, "Music," in *The American Yearbook, 1916* (New York: Appleton, 1917), pp. 741–42; Frederick H. Martens, "Music," in *The American Yearbook, 1917* (New York: Appleton, 1918), pp. 708–12.
6. Congressman Henry Bruckner of New York introduced a bill to es-

tablish a National Conservatory of Music and Art, and after a congressional hearing in June 1918, Duncan U. Fletcher of Florida introduced a revised bill in the Senate in August 1918. Jerome F. Donovan submitted an identical bill in the House. The Fletcher bill also provided for the establishment of a federal agency in music to promote community music, music education, and American compositions more effectively. The bill, however, was tied up in the Committee on Education for years. See U.S. Congress, Senate, Committee on Education, *A Bill to Establish a National Conservatory of Music and Art, Hearing on S. 561.* 66th Cong., 2d sess., 1919. (Hereafter, *Establishment of National Conservatory, Hearings,* 1919.)

7. Frederick H. Martens, "Music," in *The American Yearbook, 1918* (New York: Appleton, 1919), pp. 427, 757.

8. C. M. Tremaine, Remarks, April 12, 1918, *Music Supervisors National Conference Journal of Proceedings,* 1918:185.

9. Harvey N. Roehl, *Player Piano Treasury* (Vestal, N.Y.: Vestal Press, 1961; 2d ed., 1973), p. 29. See also "The Moral Value of Music" in chapter one.

10. American families paid an estimated $15 million annually to foreign countries (especially Germany and Austria) before the Great War to train their promising music students. *New York Times* (hereafter *NYT*), June 7, 1918, p. 9; U.S. Congress, Senate, Subcommittee of the Committee on Education and Labor, *A Bill to Establish a National Conservatory of Music, Hearing on S. 1320.* 68th Cong., 1st sess., March 25, 1924, p. 4.

11. See *Establishment of National Conservatory, Hearings,* 1919.

12. The exemption of piano manufacturing from the War Revenue Tax and the reclassification of the musical instruments industry as "essential to the national welfare" for the duration of the war resulted primarily from the efforts of George W. Pound, general manager of MICC. An attorney with Rudolph Wurlitzer Co. and former general manager of NPMA, Pound was an intimate friend of Theodore Roosevelt. During the congressional hearings on what became the Copyright Act of 1909 he had also played a role in exposing Aeolian's attempt to monopolize the perforated roll industry (see chapter two). John C. Freund, "Get Together!—Get Together," *The Music Trades* 53 (May 26, 1917): 1–6; "Trade Topics," *The Music Trades* 53 (August 18, 1917): 24; "War Industries Take Precedence in Allotments of Steel by Government," *The Music Trades* 54 (October 6, 1917): 3; *The Music Trades* 54 (November 3, 1917): 24; *The Music Trades* 54 (November 10, 1917): 28; "Music Chamber to Meet Industry Crisis," *The Music Trades* 54 (November 17, 1917): 27; "Big 'Non-Essential' Bugaboo Scotched," *The Music Trades* 54 (December 15, 1917): 27; "22nd Annual Convention of the N. P. Mfrs.' Assn.," *The Music Trades* 55 (June 8, 1918): 6–8.

13. "Piano Industry No Drain on Country's Resources in Man-Power, Materials, Fuel," *The Music Trades* 54 (December 1, 1917): 3–4; "National Music Industries Convention in New York," *The Music Trades* 75 (June 9, 1928): 13; "Music Trade as Affected by War," *NYT*, August 4, 1918, p. 18; "Why the Slump in the Piano Trade?" *NYT*, February 26, 1922, p. 27.

14. *The Music Trades* 55 (June 8, 1918): 38.

15. C. M. Tremaine, *History of National Music Week* (New York: National Bureau for the Advancement of Music, 1925), p. 9.

16. "Music Trade as Affected by War," *NYT*, August 4, 1918, p. 18; *NYT*, January 4, 1917, p. 18; *NYT*, April 7, 1918, sec. 5, p. 7; *NYT*, May 31, 1921, p. 26; *NYT*, April 23, 1922, p. 29.

17. The *New York Times Index* listed "Player Piano" as an entry separate from "Piano" for the first time in 1918. National Piano Manufacturers' bulletin quoted in *NYT*, May 18, 1919, sec. 2, p. 10; *NYT*, January 11, 1920, sec. 3, p. 8; *NYT*, November 17, 1918, sec. 7, p. 9; *NYT*, October 15, 1922, sec. 2, p. 14; *NYT*, November 6, 1922, p. 27; U.S. Labor Department Training Service, *Course of Instruction in Piano Making, with Section on Player Pianos, Pneumatic Actions, Piano Actions, and Keys* (Washington, D.C.: U.S. Government Printing Office, Training Bulletin no. 22, 1919).

18. Will Earhart, "Recent Advances in Instruction in Music in the Public Schools," Part One, *Biennial Survey of Education, 1920–22*, vol. 1 (Washington, D.C.: U.S. Government Printing Office, 1924), pp. 439–42.

19. Ibid., pp. 443–46, 447–48. See also "Present Status of Music Instruction in Colleges and High Schools, 1919–1920: Report," U.S. Department of Interior, Bureau of Education *Bulletin*, 1921, no. 9 (Washington, D.C.: U.S. Government Printing Office, 1921): 5–53.

20. "Music and the American Home," *The Outlook* 117 (October 3, 1917): 180–81, 182.

21. The reader will recall that Secretary Davis also endorsed the music-in-industry movement (chap. 1). *NYT*, May 15, 1922, p. 5; James J. Davis, "'There Should Be a Musical Instrument in Every School Room,' Says Secretary of Labor Davis" (Interview), *The Music Trades* 65 (May 19, 1923): 1.

22. Peter W. Dykema, professor of music at the University of Wisconsin and spokesman for the Committee on Community Music of the Music Teachers National Assn. in 1930, called the bureau the most significant agency stimulating music interest in the United States. See Peter W. Dykema, "Report of the Committee on Community Music," *MTNA Proceedings*, 1930:241–43.

23. Oscar Thompson and Nicolas Slonimsky, eds., *International Cyclopedia of Music and Musicians* (New York: Dodd, Mead, 5th ed., 1949), p. 1917; Alfred Dolge, *Pianos and Their Makers* (Covina, Calif.: Covina Publishing Co., 1911; reprinted, New York: Dover, 1972), vol. 1, p. 277; C. M.

Tremaine, "The National Bureau for the Advancement of Music and Its Relation to the Supervisor," *Music Supervisors National Conference Journal of Proceedings*, 1927:132–35.

24. C. M. Tremaine, "The Music Memory Contest, etc." *Music Supervisors National Conference Journal of Proceedings*, 1918:99–107; C. M. Tremaine, "National Bureau for the Advancement of Music and Its Relation to the Supervisor," pp. 132–35; Edward Bailey Birge, *History of Public School Music in the United States* (Boston: Oliver Ditson Co., 1928), pp. 210–11. See also C. M. Tremaine, "Music Memory Contests, with List of One Hundred Selections Most Frequently Used," *National Education Association Journal* 15 (February 1926): 43–44; and J. C. Seegers, "Teaching Music Appreciation by Means of the Music Memory Contest," *Elementary School Journal* 26 (February 1925): 215–23.

25. C. M. Tremaine, "National Music Week," in *The Magic of Music: An Anthology for Music Weeks and Days*, compiled and edited by Robert Haven Schauffler, pp. 4–5 (New York: Dodd, Mead, 1946).

26. Ibid., pp. 7–8; Tremaine, *History of National Music Week*, pp. 17–23.

27. Tremaine, "National Music Week," pp. 7–8; Tremaine, *History of National Music Week*, pp. 17–23; Harold E. Rainville to Radio Editor of the *New York Times*, February 17, 1937, printed in *NYT*, March 14, 1937, sec. 11, p. 6; *NYT*, April 16, 1921, p. 8.

28. Rainville to Radio Editor, *NYT*, March 14, 1937, sec. 11, p. 6; The National Music Week Committee, "How to Organize a Music Week Committee," in *Magic of Music*, ed. by Schauffler, pp. 11–16; *NYT*, April 10, 1921, sec. 6, p. 4; *NYT*, April 16, 1923, sec. 6, p. 3; *NYT*, April 23, 1923, sec. 2, p. 3; *NYT*, February 18, 1924, p. 13.

29. Peter W. Dykema, "Report of the Committee on Community Music," *MTNA Proceedings*, 1924:200–201.

30. Tremaine, "National Bureau for the Advancement of Music and Its Relation to the Supervisor," pp. 132–35.

31. Senator Fletcher's bill establishing a National Conservatory of Music was also still being debated in the Committee on Education. U.S. Congress, House, A Bill To Create a Department of Fine Arts, H.R. 5801, 68th Cong., 1st sess., January 19, 1924, *Congressional Record*, 65:1181; U.S. Congress, Senate, Subcommittee of the Committee on Education and Labor, *A Bill to Establish a National Conservatory of Music, Hearing on S.1320.* 68th Cong., 1st sess., March 25, 1924.

32. Tremaine, "National Bureau for the Advancement of Music and Its Relation to the Supervisor," pp. 132–35.

33. Ibid.

34. The National Piano Promotion Committee of the National Piano Manufacturers Association. This group will be discussed later in the chapter.

35. Charles L. Gary, *Vignettes of Music Education History* (Washington, D.C.: Music Educators National Conference, 1964), pp. 26–27.

36. P. P. Claxton to Will Earhart, January 12, 1914, quoted in Clara Josephine McCauley, *A Professionalized Study of Public School Music* (Knoxville, Tenn.: Jos. E. Avent, 1932), pp. 38–39.

37. Birge, *History of Public School Music*, pp. 201–2.

38. "The Golden Hour Plan: America's Most Serious Problem—A Possible Solution in which You May Have a Vital Part," *The Etude* 39 (April 1921): 223; "The Golden Hour," *The Etude* 39 (May 1921): 294; "What about the Golden Hour," *The Etude* 40 (March 1922): 151; "America's Greatest Present Problem," *The Etude* 44 (January 1926): 8.

39. Miller quoted in Birge, *History of Public School Music*, pp. 198–99.

40. "Report of the Subcommittee on Class Piano Instruction," *Music Supervisors National Conference Journal of Proceedings*, 1928:325.

41. "Survey Shows Piano Classes in 358 Schools," *The Musician* 33 (October 1928): 11; Joseph E. Maddy, "Report of the Committee on Piano Classes," *MTNA Proceedings*, 1930:260–63.

42. Peter W. Dykema, "Report of the Committee on Community Music," *MTNA Proceedings*, 1927:197–207.

43. Josef Hofmann, "A Musical Educational Renaissance," *The Etude* 54 (October 1936): 611–12.

44. F. L. Donelson, "The Teacher, the Pupil and the Untuned Piano," *The Etude* 48 (October 1930): 751.

45. Peter Dykema, "Report of the Committee on Community Music," *MTNA Proceedings*, 1931:158–64.

46. Corley Gibson, "Why I Believe the Piano Industry Is on the Threshold of Its Greatest Era of Prosperity," *The Music Trades* 77 (October 1929): 3.

47. I wish to thank John H. Steinway and Henry Z. Steinway, who pointed out the necessity of qualifying this seemingly bold remark. Certainly the various piano companies that *survived* the 1920s and 1930s have made a remarkable recovery, a recovery that stemmed from their production of the new (and now current) smaller, more fashionable piano styles, together with their promotion of traditional values, enjoyable music instruction, and a return to self-produced music (see chap. 6 and the epilogue). Currently, many companies are also prospering through production and sales of electronic keyboards and digital pianos with MIDI functions, though foreign manufacturers are intensely competing in both this and the traditional piano markets. As I read the history of the American piano industry, however, I conclude that the player piano trade indeed was ruined, and that the piano industry in general has not recovered the production nor the market that it enjoyed from 1909 to 1923. Upright piano production crested in 1909, player piano manufacture peaked in

1923, grand piano production in 1925. And while in 1909 there were almost three hundred purportedly separate piano manufacturing firms, there were fewer than ninety by 1929, and only thirty-six by 1933 (including mergers), a figure that has remained relatively constant to the present. That the trade never fully recovered is further shown if one considers the increase in population and the decrease in pianos produced per capita since the 1920s. See Solomon Fabricant, *The Output of Manufacturing Industries, 1899–1937* (New York: National Bureau of Economic Research, 1940), the annual *Statistical Abstract of the United States*, and the decennial *Census of the United States*.

48. Bob Pierce, comp., *Pierce Piano Atlas* (Long Beach, Calif.: Bob Pierce, publisher, 7th ed., 1977), p. 5.

49. A. B. Chase slogan quoted in *Purchaser's Guide to the Music Industries, 1977* (Englewood, N.J.: Music Trades Corp., 81st ed., 1977), pp. 16, 18. Piano industry statistics compiled from U.S. Department of Commerce, Bureau of Census, *Biennial Census of Manufacturers*, 1921–1931; Fabricant, *Output of Manufacturing Industries*, pp. 597–99.

50. The Music Industries Chamber of Commerce was composed of the following organizations: National Piano Manufacturers Association (NPMA), National Association of Music Merchants (NAMM) (formerly the National Association of Piano Dealers, until 1919), National Piano Travelers Association (NPTA), National Association of Piano Tuners (NAPT), National Association of Sheet Music Dealers (NASMD), National Musical Merchandise Association (NMMA), National Association of Musical Instrument and Accessories Manufacturers (NAMIAM), National Music Dealers Association (NMDA), National Association of Organ Manufacturers (NAOM), National Musical Supply Association (NMSA), and the National Committee for Phonograph Manufacturers.

51. *The Music Trades* 71 (May 15, 1926): 3.

52. "Procter Piano Company: A Case Dealing with the Expansion of a Piano Manufacturer into the Field of Player Pianos," *Harvard Business Review* 1 (October 1922): 116–19. "Procter" is a fictitious name, but most likely refers to Steinway & Sons.

53. "Why the Slump in the Piano Trade?" *NYT*, February 26, 1922, p. 27; "Great Slump in the Piano Trade Is Mystifying," *Current Opinion* 72 (June 1922): 830–31.

54. "Demonstration Week Campaign," *The Music Trades*, ca. 1924, quoted in "60 Years Ago," *The Music Trades* 132 (January 1984): 108; Arthur Ord-Hume, *Player Piano: The History of the Mechanical Piano and How to Repair It* (London: George Allen and Unwin, 1970), p. 41.

55. "Absence of Seasonal Slump in 1923 Due to Advertising," *The Music Trades*, ca. 1924, quoted in "60 Years Ago," *The Music Trades* 132 (January 1984): 108; M. J. Kennedy quoted in this article, also; NPMA production

figures found in NPMA, "Piano Unit Production, 1900–1976," author's collection, provided by George M. Otto, Executive Director, National Piano Manufacturers Association to author, November 11, 1980.

56. "The Piano Trade Is Now on Trial!" *The Music Trades* 72 (December 4, 1926): 3–4, 8.

57. "Piano Promotion Plan to Begin Functioning Immediately," *The Music Trades* 72 (December 11, 1926): 3. L. P. ("Perk") Bull of Story & Clark Piano Co. was one of the founders of the NPMA Piano Promotion Committee, which devised the plan. See "L. P. Bull . . 1901–1975," *The Music Trades* 123 (July 1975): 107ff.

58. "Annual Convention of the NPMA," *The Music Trades* 71 (June 12, 1926): 25.

59. "31st Annual Convention of NPMA," *The Music Trades* 73 (June 11, 1927): 17; Edward C. Boykin, " 'The Most Interesting Piano Story Ever Told,' " *The Music Trades* 77 (February 15, 1929): 9–12.

60. "Piano Promotion Body Reviews Its 1st Year Record," *The Music Trades* 75 (January 21, 1928): 8; *The Music Trades* 75 (January 7, 1928): 7; *The Music Trades* 73 (January 29, 1927): 4; "Report of the Subcommittee on Class Piano Instruction," *Music Supervisors National Conference Journal of Proceedings*, 1928:325; *NYT*, May 2, 1927, p. 26; C. M. Tremaine, "Gap between Music in Schools and Music in Homes," *The Musician* 36 (July 1931): 13.

61. Stuart Ewen, *Captains of Consciousness: Advertising and the Social Roots of the Consumer Culture* (New York: McGraw-Hill, 1976), pp. 115, 121, 132–33, 135, 162 (the entire Part 3 is helpful here); Eli Zaretsky, *Capitalism, the Family, and Personal Life* (New York: Harper & Row, 1976), pp. 57, 62, 64–65, 67–68. Though these books' interpretations are becoming dated, their discussions of the transformation of the home are still useful.

62. *The Music Trades*, ca. 1953, quoted in "30 Years Ago," *The Music Trades* 131 (November 1983): 91. For the importance of the retail dealer in the music industry, see Brian T. Majeski, "Retail Salespeople . . . The Hope of the Industry," *The Music Trades* 132 (March 1984): 16; "Tough Times Try Industry Mettle," *The Music Trades* 130 (July 1982): 28–54 passim.

63. Otto W. Miessner, "How the Economic Slump Has Affected the Music Teacher," *The Musician* 36 (June 1931): 11, 25; Otto W. Miessner, "What Is Happening to the Piano?" *MTNA Proceedings*, 1930:188; William Tonk, *Memoirs of a Manufacturer* (New York: Presto, 1926), pp. 55–56.

64. "Buying a New Piano," *The Etude* 52 (October 1934): 572; Gilbert Russell, "How to Buy a Piano," *The Etude* 43 (January 1925): 20; "Pride in the American Piano," *The Etude* 52 (November 1934): 636.

65. Byron H. Collins, "What Should I Know to Purchase a Reliable Pi-

ano?" *The Etude* 40 (October 1922): 669; Miessner, "What Is Happening to the Piano?" p. 189.

66. John C. Bostelmann, Jr., "The Visuola," *MTNA Proceedings*, 1927: 184–93; John C. Bostelmann, Jr., "A New Approach to Piano Study," *The Musician* 32 (October 1927): 13, 34; Miessner, "What Is Happening to the Piano?" pp. 189–90; Miessner, "How the Economic Slump Has Affected the Music Teacher," pp. 11, 25.

67. Frank L. Wing, *The Book of Complete Information about Pianos* (New York: Wing & Son, 1897), p. 5.

68. F. A. Hurd, "Why Some Dealers Don't Sell Players," *The Music Trades* 77 (January 12, 1929): 10.

69. Marion Reed, "How to Make the Reproducing Library Pay," *The Music Trades*, December 20, 1924, reproduced in Roehl, *Player Piano Treasury*, p. 188.

70. Alfred Dolge quoted in Harvey N. Roehl, *Player Piano Treasury*, p. 54; Robert Haven Schauffler, "Finding the Soul of the Player Piano," *The Delineator* 94 (February 1919): 51.

71. "New Foot-Propelled Welte-Mignon (Licensee) Action Quickly Finds Friends in the Trade," *The Music Trades*, December 25, 1926, reproduced in Roehl, *Player Piano Treasury*, p. 87; Hurd, "Why Some Dealers Don't Sell Players," p. 10.

72. Roy E. Waite, "The Piano's Future," *NYT*, June 18, 1933, sec. 10, p. 5; *Life* 89 (June 9, 1927): 26.

73. *The Music Trades*, ca. 1894, quoted in "90 Years Ago," *The Music Trades* 132 (April 1984): 16.

74. Robert N. Watkin, President, NAMM, to members, ca. 1924, quoted in "60 Years Ago," *The Music Trades* 132 (January 1984): 111; *The Music Trades*, ca. 1924, quoted in "60 Years Ago," *The Music Trades* 132 (April 1984): 14, 16; *NYT*, June 9, 1926, p. 18.

75. "Radio—Mad," *The Etude* 41 (February 1923): 77.

76. Quoted in Erik Barnouw, *A History of Broadcasting in the United States* (New York: Oxford University Press, 1966), vol. 1, p. 78. Barnouw's three volume work (1966–1970) is the standard history of the American radio industry. Also useful are Daniel Boorstin's observations in *The Americans: The Democratic Experience* (New York: Random House, 1973).

77. U.S. President, Committee on Social Trends, *Recent Social Trends in the United States: Report of the President's Research Committee on Social Trends*, vol. 1 (New York: McGraw-Hill, 1933; reprinted Westport, Conn.: Greenwood Press, 1970), pp. 152–57.

78. "The Music Trades Silver Jubilee," *NYT*, June 7, 1925, sec. 9, p. 16.

79. Cable Company spokesman quoted in "Chicago's Music Industry Is Huge," *Chicago Commerce* 24 (July 21, 1928): 7–8.

80. George C. Foster, statement to American Piano Co. stockholders,

quoted in *NYT,* March 26, 1925, p. 21. Edward Strumaker, president of Victor Talking Machine Co., concurred. Although the radio initially hurt phonograph sales, Victor was enjoying booming sales once the company teamed up with the radio manufacturers in 1925 and produced a combined machine, the Victrola-radio. See *NYT,* April 25, 1925, p. 25; *NYT,* May 2, 1926, sec. 9, p. 21; *NYT,* February 4, 1927, p. 30; Barnouw, *History of Broadcasting,* vol. 1, pp. 220, 233; Roland Gelatt, *The Fabulous Phonograph: From Tin Foil to High Fidelity* (Philadelphia: J. B. Lippincott, 1955), pp. 245–56, 265–69 passim.

81. Mason & Hamlin advertisement, *NYT,* March 23, 1928, p. 15.

82. Barnouw, *History of Broadcasting,* vol. 1, p. 131; Maurice Peress, program notes for *The Birth of Rhapsody in Blue: Paul Whiteman's Historic Aeolian Hall Concert of 1924,* Maurice Peress, conducting, with piano soloists Ivan Davis and Dick Hyman (Musical Heritage Society compact disc recording, no. 11238A); *NYT,* December 14, 1927, p. 32.

83. The new Steinway Hall won the Fifth Avenue Association's first prize for architectural design. *NYT,* October 12, 1925, p. 25; *NYT,* October 28, 1925, p. 28; *NYT,* December 20, 1925, sec. 10, p. 2; *NYT,* July 18, 1927, p. 1; Theodore E. Steinway, *People and Pianos: A Century of Service to Music* (New York: Steinway & Sons, 1953), pp. 65, 78.

84. Lucien Wulsin II to Alfred C. Howell, October 30, 1929, R. H. Woodford Radio File 1929–30, folder 2, Baldwin Co., Correspondence of Lucien Wulsin II, 1929, D. H. Baldwin & Co. Archives, Cincinnati Historical Society, Eden Park, Cincinnati Ohio (hereafter Baldwin Archives); Western Union cable to dealers from Baldwin Co. General Office, November 13, 1929, R. H. Woodford Radio File, 1929–30, folder 3, Baldwin Co., Correspondence of Lucien Wulsin II, 1929–30, Baldwin Archives; Baldwin Piano Co. to G. W. Lawrence, November 13, 1929, R. H. Woodford Radio File 1929, Hamilton Radio, folder 1, Baldwin Co., Correspondence of Lucien Wulsin II, 1929, Baldwin Archives; Lucien Wulsin II to William F. Wiley, August 1, 1930, Baldwin Co., Correspondence of Lucien Wulsin II, 1930 folder, Baldwin Archives; "'At the Baldwin': Radio Presentations of The Baldwin Company Prove Most Effective Method of Promoting the Piano in History of the Industry," *The Baldwin Keynote,* vol. 9, no. 2, 1929, pp. 3–7; "Baldwin to Broadcast to Millions," *The Music Trades* 77 (January 19, 1929): 5; "Baldwin Radio Feature to Be Continued and Enlarged," *The Music Trades* 78 (October 1929): 13; James E. Hiltz to Baldwin Piano Co., 1929, c/o Station WJZ, New York, Advertising/Sales Promotions 1929–30, Listener Response to "At the Baldwin" Radio Program on NBC, 1929 folder, Baldwin Archives.

85. William Geppert, "Veteran Editor Analyzes Success of 'At the Baldwin' Radio Campaign," *Musical Courier,* June 1, 1930, offprint in Box 283, vol. 76, Baldwin Archives.

86. *Christian Science Monitor* quoted in "'At the Baldwin': Radio Presentations of The Baldwin Company," p. 7.

87. Henry C. Lomb, "Prospect and Retrospect [on School Music Program]," *The Music Trades* 77 (January 12, 1929): 11. The Weydig Piano Corp., New York, offered consumers the "Radi-O-Player." See Roehl, *Player Piano Treasury*, p. 55. For the surveys indicating radio audience musical preferences, see Noble Hollister, "Jazz Feels Surge of a Higher Order," *NYT Magazine*, March 15, 1925, p. 9; "NBC Reports Radio Survey Questionaire," *NYT*, April 1, 1927, p. 28. For a comparison, in 1923, 75 percent of radio fans wanted jazz. Barnouw discusses the predominance of conservatory music on radio during the 1920s in *History of Broadcasting*, vol. 1, pp. 125–35.

88. Walter Damrosch, *My Musical Life* (New York: Charles Scribner's Sons, Golden Jubilee Edition, 1935), pp. 369–79; *NYT*, June 27, 1928, p. 28; Charles C. Alexander, *Here the Country Lies: Nationalism and the Arts in Twentieth-Century America* (Bloomington: Indiana University Press, 1980), pp. 128–29.

89. Olin Downes, "A New Musical Era," *NYT*, May 24, 1931, sec. 8, p. 8.

90. "The Ragtime Queen Has Abdicated," *NYT Magazine*, May 24, 1925, p. 21; *NYT*, June 11, 1925, p. 1.

91. In an effort to encourage the public to purchase only reliable instruments, *The Etude* magazine offered a consumer protection service to its readers in 1929. See "Better Pianos," *The Etude* 47 (June 1929): 422. For general trends, see Henry L. Mason, "How Has the Pianoforte as an Instrument Developed since 1876?—With Some Figures," *MTNA Proceedings*, 1928:134–46, and *The Etude* 48 (May 1930): 323–24; V. S. Clark, *History of Manufacturing in the United States*, vol. 3 (New York: McGraw-Hill, 1929), p. 350; Roy E. Waite to *NYT* Music Editor, June 9, 1933, printed as "The Piano's Future," in *NYT*, June 18, 1933, sec. 10, p. 5. See also Walter Rendell Storey, "The Piano Acquires Grace and Beauty," *NYT Magazine*, March 14, 1926, pp. 9, 18.

92. Steinway and Baldwin sales records taken from Henry Z. Steinway to author, January 2, 1986; *NYT*, January 26, 1930, sec. 2, p. 20; Morley P. Thompson, "Schedule of Factory Shipments," Capital Study, the Baldwin Piano Co. folder, Valuable Financial Papers Collected by M. P. Thompson file, Baldwin Archives.

93. "American Piano Co.'s Party One of the Outstanding Social Functions During the Anniversary Conventions," *The Music Trades* 71 (June 12, 1926): 17; Lloyd Graham, "The Story of the Rudolph Wurlitzer Family and Business" (unpublished manuscript in the possession of Mrs. Janet Wurlitzer Stites, Cincinnati, Ohio), pp. 99–100.

94. *Moody's Analysis of Investments: Industrials*, volumes for 1927, 1928 (New York: Moody's Investor Service, 1927, 1928).

95. *NYT,* February 9, 1928, p. 32; *NYT,* September 6, 1928, p. 41; *NYT,* December 27, 1929, p. 42.

96. "American Piano Co. in Equity Receivership," *The Music Trades* 77 (December 1929): 22.

97. *NYT,* January 31, 1930, p. 24; *NYT,* March 30, 1930, sec. 2, p. 14; *NYT,* May 22, 1930, p. 43; "American Piano Corporation," *The Music Trades* 78 (June 1930): 12–13; *NYT,* July 26, 1930, p. 2.

98. U.S. Commerce Department, Bureau of the Census, *Biennial Census of Manufacturers,* 1921, 1923, 1925, 1927, 1929; Fabricant, *Output of Manufacturing Industries,* pp. 597–99; Johnson Heywood, "Swing High, Swing Low with the Musical Instruments Industry," *Dun's Review* 47 (June 1939): 23.

99. Lumber was used not only in manufacturing cabinets, but also in making shipping crates. *NYT,* April 8, 1928, sec. 9, p. 15.

100. *Radio Retailing* survey quoted in *NYT,* January 9, 1927, sec. 8, p. 11; J. Andrew White, "Radio Music for Everybody," *The Etude* 40 (June 1922): 371–72.

101. The variety even included "party rolls," the counterpart to dirty movies. In the mid-twenties, the New York Piano Merchants' Association adopted a resolution to ban the sale of any sheet music, phonographic record, or piano-word roll, whose words were "lewd, lascivious, salacious, or suggestive." Similarly, the Q.R.S Music Co. launched a campaign against filth in popular songs, because "in recent days the output of the salacious has taken on a rawness never before dared. . . . such a number, finding its way into decent homes, is bound to have a bad effect—to hurt the sales of player-pianos and phonographs." See *NYT,* February 3, 1927, p. 3; "Q.R.S Music Co. Launches Campaign Against Filth in Popular Songs with Vigorous Circular Letter," *The Music Trades* (November 192-?), reproduced in Roehl, *Player Piano Treasury,* p. 155.

102. These devices evidently remained so popular in speakeasies, restaurants, clubs, etc., that some companies reported operating at full capactiy and even in overtime to keep up with demand. See "Busy Times at Western Electric Piano Co.," *The Music Trades* 71 (June 12, 1926), reproduced in Roehl, *Player Piano Treasury,* p. 135; "Make the Most of the New Era Prosperity," advertisement for Nelson-Wiggens Co., illustrated in Roehl, *Player Piano Treasury,* p. 132; Clayton Haswell, "Restored Jukeboxes," *Cincinnati Enquirer,* June 9, 1984, sec. D, p. 4.

103. Peter W. Dykema, "Report of the Committee on Community Music," *MTNA Proceedings,* 1930:233.

104. *NYT,* September 2, 1930, p. 20. For Thomas Tapper, see chap. 1, note 62.

CHAPTER SIX

1. "Music Renaissance Is Seen in Nation," *New York Times* (hereafter *NYT*), May 5, 1929, sec. 2, p. 2; "Nation Poll on Music Week," *NYT*, May 4, 1930, sec. 11, p. 8.

2. *The Music Trades* 79 (December 1931): 9.

3. Hermann Irion quoted in "America Turning Anew to the Piano," by Paul Kempf, in *The Musician* 34 (January 1929): 11.

4. *The Music Trades* 77 (July 1929): 37; "Merchants Assn. Seeks Fed. Aid for the Fine Arts," *The Music Trades* 77 (April 1929): 11.

5. Supporters of the bill to establish a national conservatory were the National Bureau for the Advancement of Music, the Music Industries Chamber of Commerce, the American Federation of Labor, the American Federation of Musicians, the National Council of Women, the National Federation of Music Clubs, the Federation of Protestant Churches of America, the Association of Music School Settlements of New York, Pen Women of America, the Rotary Club, Women's Universal Alliance, the American Association of Lovers of Music, and the music teachers' associations of many states. By 1924, however, the National Federation of Music Clubs had withdrawn its support in favor of a similar bill, one that would distribute the governing power of the conservatory among a commission of five rather than giving control to a single director general. U.S. Congress, Senate, *Hearing before the Committee on Education and Labor on S.561, A Bill to Establish a National Conservatory of Music and Art*, 66th Cong., 2d sess., December 1919, pp. 16, 19; U.S. Congress, Senate, *Hearing before a Subcommittee of the Committee on Education and Labor on S.1320, A Bill to Establish a National Conservatory of Music*, 68th Cong., 1st sess., March 25, 1924, pp. 8, 10, 21–22, 42, 45.

6. The words are Jacob Hayman's, a civil engineer who originated the campaign in 1914. U.S. Congress, Senate, *Hearing on S.561* (1919), p. 11.

7. The words of Senator Duncan U. Fletcher of Florida, who introduced a revised version of the bill in August 1918 (along with Jerome F. Donovan in the House) following the June 1918 hearings on the original bill, which had been submitted by Congressman Henry Bruckner of New York, October 4, 1917 (ibid., p. 7).

8. *The Music Trades* 77 (April 1929): 41; *The Music Trades* 78 (May 1930): 15; "Baldwin to Broadcast to Millions," *The Music Trades* 78 (January 19, 1929): 5 (see also chapter four); "Baldwin's New National Advertising Drive to Create Interest in the Piano as Essential to the Home," *The Music Trades* 78 (May 1930): 13; Steinway ads in *Harvard Advertising Awards, 1930* (New York: McGraw-Hill, 1931).

9. Fred P. Bassett, "Quality Production and Energetic Effort Will Tell

Piano Tale of 1930," *The Music Trades* 77 (December 1929): 19; Edward C. Boykin, "'The Most Interesting Piano Story Ever Told': Profit Plans for Every Dealer," *The Music Trades* 77 (February 15, 1929): 9, 10–11, 12.

10. "Music Industries Hold 13th Annual Convention in NYC," *The Music Trades* 78 (June 1930): 3–7; "Music Industries Chamber of Commerce," *The Music Trades* 79 (June 1931): 3–7.

11. *Business Week* was critical of the trade's attempt to discourage the used-piano market instead of organizing it. See "The Piano Industry Struck the Wrong Key," *Business Week*, January 15, 1930, pp. 13–14; "Music Industries Hold 13th Annual Convention in NYC," pp. 3–7; U.S., Department of Commerce, Bureau of the Census, *Biennial Census of Manufacturers, 1935* (Washington, D.C.: U.S. Government Printing Office, 1938): 1220, 1224.

12. "National Bureau for the Advancement of Music," *The Music Trades* 78 (December 1930): 12; Peter W. Dykema, "Report of the Committee on Community Music," *Music Teachers National Association Conference Proceedings* (hereafter *MTNA Proceedings*), 1930:241–43.

13. Gordon G. Campbell, "Future of Piano Business Is Secure," *The Music Trades* 79 (December 1931): 3; *Life* 89 (March 31, 1927): 4.

14. *NYT*, May 14, 1931, p. 27; *NYT*, July 18, 1931, p. 24.

15. Morley P. Thompson, "Financial History of the Baldwin Piano Company, since 1902," p. 14, typewritten (December 6, 1954), Baldwin Co., Financial History 1902–1954, Morley P. Thompson folder, Baldwin Archives; Lawrence M. Hughes, "A Century of Salesmanship Helps Build Steinway Name," *Sales Management* offprint for April 15, 1953, pp. 4, 5, Unprocessed Publications and Advertising Box, Steinway Factory Archives, Fiorello H. LaGuardia Community College of the City University of New York, Long Island City, New York (hereafter Steinway Factory Archives); *NYT*, May 7, 1932, p. 22.

16. Van Allen Bradley, *Music for the Millions: The Kimball Piano and Organ Story* (Chicago: Henry Regnery Co., 1957), p. 262; Lloyd Graham, "The Story of the Rudolph Wurlitzer Family and Business," p. 103, typed manuscript (May 25, 1955) in possession of Mrs. Janet Wurlitzer Stites, Cincinnati, Ohio.

17. "Pianofortissimo: In 1935 the Piano Industry Discovered Style," *Fortune* 20 (August 1939): 49; Otto W. Miessner, "What Is Happening to the Piano?" *The Musician* 36 (May 1931): 11, 22; "Pianos: Radio, Ex-Foe, Proves Ally," *Newsweek*, November 6, 1935, pp. 37–38.

18. "The Music Tradesmen Join Other Manufacturers in Plea to Hoover to Aid Country's Industries," *The Music Trades* 80 (March 1932): 3.

19. An excellent summary and bibliography of the National Recovery Administration can be found in Otis L. Graham, Jr., and Meghan Robin-

son Wander, eds., *Franklin D. Roosevelt, His Life and Times: An Encyclopedic View* (Boston: G. K. Hall & Co., 1985), pp. 274–77.

20. The members of NPMA's Code Authority for the Retail Code were Theodore E. Steinway, chairman, W. H. Alfring, and Harry Sohmer. NAMM's members were Homer L. Kitt and Delbert L. Loomis. See National Recovery Administration, "Code of Fair Competition for the Piano Manufacturing Industry," in *National Recovery Administration Codes of Fair Competition*, vol. 2, nos. 88–110 (Washington, D.C.: U.S. Government Printing Office, 1934), pp. 435–42; U.S. Department of Commerce, NRA Records Section, "National Recovery Administration Division of Review, Work Materials no. 13," March 1936, p. 381, typewritten, Perry-Casteñeda Library, University of Texas at Austin; and Lucien Wulsin, "Resumé of Piano Industry under NRA Code," *The Music Trades* 82 (February 1934): pp. 3–4.

21. Alfring also served with Theodore E. Steinway, chairman, and Harry Sohmer as a member of NPMA's Code Authority for the Retail Code. E. F. Brooks, Jr., president of Aeolian American Division, to author, August 22, 1980; E. F. Brooks, Jr., "Aeolian American Division of Aeolian Corporation, East Rochester, New York," pp. 1–4, typewritten, in author's possession; "The Piano Industry Struck the Wrong Key," *Business Week*, January 15, 1930, p. 14; *NYT*, October 9, 1930, p. 46; *NYT*, February 11, 1931, p. 37; *NYT*, September 10, 1931, p. 38; *NYT*, August 12, 1932, p. 29; "Pianos Harmonize on Economy Theme," *Business Week*, August 10, 1932, pp. 9–10; "Piano Merger Links Two Largest Makers: Union of Aeolian and American Groups Will Embrace 20 Companies," *NYT*, June 30, 1932, p. 17; "Aeolian-American Corporation Announced," *The Music Trades* 80 (August 1932): 3; *NYT*, February 24, 1933, p. 27; *NYT*, August 10, 1933, p. 31; *NYT*, August 24, 1933, p. 27; *NYT*, December 20, 1933, p. 38; *NYT*, August 10, 1934, p. 31.

22. Farny Wurlitzer, the youngest brother, who was in charge of manufacturing the coin-operated musical instruments in North Tonawanda, New York, bought the Simplex Phonograph Corp. in 1933 despite the hard times. This purchase enabled Wurlitzer to dominate the coin-operated phonograph or "jukebox" business in later years.

23. Graham, "Story of the Rudolph Wurlitzer Family and Business," pp. 103–10, 115–16, 132.

24. Interview with Henry Z. Steinway and David Rubin, senior vice president, Steinway & Sons (who worked for Baldwin under Lucien Wulsin and also knew Theodore E. Steinway), Steinway Hall, New York, December 31, 1985; Lucien Wulsin, 50th Reunion Speech, p. 6, typewritten, Harvard University and Clubs, 1959, Baldwin Archives; Robert M. Davis, *History of the Code of Fair Competition for the Piano Manufacturing In-*

dustry, February 19, 1936, pp. 10, 16, 18–19, 20 (Washington, D.C.: National Archives Microfilm Publications, Document Series of the National Recovery Administration, 1933–36, microcopy no. 213, roll no. 127, Code no. 91).

25. Interview with Henry Z. Steinway and David Rubin, December 31, 1985; "Here Are the Steinways and How They Grew," *Fortune* 10 (December 1934): 163; Davis, *History of the Code of Fair Competition for the Piano Manufacturing Industry*, pp. 10, 16, 18–19; Lucien Wulsin, "Resumé of Piano Industry under NRA Code," pp. 3–4.

26. *The Music Trades* 83 (July 1935): 19; "Adopt Trade Practice Rules at Music Industry Convention," *The Music Trades* 81 (June 1933): 3–4; "Piano Manufacturers Hold Annual Meeting," *The Music Trades* 81 (June 1933): 5.

27. Davis, *History of the Code of Fair Competition for the Piano Manufacturing Industry*, pp. 18–19, 48; Harry Meixell, "National Recovery Act and the Music Industry," *The Music Trades—National Recovery Number* 81 (December 1933): 5.

28. *The Music Trades* 81 (November 1933): 3; Hugh S. Johnson to Franklin Roosevelt, November 2, 1933, in National Recovery Administration, "Code of Fair Competition for the Piano Manufacturing Industry," p. 437; Wulsin, "Resumé of the Piano Industry under NRA Code," pp. 3–4; Davis, *History of the Code of Fair Competition for the Piano Manufacturing Industry*, p. 16.

29. Hugh S. Johnson to Franklin Roosevelt, November 2, 1933, in National Recovery Administration, "Code of Fair Competition for the Piano Manufacturing Industry," p. 436; *The Music Trades* 81 (October 1933): 5.

30. Davis, *History of the Code of Fair Competition for the Piano Manufacturing Industry*, p. 38.

31. Meixell, "National Recovery Act and the Music Industry," p. 5; *The Music Trades—National Recovery Number* 81 (December 1933): 28; Wulsin, "Resumé of Piano Industry under NRA Code," pp. 3–4.

32. The standard account of Ford and and the automobile industry during the National Recovery Administration years is Sidney Fine, *The Automobile under the Blue Eagle: Labor, Management, and the Automobile Manufacturing Code* (Ann Arbor: University of Michigan Press, 1963).

33. Bradley, *Music for the Millions*, pp. 94–95, 210, 240–44, 255–57.

34. William W. Kimball to author, December 17, 1985; Bradley, *Music for the Millions*, p. 264.

35. Henry Z. Steinway recalls that his father, Theodore E. Steinway, said that the incident that estranged Kimball and Wulsin might have been a rumored comment from Wulsin calling Kimball an "errand boy," because he was unable to act independently (as Wulsin apparently could) on NRA

protocol without first consulting the Kimball board of directors. W. W. Kimball, son of C. N. Kimball, mentioned nothing of such a remark in a letter to the author, but only that his father considered the NRA "anathema," and as a Republican, could not stand FDR. Since Wulsin "appeared to be siding with the Franklin Roosevelt gang," supporting Wulsin was impossible. Henry Z. Steinway to author, October 11, 1985; Interview with Henry Z. Steinway and John H. Steinway, March 19, 1984, Steinway Hall, New York; William W. Kimball to author, December 17, 1985.

36. Robert O. Dawson, "Report of the Administration Member," June 13, 1935, p. 1 (Washington, D.C.: National Archives Microfilm Publications, Document Series of the National Recovery Administration, 1933–36, microcopy no. 213, roll no. 127, Code no. 91).

37. Letter from C. N. Kimball, May 14, 1933, quoted in Davis, *History of the Code of Fair Competition for the Piano Manufacturing Industry*, p. 39. See also p. 22.

38. Davis, *History of the Code of Fair Competition for the Piano Manufacturing Industry*, p. 40.

39. Ibid., p. 25; Wulsin, "Resumé of Piano Industry under NRA Code," pp. 3–4.

40. Davis, *History of the Code of Fair Competition for the Piano Manufacturing Industry*, pp. 2, 18, 22, 25–27, 44; Wulsin, "Resumé of Piano Industry under NRA Code," pp. 3–4; Lucien Wulsin, "Piano Industry Gains in Year Summarized: Annual Report of NPMA," *The Music Trades* 82 (June 1934): 3; *The Music Trades* 82 (August 1934): 3.

41. Davis, *History of the Code of Fair Competition for the Piano Manufacturing Industry*, pp. 18, 20, 22.

42. Ibid., pp. 22–23, 25; Dawson, "Report of Administration Member," pp. 1–3.

43. John H. Steinway to author, October 10, 1985.

44. *The Baldwin Keynote*, vol. 11, no. 8, November–December 1933, p. 3; Wulsin, "Piano Industry Gains in Year Summarized," p. 3; *NYT*, June 6, 1934, p. 24.

45. *NYT*, April 14, 1935, sec. 2, p. 8; U.S. Congress, Senate, Committee on Finance, *Investigation of the National Recovery Administration, Hearings on S. Res. 79*, 74th Cong., 1st sess., 1935, pp. 1855–56; U.S. Congress, House, *Hearings before the Committee on Ways and Means. Extension of National Industrial Recovery Act*, 74th Cong., 1st sess., May 20–24, 1935, pp. 451–52.

46. George M. Otto, executive director, NPMA, to author, September 30, 1980; NPMA, "Piano Unit Production, 1900–1976," author's collection; Bradley, *Music for the Millions*, p. 264; *The Music Trades* 83 (June 1935): 3; *The Music Trades* 83 (August 1935): 3, 6, 8, 12.

47. *The Music Trades* 83 (June 1935): 14; "Majority of Piano Makers and Music Publishers Are in Favor of Voluntary Code," *The Music Trades* 83 (October 1935): 9.

48. Wulsin, "Piano Industry Gains in Year Summarized," p. 3.

49. *NYT*, May 22, 1931, p. 28; H. Howard Taubman, "Stokowski Finds Us Turning to Music," *NYT Magazine*, June 14, 1936, pp. 7, 19.

50. Peter Dykema, "Report of the Committee on Community Music," *MTNA Proceedings*, 1931:158–64; *NYT*, April 27, 1934, p. 24; *NYT*, May 11, 1934, p. 24. The National Music Guild, now called the International Piano Guild, has an archive in Austin, Texas. The Guild is part of the American College of Musicians, which Allison also organized. See *The Handbook of Texas*, forthcoming revised edition, s.v. "Allison, Irl," and "National Guild of Piano Teachers," by Craig H. Roell (manuscripts currently in care of the Texas State Historical Association, Austin, Texas).

51. *NYT*, May 1, 1932, sec. 8, p. 6; *NYT*, April 21, 1938, p. 17.

52. C. M. Tremaine, "The Present Status of School Music Education," *Music Educators National Conference Bulletin*, no. 16, April 1934, pp. 3ff; *NYT*, March 31, 1936, p. 16; Olin Downes, "Substantial Music on the Radio," *NYT*, December 10, 1933, sec. 10, p. 8; *NYT*, April 11, 1936, p. 18.

53. Dr. Earl Vincent Moore reported the low estimate of 20,000 unemployed musicians as made by Olin Downes of the *New York Times*. The high estimate of 70,000 was taken by musicians' union officials. See Dr. Earl Vincent Moore, *Final Report of the Federal Music Project, October 10, 1939* (Washington, D.C.: U.S. Government Printing Office, 1939), pp. 1, 4; Cornelius B. Canon, "The Federal Music Project of the Works Progress Administration: Music in a Democracy" (Ph.D. dissertation, University of Minnesota, 1963), pp. 2, 6, 9, 36; Dr. Nikolai Sokoloff, *The Federal Music Project* (Washington, D.C.: U.S. Government Printing Office, 1936), pp. 7, 9, 10; Dr. Nikolai Sokoloff, "America's Vast New Musical Awakening," *The Etude* 55 (April 1937): 221–22.

54. Charles C. Alexander, *Here the Country Lies: Nationalism and the Arts in Twentieth-Century America* (Bloomington: Indiana University Press, 1980), pp. 203–10; William F. McDonald, *Federal Relief Administration and the Arts: The Origins and Administrative History of the Arts Projects of the Works Progress Administration* (Columbus: Ohio State University Press, 1969), pp. 584–646; Janelle J. Warren, "Of Tears and Need: The Federal Music Project, 1935–1943" (Ph.D. dissertation, George Washington University, 1973).

55. "Music Is Conquering All America," *NYT Magazine*, July 31, 1938, p. 13; *NYT*, April 24, 1938, p. 14; *NYT*, October 25, 1936, p. 29; *NYT*, December 31, 1938, p. 3.

56. Roy E. Waite, "The Piano's Future: Indications That Interest in Personal Performance Is Again Rising," *NYT*, June 18, 1933, sec. 9, p. 5.

57. "Is the Piano Optimist Justified?" *The Music Trades* 77 (February 15, 1929): 4–5; Richard McClanahan, "The Salvation of the Piano Lies with Those Who Teach It," *The Musician* 35 (October 1930): 9–10; Otto B. Heaton quoted in "Piano Merchants Move to Cooperate with Teachers," *The Musician* 31 (November 1926): 12; Olin Downes, "The Question of the Piano," *NYT*, June 4, 1933, sec. 9, p. 4; Otto W. Miessner, "Suggested Remedies for the Prevailing Maladies of Music," *The Musician* 36 (July 1931): 7–8.

58. *NYT*, January 10, 1936, p. 18.

59. See chapter one.

60. Downes, "The Question of the Piano," p. 4; Walter Damrosch, *My Musical Life* (New York: Charles Scribner's Sons, 1935), p. 8.

61. Constantin von Sternberg, "Report of Piano Conference," *MTNA Proceedings*, 1908:210–13; J. Lawrence Erb, "The Problems of the Music Teacher," *MTNA Proceedings*, 1917:9–10; Clarence G. Hamilton, "The Future of Piano Study," *MTNA Proceedings*, 1931:105–6; John C. Bostelmann, Jr., "A New Approach to Piano Study," *The Musician* 32 (October 1927): 13, 34.

62. Lucien Wulsin to Mrs. Russell Davenport, February 16, 1939, Baldwin Co., Correspondence of Lucien Wulsin II, 1930, Baldwin Archives.

63. Downes, "The Question of the Piano," p. 4. See also James L. Mursell, *Human Values in Music Education* (New York: Silver, Burdett & Co., 1934), pp. 146–48, 314; Karl C. Gehrkens, "Public School Music's Contribution to Musical Education: The Present," *MTNA Proceedings*, 1926:204–13.

64. Ella Mason, "The Growth and Significance of the Piano Class," *MTNA Proceedings*, 1929:46–53; Ella Mason, "Piano Class Instruction Now Given in Schools of 880 American Cities," *The Musician* 36 (January 1931): 6; Ella Mason, "Report of the Committee on Class Instruction in Applied Music: Piano," *MTNA Proceedings*, 1932:222–26. See also Ernest R. Kroeger, "Changes in Piano Teaching in Fifty Years," *The Etude* 47 (December 1929): 885–86; Kate S. Chittenden, "Salient Changes in Music Teaching in the Last 50 Years: Piano," *MTNA Proceedings*, 1926:23–26; Sidney Silber, "Modern Piano Pedagogy," *The Etude* 53 (January 1935): 12; Henry Holden Huss, "The New Era in Piano Study," *MTNA Proceedings*, 1914:101–8; and Mrs. Crosby Adams, "Recent Developments in Teaching Children to Play the Piano," *MTNA Proceedings*, 1921:82–90.

65. Edward Bailey Birge, *History of Public School Music in the United States* (Boston: Oliver Ditson Co., 1928), p. 249.

66. National Bureau for the Advancement of Music, *Piano Classes in the Schools* (pamphlet), quoted in Norman E. Pillsbury, "Group Piano Teaching in Public Schools," *The Music Trades* 79 (December 1931): 6.

67. *NYT*, June 13, 1930, p. 25.

68. *The Music Trades* 79 (February 1931): 13; "25,000 Join Nation-Wide Radio Music Class; 4,000 Enrolling Daily for Piano Lessons," *NYT*, March 29, 1931, pp. 1, 26; *NYT*, April 1, 1931, p. 4; John Tasker Howard, "50,000 Are Enrolled to Study Lessons on the Air," *NYT*, April 5, 1931, sec. 9, p. 9; C. D. Bond, "Despite Certain Trends, Piano Interest Gains, When Proper Means Are Taken to Promote Sales," *The Music Trades* 79 (September 1931): 11–12.

69. Conductor Frank H. Damrosch claimed that "99 percent of the music teachers in the United States are totally incompetent to teach music," having no more than an "inferior instruction" in piano, who teach "parrot-like performances" rather than teaching the "real thing." See *NYT*, September 3, 1911, sec. 5, p. 13.

70. *NYT*, June 26, 1930, p. 26.

71. Osbourne McConathy, "The Public School and the Private Music Teacher," *MTNA Proceedings*, 1930:61–76; "Music Teachers National Association Endorses Group Piano Method," *The Music Trades* 78 (January 19, 1929): 3. For more on the war between private piano and school class piano teachers, see John L. Bratton, "The American Music Teacher under Changing Conditions of Today," *MTNA Proceedings*, 1929:36–45; and Sidney Silber, "Modern Piano Pedagogy," *The Etude* 53 (January 1935): 12.

72. L. P. Bull quoted in "Back to the Piano," by Olin Downes, *NYT*, August 1, 1937, sec. 10, p. 5; NPMA estimate of amateur musicians in America quoted in *Steinway News* (house organ of Steinway & Sons), no. 64, April 1, 1939, Steinway Family Archives, Steinway & Sons, New York (hereafter Steinway Family Archives); Institute of Musical Art of the Juilliard School of Music piano study reported in *Steinway News*, no. 99, February 1942; National Piano Manufacturers Association, "Piano Unit Production, 1900–1976," author's possession; *NYT*, December 17, 1935, p. 47.

73. *NYT*, April 1, 1932, p. 16; *NYT*, April 10, 1932, p. 7; *NYT*, August 1, 1935, p. 22; Mildred Adams, "Still Deeper into the Victorian Era: The Extent of Our Return to the Fashions of Earlier Days," *NYT Magazine*, August 9, 1931, pp. 12–13; Robert S. McElvaine, *The Great Depression: America, 1929–1941* (New York: Times Books, 1984), pp. 217–18, 220–21, 339; Susan Ware, *American Women in the 1930s: Holding Their Own* (Boston: Twayne Publishers, 1982), pp. xvi–xvii, 13–14.

74. Mrs. Franklin D. (Eleanor) Roosevelt, *It's Up to the Women* (New York: Frederick A. Stokes, 1933), p. 20; *NYT*, July 8, 1930, p. 1; *NYT*, November 15, 1933, p. 16.

75. R. W. Wilson, "Victorian Days that Beckon Us," *NYT Magazine*, April 30, 1933, pp. 10–11.

76. The Supreme Court upheld a New York judge's decision that a radio is a necessity in the home of a family earning $30 a week. The ruling

pertained to a man who argued that his wife had no right to charge the purchase of an expensive radio. *NYT*, November 24, 1931, p. 21.

77. On the return to traditional Victorian values, see also "Slump Has Restored Family Life," *NYT*, January 24, 1932, sec. 2, p. 1; *NYT*, February 24, 1932, p. 6; W. S. Bond, "A Message to Parents about the Piano," *The Etude* 50 (March 1932): 220; "Keystone of Our Nation—Homemade Music," *The Etude* 58 (February 1940): 77, 139; and Warren I. Susman, "The Culture of the Thirties," in his *Culture as History: The Transformation of American Society in the Twentieth Century* (New York: Pantheon, 1984), pp. 150–83.

78. Helen Harford Baldwin, "The Piano—the Soul of the Studio," *The Musician* 31 (December 1926): 15, 36; Helen Sprackling, "How to Determine Its Place in the Room," *House Beautiful* 63 (February 1928): 200–201; Mrs. Somerset Maugham, "Lighting the Piano: Some Suggestions for Dressing This Instrument So That It Becomes an Object of Decoration," *House and Garden* 47 (April 1925): 72.

79. On the emergence of style, color, and eye appeal in the consumer culture, see Roland Marchand, *Advertising the American Dream: Making Way for Modernity, 1920–1940* (Berkeley and Los Angeles: University of California Press, 1985), pp. 117–40; Jeffrey Meikle, *Twentieth Century Limited: Industrial Design in America, 1925–1939* (Philadelphia: Temple University Press, 1979), pp. 19–25

80. *NYT*, March 19, 1933, sec. 9, p. 8; *NYT*, March 26, 1933, sec. 9, p. 8; *NYT*, April 16, 1933, sec. 8, p. 12. See also Meikle, *Twentieth Century Limited*, pp. 97–99.

81. Ethel Carpenter, "Where Shall We Put That Piano," *Ladies' Home Journal* 45 (April 1928): 35, 224, 15.

82. Walter Rendell Storey, "The Piano Acquires Grace and Beauty," *NYT Magazine*, March 14, 1926, pp. 9, 18; "Pianos as Period Furniture," *House and Garden* 50 (September 1926): 80–81; Walter Rendell Storey, "Walls that Speak to Old Furnishings," *NYT Magazine*, November 12, 1933, p. 16; "Pianofortissimo: In 1935 the Piano Industry Discovered Style," *Fortune* 20 (August 1939): 46; Cyril Ehrlich, *The Piano: A History* (London: Dent, 1976), pp. 188–89.

83. *NYT*, August 29, 1930, p. 31; *The Music Trades* 78 (January 1930): 3.

84. The bridge between the baby grand and the console upright was introduced by Mathushek Piano Co. in 1931. Its "Spinet Grand" utilized period styles and little space, and was inspired by the design of the old square grand. See Theodore Gray, "Restores Piano to American Home," *The Musician* 41 (December 1936): 195–96. The revolutionary console design originated in Sweden (Lundholm of Stockholm) in 1934. Percy Brasted of Associated Piano Co. (London) bought the rights and began manufacture under the tradename "Minipiano." He arranged for the

Minipiano to be made under license in the United States by Hardman, Peck & Co. (See Ehrlich, *The Piano*, p. 190; David Wainwright, *The Piano Makers* (London: Hutchinson, 1975), pp. 155–57.

85. For details and illustrations of, and reactions to the new console, see "Pianofortissimo," pp. 45–46; Wendall Barnes, "New Pianos in New Settings," *The Etude* 55 (December 1937): 803–4, 817; "Persistent Pianos," *Business Week*, October 26, 1935, pp. 18–19; Henry Bellamann, "The Little Piano for the Modern Apartment," *Arts and Decoration* 43 (January 1936): 30–31, 43; Marion Bauer, "A Renaissance of the Piano," *Arts and Decoration* 46 (April 1937): 34–35, 42; Walter Rendell Storey, "Pianos for the Modern Interior," *NYT Magazine*, August 16, 1936, p. 12; and "Keyboards," *Time* 26 (August 1935): 54, 56.

86. "No Place for a Piano? Nonesense! Gone Are the 'Model T' Styles of Yesterday," *American Home* 21 (December 1938): 23–24.

87. "Persistent Pianos," pp. 18–19.

88. Ibid.; *The Music Trades* editorial quoted in Peter W. Dykema, "Report of the Committee on Community Music," *MTNA Proceedings*, 1936: 353; *NYT*, June 3, 1936, p. 32; *NYT*, July 28, 1936, p. 24; *NYT*, November 17, 1936, p. 49; *The Music Trades* 84 (August 1936): 4; *Steinway News*, no. 13, July 7, 1936, no. 17, September 8, 1936, and no. 21, November 25, 1936.

89. *Steinway News*, no. 5, December 15, 1935.

90. *NYT*, August 1, 1936, p. 25.

91. "Pianofortissimo," p. 119.

92. "Direct Child Appeal: This Mail Campaign, Through Human-Interest Angle, Sells 1,500 Pianos; Costs $1.92 a Name," *Printers' Ink* 181 (November 18, 1937): 24–26, 30.

93. *The Music Trades* 84 (March 1936): 8; *The Music Trades* 85 (June 1937): 6.

94. *The Music Trades* 86 (June 1938): 10; *The Music Trades* 86 (October 1938): 3; "Pianofortissimo," pp. 49, 118; *The Music Trades* 86 (December 1938): 14.

95. Lawrence H. Selz, *Consumer Investigation for National Piano Manufacturers Association* (New York: NPMA, 1938), author's collection.

96. The information in this and the following paragraphs is taken from the Selz *Consumer Investigation*. Summaries of the report also were published. See Lawrence H. Selz Organization, "Piano Merchandising," *Bulletin of the National Retail Dry Goods Association*, 22 (May 1940): 37–38; *NYT*, March 26, 1938, p. 30; and *NYT*, April 3, 1938, sec. 11, p. 5.

97. *NYT*, May 12, 1933, p. 2. See also *NYT*, March 16, 1933, p. 33.

98. *NYT*, May 10, 1937, p. 36; *NYT*, July 27, 1937, p. 36; *NYT*, August 3, 1938, p. 25; *NYT*, August 2, 1938, p. 25; *NYT*, October 26, 1938, p. 32; "Pianofortissimo," p. 45; NPMA, "Piano Unit Production, 1900–1976," author's collection.

99. "Pianofortissimo," p. 120; E. M. Kelly, " 'Dying' Music Industry Lives Anew as Millions Turn to Tune-Making," *Sales Management* 42 (January 1, 1938): 22, 24, 64.

100. Irwin Robinson of *Advertising Age* quoted in *NYT*, July 28, 1937, p. 21; "Modernly Merchandising the Piano," *The Music Trades* 86 (May 1938): 8.

EPILOGUE

1. National Piano Manufacturers Association, "Piano Unit Production, 1900–1976," author's collection.

2. Theodore E. Steinway, *People and Pianos: A Century of Service to Music* (New York: Steinway & Sons, 1953), pp. 65, 89; "Story and Clark: The First 100 Years," offprint from *The Music Trades*, January 1957, supplied to author by T. H. Krumwiede, director of piano marketing, Story & Clark Piano Co.; Van Allen Bradley, *Music for the Millions: The Kimball Piano and Organ Story* (Chicago: Henry Regnery Co., 1957), pp. 273–77.

3. Cordell Hull to Director, Cincinnati May Festival, September 28, 1939, and Lucien Wulsin to Joseph S. Graydon, October 12, 1939, Baldwin Co., Correspondence of Lucien Wulsin II, 1930–40, Correspondence Involving Baldwin and Its Financial Situation Generally, etc. folder, D. H. Baldwin & Co. Archives, Cincinnati Historical Society, Eden Park, Cincinnati, Ohio (hereafter, Baldwin Archives).

4. "Pianos to Aircraft & Vice Versa," typewritten, Advertising/Sales Promotion, 1940–50, Correspondence with Various Dealers, 1944–45, George W. Lawrence files, Baldwin Archives.

5. J. Joseph Whalan, War Production Board, to The Baldwin Piano Co., January 26, 1944, Advertising/Sales Promotion, 1940–50, Correspondence with Various Dealers, 1944–45, Philip Wyman files, Baldwin Archives.

6. Steinway, *People and Pianos*, p. 87; George W. Lawrence to J. M. Wylie, February 29, 1944, Advertising/Sales Promotion, 1940–50, Correspondence with Various Dealers, 1944–45, from files of George W. Lawrence folder, Baldwin Archives; "Story and Clark: The First 100 Years."

7. NPMA, "Piano Unit Production, 1900–1976," author's collection.

8. David Wainwright asserts that the gramophone, radio, Great Depression, and finally the cinema devastated the trade. Cyril Ehrlich affirms this, arguing that the piano industry was "crippled by alternative sources of entertainment, erosion of the instrument's social status, and by the crash and depression of the 1930s. It must be emphasized that the blows came in that order." See David Wainwright, *The Pianomakers* (London:

Hutchinson, 1975), p. 153; Cyril Ehrlich, *The Piano: A History* (London: Dent, 1976), p. 184.

9. Olin Downes, "Is Music 'Education'?" *New York Times* (hereafter *NYT*), August 4, 1935, sec. 9, p. 5.

10. Eleanor Roosevelt quoted in *NYT Magazine*, August 10, 1930, pp. 2, 19.

11. James Truslow Adams, "Our Way of Life Yesterday and Today: The Symbolic Evening at Home Has Been Annihilated in Ameria by Mechanical Devices," *NYT Magazine*, August 3, 1930, pp. 4–5, 19; Gertrude Borchard, "The Player Piano as Teacher's Aid," *The Musician* 24 (January 1919): 18, 42.

12. The Baldwin Piano Co., *Baldwin Course in Piano Salesmanship*, unit 3, *How to Demonstrate a Piano* (Cincinnati: Baldwin Piano Co., 1931), p. 5, and unit 5, *Prospect Getting Plans*, p. 5, Advertising/Sales Promotion, 1920–30 file, Baldwin Archives.

13. The Baldwin Co., *Baldwin Course in Piano Salesmanship*, unit 1, *The Piano—What It Does*, p. 7.

14. Ibid., pp. 8–10; "Reasons Why People Buy Pianos," in William A. Mills, *Merchandising Music: Sales Training Manual for Music Salesmen*, (New York: National Association of Music Merchants, Inc., in cooperation with Business Education Service of the U.S. Office of Education, 1946), pp. 96–99.

15. Baldwin Co., *Baldwin Course in Piano Salesmanship*, unit 1, *The Piano—What It Does*, pp. 10–13; Mills, *Merchandising Music*, p. 15.

16. For a variety of approaches addressing the consequences of consumerism, see Daniel Horowitz, *The Morality of Spending: Attitudes toward the Consumer Society in America, 1875–1940* (Baltimore: The Johns Hopkins University Press, 1985), which is especially valuable for its review of the scholarly literature; Kathy Peiss, *Cheap Amusements: Working Women and Leisure in Turn-of-the-Century New York* (Philadelphia: Temple University Press, 1986); John F. Kasson, *Amusing the Million: Coney Island at the Turn of the Century* (New York: Hill and Wang, 1978); Richard Wightman Fox and T. J. Jackson Lears, eds., *The Culture of Consumption: Critical Essays in American History, 1880–1980* (New York: Pantheon Books, 1983); Alice Goldfarb Marquis, *Hopes and Ashes: The Birth of Modern Times, 1929–1939* (New York: The Free Press, 1986); and Roland Marchand, *Advertising the American Dream: Making Way for Modernity, 1920–1940* (Berkeley and Los Angeles: University of California Press, 1985).

17. Steinway & Sons advertisement, "A Song for Parents," illustrated in *Harvard Advertising Awards, 1930* (New York: McGraw-Hill, 1931): 24.

Select Bibliography

This bibliography makes no attempt to encompass all primary and secondary sources used in this study. Rather, it contains only those items that I have drawn on for factual material, that have influenced my interpretations, or that represent significant points of view in the historiography of the music industry and the consumer culture. For a guide to the specific collections, periodicals, articles, and books, the reader should rely on the extensive notes to the text chapters. For the convenience of the reader, the source material is categorized topically.

Archive and Manuscript Collections

Archival sources for the music industry are limited. I have written to all extant piano companies regarding their records. With the few exceptions noted, these firms report that they have disposed of their documents pertaining to the period under study. Another invaluable source would have been the records of the National Piano Manufacturers Association of America. Unfortunately, aside from piano unit production figures, no archive exists for the pre–World War Two years. As the executive director, George M. Otto, put it, "most of the records of the Association have long gone the way of most paper." The NPMA was not affiliated with the National Association of Manufacturers, so no NPMA records were kept there. Even the papers of Lucien Wulsin II contained virtually no information regarding the association of which he was president for four consecutive terms. The files of the National Association of Music Merchants contain information relating generally to music in America, though not specifically regarding the piano.

The D. H. Baldwin & Co. papers and the papers of Lucien Wulsin I and Lucien Wulsin II are large, crucial, and well-organized collections under the care of the Cincinnati Historical Society. The Steinway Family Archive housed in Steinway Hall in New York contains a wealth of cultural materials, though many of the business records have been destroyed. Some of this lost information can be found in the Steinway & Sons Factory Archive, Fiorella H. LaGuardia Community College, Long Island City. Mrs. Janet Wurlitzer Stites maintains a small Wurlitzer family archive in Cincinnati. She has informed me that many of the Rudolph Wurlitzer Co. factory papers recently have been acquired by the University of Illinois at De Kalb, but they were unavailable for this study. The records of Story & Clark Piano Co. in Grand Haven, Michigan are unorganized and contain mostly customer registration numbers for warranty purposes. The most exhaustive coverage of the music industry can be found in *The Music Trades*, published continually since 1890. Original records are located in *The Music Trades* archive, Englewood, New Jersey, although the Music Division of the New York Public Library at Lincoln Center houses a microfilm copy of the journal.

The papers of the Music Educators National Conference (formerly, the Music Supervisors) are found in the MENC Historical Center, McKeldin Library, University of Maryland at College Park. The Music Teachers National Association has no records available for examination. Both organizations published extensive annual proceedings, however. The papers of Charles Milton Tremaine at the Bentley Historical Library, University of Michigan, primarily contain his work with the National Music Camp at Interlochen, Michigan, not with the National Bureau for the Advancement of Music. The National Guild of Piano Teachers operates its archive in Austin, Texas. In addition, the University of Texas Archives, Austin, houses a collection of State Music Reports of the Works Progress Administration.

Government archives had relatively little information, though congressional hearings, reports, and other published documents did reward the diligent search. I also canvassed presidential papers from the period for relevant items and will incorporate them into a future article on the social and political role of music in the White House from McKinley to Truman. Other disappointing archival deadends include the Piano Technicians Guild, the National Music Council, the National Council of Music Importers and Exporters, the National Piano Travelers Association, and the National Association of Musical Merchandise Wholesalers (presently the Music Distributors Association).

Trade Publications, Association Proceedings, Newspapers, and Yearbooks

The American Yearbook.
The Baldwin Keynote.
Baldwin's Musical Review.
Dealer's Handbook of Pianos and Their Makers. (Title/publisher vary.)
The Etude.
Moody's Analysis of Investments: Industrials.

Music Supervisors National Conference Journal of Proceedings (*MSNC Proceedings*).
Music Teachers National Association Conference Proceedings (*MTNA Proceedings*).
The Music Trades.
The Music Trades Corp. *Purchasers' Guide to the Music Industries.* (Title varies.)
Musical Age.
Musical Courier.
The Musician.
New York Times.
Piano Trade Magazine.
Pierce, Bob, comp. *Pierce Piano Atlas.* Long Beach, Calif.: Bob Pierce, Publisher, 7th ed., 1977.
Pierre Key's Music Year Book.
The Standard Advertising Register.
Steinway News.
Taylor, S. K., comp. *The Musician's Piano Atlas.* Supplement No. 1. Macclesfield, Cheshire: Omicron Publishing Ltd., 1984.

Interviews and Correspondence

Brooks, E. F., Aeolian American Division, Aeolian Corp., personal letter, August 22, 1980.
Clinton, Mariann H., Music Teachers National Association, personal letter, September 11, 1980.
Dillon, Donald W., Music Educators National Conference, personal letter, August 22, 1980.
Gard, William R., National Association of Music Merchants, personal letter, July 30, 1980.
Haley, Tom, National Association of Manufacturers, personal letter, July 28, 1980.
Hershman, Jerome, National Council of Music Importers and Exporters, personal letter, September 18, 1980.
Kimball, William W., personal letter, December 17, 1985.
Krumwiede, T. H., Story & Clark Piano Co., personal letter, August 29, 1980.
Otto, George M., National Piano Manufacturers Association of America, personal letter, September 30, 1980.
Rubin, David. Steinway Hall, New York. Interview, December 31, 1985.
Steinway, Henry Z. Steinway Hall, New York. Interviews: March 19, 1984;

December 31, 1985; December 29, 1987. Also numerous personal letters.

Steinway, John H. Steinway Hall, New York. Interview, March 19, 1984. Also numerous personal letters.

Stites, Janet Wurlitzer. Cincinnati. Interview, March 14, 1984, and personal letters.

Whitlock, Jan B., American Music Conference, personal letter, October 17, 1980.

Government Documents

Davis, Robert M. *History of the Code of Fair Competition for the Piano Manufacturing Industry, 19 February 1936*. Washington, D.C.: National Archives Microfilm Publications, Document Series of the National Recovery Administration, 1933–36, microcopy no. 213, roll no. 127, Code no. 91.

Earhart, Will. "Recent Advances in Instruction in Music in the Public Schools." Vol. 1, part 1. *Biennial Survey of Education, 1920–22*. Washington, D.C.: U.S. Government Printing Office, 1924.

Manchester, Arthur L. "The Status of Music Education in the United States." *U.S. Bureau of Education Bulletin*, 1908, no. 4, pp. 1–85.

Moore, Earl Vincent. *Final Report of the Federal Music Project, 10 October 1939*. Washington, D.C.: U.S. Government Printing Office, 1939.

National Recovery Administration. *National Recovery Administration Codes of Fair Competition*. Vol. 2. Nos. 88–110. Washington, D.C.: U.S. Government Printing Office, 1934.

Pierce, Anne E., and Robert S. Hilpert. "Instruction in Music and Art." *U.S. Bureau of Education Bulletin*, no. 17, 1932.

Sokoloff, Nikolai. *The Federal Music Project*. Washington, D.C.: U.S. Government Printing Office, 1936.

U.S. Congress. House. A Bill Prohibiting Fraud upon the Public by Requiring Manufacturers to Place Their Own Names upon Manufactured Articles. H.R. 16844, 62d Cong., 2d sess., 1912. *Congressional Record*, 48:677, 7740–42.

———. A Bill Requiring Manufacturers to Certify to the Materials of and Place their Names upon the Products They Produce. H.R. 2970, 63d Cong., 1st sess., 1913. *Congressional Record*, 50:227.

———. *A Bill to Authorize and Consolidate the Acts Respecting Copyright*, H.R. 28192 [The Copyright Act of 1909]. 60th Cong., 2d sess., 1909.

———. A Bill to Create a Department of Fine Arts, H.R. 5801. 68th Cong., 1st sess., January 19, 1924. *Congressional Record*, 65:1181.

———. Committee on Patents. *Creating a Bureau of Fine Arts, Report to*

Accompany H.J. Res. 671 [To Create a Bureau of Fine Arts in the Department of Interior for the Promotion of Art and Literature]. H. Rept. 2486, 75th Cong., 3d sess., 1938.

———. Committee on Patents. *Revision of Copyright Laws, Hearings, Revised Copy for Use of the Committee on Patents.* 74th Cong., 2d sess., 1936.

———. Committee on Patents. *To Amend and Consolidate the Acts Respecting Copyright.* H. Rept. 2222, 60th Cong., 2d sess., 1909.

———. Committee on Patents. *To Amend the Copyright Act of 1909, Hearings on H.R. 6250 and H.R. 9137.* 68th Cong., 1st sess., 1924.

———. Committee on Rules. *Consideration of the House Joint Resolution to Create a Bureau of Fine Arts. Report to Accompany H. Res. 526.* H. Rept. 2680, 75th Cong., 3d sess., 1938.

———. Committee on Ways and Means. *Hearings on the Extension of National Industrial Recovery Act.* 74th Cong., 1st sess., 1935.

———. Extension of Remarks on H.R. 2970, A Bill Requiring Manufacturers to Certify to the Materials of and Place Their Names upon the Products They Produce. 63d Cong., 2d sess., January 21, 1914. *Congressional Record*, 51: Appendix, pp. 79–82.

U.S. Congress. Senate and House, conjointly. Committee on Patents. *To Amend and Consolidate the Acts Respecting Copyright, Hearings on S. 9440 and H.R. 28192.* 60th Cong., 1st sess., 1908.

———. Committee on Patents. *To Amend and Consolidate the Acts Respecting Copyright, Hearings on S. 6330 and H.R. 19853.* 59th Cong., 1st sess., 1906.

U.S. Congress. Senate. Committee on Education and Labor. *Bureau of Fine Arts—Hearings before a Subcommittee on S. 3296, A Bill to Provide for a Permanent Bureau of Fine Arts.* 75th Cong., 3d sess., 1938.

———. Committee on Education and Labor. *Hearing before a Subcommittee of the Committee on Education and Labor on S. 1320, A Bill to Establish a National Conservatory of Music.* 68th Cong., 1st sess., 1924.

———. Committee on Education and Labor. *Hearing before the Committee on Education and Labor on S. 561, A Bill to Establish a National Conservatory of Music and Art.* 66th Cong., 2d sess., 1919.

———. Committee on Finance. *Investigation of the National Recovery Administration, Hearings on S. Res. 79.* 74th Cong., 1st sess., 1935.

———. *To Amend and Consolidate the Acts Respecting Copyright.* S. Rept. 1108, 60th Cong., 2d sess., 1909.

U.S. Department of Commerce. Bureau of Census. *Biennial Census of Manufacturers*, 1905, 1914, 1921–1939.

———. Bureau of Census. *13th Census of the United States, 1910.* Vol. 8, Manufactures, 1909. Washington, D.C.: U.S. Government Printing Office, 1913.

———. Bureau of Census. *Historical Statistics of the United States from Colonial Times to the Present.* Washington, D.C.: U.S. Government Printing Office, 1975.

———. NRA Records Section. National Recovery Administration Division of Review. *NRA Work Materials* No. 13, March 1936. Perry-Castañeda Library, University of Texas at Austin. (Typewritten.)

U.S. Department of Commerce and Labor. Bureau of Manufacturers. Anderson, George E. "Brazil, Good Field for American Pianos." *Monthly Consular and Trade Reports,* no. 349, October 1909.

———. Burrill, H. R. "Piano Trade in Australia." *Monthly Consular and Trade Reports,* no. 318, March 1907.

———. "Piano Markets in India and Brazil." *Monthly Consular and Trade Reports,* no. 314, November 1906.

U.S. Department of the Interior. Bureau of Education. "Present Status of Music Instruction in Colleges and High Schools, 1919–20: Report." *Bureau of Education Bulletin,* no. 9, 1921.

U.S. Department of Labor. *Training Service Course of Instruction in Piano Making, with Section on Player Pianos, Pneumatic Actions, Piano Actions, and Keys.* Washington, D.C.: U.S. Government Training Bulletin No. 22, 1919.

U.S Post Office Department. Inspectors Division. *Information and Instructions for Guidance of Post-Office Inspectors in Investigation of Cases Relating to "Piano Contests."* Washington, D.C.: U.S. Government Printing Office, 1916.

U.S. President. Committee on Social Trends. *Recent Social Trends in the United States: Report of the President's Research Committee on Social Trends.* Vol. 1. New York: McGraw-Hill, 1933; reprinted Westport, Conn.: Greenwood Press, 1970.

Business History

Albion, Mark, and Paul Farris. *The Advertising Controversy: Evidence on the Economic Effects of Advertising.* Boston: Auburn House, 1981.

Borden, Neil. *The Economic Effects of Advertising.* Chicago: R. D. Irwin, 1942.

Bruchey, Stuart W., ed. *Small Business in American Life.* New York: Columbia University Press, 1980.

Chandler, Alfred D., Jr. *Strategy and Structure: Chapters in the History of the Industrial Enterprise.* Cambridge: MIT Press, 1962.

———. *The Visible Hand: The Managerial Revolution in American Business.* Cambridge: Harvard University Press, 1977.

Curti, Merle. "The Changing Concept of 'Human Nature' in the Literature of American Advertising." *Business History Review* 41 (Winter 1967): 335–57.

Drucker, Peter. *Management: Tasks, Responsibilities, Practices.* New York: Harper and Row, 1974.

Flink, James J. *America Adopts the Automobile, 1895–1910.* Cambridge: MIT Press, 1970.

Fox, Stephen. *The Mirror Makers: A History of American Advertising and Its Creators.* New York: William Morrow, 1984.

Givens, C. C., Jr. *Modern Advertising: Its Importance to the Retailer and His Community.* New York: C. C. Givens, Jr., 1928.

Hotchkiss, George Burton, and Richard B. Franken. *The Leadership of Advertised Brands.* New York: Doubleday, Page & Co., 1923.

Hower, Ralph. *History of an Advertising Agency: N. W. Ayer & Son at Work, 1869–1949.* Cambridge: Harvard University Press, 1949.

Jerome, Harry. *Mechanization in Industry.* New York: National Bureau of Economic Research, no. 27, 1934.

Lamoreaux, Naomi. *The Great Merger Movement in American Business, 1895–1904.* New York: Cambridge University Press, 1985.

McCraw, Thomas K. "Rethinking the Trust Question." In *Regulation in Perspective,* edited by Thomas K. McCraw, pp. 1–55. Cambridge: Harvard University Press, 1981.

Pease, Otis. *The Responsibilities of American Advertising: Private Control and Public Influence, 1920–1940.* New Haven: Yale University Press, 1958.

Pope, Daniel. *The Making of Modern Advertising.* New York: Basic Books, 1983.

Prothro, James Warren. *The Dollar Decade: Business Ideas in the 1920s.* Baton Rouge: Louisiana State University Press, 1954.

Raucher, Alan R. *Public Relations and Business, 1900–1929.* Baltimore: Johns Hopkins University Press, 1968.

Robertson, James Oliver. *America's Business.* New York: Hill and Wang, 1985.

Schudson, Michael. *Advertising, The Uneasy Persuasion: Its Dubious Impact on American Society.* New York: Basic Books, 1984.

Shaw, Livermore. "The Success of Industrial Mergers." *Quarterly Journal of Economics* 50 (November 1935): 68–96.

Tolbert, Charles, Patrick M. Horan, and E. M. Beck. "Stratification in a Dual Economy." *American Sociological Review* 43 (October 1978): 704–20.

———. "The Structure of Economic Segmentation: A Dual Economy Approach." *American Journal of Sociology* 85 (March 1980): 1095–1116.

The Consumer Culture

Abbot, Lawrence F. "Mechanical Music." *The Outlook* 140 (May 13, 1925): 52–53.

Adams, James Truslow. "Our Way of Life Yesterday and Today: The Symbolic Evening at Home Has Been Annihilated in America by Mechanical Devices." *New York Times Magazine*, August 3, 1930, pp. 4–5, 19.

Andrews, Benjamin R. "The Home Woman as a Buyer and Controller of Consumption." *Annals of the American Academy of Political and Social Science* 143 (May 1929): 41–48.

Barnouw, Erik. *A History of Broadcasting in the U.S.* 3 vols. New York: Oxford University Press, 1966–70.

Barzun, Jacques. *Music in American Life.* Garden City, N.Y.: Doubleday, 1956.

Benjamin, Walter. "The Work of Art in the Age of Mechanical Reproduction." In *Illuminations*, edited by Hannah Arendt, translated by Harry Zohn, pp. 217–51. New York: Harcourt, Brace & World, 1968.

Benson, Susan Porter. "Palace of Consumption and Machine for Selling: The American Department Store, 1880–1940." *Radical History Review* 21 (Fall 1979): 199–221.

Boorstin, Daniel J. *The Americans: The Democratic Experience.* New York: Random House, 1973.

―――. *The Image: A Guide to Pseudo-Events in America.* New York: Atheneum, 1961; reprinted 1977.

Braine, Robert. "Canned Music." *The Etude* 50 (February 1932): 136.

Coben, Stanley. "The Assault on Victorianism in the Twentieth Century." *American Quarterly* 27 (1975): 604–25.

Cohen, David L. *The Good Old Days: A History of American Morals and Manners as Seen through the Sears, Roebuck Catalogs 1905 to the Present.* New York: Simon and Schuster, 1940.

Covert, Catherine L., and John D. Stevens. *Mass Media between the Wars: Perceptions of Cultural Tension, 1918–1940.* Syracuse, N.Y.: Syracuse University Press, 1984.

Dale, Lawrence. "The Piano and the New Competition." *Commerce and Finance* 19 (January 1, 1930): 13, 15.

"The Democracy of Music Achieved by Invention." *Current Literature* 42 (June 1907): 670–73.

Dewhurst, J. Frederick, and Associates. *America's Needs and Resources.* New York: Twentieth Century Fund, 1947.

Downes, Olin. "Mechanism and Art: Serious Problems Raised by New Device—Injurious Effect on the Progress of Music." *New York Times*, January 25, 1930, sec. 8, p. 8.

―――. "Radio and the Public Taste: Demand for Better Programs Increasing—Their Effect on the Concert Situation." *New York Times*, May 20, 1928, sec. 8, p. 6.

Dulles, Foster Rhea. *America Learns to Play*. New York: D. Appleton-Century, 1940.

Erenberg, Lewis A. *Steppin' Out: New York Nightlife and the Transformation of American Culture, 1890–1930*. Chicago: University of Chicago Press, 1981.

Ewen, Stuart. *Captains of Consciousness: Advertising and the Social Roots of the Consumer Culture*. New York: McGraw Hill, 1976.

Fass, Paula S. *The Damned and the Beautiful: American Youth in the 1920s*. New York: Oxford University Press, 1977.

Flink, James J. *The Car Culture*. Cambridge: MIT Press, 1975.

Fox, Richard Wightman, and T. J. Jackson Lears, eds. *The Culture of Consumption: Critical Essays in American History 1880–1980*. New York: Pantheon Books, 1983.

Gelatt, Roland. *The Fabulous Phonograph, 1877–1977*. New York: Collier, 2d rev. ed., 1977.

Giedion, Siegfried. *Mechanization Takes Command*. New York: W. W. Norton, 1948.

Hall, James B., and Barry Ulanov, eds. *Modern Culture and the Arts*. New York: McGraw-Hill, 1967.

Harris, Neil. "The Drama of Consumer Desire." In *Yankee Enterprise*, edited by Otto Mayr and Robert C. Post, pp. 196–211. Washington, D.C.: Smithsonian Institution Press, 1981.

Hendon, William S., and James L. Shanahan. *Economics of Cultural Decisions*. Cambridge: Abt Books, 1984.

Henry, Jules. *Culture Against Man*. New York: Random House, 1963.

Horowitz, Daniel. *The Morality of Spending: Attitudes toward the Consumer Society in America, 1875–1940*. Baltimore: Johns Hopkins University Press, 1985.

Juster, Thomas. *Anticipation and Purchases: An Analysis of Consumer Behavior*. Princeton, N.J.: Princeton University Press, 1964.

Lynd, Robert S., and Helen Merrell Lynd. *Middletown: A Study in Modern American Culture*. New York: Harcourt, Brace & World, 1929.

Maguire, Helena. "Autopianos and Automobiles." *The Musician* 19 (December 1914): 809.

Marchand, Roland. *Advertising the American Dream: Making Way for Modernity, 1920–1940*. Berkeley and Los Angeles: University of California Press, 1985.

McLuhan, Marshall. *The Mechanical Bride: Folklore of Industrial Man*. New York: Vanguard, 1951.

Meikle, Jeffrey. *Twentieth-Century Limited: Industrial Design in America, 1925–1939*. Philadelphia: Temple University Press, 1979.

"'Murder' of Music Laid to Machines." *New York Times*, July 19, 1933, p. 20.

"Music Ex Machina." *The Atlantic Monthly* 112 (November 1913): 714–16.

Perrett, Geoffrey. *America in the Twenties: A History*. New York: Simon and Schuster, 1982.

Priestly, J. B. "Having Sold the Piano." *Saturday Review* 141 (June 5, 1926): 673–74.

Rice, Diana. "Mechanical Music Has Not Yet Won a Victory." *New York Times*, July 1, 1928, sec. 8, p. 10.

Rodgers, Daniel T. *The Work Ethic in Industrial America, 1850–1920*. Chicago: University of Chicago Press, 1978.

Rorty, James. *Our Master's Voice*. New York: John Day, 1934; Arno reprint, 1967.

Schauffler, Robert Haven. "Canned Music—The Phonograph Fan." *Collier's* 67 (April 23, 1921): 10–11, 23–24.

———. "The Mission of Mechanical Music." *Century Magazine* 89 (December 1914): 293–98.

Sousa, John Philip. "Sousa's Protest against 'Canned Music.'" *Current Literature* 41 (October 1906): 426–28.

———. "The Menace of Mechanical Music." *Appleton's Magazine* 8 (September 1906): 7.

Susman, Warren I. *Culture As History: The Transformation of American Society in the Twentieth Century*. New York: Pantheon Books, 1985.

Toffler, Alvin. *The Culture Consumers: A Study of Art and Affluence in America*. New York: St. Martin's Press, 1964.

Weber, Joseph N. "Canned Music." *American Federationist* 38 (September 1931): 1063–70.

Weinberger, Julius. "Economic Aspects of Recreation." *Harvard Business Review* 15 (Summer 1937): 448–63.

Whiting, Arthur. "The Mechanical Player." *Yale Review* 8 (July 1919): 828–35.

Williamson, Judith. *Decoding Advertisements: Ideology and Meaning in Advertising*. Boston: Marion Boyars, 1978.

Yellis, Kenneth A. "Prosperity's Child: Some Thoughts on the Flapper." *American Quarterly* 21 (Spring 1969): 44–64.

Zaretsky, Eli. *Capitalism, the Family, and Personal Life*. New York: Harper Colophon Books, 1976.

Music History, Appreciation, and Study

Alexander, Charles C. *Here the Country Lies: Nationalism and the Arts in Twentieth-Century America.* Bloomington: Indiana University Press, 1980.

Artrim, Doron K. "The Piano as a Barometer of Musical Conditions." *Musical Observer* 30 (April 1931).

Atta, H. L. *The Piano Player.* Dayton: Ohio Printing Co., 1914.

Baldwin, Ralph L. "An Unsuspected Popular Instinct for Musical Education." *MTNA Proceedings,* 1913, pp. 179–84.

Berlin, Edward A. *Ragtime: A Musical and Cultural History.* Berkeley and Los Angeles: University of California Press, 1980.

Birge, Edward Bailey. *History of Pubic School Music in the United States.* Boston: Oliver Ditson Co., 1928.

———. "Music-Appreciation in Public Schools." *MTNA Proceedings,* 1909, pp. 142–44.

Blesh, Rudi. "Scott Joplin." *American Heritage* 26 (June 1975): 27–32, 86–91.

———. "Scott Joplin: Black-American Classicist." In *The Collected Works of Scott Joplin,* edited by Vera Brodsky Lawrence, vol. 1, pp. xiii–xl. New York: New York Public Library, 1972.

Blesh, Rudi, and Harriet Janis. *They All Played Ragtime.* New York: Oak Publications, rev. ed., 1971.

Borchard, Gertrude. "The Player Piano as Teacher's Aid." *The Musician* 24 (January 1919): 18.

Bostelmann, John C., Jr. "A New Approach to Piano Study." *The Musician* 32 (October 1927): 13, 34.

Canon, Cornelius B. "The Federal Music Project of the Works Progress Administration: Music in a Democracy." Ph.D. dissertation, University of Minnesota, 1963.

Clark, Kenneth S. *Music in Industry.* New York: National Bureau for the Advancement of Music, 1929.

Coleman, Satis N. *Your Child's Music.* New York: John Day Co., 1939.

Cooke, James Francis, ed. *Master Rules for Successful Piano Practice.* Philadelphia: Theodore Presser Co., 1910.

Damrosch, Walter. *My Musical Life.* New York: Charles Scribner's Sons, Golden Jubilee Edition, 1935.

Davidson, Archibald T. *Music Education in America.* New York: Harper and Bros., 1928.

Davis, James J. " 'There Should Be a Musical Instrument in Every School Room,' Says Secretary of Labor Davis" (Interview). *The Music Trades* 65 (May 19, 1923): 1.

Davis, Ronald L. *A History of Music in American Life.* Vol. 2, *The Gilded*

Years, 1865–1920, and Vol. 3, *The Modern Era, 1920–Present*. Malabar,
Fla.: Krieger, 1980–81.

"Days of Glory Reviewed for the Piano: New Teaching Modes
Repopularizing the Instrument, Once a Social Asset." *New York Times
Magazine*, May 31, 1931, p. 16.

Dykema, Peter W. "Music as Recreation." *Playground* 17 (January 1924):
533–37, 553, 556.

Eisenberg, Jacob. "Apathy toward Piano Study: Causes and Remedies."
The Musician 27 (November 1922): 17, 30.

Elson, Louis C. *The History of American Music*. New York: Macmillan,
1904.

Ewen, David. *American Popular Songs from the Revolutionary War to the
Present*. New York: Random House, 1966.

―――. *The Life and Death of Tin Pan Alley: The Golden Age of American
Popular Music*. New York: Funk and Wagnalls, 1964.

Fellows, A. "Creative Music and the Bad Boy." *Progressive Education* 8
(April 1931): 348–49.

Fisher, William Arms. *Music Festivals in the United States: An Historical
Sketch*. Boston: American Choral and Festival Alliance, 1934.

Fullerton, L. Waldo. "Music and the War." *The Outlook* 112 (January 19,
1916): 151–52.

Gabrielle, Elliot. "Music at the Front: An Interview with Walter Damrosch." *The Outlook* 120 (October 12, 1918): 286–87.

Gary, Charles L. *Vignettes of Music Education History*. Washington, D.C.:
Music Educators National Conference, 1964.

Grabel, Virgel, Jr. "How American Industries Are Utilizing Music." *The
Etude* 41 (May 1923): 303–4, 351.

Grew, Sydney. *The Art of the Player Piano*. New York: E. P. Dutton, 1922.

Hanson, Howard. "Music's Place in the 'New Deal.'" *The Musician* 38
(July 1933): 7–8.

Haskins, James, with Kathleen Benson. *Scott Joplin: The Man Who Made
Ragtime*. New York: Stein and Day, Scarborough Books Edition, 1980.

Hasse, John Edward, ed. *Ragtime: Its History, Composers, and Music*.
New York: Schirmer Books, 1985.

Hitchcock, H. Wiley. *Music in the United States: A Historical Introduction*.
Englewood Cliffs, N.J.: Prentice Hall, 2d ed., 1974.

"Is Music an Effeminate Art?" *Current Opinion* 75 (November 1923):
586–87.

Kirk, Elise K. *Music at the White House: A History of the American Spirit*.
Urbana: University of Illinois Press, 1986.

Kobbe, Gustav. *The Pianolist—A Guide for Pianola Players*. New York:
Moffat, Yard & Co., 1907; 4th ed., 1912.

Kroeger, Ernest R. "Changes in Piano Teaching in Fifty Years." *The Etude* 47 (December 1929): 885–86.

Lewis, Leo Rich. "Music-Education and 'Automatics.'" *The Atlantic Monthly* 101 (March 1908): 383–87.

Lubin, Ernst. *The Piano Duet.* New York: Da Capo Press, 1970.

Marin, C. S. "The Campaign for the Federal Art Bill." *Communist* 17 (June 1938): 562–70.

Mason, Ella. "The Growth and Significance of the Piano Class." *MTNA Proceedings*, 1929, pp. 46–53.

Maxwell, Leon R. "Music as War Ammunition." *MTNA Proceedings*, 1918, 68–77.

McCall, A. B. "Girl's Education in Music." *Woman's Home Companion* 39 (March 12, 1912): 27.

McCauley, Clara Josephine. *A Professionalized Study of Public School Music.* Knoxville: Jos. E. Advent, 1932.

McConathy, Osbourne. "The Public School and the Private Music Teacher." *MTNA Proceedings*, 1930, pp. 61–76.

McCue, George, ed. *Music in American Society, 1776–1976.* New Brunswick, N.J.: Transaction Books, 1977.

McDonald, William F. *Federal Relief Administration and the Arts: The Origins and Administrative History of the Arts Projects of the Works Progress Administration.* Columbus: Ohio State University Press, 1969.

Mero, Yolanda. "Musical Democracy vs. Pianism." *The Musician* 22 (June 1917): 494.

Miessner, Otto W. "How the Economic Slump Has Affected the Music Teacher." *The Musician* 36 (June 1931): 11, 25.

Mursell, James L. *Human Values in Music Education.* New York: Silver, Burdett & Co., 1934.

"Music and Labor: Symposium." *The Etude* 41 (June 1923): 867–68.

"Music and the American Home." *The Outlook* 117 (October 3, 1917): 180–83.

"Music as a Spur to Production." *Playground* 16 (January 1923): 461–62.

Music in Industry: A Manual on Music for Work and for Recreation in Business and Industry. Chicago: Industrial Recreational Assn., 1944.

Nash, Grace Helen. "Modern Trends in Piano Teaching." *MTNA Proceedings*, 1930, pp. 158–66.

"Our Government Surveys Public School Music." *The Musician* 38 (September 1933): 6.

Pearsall, Ronald. *Edwardian Popular Music.* Cranbury, N.J.: Associated University Presses, 1975.

———. *Victorian Popular Music.* London: David and Charles Publishers, Ltd., 1973.

Pupin, A. "Formation of Character through a Proper Study of Music." *The Musician* 14 (February 1909): 67.

"The Ragtime Queen Has Abdicated." *New York Times Magazine*, May 24, 1925, p. 21.

Randolph, Harold. "The Feminization of Music." *MTNA Proceedings*, 1922, pp. 194–200.

Schafer, William J., and Johannes Riedel. *The Art of Ragtime: Form and Meaning of an Original Black American Art.* Baton Rouge: Louisiana State University Press, 1973.

Schauffler, Robert Haven. "Finding the Soul of the Player Piano." *The Delineator* 94 (February 1919): 51.

Schonberg, Harold. *The Great Pianists from Mozart to the Present.* New York: Simon and Schuster, 1963.

Schullian, Dorothy M., and Max Schoen, eds. *Music and Medicine.* New York: Henry Schuman, 1948.

Schwab, Charles M. "Music, the Great Humanizer." *The Etude* 43 (December 1925): 839–40.

Scott, Frank A. "A Survey of Home Music Study." *MTNA Proceedings*, 1919, pp. 171–77.

Seeger, Charles. "Music and Class Structure in the U.S." *American Quarterly* 9 (Fall 1957): 281–94.

Seegers, J. C. "Teaching Music Appreciation by Means of the Music-Memory Contest." *Elementary School Journal* 26 (February 1925): 215–23.

Sherwood, H. N. "Character Education through Music." *School and Society* 25 (January 29, 1927): 124–28.

Silber, Sidney. "Modern Piano Pedagogy." *The Etude* 53 (January 1935): 12.

Sokoloff, Nikolai. "America's Vast New Musical Awakening." *The Etude* 55 (April 1937): 221–22.

Spalding, Walter R. "Is Music a Non-Essential?" *The Outlook* 118 (March 20, 1918): 441–42.

———. "Music a Necessary Part of the Soldier's Equipment." *The Outlook* 119 (June 5, 1918): 223–24.

Sunderman, Lloyd Frederick. *Historical Foundations of Music Education in the United States.* Metuchen, N.J.: Scarecrow Press, 1971.

Surette, Thomas Whitney. *Music and Life.* Boston: Houghton Mifflin Co., 1917.

———. "Music for Children." *The Atlantic Monthly* 117 (March 1916): 356–65.

"Survey Shows Piano Classes in 358 Schools." *The Musician* 33 (October 1928): 11.

Tapper, Thomas. *The Education of the Music Teacher.* Philadelphia: Theodore Presser Co., 1915.

Tremaine, C. M. "Gap between Music in Schools and Music in Homes." *The Musician* 36 (July 1931): 13.

_____. *History of National Music Week.* New York: National Bureau for the Advancement of Music, 1925.

_____. "The Music Memory Contest, etc." *MSNC Journal of Proceedings,* 1918, pp. 99–107.

_____. "Music Memory Contests, with List of One Hundred Selections Most Frequently Used." *National Education Association Journal* 15 (February 1926): 43–44.

_____. "The National Bureau for the Advancement of Music and Its Relation to the Supervisor." *MSNC Journal of Proceedings,* 1927, pp. 132–35.

_____. "National Music Week." In *The Magic of Music: An Anthology for Music Weeks and Days,* edited and compiled by Robert Haven Schauffler, pp. 4–5. New York: Dodd, Mead, 1946.

_____. "The Present Status of School Music Education." *Music Educators National Conference Bulletin,* no. 16, April 1934.

Turner, Chittenden. "Music and the Women's Crusade." *Arts and Decoration* 19 (September 1923): 29, 70.

Ulrich, Homer. *A Centennial History of the Music Teachers National Association.* Cincinnati: MTNA, 1976.

"Unemployed Arts: The WPA's Four Arts Projects." *Fortune* 15 (May 1937): 108–17.

Van de Wall, Willem. "The Musician's Contribution to Modern Mental Health." *MTNA Proceedings,* 1924, pp. 145–59.

Warren, Janelle J. "Of Tears and Need: The Federal Music Project, 1935–1943." Ph.D. dissertation, George Washington University, 1973.

White, William Braid. *The Player-Pianist.* New York: Edward L. Bill, 1910.

"Why Should a Young Girl Take Up the Study of Music?" *The Musician* 14 (February 1909): 72.

Wilson, David Miller. *The Player Piano, Its Construction and How to Play.* New York: Pitman & Sons, 1923.

Witherspoon, Herbert. "Music as a Vital Factor in Education." *MTNA Proceedings,* 1926, pp. 54–65.

York, Francis L. "The Influence of the Pianoforte on the General Development of Music." *MTNA Proceedings,* 1910, p. 67.

Zanzig, Augustus D. *Music in American Life.* New York: Oxford University Press, prepared for the National Recreation Association, 1932.

_____. "Music Settlement Schools." *MTNA Proceedings,* 1922, pp. 62–66.

The American Piano Industry and Music Trades

Aeolian Co. *Catalog of Metrostyle and Themodist Music for the Pianola and Pianola Piano.* New York: The Aeolian Co., 1906.

———. *Catalog of Music for the Pianola and Pianola Piano.* New York: The Aeolian Co., 1905.

American Piano Co. *A Catalogue of Music for the Ampico.* New York: American Piano Co., 1923.

"American Pianos." *Antiquarian* 3 (October 1924): 12–13.

Ayars, Christine Merrick. *Contributions to the Art of Music in America by the Music Industries of Boston, 1640 to 1936.* New York: H. W. Wilson, 1937.

"Baldwin Radio Feature to Be Continued and Enlarged." *The Music Trades* 78 (October 1929): 13.

"Baldwin's New National Advertising Drive to Create Interest in the Piano as Essential to the Home." *The Music Trades* 78 (May 1930): 13.

"Baldwin to Broadcast to Millions." *The Music Trades* 77 (January 19, 1929): 5.

Barnes, Wendall. "New Pianos in New Settings." *The Etude* 55 (December 1937): 803–6.

Bauer, Marion. "A Renaissance of the Piano." *Arts and Decoration* 46 (April 1937): 34–35, 42.

Bent, George Payne. *Tales of Travel, Life and Love: An Autobiography.* Los Angeles: The *Times-Mirror* Press, 1924.

"Big 'Non-Essential' Bugaboo Scotched." *The Music Trades* 54 (December 15, 1917): 27.

Bowers, Q. David. *Put Another Nickel In: A History of Coin-Operated Pianos and Orchestrions.* Vestal, N.Y.: The Vestal Press, 1966.

Boykin, Edward C. " 'The Most Interesting Piano Story Ever Told' " [Piano Promotion Plan of NPMA]. *The Music Trades* 77 (February 15, 1929): 9–12.

Bradley, Van Allen. *Music for the Millions: The Kimball Piano and Organ Story.* Chicago: Henry Regnery Co., 1957.

Brooks, E. F., Jr. "Aeolian American Division of Aeolian Corporation, East Rochester, New York." (Author's collection, typewritten.)

Carson, Gerald. "The Piano in the Parlor." *American Heritage* 17 (December 1965): 54–59, 91.

"Certain Limitations in the Application of Scientific Management." *Harvard Business Review* 4 (October 1925): 106–11.

"Chicago's Music Industry Is Huge." *Chicago Commerce* 24 (July 21, 1928): 7–9, 29–30.

Chickering & Sons. *The Jonas Chickering Centennial Celebration.* New York: Cheltenham, 1924.

Chilton, Carroll Brent. "A Musical Caliban." *The Independent* 62 (April 11, 1907): 838–44.

Clark, V. S. *History of Manufacturing in the United States.* Vol. 3. New York: McGraw-Hill for the Carnegie Institution of Washington, 1929.

Coiner, Charles T. "How Steinway Uses Modern Art." *Advertising Arts* (supplement to *Advertising and Selling*), April 2, 1930, p. 17.

Collins, Byron H. "What Should I Know to Purchase a Reliable Piano?" *The Etude* 40 (October 1922): 669.

Cooke, James Francis. "The Piano as a Home Investment." *The Etude* 47 (February 1929): 91.

———. "The Piano Triumphs: An Editorial Discussion of the Recent Amazing and Highly Gratifying Developments in the Piano Industry." *The Etude* 71 (October 1953): 15, 20, 58–59.

Dealer's Handbook of Pianos and Their Makers. Tulsa, Okla.: Robert G. Anderson, 1972.

DeVore, Nicholas. "Music Industry Prepares for an Upswing." *The Musician* 46 (September 1941): 136, 139.

"Direct Child Appeal: This Mail Campaign, Through Human-Interest Angle, Sells 1,500 Pianos; Costs $1.92 a Name." *Printers' Ink* 181 (November 18, 1937): 24–26, 30.

"Discriminating Player-Pianos." *The Literary Digest* 47 (July 12, 1913): 52.

Dolge, Alfred. *Pianos and Their Makers.* Vol. 1. *A Comprehensive History of the Development of the Piano from the Monochord to the Concert Grand Player Piano.* Covina, Calif.: Covina Publishing Co., 1911; reprinted, New York: Dover, 1972. Vol. 2. *Development of the Piano Industry in America since the Centennial Exhibition at Philadelphia, 1876.* Covina, Calif.: Covina Publishing Co., 1913.

Downes, Olin. "The Question of the Piano." *New York Times*, June 4, 1933, sec. 9, p. 4.

Ehrlich, Cyril. *The Piano: A History.* London: Dent, 1976.

Encyclopedia Britannica. 11th ed., 1911. S.v. "Pianoforte," by Alfred J. Hipkins and Kathleen Schlesinger.

Erwin, Paul. "Preliminary Draft of Baldwin Early Years." D. H. Baldwin & Co. Archives, Cincinnati Historical Society. (Typewritten.)

Fabricant, Solomon. *Employment in Manufacturing, 1899–1939: An Analysis of Its Relation to the Volume of Production.* New York: National Bureau of Economic Research, Inc., no. 41, 1942.

———. *The Output of Manufacturing Industries, 1899–1937.* New York: National Bureau of Economic Research, Inc., no. 39, 1940.

Fisher, William Arms. *One Hundred and Fifty Years of Music Publishing in the U.S.* Boston: Oliver Ditson, 1933.

"From Fighting Crooks to Staging Trade Shows: A Look at NAMM's Evolution and the Role of Trade Shows in the Music Industry." *The Music Trades* 131 (May 25, 1983): 76.

Gaines, James R. *The Lives of the Piano*. New York: Holt, Rinehart & Winston, 1980.

Geppert, William. *The Official Guide to Piano Quality*. New York: Eilert Printing Co., 1916.

Gill, Dominic, ed. *The Book of the Piano*. Ithaca: Cornell University Press, 1981.

Givens, Larry. *Re-Enacting the Artist: The Story of the Ampico Reproducing Piano*. Vestal, N.Y.: The Vestal Press, 1970.

Good, Edwin M. *Giraffes, Black Dragons, and Other Pianos: A Technological History from Cristofori to the Modern Concert Grand*. Stanford, Calif.: Stanford University Press, 1982.

Gow, George Coleman. "The Pros and Cons of the Mechanical Player." *MTNA Proceedings*, 1910, pp. 77–87.

Graham, Lloyd. "The Story of the Rudolph Wurlitzer Family and Business." May 25, 1955. Manuscript in possession of Mrs. Janet Wurlitzer Stites, Cincinnati, Ohio. (Typewritten.)

"Great Slump in the Piano Trade Is Mystifying." *Current Opinion* 72 (June 1922): 830–31.

Grover, David S. *The Piano: Its Story from Zither to Grand*. London: Robert Hale, 1976, and New York: Charles Scribner's Sons, 1978.

Harrison, Sidney. *Grand Piano*. London: Faber and Faber, 1976.

Hawkins, Herbert B. "Determining Piano [Production] Costs." *Journal of Accountancy* 35 (February 1923): 115–23.

"Here Are the Steinways and How They Grew." *Fortune* 10 (December 1934): 99–105.

Heywood, Johnson. "Swing High, Swing Low with the Musical Instruments Industry." *Dun's Review* 47 (June 1939): 22–26.

Hickey, Michael J. "Trade Conditions and Probabilities." *American Industries* 19 (April 1919): 10–18.

Hollis, Helen Rice. *The Piano: A Pictorial Account of Its Ancestry and Development*. New York: Hippocrene, rev. ed., 1984.

Hoover, Cynthia Adams. "Music and Musical Instruments." In *1876: A Centennial Exposition*, edited by Robert C. Post, pp. 138–43. Washington, D.C.: Smithsonian Institution, 1976.

————. "The Steinways and Their Pianos in the Nineteenth Century." Offprint from *Journal of the American Musical Instrument Society*, vol. 7, 1981.

Hughes, Lawrence M. "A Century of Salesmanship Helps Build Steinway Name." Offprint from *Sales Management*, April 15, 1953.

Hume, Paul, and Ruth Hume. "The Great Chicago Piano War." *American Heritage* 21 (October 1970): 16–21.

Hurd, F. A. "Why Some Dealers Don't Sell Players." *The Music Trades* 77 (January 12, 1929): 10.

Jacobs, C. Albert, Jr. "The Piano Industry: Its Past, Present and Future." *Bulletin of the National Retail Dry Goods Association* 22 (May 1940): 33–36.

Johnson, Barbara. "Ayer-Steinway 69-Year History Resulted in 'Immortal' Ads." *Advertising Age*, August 25, 1969, p. 255.

Kastl, Norma. "Pianos and Radios as Furniture." *Parents' Magazine* 14 (October 1939): 48–49, 56, 62.

Kelly, E. M. " 'Dying' Music Industry Lives Anew as Millions Turn to Tune-Making." *Sales Management* 42 (January 1, 1938): 22, 24, 64.

Kempf, Paul. "America Turning Anew to the Piano." *The Musician* 34 (January 1929): 11.

"Keyboards." *Time* 26 (August 1935): 54, 56.

"Kimball's 125 Year Saga: The Rise, Fall, and Regeneration of One of the Industry's Most Distinguished Participants." *The Music Trades* 130 (October 1982): 46–54, 96.

Kuznets, Simon. *Seasonal Variations in Industry and Trade.* New York: National Bureau of Economic Research, no. 22, 1933.

Loesser, Arthur. *Men, Women and Pianos: A Social History.* New York: Simon and Schuster, 1954.

Majeski, John F. "Steinway." Part 1. "125 Years of Service to Music Worldwide." Part 2. "Building Music's Most Famous Name." *The Music Trades* 126 (April, August 1978): 54–65, 68–78.

"Majority of Piano Makers and Music Publishers Are in Favor of Voluntary Code." *The Music Trades* 83 (October 1935): 9.

Margolius, Sidney. "How to Build Up Pianos: Piano Business Staging Remarkable Comeback Due Largely to Upswing in Musical Interest, Better Styling." *Retailing* (Executive Edition) 11 (January 9, 1939): 4–5.

Martin, Jane, comp. *Reminiscences of Morris Steinert.* New York: G. P. Putnam's Sons, 1900.

Mason, Henry L. "How Has the Pianoforte as an Instrument Developed since 1876?—With Some Figures." *MTNA Proceedings*, 1928, pp. 134–46.

Maugham, Mrs. Somerset. "Lighting the Piano: Some Suggestions for Dressing this Instrument So that It Becomes an Object of Decoration." *House and Garden* 47 (April 1925): 72, 126.

Meixell, Harry. "National Recovery Act and the Music Industry." *The Music Trades—National Recovery Number* 81 (December 1933): 5.

Miessner, Otto W. "What Is Happening to the Piano?" *MTNA Proceedings*, 1930, pp. 181–97.

Mills, William A. *Merchandising Music: Sales Training Manual for Music Salesmen.* New York: National Association of Music Merchants, Inc., in cooperation with Business Education Service of the U.S. Office of Education, 1946.

"Music Chamber [of Commerce] to Meet Industry Crisis." *The Music Trades* 54 (November 17, 1917): 27.

"National Bureau for the Advancement of Music." *The Music Trades* 78 (December 1930): 12.

The New Grove Dictionary of Music and Musicians. 1980 ed. S.v. "Pianoforte," by William J. Conner, Cyril Ehrlich, et al. S.v. "Player piano," by Frank W. Holland.

"No Place for a Piano? Nonsense! Gone Are the 'Model T' Styles of Yesterday." *American Home* 21 (December 1938): 23–24.

Ord-Hume, Arthur W. J. G. *Pianola: The History of the Self-Playing Piano.* London: George Allen & Unwin, 1984.

———. *Player Piano: The History of the Mechanical Piano and How to Repair It.* London: George Allen & Unwin, 1970.

Paderewski, Ignacy Jan, and Mary Lawton. *The Paderewski Memoirs.* New York: Charles Scribner's Sons, 1939.

Parton, James. "The Piano in the United States." *The Atlantic Monthly* 20 (July 1867): 82.

"Persistent Pianos." *Business Week*, October 26, 1935, pp. 18–19.

"Piano Comeback." *The Literary Digest* 122 (August 22, 1936): 36–37.

"Piano Comeback." *Newsweek* 14 (August 14, 1939): 42.

"Pianofortissimo: In 1935 the Piano Industry Discovered Style." *Fortune* 20 (August 1939): 44–49, 118–20.

"Piano Industry No Drain on Country's Resources in Man-Power, Materials, Fuel." *The Music Trades* 54 (December 1, 1917): 3–4.

"The Piano Industry Struck the Wrong Key." *Business Week*, January 15, 1930, pp. 13–14.

"Piano Merchants Move to Cooperate with Teachers." *The Musician* 31 (November 1926): 12.

"Piano-Players and Player-Pianos." *The Literary Digest* 47 (September 20, 1913): 468–69.

"Piano Players, Human and Mechanical." *The Literary Digest* 46 (June 21, 1913): 1376.

"Piano Promotion Body Reviews Its First Year Record." *The Music Trades* 75 (January 21, 1928): 8.

"Piano Promotion Plan to Begin Functioning Immediately." *The Music Trades* 72 (December 11, 1926): 3.

"Pianos: Radio, Ex-Foe, Proves Ally." *Newsweek* 6 (November 6, 1935): 37–38.

Piano Travelers' Association Book. New York: Rand, McNally, 1915.

"Price Revision in Falling Markets." *Harvard Business Review* 6 (April 1928): 359–62.

"Proctor Piano Company." *Harvard Business Review* 1 (October 1922): 116–19.

Q.R.S Music Co. *Q.R.S Player Rolls Classified Catalog.* Chicago: The Q.R.S Music Co., 1925.

"Recording the Soul of Piano Playing." *Scientific American* 137 (November 1927): 422–23.

"Rising Piano Sales Point to Renaissance of Music." *Business Week*, January 13, 1932, pp. 11–12.

Roehl, Harvey N. *Player Piano Treasury: The Scrapbook History of the Mechanical Piano in America as Told in Story, Pictures, Trade Journal Articles and Advertising.* Vestal, N.Y.: The Vestal Press, 1961; 2d ed., 1973.

Rubinstein, Artur. *My Young Years.* New York: Alfred Knopf, 1973.

Seligman, Edwin R. A. *The Economics of Instalment Selling: A Study in Consumers' Credit.* Vol. 1. New York: Harper and Brothers, 1927.

Selz, Lawrence H. *Consumer Investigation for National Piano Manufacturers Association.* New York: NPMA, 1938.

_____. "Piano Merchandising." *Bulletin of the National Dry Goods Association* 22 (May 1940): 37–38.

Spillane, Daniel. *History of the American Pianoforte: Its Technical Development and the Trade.* New York: Daniel Spillane, 1890; reprinted, New York: Da Capo Press, 1969.

Steinway & Sons. *The Steinways of Today.* New York: William Bradford Press for Steinway & Sons, n.d. [ca. 1930s].

Steinway, Charles H. "Building Up Prestige and What It Entails." Offprint from *Printers' Ink*, November, 1912.

Steinway, Theodore E. *People and Pianos: A Century of Service to Music.* New York: Steinway & Sons, 1953; 2d ed., 1961.

"Story & Clark: The First 100 Years." Offprint of the *The Music Trades* for January 1957.

"Swing and Upswing." *Time* 33 (June 19, 1939): 68.

Thompson, Morley P. "Financial History of the Baldwin Company since 1902." D. H. Baldwin & Co. Archives, Cincinnati Historical Society. (Typewritten.)

Tonk, William. *Memoirs of a Manufacturer.* New York: Presto Publishing Co., 1926.

"Truck Technique Helps Boom Piano Sales in Farm Areas." *Life* 9 (August 1940): 49–53.

Wainwright, David. *The Piano Makers.* London: Hutchinson, 1975.

Waite, Roy E. "The Piano's Future." *New York Times*, June 18, 1933, sec. 10, p. 5.

Walter, William E. "The Industry of Music-Making." *The Atlantic Monthly* 101 (January 1908): 91–96.

Weinrott, Lester A. "Play That Player Piano." *Chicago History* 4 (Summer 1975): 79ff.

White, William Braid. "The Decline of the American Piano Industry." *The American Mercury* 28 (February 1933): 210–13.

―――. *The Player Piano Up to Date.* New York: Edward L. Bill, 1914.

Wing, Frank L. *The Book of Complete Information about Pianos.* New York: Wing & Son, 1897.

Wolman, Leo. *Ebb and Flow in Trade Unionism.* New York: National Bureau of Economic Research, Inc., no. 30, 1936.

―――. *The Growth of American Trade Unions, 1880–1923.* New York: National Bureau of Economic Research, Inc., no. 6, 1924.

Wulsin, Lucien. *Dwight Hamilton Baldwin (1821–1899) and the Baldwin Piano.* New York: Newcomen Society in North America and Princeton University Press, July 1953.

―――. "A Piano Man Looks Back." *The Music Trades* 111 (February 1963): 38–44.

―――. "Resumé of Piano Industry under NRA Code." *The Music Trades* 82 (February 1934): 3–4.

Victorian Home and Family Life

Beecher, Catharine E., and Harriet Beecher Stowe. *The American Woman's Home.* New York: J. B. Ford, 1869; reprint, Watkins Glen, N.Y.: American Life Foundation Library of Victorian Culture, 1979.

Chafe, William. *The American Woman: Her Changing Social, Economic, and Political Roles, 1920–1970.* New York: Oxford University Press, 1975.

Chester, E. *Girls and Women.* The Riverside Library for Young People, no. 8. New York: Houghton, Mifflin, 1890.

Cott, Nancy F. *The Bonds of Womanhood.* New Haven: Yale University Press, 1977.

Cowan, Ruth Schwartz. "The 'Industrial Revolution' in the Home: Household Technology and Social Change in the 20th Century." *Technology and Culture* 17 (January 1976): 1–22.

Dale, Daphne. *Our Manners and Social Customs: A Practical Guide.* Chicago: Elliot and Beezley, 1892.

Degler, Carl N. *At Odds: Women and the Family in America from the Revolution to the Present.* New York: Oxford University Press, 1980.

Dingwall, Eric John. *The American Woman.* New York: Rinehart and Co., 1957.

Dunbar, Janet. *The Early Victorian Woman: Some Aspects of Her Life.* London: George G. Harrap, 1953.

Dutton, Ralph. *The Victorian Home: Some Aspects of 19th-Century Taste and Manners.* London: Batsford, 1954.

Green, Harvey. *The Light of the Home: An Intimate View of the Lives of Women in Victorian America.* New York: Pantheon, 1983.

Handlin, David P. *The American Home: Architecture and Society, 1815–1915.* Boston: Little, Brown & Co., 1979.

Houghton, Walter E. *The Victorian Frame of Mind, 1830–1870.* New Haven: Yale University Press, 1957.

Howe, Daniel Walker, ed. *Victorian America.* Philadelphia: University of Pennsylvania Press, 1976.

Humphreys, Mary Gay. *The House and Home, A Practical Book.* Vol. 2. New York: Charles Scribner's Sons, 1896.

Mintz, Steven. *A Prison of Expectations: The Family in Victorian Culture.* New York: New York University Press, 1983.

Rodgers, Daniel T. *The Work Ethic in Industrial America, 1850–1920.* Chicago: University of Chicago Press, 1978.

Sklar, Kathryn Kish. *Catharine Beecher: A Study in American Domesticity.* New York: Norton, 1976; first published by Yale University Press, 1973.

Wilson, P. W. "Victorian Days that Beckon Us." *New York Times Magazine,* April 30, 1933, pp. 10–11.

Woloch, Nancy. *Women and the American Experience.* New York: Alfred A. Knopf, 1984.

Wright, Gwendolyn. *Moralism and the Model Home: Domestic Architecture and Cultural Conflict in Chicago, 1873–1913.* Chicago: University of Chicago Press, 1980.

Ziff, Larzer. *The American Eighteen Nineties: Life and Times of A Lost Generation.* Lincoln: University of Nebraska Press, 1979.

Index